CROSSO

FICTION

How Picturebooks Work
by Maria Nikolajeva and Carole Scott

Brown Gold
Milestones of African American Children's Picture Books, 1845–2002
by Michelle H. Martin

Russell Hoban/Forty Years
Essays on His Writing for Children
by Alida Allison

Apartheid and Racism in South African Children's Literature
by Donnarae MacCann and Amadu Maddy

Empire's Children
Empire and Imperialism in Classic British Children's Books
by M. Daphne Kutzer

Constructing the Canon of Children's Literature
Beyond Library Walls and Ivory Towers
by Anne Lundin

Youth of Darkest England
Working Class Children at the Heart of Victorian Empire
by Troy Boone

Ursula K. Le Guin Beyond Genre
Literature for Children and Adults
by Mike Cadden

Twice-Told Children's Tales
edited by Betty Greenway

Diana Wynne Jones
The Fantastic Tradition and Children's Literature
by Farah Mendlesohn

Childhood and Children's Books in Early Modern Europe, 1550–1800
edited by Andrea Immel and Michael Witmore

Voracious Children
Who Eats Whom in Children's Literature
by Carolyn Daniel

National Character in South African Children's Literature
by Elwyn Jenkins

Myth, Symbol, and Meaning in *Mary Poppins*
The Governess as Provocateur
by Georgia Grilli

A Critical History of French Children's Literature, Vols. 1 & 2
by Penny Brown

Once Upon a Time in a Different World
Issues and Ideas in African American Children's Literature
by Neal A. Lester

The Gothic in Children's Literature
Haunting the Borders
edited by Anna Jackson, Karen Coats, and Roderick McGillis

Reading Victorian Schoolrooms
Childhood and Education in Nineteenth-Century Fiction
by Elizabeth Gargano

Soon Come Home to This Island
West Indians in British Children's Literature
by Karen Sands-O'Connor

Boys in Children's Literature and Popular Culture
Masculinity, Abjection, and the Fictional Child
by Annette Wannamaker

Into the Closet
Cross-dressing and the Gendered Body in Children's Literature
by Victoria Flanagan

Russian Children's Literature and Culture
edited by Marina Balina and Larissa Rudova

The Outside Child In and Out of the Book
by Christine Wilkie-Stibbs

Representing Africa in Children's Literature
Old and New Ways of Seeing
by Vivian Yenika-Agbaw

The Fantasy of Family
Nineteenth-Century Children's Literature and the Myth of the Domestic Ideal
by Liz Thiel

From Nursery Rhymes to Nationhood
Children's Literature and the Construction of Canadian Identity
by Elizabeth A. Galway

CROSSOVER
FICTION

Global and Historical Perspectives

SANDRA L. BECKETT

Routledge
Taylor & Francis Group

NEW YORK AND LONDON

First published 2009
by Routledge
270 Madison Ave, New York, NY 10016

Simultaneously published in the UK
by Routledge
2 Park Square, Milton Park, Abingdon, Oxon OX14 4RN

Routledge is an imprint of the Taylor & Francis Group, an informa business

Transferred to Digital Printing 2009

© 2009 Taylor & Francis

Typeset in Minion by Swales & Willis Ltd., Exeter, Devon

Library of Congress Cataloging in Publication Data
Beckett, Sandra L., 1953–
Crossover fiction : global and historical perspectives / by Sandra L. Beckett.
p. cm. — (Children's literature and culture ; 56)
Includes bibliographical references and index.
1. Children's stories—History and criticism. 2. Fiction—History and criticism. 3.
Books and reading—History. I. Title.
PN1009.A1B42 2008
809.3—dc22
2008003925

ISBN10: 0–415–98033–X (hbk)
ISBN10: 0–415–87936–1 (pbk)
ISBN10: 0–203–89313–1 (ebk)

ISBN13: 978–0–415–98033–3 (hbk)
ISBN13: 978–0–415–87936–1 (pbk)
ISBN13: 978–0–203–89313–5 (ebk)

For Paul and my three J's

Contents

Series Editor's Foreword

Dedicated to furthering original research in children's literature and culture, the Children's Literature and Culture series includes monographs on individual authors and illustrators, historical examinations of different periods, literary analyses of genres, and comparative studies on literature and the mass media. The series is international in scope and is intended to encourage innovative research in children's literature with a focus on interdisciplinary methodology.

Children's literature and culture are understood in the broadest sense of the term 'children' to encompass the period of childhood up through adolescence. Owing to the fact that the notion of childhood has changed so much since the origination of children's literature, this Routledge series is particularly concerned with transformations in children's culture and how they have affected the representation and socialization of children. While the emphasis of the series is on children's literature, all types of studies that deal with children's radio, film, television, and art are included in an endeavor to grasp the aesthetics and values of children's culture. Not only have there been momentous changes in children's culture in the last fifty years, but there have been radical shifts in the scholarship that deals with these changes. In this regard, the goal of the Children's Literature and Culture series is to enhance research in this field and, at the same time, point to new directions that bring together the best scholarly work throughout the world.

Jack Zipes

Acknowledgments

I am particularly indebted to the many authors around the globe who graciously discussed their work with me. I would also like to express my sincere thanks to the many friends and colleagues who have contributed in some way to this book, in particular Harald Bache-Wiig, Nina Christensen, Corrado Federici, Yukiko Fukumoto, Claude Girault, Maija-Liisa Harju, Lena Kåreland, Angela Lebedeva, Ann Lawson Lucas, Helma van Lierop-Debrauwer, Maria Nikolajeva, Jean Perrot, Rolf Romören, Svein Slettan, Larissa Tumanov, Thomas van der Walt, Anne de Vries, and Jack Zipes. My deep gratitude goes to the staff at the International Youth Library in Munich and the International Institute for Children's Literature, Osaka, notably Jochen Weber and Yasuko Doi. I wish to acknowledge the generous financial support of the Social Sciences and Humanities Research Council of Canada, Brock University Chancellor's Chair for Research Excellence, the Humanities Research Institute at Brock University, and Brock University Experience Works. Very special thanks go to my research assistants, Lindsay Clark and Carlene Thomas, who have enthusiastically shared my passion for crossover fiction.

defines "crossover literature" as "children's books which appeal to adults."[18] This definition is implied when the restrictive term "kidult fiction" is used synonymously for crossover fiction. However, the term is sometimes reserved exclusively for young adult fiction that is read by adults. Pointing out that "people use the term 'crossover' in different ways," the British author Linda Newbery stated, in an interview posted on the Wordmavericks website, that she feels "a 'crossover' book isn't an older teenage novel," but rather "a book which appeals to children, like Philip Pullman's *His Dark Materials*, or *Alice in Wonderland*, and equally to adults." There is a tendency to equate crossover with fantasy, which admittedly plays a major role in the current phenomenon, but, in fact, almost every genre can cross between child and adult audiences. Thus, even when the "crossover" tag is applied only to one-way traffic, it is not necessarily used to refer to all the traffic in that direction.

Although a few scholars have criticized this limited use of the term,[19] the media has rarely recognized that crossover literature is not a one-sided phenomenon or a one-way border crossing. An article in the U.K. newspaper the *Observer* in 2004 points out this oversight: "What is not acknowledged, though, is that the traffic flows in the opposite direction—crossover fiction is also adult fiction that appeals to children."[20] One critic goes perhaps a little too far in this direction, describing bookshops that are "already choc full of crossover titles." She offers the following very broad definition: "Any novel that can be comprehended by someone with a reading age of eight could legitimately be classified as a crossover title. And that includes a substantial portion of books currently marketed for adults."[21] At least the author of this article recognizes that adult books also cross over to young readers. Prior to *Harry Potter*, the crossover took place predominantly in that direction. Children have been appropriating adult books for generations. Classics like *Robinson Crusoe*, *Oliver Twist*, *Treasure Island*, *Don Quijote*, and *Les trois mousquetaires* became the property of young readers. Publishers have been repackaging adult fiction for children for almost as long. Critics talk about the latest trend of signing up mainstream authors who can straddle the adult-child literary divide to write young adult novels. In fact, publishers in France, Spain, and other countries have been doing this for decades. Authors and readers have always crossed the borders in both directions, with or without the help of publishers.

The term "crosswriting" was widely used by critics, even beyond English-speaking borders, before the widespread adoption of the term "crossover fiction." Crosswriting, in the broad sense of the term, includes authors who write for both child and adult audiences in separate works. The list of renowned authors who have written for both readerships is extensive and distinguished. It even includes a few Nobel Laureates, such as Rudyard Kipling, Selma Lagerlöf, Gabriela Mistral, Toni Morrison, and Isaac Bashevis Singer. Among the many primarily adult authors who have also published for children are Margaret Atwood, Ray Bradbury, E. E. Cummings, Charles Dickens, T. S. Eliot, William Faulkner, Ian Fleming, Graham Greene, Nathaniel Hawthorne, Ted Hughes,

Aldous Huxley, James Joyce, Rudyard Kipling, Mordecai Richler, Gabrielle Roy, Salman Rushdie, John Ruskin, Carl Sandburg, Gertrude Stein, Robert Louis Stevenson, William Makepeace Thackeray, Mark Twain, H. G. Wells, E. B. White, T. H. White, Oscar Wilde, and Virginia Woolf. The English-speaking world is often cited as having a particularly high number of important adult authors who have written for children. The author of the article "When Majors Wrote for Minors," published in 1952, actually claims that "almost every major writer of the nineteenth century [in English and American literatures] wrote for children as well as for adults."[22]

English-language literature does not, however, have a monopoly on cross-writers. The number of authors of adult fiction who have written for a juvenile audience in France is equally impressive, and it includes the names of some of the country's most prominent poets, playwrights, and novelists, including Marcel Aymé, Henri Bosco, Michel Butor, Colette, Georges Duhamel, Marguerite Duras, Paul Eluard, Jean Giono, Julien Green, Max Jacob, Eugene Ionesco, J. M. G. Le Clézio, François Mauriac, André Maurois, Daniel Pennac, Jacques Prévert, Claude Roy, Antoine de Saint-Exupéry, Samivel, Georges Sand, Jules Supervielle, Michel Tournier, and Marguerite Yourcenar. Many other countries also provide illustrious examples, such as Isabel Allende, Peter Bichsel, Heinrich Böll, Bertolt Brecht, Clemens Brentano, Italo Calvino, Karel Čapek, Anton Chekhov, Umberto Eco, Natalia Ginzburg, Peter Härtling, E. T. A. Hoffmann, Erich Kästner, Selma Lagerlöf, Clarice Lispector, Ana Maria Machado, Carmen Martín Gaite, José Renato Monteiro Lobato, Rosa Montero, Elsa Morante, and Erwin Strittmatter. Some of these authors, for example, Bosco, Lagerlöf, Saint-Exupéry, and Tournier, are first and foremost novelists for adults, but their most celebrated works are children's books.

There are also authors who have written extensively for both audiences, but who are nonetheless probably best known for their children's books, including Louisa May Alcott, Roald Dahl, Michael Ende, Madeleine L'Engle, Kenneth Grahame, Russell Hoban, Erich Kästner, C. S. Lewis, A. A. Milne, José Renato Monteiro Lobato, and E. B. White. Children's books by these writers generally appeal as much to adults as to children. A smaller category of authors are equally well known in the fields of children's and adult fiction, for example Ursula Le Guin, Luigi Malerba, João Pedro Mésseder, Jürg Schubiger, and Yuri Olesha. Authors who have won major prizes in both the adult literature and children's literature categories have been relatively few. Peter Härtling, one of the few major German authors of literary fiction to have always written for children and young adults as well as adults, won the special Deutscher Jugendliteraturpreis (German Youth Literature Award) for his collected children's works in 2001, as well as the Eichendorff Prize in 2000 and the Deutscher Bücherpreis (German Book Award) for his collected works in 2003. When authors publish works for both adults and children, their most loyal fans may read all of their books, regardless of the intended audience. Many readers seek out other books by writers that they have enjoyed, expecting to obtain a similar pleasure from all the praise of poets like Alfonso Gatto and Andrea Zanzotto and writers like Italo Calvino and Luigi Malerba.[39]

In most Western countries, it was not enough just to establish definite boundaries between adult and children's fiction. Although publishers had originally been content to bring out either books for adults or books for children, lumping together children and adolescents, they began in the 1960s and 1970s to divide children's literature into ever narrower categories. As Salman Rushdie put it in 1992, "the world of books has become a severely categorized and demarcated affair, in which children's fiction is not only a kind of ghetto but one subdivided into writing for a number of different age groups."[40] Many children's authors feel that these narrow age categories correspond more to commercial necessities than to any kind of psychological or sociological realities. Dominique Demers wonders, tongue in cheek, if she is supposed to write for a certain age group, for example eight to ten, in the same way that advertising agencies target suburban consumers in a particular age and salary range. She points out how ridiculous it would be to ask someone what would be a good book for a 67-year-old man. The illusion that children should be defined mainly in terms of age category constitutes, as Demers rightly puts it, "one of the great contemporary myths."[41] The current crossover trend is effectively deconstructing that myth.

In conjunction with a move to specialization, children's literature annexed an increasingly large public by introducing new age categories at both ends of the spectrum, that is, for babies and for young adults or "grands adolescents" in Quebec. These new age categories were also carved out in a very specific manner, for example, twelve to eighteen months or eighteen to twenty-five years. Paradoxically, at the upper end of the spectrum, the border between children's and adult fiction is once again blurred. The current growing intersection of readerships is in stark contrast to the narrow categorization that reduces young readers to, and confines them within, a specific age group. Young readers are becoming more sophisticated and teenagers in particular seem to be reading up. "The growing exodus of young adults to adult books," which one critic describes in the Canadian context, is a widespread contemporary phenomenon.[42]

In many Western countries, children's publishing became quite profitable and often kept publishers financially viable. However, it took the runaway financial success of *Harry Potter* to change the status of children's books in the literary world. Previously, children's books had been excluded from "real" literature and considered a minor or sub-genre. The negative "self-image" of children's literature is discussed at length in Shavit's 1987 study.[43] The low status of children's fiction has been the subject of much debate in many countries for decades. In an article devoted, in 1956, to ten major French authors who also wrote for children, Gabriel d'Aubarède laments the fact that children's literature is "too often considered a minor genre."[44] However, the author himself seems unintentionally to promote this attitude by first referring to three members of the prestigious Académie française (Georges Duhamel, André Maurois, and Daniel-Rops), as if in a deliberate attempt to give his article more weight and the subject more credibility. The remaining authors seem to be mentioned in descending order of perceived importance, beginning with Marcel Aymé. In a similar manner, Tournier deplores the fact that "a children's book is not considered a literary work," while at the same time reinforcing this view of children's literature as a minor, insignificant genre by referring to it as "pseudo-literature."[45] Until recent decades, children's literature was generally excluded from serious critical and theoretical scholarship. Even in countries where children's literature enjoyed a more respected status, as in the Scandinavian countries, it was a very distinct genre that was separated from general literature.

Until quite recently, in most countries, children's authors had a very low status in the press as well as in literary journals. There was a widespread view that an author only became a full-fledged writer when he or she was published for adults. Children's authors and children's literature scholars around the globe have struggled to change this opinion. In Quebec, the children's author Denis Côté has insistently questioned the distinction made between "les auteurs jeunesse" (children's authors) and "les écrivains" (writers), the latter term being reserved for authors who write solely or primarily for adults.[46] When a best-selling young adult trilogy by Dominique Demers was published for adults as *Marie-Tempête*, the author of the preface revisited the question of the existence of "children's authors" and concluded that there are only "writers, period" (9). The British author Aidan Chambers, on the other hand, distinguishes between "writers," who write for a specific audience and their needs, and "authors," who write for themselves and are primarily interested in producing art and ask themselves how a story can be told in such a way that it has more layers of meaning.[47] There have been many attempts to define the word "writer" and to establish who it should include. In a book published in France in 2000, Dominique Noguez coined the term *grantécrivain*, which could be translated as "greatwriter." She describes the *grantécrivain*, a species she feels is particularly typical of France, as a writer whose greatness is recognized and mythologized during his or her lifetime and who plays a major role not only in the literary world, but also on the cultural scene and in public life in general.[48] Although this concept might seem to exclude children's authors, many of the French writers that, according to Noguez's definition, would be classifed as *grantécrivains* have written for children as well as adults. Attitudes vary greatly from one country to another, even within the Western world. In Italy, as in France, many renowned authors of adult fiction have also been acclaimed as children's authors.

In Italy, children's books written by mainstream authors are cited on an equal basis with their works for adults in biographies and literary histories, but in many cultures the studies devoted to the works of major authors who have written for both audiences completely ignore their texts for children. According to Dagmar Grenz, this is the case for Erich Kästner in Germany. On the other hand, E. T. A. Hoffmann's two fairy tales for children have always received the same attention as his works for adults, although Grenz is quick to add that the fact they are addressed to children "has mostly been neglected or denied."[49] Pointing to the example of Roald Dahl, whose children's books are generally ignored in works devoted to the writer's adult fiction, Peter Hunt insists that this "demonstrates how deep is the division between literature and popular culture." This is especially true when you consider that Dahl is "probably the most successful worldwide children's author of the twentieth-century."[50] It is even more disturbing when a crosswriter neglects his own children's books. Despite the importance that Michel Tournier attributes to his children's texts, the only reference to them in his autobiography is a brief endnote mentioning the existence of *Friday and Robinson.*

Mainstream Italian authors who also write for young readers have never suffered noticeably from the negative image that has often stigmatized their counterparts in other countries, causing them to take a defensive stance about their writing when it is categorized for children. The Italian situation was the exception rather than the rule, however. Authors who wrote primarily for adults often tended to speak about their works read by children, regardless of their success, somewhat reluctantly, indeed apologetically. Some, like Arthur Ransome, even denied repeatedly that they wrote for children. Tournier continues to deny vehemently that he writes children's books. Many authors who publish in both markets have taken great care not to allow themselves to be categorized as "children's authors." The message that had obviously reached many writers was that it was acceptable to be published for children, but, at all costs, avoid calling yourself a children's author. The refusal to divide one's work into adult and juvenile fiction, and the resulting ambiguity, could be interpreted as a deliberate attempt to avoid this categorization. That may still be the case for a large number of those who prefer to be viewed as "crossover authors."

Writers who more or less willingly embraced the "children's author" label were sometimes marginalized, even completely excluded from the canon, in spite of receiving prestigious awards for adult novels. A notable example is the French writer Henri Bosco, who has been somewhat marginalized by literary histories even though he won the prestigious Prix Théophraste Renaudot in 1945 for his adult novel *Le Mas Théotime* (*The Farm Théotime*). That same year, he published his best-known and most translated work, *The Boy and the River,* which became a French children's classic with sales of more than three million copies. The original edition of the novel was not published for a young audience, but when Gallimard brought out a children's edition in 1953, Bosco himself began calling it a children's book and speaking of his status as a children's author. A number of scholars are convinced that Bosco's reputation as a children's author, which was firmly established in 1959 when he won the Grand Prix de la Littérature pour les Jeunes, irreparably compromised his status in the adult canon.

Many writers adopt a pseudonym when they begin writing children's books. One cannot help wondering if they are afraid that their status as a mainstream writer would be tarnished if their name was associated with a children's book. It is also possible, however, that the pen name reflects a feeling of split personality. Although the majority of writers say that they do not feel any different when they write for one audience or the other, there are exceptions. Lian Hearn, the author of the bestselling crossover series Tales of the Otori, is well known in Australia as an author of children's books under the name Gillian Rubenstein. The series was so strikingly different from anything she had written previously that she felt the need for a new name. In her case, changing genres called for a new identity. There was an added benefit for Hearn, who dislikes publicity and could now refuse interviews "because Lian Hearn doesn't exist."[51] Hearn/Rubenstein did not need to worry about the stigma attached to writing children's books, as attitudes have changed dramatically in the past few years. Commenting, in 2002, on the sudden rise in adult authors writing young adult fiction, Lois Lowry, two-time winner of the Newbery Medal, said: "In the past, there's been an attitude that writing for children is a lesser art. So for these highly respected authors to be taking it up *may* indicate that that attitude is changing."[52] If there was still some doubt about the attitude shift in 2002, it has been clearly erased in the ensuing years. In 2003, kidult fiction was so fashionable and lucrative that Britain's trendy *Jack* magazine published an article titled "Should I Quit My Job and Pursue a Career Writing Children's Books for Adults?"[53]

What is new about crossover literature is the hype and the media attention that it has been receiving in recent years. Crossover fiction is now recognized as a distinct literary genre and a marketing category by critics, publishers, booksellers, writers, and readers. Recent literary encyclopedias have included substantial entries on the subject.[54] In today's culture, crossover literature is very much in vogue. Throughout history, readers' responses to books have often been dictated by fashion. There are trendy books, such as Dan Brown's *The Da Vinci Code*, that you dare not admit you haven't read. Publishers, too, are extremely fashion conscious. One journalist claims that is why, in 1996, so many publishers "turned down a struggling writer's novel about a young wizard at a boarding school. Children's novels weren't fashionable. Nor were wizards. Nor boarding schools."[55] The unprecedented success of the Harry Potter books convinced publishers, as well as the media, to change their opinion. Full-page spreads are now devoted to authors who, not long ago, would have been royally ignored. Initially, crossover fiction was seen essentially as a financial success, epitomized by *Harry Potter*. It was not long, however, before it firmly established itself as a critical success as well, notably with the third novel in Philip Pullman's *His Dark Materials*. *The Amber Spyglass* was followed by other award-winning bestsellers like Mark Haddon's *The Curious Incident of the Dog in the Night-Time*. Even critics who generally disdain most bestsellers as pulp fiction, are now praising bestselling crossovers. They seem to overlook the fact that prior to Pullman, earlier authors such as Jostein Gaarder had already achieved the rare combination of commercial success and the approbation of the literary establishment. Literary triumphs as well as commercial hits, crossover books have brought new energy and excitement to literature and the world of books.

Chapter One
Adult-to-Child Crossover Fiction

sometimes I apply myself so well and have so much talent that what I write can
also be read by children. When my pen is less lucky, what it writes is only good
enough for adults.

Michel Tournier, "Michel Tournier: avant tout, plaire aux enfants"

Until J. K. Rowling's Harry Potter series set in motion an extraordinary child-
to-adult crossover craze that took the entire world by storm, books generally
crossed over in the other direction. Children have long laid claim to adult fiction,
as we saw in the introduction. In fact, this type of readership transgression has
been going on almost as long as books have existed. Many of the world's great
classics were appropriated very early on by children, even though they were
not written with young readers in mind. Some works very quickly assumed the
status of crossover works. A number of them became almost the sole property
of children, a prime example being Daniel Defoe's *Robinson Crusoe*, which is
read by children around the world, but very rarely by adults in any country. First
published in 1719, Defoe's most celebrated work was not meant for children,
but became a classic of children's literature and inspired countless adaptations,
abridged versions, and retellings or Robinsonnades. Abridged versions of the
great classics of world literature accounted for a large percentage of children's
reading material well into the twentieth century. The creation of a distinct body
of children's literature did not put an end to the process of abridgement or
adaptation, which continues to be widely used to make adult fiction accessible
to children. Although many of the novels mentioned below were adapted,
children often read the integral texts and, in some cases, they continue to do so
today.

Miguel de Cervantes's *Don Quijote de la Mancha*, published in two parts in
1605 and 1615, is the most influential and emblematic work in the Spanish
literary canon and a founding work of modern Western literature, yet it has
often been adapted for children around the world. The much-shortened
children's editions of what has been called the first modern novel focus on some

of the best-known adventures of the mad knight errant and his squire Sancho Panza. Since the first part of John Bunyan's famous Christian allegory *The Pilgrim's Progress* was published in England in 1678, it has inspired numerous retellings and adaptations for children. Although few children read it today, it was a staple of the children's library for more than two hundred years. Jonathan Swift's social satire *Gulliver's Travels* was published for adults in 1726, but it was almost immediately abridged for children. The juvenile editions, which generally retain only the Lilliputian and Brobdingnagian sections, emphasize the adventure and fantasy elements while eliminating the social and political satire. Like *Don Quixote, Gulliver's Travels* continues to be widely reissued for children today.

Throughout the nineteenth century, a large number of adult novels crossed over into the domain of juvenile literature. Sir Walter Scott's historical novels, such as *Rob Roy* (1817) and *Ivanhoe* (1820), appealed to young readers interested in tales of medieval adventure and heroism. Mary Shelley's gothic classic *Frankenstein*, which she completed at the age of nineteen, gained immediate popular success when it was published in 1818. What has been called the first science fiction novel continues to appeal to teenagers, who are familiar with popular versions of the myth that spawned a complete genre of horror stories and films. The situation is somewhat similar for Bram Stoker's influential horror novel *Dracula*, published toward the end of the century, in 1897. James Fenimore Cooper's adventure novels—in particular his most famous work, *The Last of the Mohicans* (1826)—were popular with a broad audience throughout the nineteenth century and with a narrower audience of adolescents in the twentieth century. The novels written by the Brontë sisters—Emily's *Wuthering Heights* (1847) and Charlotte's classic romance novel *Jane Eyre* (1847), which was a bestseller in its day—have long been among the first adult novels to be read by adolescents. Nathaniel Hawthorne's novel *The Scarlet Letter* (1850) is still widely read in American secondary schools. Charles Dickens's most famous novels, *Oliver Twist* (1837–39), *A Christmas Carol* (1843), and *David Copperfield* (1849–50), were written for adults, but were popular with readers of all ages. Alexandre Dumas's immensely successful historical novels, which first appeared serially in periodicals, were quickly appropriated by young readers. *Les trois mousquetaires* (1844) became a children's classic and one of the best-loved novels in literary history. Few children today read the integral texts of Dumas's lengthy novels, but they know them through film or television adaptations. Herman Melville's lengthy whaling adventure *Moby Dick* (1851) has been adapted many times for children. In her afterword to *Uncle Tom's Cabin*, Harriet Beecher Stowe suggests that children even read the novel in its original 1851 serialized version in the abolitionist newspaper *The National Era*. The highly successful and influential novel inspired numerous adaptations and abridged editions for children. H. G. Wells's earlier science fiction novels, called "scientific romances," have always had appeal for adolescents, notably *The Time Machine* (1895), *The Invisible Man* (1897), and *The War of the Worlds*

(1898). Another late nineteenth-century novel widely read by adolescents is Joseph Conrad's *Heart of Darkness*, published in 1899. The nineteenth century was particularly rich in adult-to-child crossovers.

These novels were never intended to be crossover books, however. The authors did not consciously seek to address young readers, but often their books contained themes that other adults saw as useful vehicles for conveying religious, patriotic, psychological, or moral values to children. While many of these books were adapted for children in order to offer them "great literature," it was often with a didactic intention. These adaptations therefore reveal much about contemporary attitudes and expectations with regard to young readers and childhood in general. However, as mentioned, children were not always reading these books under duress or in abridged editions. Although many adult classics were adapted for children in a process critics often refer to as "dumbing down," a large number of integral texts were also appropriated by young readers.[1] Children may not understand all the layers of meaning in these works, but then neither do all adults, and that is not necessary when readers are gripped by the story. The Irish critic Declan Kiberd, among others, feels that subversive texts, such as *Gulliver's Travels*, were deliberately relegated to children's literature to get them out of the mainstream.[2] As we shall see, some novels are so completely appropriated by a young audience that they end up disappearing from adult catalogues. A large number of the works cited, however, have retained their popularity with both audiences. In many cases, the crossover appeal remained strong in the twentieth century due to popular film adaptations.

The crossing over of adult novels continued into the twentieth century, but it was much less prominent. In the early part of the century, many of the distinctions that would later be made between children's and adult fiction still did not exist. Books about children were not yet generally assumed to be for children. Jack London's novella *The Call of the Wild*, which brought the American author international fame, is often mistakenly classified as a children's book because of its popularity with young readers. The story was serialized in *The Saturday Evening Post*, to popular acclaim, in the summer of 1903, before being published in book form by Macmillan. Like *The Call of the Wild*, *White Fang* and *The Sea-Wolf* are also generally thought to be addressed to boys and young men, but in reality, London's authentic outdoor adventures appeal to a wide audience of readers of both sexes and all ages. His crossover appeal is due in part to the fact that he was among the first writers to work with the movie industry and saw a number of his novels made into films. *The Sea-Wolf*, released in 1913, was one of the first American feature films.

As writers and critics adopted modernism and shied away from popular authors who appealed to young readers, books about children were often marketed only for a juvenile audience by the rapidly developing children's publishing industry. Although Lucy Maud Montgomery's first novel, *Anne of Green Gables*, came to be considered a children's book, it was not originally written or published as such. The L. C. Page Company in Boston issued the first edition, in 1908, in a format clearly intended for a general audience. The sophisticated cover illustration, which portrays a mature young woman in profile, would have little appeal for children. The novel was an immediate international success with a wide and diverse readership, as were the sequels. As a popular woman's writer whose books appealed to children, Montgomery was not viewed as a serious writer by the literary establishment. Her books continued to sell well throughout the twentieth century, but they were increasingly considered, by critics and the readers they influenced, to be primarily for a young audience.

Some books written and published for adults were read by a male or female audience of all ages. Like *Anne of Green Gables*, *Maria Chapdelaine*, another classic of Canadian literature, was particularly popular with women and girls. Written by the expatriate Frenchman Louis Hémon, the story of a young woman living on a remote farm in northern Quebec was first serialized in the Paris magazine *Le Temps* in 1914. It was first published in book form in Montreal in 1916, initially without much success, and then appeared in Paris in 1921. The novel eventually became a bestseller on both sides of the Atlantic. Translated into more than twenty languages, *Maria Chapdelaine* has enchanted millions of readers, both young and old, around the world. The novel has been made into a film several times, most recently by the famous Quebecois director and screenwriter Gilles Carle in 1983. Among the books that appealed chiefly to men and boys were the military adventure tales of C. S. Forester. The famous eleven-book series about Captain Horatio Hornblower and naval warfare during the Napoleonic era, which Forester began publishing in 1937, was a favourite with adolescent boys.

Popular genre fiction, such as horror, detective, romance, fantasy, and science fiction, has always crossed between adult and child audiences. Detective fiction fans of all ages read Agatha Christie's Miss Marple novels or Conan Doyle's Sherlock Holmes's stories. The same can be said of the bestselling historical mysteries by the hugely popular Russian author Boris Akunin (pseudonym of Grigory Shalvovich Chkhartishvili), who began writing his famous Adventures of Erast Fandorin in 1998, with *Azazel*, translated into English as *The Winter Queen*. Young enthusiasts of historical fiction do not limit themselves to the children's novels of the popular British author Eleanor Hibbert, who is better known to readers as Jean Plaidy, Victoria Holt, and Philippa Carr. The enormously popular horror stories of Stephen King, who revived interest in modern horror fiction, have a very broad readership. We know what a wide following King has among adolescents in North America, but he enjoys tremendous international popularity as well. In Germany, for example, he is the favourite author among young people.[3]

The fantasy genre has always had a wide crossover audience. Many fantasy authors, such as Ursula Le Guin and Madeleine L'Engle, write for both adults and children, and their most loyal fans tend to read the novels written for both audiences. T. H. White wrote a few children's books, but he is best known for his tetralogy *The Once and Future King*, a retelling of the legend of King Arthur. Although the later novels in the series are more adult, the first book, *The Sword in the Stone*, which was originally published in 1938 as a stand-alone work, is very popular with young readers. The novel inspired both the musical *Camelot* and Disney's 1963 animated film *The Sword in the Stone*.

Fantasy authors who write only for adults have also had significant crossover appeal. On its website, Suite101.com makes the claim that "all ages high fantasy" is a large sub-genre of fantasy. However, many fantasy works that seem to fall into this category were not intended to be read by children. The surreal gothic-pastiche masterpiece Gormenghast books, by the English author Mervyn Peake, occupy a unique place in the world of fantasy literature. The three existing books, *Titus Groan* (1946), *Gormenghast* (1950), and *Titus Alone* (1959), are often erroneously referred to as a trilogy, but they were intended to be part of a lengthy cycle that was interrupted by the author's untimely death. Like the books of Dickens, with whom Peake has been compared, the demanding, dark series captivates and draws into its strange world young readers as well as adults. Contrary to many fantasy authors, however, Peake was not pleased to have attracted a wide following of young readers. Conversely, Anne McCaffrey, an American author who lives in Ireland, is delighted that her bestselling science fiction and fantasy books, most of which are published for adults, are widely read by readers of all ages, including "girls of 10 and grandmothers of 90."[4] In 1968, McCaffrey published *Dragonflight*, the first novel in her hugely successful Dragonriders of Pern series, an extensive fantasy/science fiction series that now consists of eighteen novels or novellas and several short stories, several of which have been collected into two compilations. Apparently, *Dragon's Kin*, written in collaboration with her son Todd, was really meant to be a young adult novel, but because it is part of the Pern series, it was published under the standard Del Rey label.

David Gemmell is considered by many to be Britain's finest heroic fantasy writer. His first novel, *Legend*, which introduced the eleven-novel Drenai series (1984–2004), has become a fantasy classic. Gemmell's complaints about the low status of fantasy could be applied equally to children's literature. At the outset of his career, his publishers warned him: "Fantasy isn't considered literature. . . . Never win the Booker."[5] Gemmel points to works like J. R. R. Tolkien's *Lord of the Rings* and Mervyn Peake's Gormenghast trilogy to illustrate that the genre cannot be condemned on the basis of the quality of the writing. He feels that "the stigma of fantasy" continues to frighten publishers, prompting them to bill books under some other category. According to him, J. K. Rowling's novels are marketed as crossover fiction to avoid the fantasy label. Likewise, he contends that Michael Crichton's *Timeline*, in spite of the time travel, is marketed as a "thriller," Philip Pullman's trilogy as "imaginative fiction," and Terry Pratchett's *Discworld* series as "humour."[6] Fantasy was nonetheless the catalyst of the recent crossover phenomenon that has given children's literature a new status and secured it a place in mainstream literature.

There are clear signs that the attitude toward fantasy is changing in the world of adult literary fiction as well. The British author Susanna Clarke's debut novel, *Jonathan Strange & Mr Norrell*, a hefty literary fantasy of 782 pages published in 2004, not only won the Hugo Award for Best Novel and World Fantasy Award in 2005, but was also longlisted for the Booker and shortlisted for the *Guardian* and the Whitbread first novel awards in 2004. The novel garnered a vast readership among people who do not usually like fantasy. Neil Gaiman's endorsement on the back cover describes it as "unquestionably the finest English novel of the fantastic written in the last seventy years." The historical detail, period spellings, and copious, witty, faux scholarly footnotes bring a new slant to fantasy. During the ten years that Clarke worked on her historical fantasy about two magicians who vie for power in early nineteenth-century London, magicians became a hot literary commodity. *Jonathan Strange & Mr Norrell* was published by Bloomsbury, Rowling's U.K. publisher, and has been widely referred to as "*Harry Potter* for adults." A number of reviewers deny this claim and one wryly points out that "*Harry Potter* is *Harry Potter* for adults."[7] There are nonetheless a number of similarities between Clarke's novel and Rowling's series, including an enchanting mix of magic and the mundane. *Jonathan Strange & Mr Norrell* was the object of a huge marketing campaign. This has been the case for other important debut novels, but, as a writer for *The New York Times* pointed out, this is unusual for one "that is uncompromisingly literary without being shy about taking the [fantasy] genre seriously."[8] *Jonathan Strange & Mr Norrell* was extraordinarily successful, appearing on both the *New York Times* (it went to number one) and *The Sunday Times* bestseller lists. Although one reviewer says "it is not for children, unless they are children who really, really love footnotes,"[9] Clarke's wide audience of readers includes teenagers who have read *Harry Potter* and are looking for a more sophisticated take on the world of magic.

From classics to modern fantasy, today's young readers continue to borrow fiction that was written for an adult audience. In some cases, this adoption is facilitated by publishers who repackage adult works to make them more appealing to a young audience. However, for many young readers, much of the appeal of these books lies in the fact that they are intended for adults.

Teenagers Reading Up

Philip Pullman reminds us that "children don't just read children's books." He is firmly convinced that children should be presented with adult books, mentioning a P. G. Wodehouse book that he received when he was twelve or thirteen.[10] For some teenagers, reading "adult fiction" is, as it has always been, a case of doing things which make them feel more grownup. The adult-to-adolescent crossover may depend more on social and behavioural factors than on literary ones. Ralf Isau refers to it as "the typical 'I-am-not-too-young-for-that'-Syndrome."[11] While that may be true for more popular genres, like the

readers learning English. Adult novels that cross over very often deal with child-hood and adolescence. Sandra Cisneros's internationally acclaimed novel *House on Mango Street*, which was published in 1983, describes the life of a young Mexican-American girl growing up in a working-class Chicago neighbourhood. The novel became the representative Chicano work in the canon, but it was also adopted by both Latino and non-Latino teenagers, and is now widely taught to middle and high school students. The same is true of the novel *Bless Me, Ultima* (1972), by the acclaimed Chicano author Rudolfo Anaya. His coming-of-age story of a young Mexican-American boy is included in anthologies for young readers.

The 1990s saw an increasing number of adult novels and short story collec-tions adopted by young readers. The collection of short stories *Dulle Griet* (Mad Meg), whose title is borrowed from Pieter Breughel the Elder's famous painting, was published by the Afrikaans author Riana Scheepers in 1991. According to the author, the collection is widely read by young people, especially for the sex and erotic content. For the same reason, her novella *Die heidendogters jubel* (The daughters of the heathen Jubilate, 1995), about three girls captured and held willingly in an army camp, was appropriated by young readers, in particular girls from sixteen to eighteen years of age. The public outcry against the sex in the book (the three girls also engage in lesbian sex) no doubt increased its appeal with young readers, and the author believes it has a wider audience among young readers than adults.[25] *The Dancers Dancing*, by acclaimed Irish novelist Éilis Ní Dhuibhne, was published for adults in 1999, but it is read by teenagers and found in the young adult section of some bookstores. It tells the story of a group of pubescent Irish girls who leave their homes in Dublin and Derry, in 1972, to study the Irish language in Donegal, where their new-found freedom allows them to grow up. In 1992, the Danish author Peter Høeg published the international bestseller *Frøken Smillas fornemmelse for sne* (*Miss Smilla's Feeling for Snow*), a thriller, in which the protagonist investigates the death of a neighbour's child. Although the novel was marketed for adults, it was widely read by teenagers, particularly in the Nordic countries. Some critics have said that the 1994 novel *De rode strik* (The red bow), by the Dutch author Mensje van Keulen, could be read by people from the age of eight to eighty. The author herself does not agree because she feels the book is too cruel for children, but she admits it could be read by adolescents. David Guterson's award-winning bestseller *Snow Falling on Cedars*, which was also published in 1994, is a popular novel in high school English classes throughout the United States, despite the violence and sexual content that caused it to be banned in some places. Influenced by *To Kill a Mockingbird*, Guterson's novel deals with racism in a fictional community of the Pacific Northwest, where Kabuo Miyamoto, a Japanese American, is accused of killing a fisherman amid post-World War II anti-Japanese sentiments. The 1999 film adaptation of the novel, which was nominated for an Academy Award for Best Cinematography, was rated PG-13.

In 2001, the Italian author Niccolò Ammaniti published the thriller *Io non ho paura* in Einaudi's Stile Libero series, which is devoted to emerging authors of fiction. The English translation, *I'm Not Scared*, appeared in 2003 as general fiction by Canongate, although it was hailed as a crossover novel. Ammaniti had already published several works for adults, but it was *I'm Not Scared* that earned him the reputation of Italy's best novelist of his generation and spawned comparisons with Italo Calvino. Set in the summer of 1978, the year in which Italian kidnappings reached an all-time high of nearly 600, including the famous case of Aldo Moro, the novel tells the gripping story of a nine-year-old boy who discovers a child chained up at the bottom of a hole near his small rural hamlet. The powerful coming-of-age story recounts the loss of innocence of the young boy when he learns that those closest to him are Mafiosi involved in kidnapping. *I'm Not Scared*, which has sold more than one million copies, remained on bestseller lists in Italy for several years after its release. It has also won many literary awards, including the prestigious Viareggio-Rèpaci Prize, which Ammaniti was the youngest author ever to win in 2001. Publication rights were bought in about twenty-four countries worldwide and *I'm Not Scared* was not long becoming an international bestseller as well. Critics everywhere have given the novel rave reviews, praising its literary quality and notably the lyrical, elegant prose. The film version, by Oscar-award winning Italian director Gabriele Salvatores, has also been a huge success and explains the novel's record-breaking presence on bestseller lists. Two days after the film premiered at the Berlin Film Festival in February 2003, thirty-two countries had purchased the film, which constituted the country's official entrant for Best Foreign Film at the Academy Awards in 2004. The film's crossover appeal was acknowledged, although it was rated R for disturbing images and language. In English-speaking countries, the screen adaptation was released by Miramax Films prior to the book, so many readers came to the novel after seeing the film.

The German-based Bosnian writer Saša Stanišić was born in Višigrad, in what is now Bosnia-Herzegowina, and emigrated with his family to Germany at the age of fourteen, during the Yugoslavian civil war. In 2005, Stanišić won the readers' choice award in the Ingeborg Bachemann Competition, the most important literary competition in the German-speaking countries, held yearly in Austria. The competitors are generally young authors, many of whom are about to, or have just recently, published their first book. Public interest in the competition is immense and Stanišić drew a large following in Germany and Austria, where he is currently official writer for the town of Graz. His first novel, *Wie der Soldat das Grammofon repariert* (How the soldier repairs the gramophone), was considered *the* literary debut of fall 2006. It met with wide critical acclaim and was shortlisted for the Deutscher Buchpreis, awarded to the best novel written in German. The novel was brought out by Luchterhand Literaturverlag, a German publisher of adult fiction that has no special place in its program for young adult books. Stanišić's novel was therefore unique in their publishing program, as many of his readers are adolescents. The autobiographical novel tells the story of Aleksandar, who, as a child growing up in Višegrad, has difficulty keeping his imagination in check and conforming to the provincial town's conventions. When the war begins, his family flees to Germany, where his gift for storytelling keeps Bosnia alive for them. As an adult, he returns to his childhood home, where he must confront the aftermath of a devastating war. The tragi-comic novel about one child's experience of the Bosnian war appeals to both adults and young readers. Karsten Rösel, in charge of press and publicity at Luchterhand Literaturverlag, told me in an e-mail message on September 11, 2007 that the audience at the author's readings is largely made up of young people, especially between the ages of twenty and thirty, but also consists of older adults interested in that period of Yugoslavian history.

Awards and reviews often play a role in the crossover of adult novels to a young adult audience. K. Sello Duiker, a South African author born in Soweto at the height of apartheid, published his debut novel *Thirteen Cents* in 2000. The coming-of-age story about a young Cape Town street child named Azure, who is a helpless victim of adult exploitation, got very positive reviews, in which there was no indication that it was intended for teenagers. The novel was nonetheless entered for the Noma Award for African Literature in the children's and young adult section. Many readers read the book in that context, but a number of critics felt that it should not have been entered since it was definitely not a book for young people. This view seemed to be confirmed when the novel won the 2001 Commonwealth Writers' Prize for Best First Book, Africa Region. The somewhat ambivalent status of this disturbing novel resulted in an audience of both adults and teenagers.

Duiker's second novel, *The Quiet Violence of Dreams*, about a young black man from a middle-class family who comes to terms with his sexuality, was awarded the Herman Charles Bosman Prize and was runner-up for *The Sunday Times* Literary Award in 2001. The author told his Dutch publishers that, in the South African context, he was writing "for people between 23 and 30 years of age—people in [his] age group" because they have to confront so many changes. Through the eyes of a young black man, Duiker explores contemporary youth culture. The author considered it "a rite-of-passage novel" which shows that young Africans are not really any different from young people elsewhere.[26] Duiker's third novel *The Hidden Star*, published posthumously by Umuzi in 2005, recasts African folklore in a modern realistic setting, telling the story of a young girl who finds a magical stone. On their website, the publisher markets it as "a timeless tale that will appeal to adults and children alike." This deliberate marketing for both readerships may reflect the publisher's attempt to find as large a market as possible for Duiker's final novel. At the time of his death in 2005 (he committed suicide), the 27-year-old author was considered the most promising of the emerging generation of post-apartheid black writers, and had a wide and loyal following, particularly among a younger generation of readers.

In 2002, *Books for Keeps*, a British magazine that reviews children's books, added to their review section a fourteen-plus category, which includes adult titles in addition to young adult titles. In her editorial for that issue, Rosemary Stone explains the change: "This has been prompted by new developments in publishing for older readers which have seen the emergence of 'crossover' titles which are marketed to appeal to both teenage and adult readers and by the increasing number of novels with 'contentious' subject matter." She rightly points out that this new category once again raises the question of "the usefulness and validity of such inevitably arbitrary divisions."[27] In fact, *Books for Keeps* had always included adult titles from time to time. The first issue, published in 1980, reviewed Douglas Adams's science fiction comedy *The Hitch-Hiker's Guide to the Galaxy* (1979), which developed into an international multimedia phenomenon. *Books for Keeps* has always considered the age categories used in their review sections as somewhat artificial, just as they do the division between children's and adult books.

This view is shared by the American Library Association, which states on their website that they created the Alex Awards "to recognize that many teens enjoy and often prefer books written for adults." First given in 1998, they became an official ALA Award in 2002. The awards recognize ten books "written for adults that have special appeal to young adults, ages 12 through 18." Often the novels awarded have young protagonists and many are coming-of-age stories that appeal to teenage readers. Orson Scott Card's *Ender's Shadow* (1999), a 2000 winner, is a science fiction novel about a young orphan recruited to attend the elite Battle School where future warriors are trained who will lead humanity's fleets against alien invaders. A number of the winners are much-acclaimed literary novels. The 2001 list included Tracy Chevalier's *The Girl with a Pearl Earring* (1999), narrated by the sixteen-year-old servant Griet, who serves as Vermeer's model for the famous painting. In 2004, Mark Haddon's celebrated novel *The Curious Incident of the Dog in the Night-Time* received the award. The 2006 list featured a number of notable novels, including Judy Fong Bates's *Midnight at the Dragon Café*, which tells the story of a young Chinese girl whose life is torn apart by dark family secrets in a small Ontario town in the 1950s, and Kazuo Ishiguro's *Never Let Me Go*, which was also shortlisted for the Booker Prize. Another title on the 2006 list was *Anansi Boys*, by Neil Gaiman, who had already received the award in 2000 for *Stardust*, a novel that makes fantasy accessible to a wide audience. Some teenagers had already read Gaiman's first adult novel *Neverwhere*, published in 1996, and many more were familiar with his popular series of graphic novels, *The Sandman*, which one critic has called "the best piece of fiction" of the day.[28] The fact that many teenagers are reading adult novels is certainly nothing new, but they are now actively being encouraged to do so by critics, organizations, publishers, and bookstores.

The Marketing of Adult Books for Young Readers

In the past, many adult novels have been adopted by children and young adults without any effort on the part of publishers. In recent years, however, publishers have begun taking a very proactive role in promoting adult fiction to young readers, sometimes with massive marketing campaigns. The role of publishers and the marketplace will be dealt with in chapter six, but it is useful to examine a few notable titles within the context of other adult-to-child crossovers. A notable recent example is Yann Martel's *Life of Pi* (2001), which won the Man Booker Prize in 2002. It turned a previously unknown Spanish-born Canadian author into a bestselling author whose novel has sold in excess of six million copies in forty territories worldwide. The novel sold exceedingly well in both the adult and young adult markets. Jamie Byng, whose Scottish publishing house Canongate brought out the novel in Britain, rejoiced that a book capable of changing a person's way of thinking was "out-selling all the commercial trash" and "enjoying such an enormous readership."[29] Putting it in the tradition of works like *Robinson Crusoe, Gulliver's Travels,* and *Moby Dick,* Margaret Atwood describes *Life of Pi* as "a boys' adventure for grownups."[30] However, the magic realist fable about a sixteen-year-old boy, Pi Patel, and a 450-pound Bengal tiger, Richard Parker, adrift at sea on a lifeboat for 227 days was praised for its ability to charm young and old alike. In the United States, Harcourt classified the novel as both fiction and juvenile fiction. The Harvest Books imprint published a student edition in 2004. In 2005, the Croatian artist Tomislav Torjanac won an international competition to illustrate the novel and the result was a lavishly produced edition with forty colour illustrations. Martel's novel was adapted as a play that was classified as "family theatre" for eight years of age to adult by the Brewery Theatre in the United Kingdom, and as a film that is scheduled to be released by Fox 2000 Pictures in 2009. "*Life of Pi* has reached far beyond the market for the most successful literary fiction and become a phenomenon with entirely its own momentum," said David Graham, managing director of Canongate.[31] Unlike any previous Booker Award winner, *Life of Pi* had wide appeal for young readers.

The Man Booker Prize-winning novel the following year, D. B. C. Pierre's debut novel *Vernon God Little* (2003), also crossed over to a young adult audience. A customer review on Amazon.com on July 6, 2006, by a male young adult reader from Australia using the name Hacksshadows, pronounced it "one of those rare books that would appeal to young adult male readers." Pierre deals with the almost taboo subject of school violence in this story of a marginalized Texas teenager running from the law in the wake of a Columbine-style school shooting. The novel is a darkly comic satire of American society that was likened by the Booker judges to Salinger's *Catcher in the Rye.* The postmodern novel is narrated in the idiomatic adolescent voice of fifteen-year-old Vernon Gregory Little, whose vision of the adult world that surrounds him is savagely satiric. Martel's and Pierre's novels indicate that the gap is narrowing between award-winning literary fiction and popular crossover fiction.

In 2002, with a great deal of hype, Bloomsbury, the U.K. publisher of the Harry Potter books, published *The Little Friend*, the long-awaited follow-up to Donna Tartt's 1992 debut novel and literary sensation *The Secret History*. The Southern gothic novel is a combination of thriller and Bildungsroman about a very unusual twelve-year-old girl, who is obsessed by death and with solving her brother's murder, which took place when she was just a baby. *The Little Friend* has been described as "a grownup book that captures the dark, *Lord of the Flies* side of childhood and classic children's literature," and also as a book that "can sometimes seem more like a young-adult adventure novel."[32] Despite reviews connecting it to the young adult novel, *The Little Friend* did not capture a large crossover market.

Also in 2002, the Canadian screenwriter Lori Lansens published her first novel, *Rush Home Road*, to a great deal of international critical acclaim. The story of an elderly black woman who finds an abandoned five-year-old on the steps of her trailer park home had sold in eleven territories before the manuscript was even edited. When Lansens published her second novel, *The Girls*, in 2005, she assumed it was for the same adult readership. Inspired by a documentary on the conjoined Schappell sisters, Lansens tells the story of Rose and Ruby Darlen, craniopagus twins from a small town in Ontario. Composed as a memoir that marks the sisters' thirtieth birthday, it is a remarkable dual narrative told from the perspectives of both girls, who have very different personalities although they share the same body. The book was an almost instant success. During promotional tours across Canada, Lansens learned that the 457-page novel was appealing to a younger audience of girls, who liked the confessional format, particularly the twins' memories of their childhood. An anecdote related by the author underscores its crossover appeal. One thirteen-year-old told Lansens that "it was the first hardcover she ever bought . . . with her own money," and asked her to sign it to her grandmother. Lansens suggested to her publisher, Knopf Canada, that the book also be promoted to a young adult audience, so when Vintage Canada printed *The Girls* in paperback in 2006, it was also pitched at a young adult market.

Adult novels are also being promoted for a young adult audience in many bookstores. That is not only true of award-winning bestsellers like *Life of Pi*, but also lower profile adult novels of high literary quality. These books are often rites-of-passage novels with adolescent protagonists. For example, Miriam Toews's *A Complicated Kindness* (2004), the irreverent coming-of-age story about a wry sixteen-year-old who rebels against the conventions of a strict Mennonite community in rural Manitoba, is displayed in young adult sections of some Canadian bookstores.

In a 2006 article devoted to "How Publishers are Re-branding Adult Fiction for Younger Readers," Andre Mayer rightly states that "the fact that teenagers are picking up ostensibly grown-up fiction is hardly novel." Evoking his childhood memory of spending recesses in Grade 7 "thumbing through Sidney Sheldon's salacious trash with other curious 12-year-olds," he points out that "the difference nowadays is that publishers and vendors are becoming more proactive with young bookworms."[33] Many contemporary adult novels are being successfully marketed for young readers. Marion Garner, publisher at Vintage Canada, agrees that "it isn't a new phenomenon in terms of seeing that there's an appeal, but consciously deciding to target those readers is relatively new."[34] Although there is now much more hype and high-profile marketing in promoting a promising adult-to-child crossover, publishers have, in fact, long been involved in this kind of border crossing, as we shall see in the following sections.

From Adult Novel to Children's Series

A number of modern children's classics were originally published for adults and subsequently marketed for children as well. One such novel provides a particularly interesting case of an adult novel becoming a children's classic, because it also constitutes the first novel in a very popular five-book series for children. The first edition of Henri Bosco's *The Boy and the River*, published by Charlot in Algiers in 1945, was not intended for children. There was no indication that the author considered it suitable for young readers until the discovery, in 1995, of a letter he had written to a friend on July 11, 1945, shortly after the book's appearance. The letter describes the novel's intended audience as "children, adolescents, and poets." The first children's edition was not published until 1953, when it was taken over by Gallimard and appeared in their children's series La Bibliothèque blanche. Although Bosco's *The Boy and the River* has remained unchanged since its publication at the end of the war, except for modifications of a paratextual nature, its physical appearance and its image in the minds of readers, critics, and perhaps even the author, evolved significantly over the years. Since 1953, Bosco's novel has appeared in most of Gallimard's important series of children's fiction, generally as one of the first titles to launch the new series. At the same time, the bestselling "children's book" has never stopped appealing to a crossover audience, and it continues to be reissued for adults as well.

The success of the first children's edition of *The Boy and the River* seems to have inspired Bosco to continue the story because, between 1956 and 1958, he published the four remaining novels of what is generally referred to as the Pascalet cycle. The first sequel written by Bosco was *La clef des champs* (The key to the fields), which was published in Algiers in 1956. Like the original edition of *The Boy and the River*, it was not targeted at young readers. It is a beautiful bibliophilic edition, illustrated with original watercolours by Jacques Houplain. Two years later, *La clef des champs* was republished, under the title *Pascalet*, in La Bibliothèque blanche series, where it became the fifth novel in the cycle. Thus the opening and closing stories of the series both have a crossover readership. Although *The Boy and the River* continues to appear in editions for both adults and children, since *Pascalet*'s appearance in the children's series, the novel has not been reissued for adults. Because the rare, original edition is unobtainable, *La clef des champs* has been effectively eliminated from the adult catalogue.

Three of the sequels, *Le renard dans l'île* (*The Fox in the Island*, 1956), *Barboche* (1957)—later published as *Le chien Barboche* (The dog Barboche), and *Bargabot* (1958), were undoubtedly written specifically for Gallimard's children's series and have appeared only in children's editions. However, the highly poetic *Barboche*, which tells the story of the dreamlike journey that Pascalet makes with his dog Barboche and his aged Tante Martine to the village of her childhood, just as his own childhood comes to an end, is generally considered to be the most difficult novel of the series and consequently the least accessible to young readers. The French author Samivel, who also wrote for both children and adults, suggested perspicaciously that *Barboche* is only considered difficult for children because adults commonly underestimate young readers.[35] Furthermore, it was for this novel that Bosco was awarded the Grand Prix de la Littérature pour les Jeunes in 1959. The author nonetheless intended *Barboche* to be a crossover novel that would be read by adults as well. The manuscript is preceded by a page entitled "foreword for grown-ups," which was eliminated, probably by the editor, when the book was published.[36]

Almost twenty years after its release for adults, Bosco's *L'Âne Culotte* (The donkey Culotte, 1937) was also published in a children's edition by the Club des Jeunes Amis du Livre. Unfortunately, this edition, which has been out of print for years, is the only integral version of *L'Âne Culotte* published for children. Like *The Boy and the River*, this novel continues to be reprinted regularly for both children and adults. From the 1950s onward, the author would speak of *L'Âne Culotte* as his first "children's book," stating that if the tale has the good fortune to appeal "to grown-ups," it is nonetheless "a children's book."[37] However, *L'Âne Culotte*'s status as a crossover text is clearly indicated in Bosco's adult novel *Un rameau de la nuit* (*The Dark Bough*), which was published in 1950, several years before the former appeared in a children's edition. The author embeds in *The Dark Bough* a *mise en abyme* of the reception that he envisaged for the novel: the adult protagonist carries a copy of *L'Âne Culotte* in his knapsack on a long walking tour and reads it to his hostess and her young nephew, who are equally enchanted by the story.[38]

The appropriation of *L'Âne Culotte* by young readers is a rather curious phenomenon and its status as a children's book highly problematic. Whereas *The Boy and the River* introduces a cycle in which all the novels were published in children's editions, *L'Âne Culotte* is the first volume of a trilogy in which the other two novels are exclusively for an adult readership. In fact, the first sequel, *Hyacinthe*, is one of the author's most difficult novels. Bosco's trilogy constitutes a rare example of a series of books in which one is published for children and the other two for adults only.

underwent some rewriting for the new audience. The excerpt became a thin soft-cover book for young children. Because the rewriting process of the excerpt was not extensive, *Na reke Angare* has been included here rather than in the chapter devoted to the rewriting of texts for another audience. Rasputin was one of the major writers of Russian literature during the Soviet period, and the adult novella deals with the decline of the traditional Russian village in the wake of Soviet "improvements." Five years after his native Siberian village was flooded as part of a hydroelectric project, the protagonist of "Downstream," a frustrated writer who has been criticized by the Writers' Union, travels down the Angara River and recalls moments of his past. Viktor's most vivid memory, which constitutes an analepsis in the novella, is his nocturnal trip to the river on his sixth birthday to watch the annual breakup of the ice. The narrator explains the significance of this precious memory, which would later become the subject of the children's book: "Memories linked to the river lived within him distinct from other memories; they lived like a warm, heartfelt sorrow beside which he would often rest and warm himself before moving on. He understood: childhood had preserved them—everything relating to first impressions is preserved for a long time, perhaps forever, but the crux of the matter was that out of many other things childhood had set precisely these apart" (387). The children's story contains none of the sadness, frustration, and anguish of the novella, as it focuses on the young Viktor and his idyllic, carefree childhood on the Angara River, in particular the anticipation of the ice breakup.

In 2003, an excerpt from John Irving's adult novel *A Widow for One Year* (1998) was published by Diogenes, with illustrations by the Swiss illustrator Tatjana Hauptmann, as *Ein Geräusch, wie wenn einer versucht, kein Geräusch zu machen*. The picturebook appeared the following year in English, under the title *A Sound Like Someone Trying Not to Make a Sound*. The Swiss publisher suggests that nothing could be more natural than a children's book by John Irving, in light of the importance of the themes of childhood, adolescence, and coming of age in his adult novels. The blurb on the Diogenes website states that "sometimes children's stories are hidden within stories for adults—one has only to discover them." It was Diogenes director Winfried Stephan's idea to extract from *A Widow for One Year* the "children's story" that the fictional, unsympathetic children's author Ted Cole tells his daughter. The rather strange tale deals with the fears that children experience at night. The young protagonist Tom wakes up frightened after hearing a strange noise. Much of the story's charm derives from the boy's extraordinarily descriptive imagination, as he attempts to explain to his father what the noise sounded like. After several absurd possibilities, such as "a monster with no arms and no legs," he describes it as "a sound like someone trying not to make a sound." His father's simple explanation—there is a mouse in the wall—reassures Tom, but terrifies his younger brother who doesn't know what a mouse is and stays awake imagining his own monster. Tatjana Hauptmann, who has been working with Diogenes for many years, was commissioned to do the illustrations for the picturebook because they considered her style most in tune with the story. Anna von Planta, editor at Diogenes, told me in an e-mail message on February 5, 2007, that Irving himself loved Hauptmann's illustrations. In her shadowy, moonlit pencil drawings of Tom wandering through the dark, sleeping house, attentive viewers will notice bulges in the wall and fluttering clothing that suggest hidden horrors in keeping with the boy's strange descriptions. The Swiss publisher does not specify an age category for the picturebook, but the American publisher indicates ages four and up, and reviews generally recommend it for preschool to about age six. A number of critics feel that the text is too complex for the intended audience, while some also believe that, in spite of the father's reassuring explanation, there is too much emphasis on frightening details for this age category. In any case, the picturebook that turned Irving into a children's author has strong appeal with adults.

The Crossover of Novellas for Adults

Sometimes an entire adult novella is repackaged for children. Le Clézio's *Pawana*, a work originally written for the stage and published for adults in 1992, was reissued for children in 1995, with illustrations by Georges Lemoine. It appeared in Gallimard's Lecture Junior series for children nine years old and up. The story has been more successful in the children's edition than in the adult edition, reminding us of the appropriation by young readers of novels such as *Robinson Crusoe* and *Treasure Island*, which Le Clézio himself devoured as a child. The crossover novella *Pawana* reflects the aspiration that Le Clézio has harboured since childhood, that of writing an adventure story in the manner of Jules Verne, Robert-Louis Stevenson, Jack London, and Herman Melville.

    Pawana combines a quest for treasure reminiscent of Stevenson and a story of nineteenth-century whalers not unlike Melville's (*pawana* is a Nattick word for whale). Like Captain Achab of *Moby Dick*, the captain of the *Léonore*, based on the historical figure Charles Melville Scammon, is obsessed by a quest, in this case for the secret lagoon in Baja California where the grey whales come year after year to give birth to their young. John of Nantucket embarks, as a cabin boy, on Captain Scammon's whaler, where he will be initiated not only to his profession as a harpoonist, but also to love (by the native girl Araceli) and death (the massacre of the whales and the murder of Araceli by the Spaniard who had bought her as his mistress and a slave for his prostitutes). The passage to adulthood that Le Clézio depicts in almost all of his fiction explains much of *Pawana*'s appeal for young readers. In his watercolours, Lemoine does not underplay the violence or sex in the text, devoting a troubling doublespread in red hues to the bloody carnage in the lagoon and, a few pages later, presenting a striking nude portrait of Araceli.

    Gallimard also published a children's edition of an adult novella by the celebrated French author Marguerite Yourcenar, who was the first woman to be elected to the Académie Française. In 2003, *Une belle matinée* (A lovely by the Brazilian scholar Gloria Pondé, to mark the twenty-fifth anniversary of the death of a major author who had never distinguished between young and adult audiences. Mello was an appropriate choice as illustrator because he believes that a good story should always interest adults as well as children.[51]

Guimarães Rosa is a difficult author even for adults, so *Fita verde no cabelo* is a very challenging text for young readers, even with the assistance of Mello's visual interpretation. The words "nova velha estória" (new old story), which appear in parentheses under the title of "Fita verde no cabelo" in *Ave, palavra*, receive the status of a subtitle in the picturebook. They alert readers to the intertextual play in this story about a little girl who is called Green Ribbon (Fita-Verde) because she wears an imaginary green ribbon in her hair. In this enigmatic retelling, Guimarães Rosa approaches the story of Little Red Riding Hood from an existentialist perspective, and Mello deliberately highlights this aspect of the text in his illustrations for the 1992 edition, even though it is targeted at young readers. In the crucial bed scene, Green Ribbon confronts death in the form of her grandmother, and experiences the angst that results from sudden awareness of the absurd human condition. Young readers will not understand all the levels of meaning in Guimarães Rosa's sophisticated retelling (nor will many cultivated adults), but it illustrates how complex metaphysical issues can be communicated to readers of all ages through a familiar tale like "Little Red Riding Hood."

The German-speaking market also offers examples of adult short fiction repackaged for children. The picturebook *Einer, der nichts merkte* (The man who noticed nothing), illustrated by Käthi Bhend, was published in 2003 by Atlantis in Switzerland. It is an excerpt from the prose text "Lampe, Papier und Handschuh" (Lamp, paper and glove), which the Swiss modernist writer Robert Walser published for adults in *Der Spaziergang* (*The Walk*) in 1917. Walser is considered a major writer throughout continental Europe, but he is virtually unknown in the English-speaking world and the picturebook did not appear in an English translation. A master of short fiction, Walser wrote miniature texts in terse, solid prose, so it is perhaps not surprising that Bhend conceived the idea of illustrating this text for children. However, the whimsical story of a strange, distracted man who is completely unaware of everything around him, including his wife and children, seems little suited to children. There is even an allusion to his ignored wife's adulterous behaviour. Bhend's dreamy, rather surreal illustrations render, in a sophisticated and evocative manner, the apparently simple narrative of a man who becomes increasingly detached from the world around him, eventually disappearing completely. The use of traditional planograph technique, in which colours are printed separately, makes each book "an original," as the publisher points out on the copyright page. Today the use of this technique in books is rare, but it has been used to great effect in a number of recent German-language books, whose high aesthetic quality is appreciated by readers of all ages. The age recommendation is six years and up, and the picturebook is promoted "for all ages." The publisher places this picturebook in what they call a "typical Swiss literary tradition," one that includes the "children's stories" by Peter Bichsel and Jürg Schubiger, texts that appeal to adults as well as children. While most critics think Bhend's illustrations make the text accessible to children, at least one reviewer wonders if such a "rarity" as this "Robert Walser picturebook" can really find a permanent place in children's literature.[52]

In the charming picturebook *Die Prinzessin kommt um vier* (The princess comes at four, 2000), the well-known illustrator Rotraut Susanne Berner illustrates a parable by the German author Wolfdietrich Schnurre. He was one of the founding members of the famous Gruppe 47, a post-war literary association in Germany that included such well-known authors as Heinrich Böll, Gunter Grass, and Erich Kästner. In addition to numerous short stories and other texts for adults, Schnurre began, in the 1960s, to write children's books, which he partially illustrated himself. The short story, originally titled simply "Die Prinzessin," was published for adults in 1959 in the volume *Das Los unserer Stadt* (The lot of our city). Again, this is not a story that would seem particularly appropriate for children. As in Walser and Bhend's picturebook, the protagonist is a man rather than a child, although his short stature and his clothes give him a childlike look in Berner's illustrations. For contemporary German readers, the rhythmic text has a very special tone that is elegant and somewhat old-fashioned, as is the protagonist himself.[53] It is, as the new subtitle, "Eine Liebesgeschichte," indicates, "a love story," although it is by no means an ordinary love story. This startling, unsentimental love story between a bachelor and a lonely female hyena who claims to be an enchanted princess, is illustrated with humour and tenderness by Berner. Like Bhend's illustrations for Walser's text, Berner's also use original planograph technique, and the exceptional aesthetic quality of this picturebook adds to its appeal with young and old alike. Berner seems to situate the picturebook in a crossover context by filling the protagonist's library with books by authors read by both children and adults, for example, Calvino, Carroll, Grimm, London, Melville, and Orwell. A copy of *Alice in Wonderland* lies conspicuously on the floor by the bookshelf, emblematic of the strange world into which this story draws young and old alike, while the copy of the Grimms' fairy tales on the couch suggests that this strange love story is a fairy tale for all ages.

The preceding examples constitute only a very small sampling of the many adult tales and short stories that have been repackaged for children. While some works cross over to very young children in picturebook format, others appear in juvenile collections of short fiction for older readers. As in the case of several of Tournier's stories, some adult texts appear in multiple formats for young readers of different age groups.

The Crossover of Stories from Magazines, Journals, and Newspapers

Stories published for adults in magazines, literary journals, or newspapers sometimes appear subsequently for young readers. An early example of this transposition in England is Reverend Charles Kingsley's children's novel *The Water-Babies: A Fairy Tale for a Land-Baby*, which was written in 1862–63 as a serial for *Macmillan's Magazine*. Kingsley's satirical views seem to be aimed at the readers of *Macmillan's Magazine* rather than at children, although the story of Tom the chimney sweep was written for his four-year-old son. Published in its entirety as a children's novel in 1863, it was very popular and remained a mainstay of children's literature well into the twentieth century.

A similar phenomenon occurred in nineteenth-century America. Several works by Samuel Clemens, who wrote under the pen name Mark Twain, were serialized in magazines before appearing in book form. When Twain began *The Adventures of Tom Sawyer* (1876), he did not consider that he was writing for children. After William Dean Howells, editor of the *Atlantic Monthly*, convinced him that it was a boys' book, the author promoted it as a book for readers of all ages. Although sales of *Tom Sawyer* were initially rather lukewarm, by the time of the author's death it was both a bestseller and an American classic. A sequel, *Tom Sawyer, Detective* (1896), was serialized in *Harper's Magazine*, which Twain considered to be one of the most important forums for his work. Like *Tom Sawyer*, *The Adventures of Huckleberry Finn* also appealed equally to children and adults. Excerpts were first published in serialized form in *The Century Magazine* in 1884–85 and the following year it appeared in book form as the first production of Clemens's own publishing company. Unlike *Tom Sawyer*, in which a mature narrator recalls his youth, *Huckleberry Finn* is narrated in the first person by the teenage Huck, which increases its appeal for young readers. Generally considered to be Twain's masterpiece, the book has never been out of print and has sold well over twenty million copies in over fifty languages. Clemens consistently refused to write exclusively for one audience or the other.

In the twentieth century, many children's books had their origins in adult texts originally published in newspapers, journals, or magazines. Italo Calvino's Marcovaldo stories offer a unique variation on this type of crossover. The first stories were published in the daily Communist newspaper *L'Unità* between 1952 and 1956 for a general adult readership. In 1963, additional stories, written specifically for children, were published in the leading children's newspaper *Il Corriere dei Piccoli*. Later Calvino collected all of the Marcovaldo stories, wrote four more, and published them in a volume in 1963. The book was published in two different versions, an edition for adults and an illustrated edition for children. Calvino's Marcovaldo stories were therefore written and published for both adult and child readerships.

Several of Tournier's texts initially crossed over in this manner, including "Amandine ou les deux jardins" ("Amandine, or The Two Gardens"), one of his most popular tales, and, in the author's view, one of his best works. "Amandine" appeared in the magazine *Elle* in 1974, before being published for children by Éditions G. P. Rouge et Or in 1977, with illustrations by Joëlle Boucher. It was the author's first work to appear for a dual readership of children and adults. A year after the picturebook was published, Tournier included "Amandine" in his adult collection *The Fetishist*, where it was subtitled "an initiatory tale." Without understanding the transformation, the ten-year-old protagonist experiences the onset of menstruation, a scene that the author anticipated would cause the "censors to murmur in protest."[54] For the most part, however, the sexual initiation is presented indirectly, through the maturation of Amandine's two cats, who turn out to be female cats in spite of their androgynous names. Only young readers who are emotionally ready will decode the subtle sign that Amandine has reached puberty.

Another of Tournier's well-known children's stories, "La Fugue du petit Poucet" ("Tom Thumb Runs Away"), was also originally published in *Elle* in 1972, under a slightly different title. It subsequently followed the opposite route to "Amandine," appearing for adults in *The Fetishist* a year before it came out as a children's book in 1979, with illustrations by Alain Gauthier. "Tom Thumb Runs Away" offers a modern, provocative, and, for some, scandalous reading of Perrault's well-known tale, a homage to the author who appears at the head of the novelist's list of the world's greatest writers. Tournier has said that he would gladly trade all of the theatre of the great French classic dramatist Pierre Corneille for Perrault's "Puss in Boots."[55] In his subversive retelling of "Little Thumbling," Pierre Poucet abandons his insensitive Parisian parents and runs away to the forest, where he is taken in by M. Logre (from *l'ogre*, "the ogre" in French) and his seven charming daughters. Tournier's ogre is a gentle, androgynous hippy-like figure who promotes vegetarianism, ecology, and pacifism, and frightens adults rather than children.

Thus "Amandine" and "Tom Thumb Runs Away" were not only published as children's books after appearing in an adult magazine, but they were also issued in collections of short fiction for adults. Nor was that the end of their crossover. Subsequently they both appeared in collections for children, first in the paperback *Sept contes*, then in *Le miroir à deux faces* (The mirror with two sides, 1994), a lavish picturebook published by Seuil Jeunesse with sumptuous illustrations by Alain Gauthier. The tale "Le Miroir à deux faces" appeared in a journal before it became the title tale of the picturebook of the same name and was therefore previously familiar only to a very limited adult audience. The author also told me he was considering including it in an adult version of *La couleuvrine*, thus reversing the procedure that had produced *Barbedor*.[56] Tournier is a master at recycling his fiction for readers of all ages.

Robert Cormier's anthology *Eight Plus One*, published for young adults in 1980, contains short stories that originally appeared in such publications as the *Saturday Evening Post*, *The Sign*, and *Redbook*. In later years, many of the stories in the collection were published in school textbooks and anthologies for young readers. A series of monthly stories that Bart Moeyaert wrote about his six older brothers and himself for the *Nieuw Wereldtijdschrift* (New World Magazine), the leading literary journal of Flanders, and the newspaper *De Standaard der Letteren*, were later adapted for the stage before being published, in 2000, as a young adult book entitled *Broere: de oudste, de stilste, de echste, de verste, de liefste, de snelste en ik* (*Brothers: the oldest, the quietest, the realest, the farthest, the nicest, the fastest, and I*). In 2001, the book won the Woutertje Pieterse Prize, which is awarded to the best young people's literary book in the Dutch language. The prize and the foundation that awards it were established by a number of critics who felt that children's books should be assessed with the same criteria as adult literature. Woutertje Pieterse is the name of the eponymous child protagonist of a famous nineteenth-century Dutch novel for adults. The crossover appeal of Moeyaert's work is indicated by the success of both the book and the stage production, in which the author himself played the narrator. A CD with the studio recording of the theatre production was sold with the first edition of the book, and, by popular demand, it was again included with the fifth edition.

For the most part, the short fiction considered thus far was all written, illustrated, and published in the same country. That is not always the case, however. Some adult texts spawn picturebooks in other countries. The text of the award-winning picturebook *La composición* (*The Composition*), published in 2000, was written for adults by the Chilean author Antonio Skármeta, under the title "Tema de clase" (Class topic), at the height of Pinochet's military dictatorship in Chile in the late 1970s. The first version was published in a Sunday edition of the French newspaper *Le Monde*, but subsequently appeared in newspapers in many other countries, as well as in short story collections for adults. A radio version of the story was selected "Radio Drama of the Month" in Germany, where Skármeta spent many years in exile, and was also a finalist in the Prix Italia. In an article entitled "Cuando la ficción nace del infierno" (When fiction is born of hell), the author says that he would like *The Composition* to be read as fiction, but states that compositions of this type were quite common and are remembered by adults who were children under Pinochet's reign.[57] Although the text was originally published for adults, the author seems to address his Chilean compatriots of all ages. The idea of turning the story into a children's book originated with Verónica Uribe, co-founder of Ediciones Ekaré, the first Venezuelan publishing house to specialize in children's books. The author made minor changes to the text for the picturebook edition, which is recommended for nine years and up. The terrifying impact of a repressive dictatorship on children and their families is powerfully presented in deceptively simple prose, which is quite accessible to children. *The Composition* won the 2003 UNESCO Prize for Children's and Young People's Literature in the Service of Tolerance in the category of books for children under thirteen years of age. Skármeta demonstrates that political reality can be dealt with very successfully in a picturebook, just as Roberto Innocenti does in *Rosa*

Blanca, in which a German girl discovers the horror of Nazi concentration camps. The Spanish artist Alfonso Ruano uses a stark, harsh hyperrealism, not unlike that of Innocenti's, in his edgy, detailed illustrations that create a dramatic, tension-filled atmosphere into which readers of all ages are drawn.

Specific commissions by journals or magazines have resulted in a number of successful crossover texts. Although Tournier feels that children should be given *contes* rather than *nouvelles*, since the latter is a "brutal, realistic genre" that lacks profound meaning,[58] he nonetheless includes two *nouvelles* from *The Fetishist* in children's editions. The first was "L'aire du Muguet" ("The Lily of the Valley Rest Area"), which appeared in 1982, prior to his collection of *contes* for children, in the Folio Junior series with illustrations by Georges Lemoine. The story was the result of a disconcerting commission the author received from a luxury magazine requesting a page based on an aerial photograph of a highway that cut through rural Normandy. It is the story of Pierre, a twenty-year-old long-haul trucker who, at a truck stop, sees Marinette in a field on the other side of the fence that separates their worlds. Hoping to meet her, he leaves his world of the highway to take the small country roads of her world, with tragic results. The rather lengthy, 71-page story, with its adult protagonist and tragic ending, tends to be read by older children.

L'homme qui plantait des arbres (*The Man Who Planted Trees*) was the result of a commission that Jean Giono, a member of the prestigious Académie Goncourt, received in 1953 from *The Reader's Digest* to write a story for their series "The Most Unforgettable Character I've Met." Giono tells the story of a gentle shepherd, Elzéard Bouffier, who, throughout two world wars, continues patiently and persistently to plant trees, miraculously transforming a desolate, barren landscape into one filled with renewed life and hope. The story has a rather unusual publication history. When the publisher, who wanted a true story, objected to Giono's fictional piece, the author waived his rights, making the story available to anyone who wished to publish it. In March 1954, it appeared in *Vogue* as "The Man Who Planted Hope and Grew Happiness." Within a few years, the story had been translated into more than a dozen languages, and was inspiring reforestation efforts around the world. *The Man Who Planted Trees* is a simple, timeless ecological fable that demonstrates, in a powerful and unforgettable manner, what one person can do to save the earth. Although Giono is the author of a large body of acclaimed adult fiction, he is probably best known to English-language readers for this relatively short story that has been published for both children and adults. The first trade edition of *The Man Who Planted Trees* was published in the United States by Chelsea Green in 1985, and since that time it has sold more than a quarter of a million copies. To mark National Arbor Day 2005 in the United States, Chelsea Green released a special twentieth anniversary edition with a new foreword by Wangari Maathai, winner of the 2004 Nobel Peace Prize and founder of the African Green Belt Movement. When the *Guardian* in Britain asked well-known authors, prior to Christmas 2006, what book they would recommend as the "greatest gift," Michael Morpurgo chose *The Man Who Planted Trees*, which he had read as a young man.[59] Paradoxically, Giono's internationally acclaimed story was not well known in France until it was published for children by Gallimard in 1983. *The Man Who Planted Trees* has been far more successful as a children's book than the only text Giono wrote specifically for young readers, *Le petit garçon qui avait envie d'espace* (The little boy who longed for space), commissioned by a Swiss chocolate company in 1949. The highly acclaimed Canadian animated short children's film adapted from *The Man Who Planted Trees* by Frédéric Back in 1987 (the film won an Oscar that year) undoubtedly helped to turn the adult short story into a very successful crossover work. A children's edition was published with Back's pastel and pencil drawings for the film in 1989.

"Auggie Wren's Christmas Story," published in *The New York Times* by Paul Auster on Christmas Day 1990, is an unusual, highly unsentimental Christmas story, told to the narrator of the frame story by a colourful character who works in a cigar shop. In 1998, the French author-illustrator Jean Claverie illustrated the tale for children, and, in 2003, the publisher Sudamericana brought out the innovative picturebook *El cuento de Navidad de Auggie Wren*, illustrated by the acclaimed Argentine illustrator Isol. Despite the shift in target audience, the textual layering becomes even more complex in the Argentine picturebook, because the illustrations are inspired not only by Auster's tale, but also by Wayne Wang's award-winning 1995 film adaptation, *Smoke*, which was an enormous box-office success in Europe and Asia. Adults who are familiar with the film will recognize the actors William Hurt and Harvey Keitel in Isol's caricatural representation of the main characters. A more subtle allusion to the film is found in her palette, composed mainly of various shades of brown that evoke a smoke-filled atmosphere. Although Isol has said that she does not work with children in mind because she cannot know what they think, she admits that her own child influences her work.[60] For some critics, Isol's collaboration makes *Auggie Wren's Christmas Story* a children's book (it is recommended for nine years and up), while for others, Auster's text makes this book too difficult for children. The English edition, which appeared in 2004, is rightly catalogued as general fiction by Henry Holt, because readers of all ages will return to the charming parable Christmas after Christmas. Isol's playful and quirky, yet sophisticated and thoughtful treatment of Auster's text results in a picturebook with strong crossover appeal.

One very unusual example of this type of crossover can be found in the writing of the highly regarded Danish author Louis Jensen, who began his career writing experimental poetry for adults. In 1983, he wrote his first children's story, and he now writes for children, young adults, and adults. Although Jensen's work is crossover literature, it is not generally discussed as such. His magnum opus is a collection of 1001 short stories, reminiscent of *The Thousand and One Nights*. Some of these stories are published monthly in a magazine directed primarily at adults, but in book format they are published for children.

The author's intention is to publish ten volumes of one hundred stories each, plus one additional story. To date, Jensen has published six volumes of one hundred stories each; the first, titled simply *Hundrede historier* (A hundred stories), appeared in 1992, while the most recent, *Hundrede helt & aldeles firkantede historier* (A hundred completely and entirely square stories), was published in 2007. Lise Kildegaard published translations of three square stories from the fourth volume in a 2007 issue of *Translations*, an academic journal that does not typically publish children's literature.[61] Jensen has created a new subgenre, the quintessential short story. Each of Jensen's hundreds of stories is composed of a few sentences arranged in the shape of a perfect square in the centre of a page. Story and graphic design are intimately linked in these poems that give a modern form and new meaning to the literary tradition of the fairy tale. There is something for everyone in these magical stories, with their wide range of tones (from absurd to serious) and subjects (from rubber boots to giants). Children and adults alike will delight in the love story about a small loaf of rye bread and a French baguette. Rather than writing in "a particularly child-orientated way," Jensen strives for "that combination of simplicity and complexity which would enable anyone to read the story. Children and adults."[62] Jensen himself acknowledges that his square stories are enjoyed by multiple audiences. Accompanied by two musicians, the author does readings intended for adults.

Stories published for adults in magazines, journals, and newspapers have resulted in a wide variety of children's stories, many published in picturebook format. Often these texts cross cultural borders in the crossover process. Giono's story was written for the adult readers of an American magazine, but became a children's film in Canada and a children's book in France. Skármata's story was first published for adults in a French newspaper, then became a radio drama in Germany, before being published for children as a picturebook in both France and Venezuela. Auster's story was published in an American newspaper, but appeared as a picturebook in Argentina. In the case of these texts, the crossover from adult to child does not result from the crossing of cultural borders, as it does with some of the works discussed in chapter six. After its publication for children in Argentina, the picturebook *Auggie Wren's Christmas Story* was published with equal success in the English-speaking market.

The Crossover of Adult Poetry and Songs

Many poets are read by a wide crossover audience. This is particularly true of well-known poets published for adults. A notable nineteenth-century example is Edgar Allan Poe, who even managed to cross cultural borders as a crossover poet. In many cases, major national poets are read by all ages, sometimes even by more than one language group. Johan Ludvig Runeberg, a nineteenth-century Finno-Swedish poet, is considered the national poet of Finland, where he is read by all ages. Many adult poets have been deliberately published for children, either in anthologies or separately in picturebook format. That is the case for the popular French poet Jacques Prévert, who was always a great favourite with teenagers in the Francophone world. Since his death in 1977, Prévert's poetry has been the object of numerous books for very young readers. The following examples demonstrate the diverse ways in which poetry initially published for adults has crossed over to a young audience.

Tournier adds Victor Hugo to the list of "masters" who represent his literary ideal, that is, "authors who never write for children," but who "write so well that children can read them."[63] In a rather unusual example of another author's text appearing in a compilation of short stories by a single author, Tournier includes Hugo's "L'Aigle du casque" ("The Eagle on the Helmet")—part of the famous epic La Légende des siècles (The Legend of the Centuries)—along with his retelling, "Angus," in the children's collection Les contes du médianoche (Tales of the midnight love feast). A rereading of the poem on the hundredth anniversary of Hugo's death in 1985 inspired Tournier to write the tale "Angus" to fill in an important "blank" left by the poet. Angus was first published as a children's book in 1988, with illustrations by Pierre Joubert and an afterword in which the author explains its genesis and begs Hugo's spirit to forgive the poetic licence he has taken in a tale meant to be "a humble act of homage to the greatest of all French poets" (Midnight 163). The afterword was appended to the tale, in the form of a long note, in both of Tournier's collections, thus inviting adult and juvenile audiences alike to read or reread the poem that had inspired "Angus." However, by including Hugo's poem in the children's collection and thus facilitating a comparative reading of the original and the hypertext, Tournier creates a text which has, in the author's own words, "pedagogical" potential.[64]

The works of numerous celebrated poets for adults have found their way into children's literature many years after their initial publication. My Life with the Wave, based on a surrealist prose poem by the acclaimed Mexican poet Octavio Paz, was translated and adapted for children by Catherine Cowan and published in the United States in 1997, a few years after he had won the Nobel Prize. In the poem, which first appeared in the collection ¿Aguila o sol? (Eagle or Sun?) in 1951, a man, while at the beach, is seduced by an ocean wave that insists on following him home to Mexico City. Their turbulent love affair turns ugly after the wave nearly drowns him; when the cold weather turns her into "a statue of ice," he sells the frozen wave to a barman friend who chops up the ice to keep bottles cold. In Paz's fantastic prose poem, the wave is a metaphorical image of a woman in love. In the picturebook, the man is replaced by a boy who takes the she-wave home as a pet, but she proves to be an unpredictable playmate. Buehner's dynamic and dramatic spreads in rich oil and acrylic paint convey the power and movement of the free-spirited blue-green wave. The story loses its anguish and cruelty in Cowan's adaptation, because, although the boy gets angry with the wave, he is quite sad when the statue of ice is merely returned to the sea. Cowan renders the ending even more reassuring for children by adding a final scene in which the boy, who misses his capricious friend, dreams of bringing home a cloud. For the attentive viewer, however, the illustrator adds a disturbing note in a visual detail that will bring a smile to the lips of adult co-readers. As the boy imagines "soft and cuddly" clouds that would be much better behaved than a wave, decidedly ominous shapes appear in a patch of sky glimpsed through a window.

In 1996, Beltz & Gelberg started the current German trend of publishing adult poetry for children with a series of picturebooks based on poems by the Austrian poet Ernst Jandl and illustrated by the German illustrator Norman Junge. One of the most important German-language lyric poets of our time, Jandl is considered to be the founder of German nonsense poetry. He plays with the German language in many different ways, often on the level of single letters or phonemes. Jandl's minimalist poems are simple enough for the earliest readers. However, since most of his poems are better heard than read, they are ideal as picturebook texts for pre-readers. In the final years of his life, Jandl seems to have taken an interest in children's books, working with Junge on the picturebooks. The first poem to undergo this transformation was *Immer höher* (Higher and higher, 1996), an accumulative poem in which a man stands on an armchair, the armchair on the table, the table on the house, the house on a mountain, the mountain on the world, and the world on the night. Junge's illustrations of a little man in a suit standing very straight on the armchair as objects climb one on top of another are quite comical for readers of all ages.

The next picturebook, *Fünfter sein* (Fifth), based on a 1970 poem by Jandl, attracted a great deal of attention when it was published in 1997. It appeared in English as *Next Please* in 2001 in Britain and in 2003 in the United States. Junge had originally created the images when the poem was made into an animated film for television in 1993. The book won the international Bologna Ragazzi award in 1998 and was also nominated for the Deutscher Jugendliteraturpreis. Five broken toys sit on straight-backed wooden chairs in a dark waiting room, lit only by a bare, swinging light bulb. They apprehensively wait their turn to go through a mysterious closed door, from which light pours each time it opens to allow a repaired toy to exit and a new patient to enter. With remarkable simplicity and sobriety, the author and illustrator create the atmosphere of anxiety and apprehension that pervades a doctor's waiting room. The illustrator humorously captures the range of emotions of an anxious child on the faces and in the body language of the waiting toys. Only when the fifth and last toy, a Pinocchio puppet with a broken nose, is called, is the viewers' perspective shifted to allow them to see inside a brightly lit office where a jolly doctor smiles reassuringly at his next patient in front of shelves of toy parts. The text is complemented perfectly by Junge's rather ominous, yet comical pen and coloured-pencil art that uses cross-hatching as well as varying degrees of light and shadow to create a very atmospheric story.

Jandl's third poem to be published as a picturebook by Beltz & Gelberg was *Antipoden: Auf der anderen Seite der Welt* (Antipodes: On the other side of the world, 1999). The picturebook suggests how easy it is to reach the people on the opposite side of the earth: by going straight down. Instead of going higher and higher, Jandl goes lower and lower in this poem: under several sheets of paper is a table, then a floor, then a room, then a cellar, then a globe, then a cellar, then a room, then a floor, then a table, then sheets of paper. Junge's illustrations once again place the poem in a child's context. The cover illustration depicts a little girl who has sawed a hole in her floor and seems to have come up under the feet of the kangaroo with boxing gloves that is pictured beside her. Jandl's most famous poem, "Ottos Mops," which was written in 1963, appeared as a picturebook in 2001, a year after the poet's death. This dazzling masterpiece, about the dog Mops and his master Otto, uses only the vowel "o." The challenge of translating such a poem no doubt explains why the picturebook has not appeared in English. However, in order to honour what would have been Jandl's eightieth birthday in 2005, a competition was held to find the best English translation of "Otto's Mops." The popularity of the poem was indicated by the number of submissions that poured in from all corners of the globe, and not only in English. The poems were judged according to "their respect of the single-vowel principal, basic narrative thrust and general Mopsian spirit." The title of the winning poem was "Fritz's Bitch," by Brian Murdoch, while the runners up were "Prue's Poodle," "Mao's Chow," and "Doug's Pug,"[65] any of which respect more faithfully Jandl's wordplay than the title "Bob's Pug," which appears on the Beltz & Gelberg website.

In 1998, one year before the 250th anniversary of Germany's most important poet, the children's publisher Carl Hanser published the picturebook *Das Hexen-Einmal-Eins* (The Witch's One-Time-One), an excerpt from the tragedy *Faust*, Goethe's most famous work and, according to many, the greatest work of German literature, illustrated by one of Germany's best loved illustrators, Wolf Erlbruch. In the first book, published in 1808, Mephisto lets a witch rejuvenate the love-sick Faust, rekindling the sexual fire of youth. Most children will have no knowledge of the poem's context, but that does not detract from their enjoyment of the magical counting spell that the witch recites as she prepares the potion. The mysterious beings and objects associated with the witch's incantatory verses in Goethe's description of the witch's kitchen are scattered across the pages, as Erlbruch offers readers of all ages a magical world to explore, whether they are familiar with *Faust* or not. A review in *Der Tagesspiegel*, cited on the Carl Hanser website, calls the picturebook "Goethe for children," and it was awarded the Bologna Ragazzi award in 1999. However, the publisher emphasizes the book's crossover appeal for a particular group of readers, one that is not determined by age, but rather by perspective. As the publisher puts it, "For those who, like Faust, look closely enough, suddenly everything becomes very light and playful. A fantastic game begins, for grown-ups, too. . . ."

In 2004, the German publisher Aufbau brought out the picturebook *Das große Lalulā* (The Big Lalula), based on a poem by Christian Morgenstern and illustrated once again by Norman Junge. Written in 1890 and published in the collection *Galgenlieder* (Songs of the gallows) in Monaco in 1905, "Das große Lalulā" is one of Morgenstern's most important and most popular poems. Along with many of his "Galgenlieder," it acquired an essential place in the German lyrical canon. Morgenstern was a master of language play, and in this case the wordplay appeals to readers of all ages. This striking example of a phonetic poem or sound text retains the characteristic features of a traditional stanza poem, but the content is void of meaning. The majority of the sound sequences show very little affinity with the German language, but there is a recognizable similarity with those of nursery rhymes. The result is a playful, nonsensical poem that charms children. According to the author, the Lalulā song encodes a chess endgame, but even with the poet's precise explanation, adults familiar with the game of chess will have difficulty reading the poem in this manner. Junge's wonderful visual interpretation of the phonetic rhapsody, a joyful succession of fanciful images, is a brilliant blend of childlike fantasy, humour, playfulness, and the grotesque. In the picturebook, Junge brings to Morgenstern's nonsensical poem a similar ludic, joyful quality that charms all ages.

A striking example of adult-to-child crossover poetry was brought out by the Portuguese publisher Caminho in 2005. The innovative picturebook *Palavra que voa* (A word that flies), is based on the poem "Papagaio" (Kite) by João Pedro Mésseder, who has published extensively for both adults and children, and illustrated by the Mozambique-born illustrator Gémeo Luís (the pseudonym of Luís Mendonça). The title of the picturebook is taken from the first two lines of the poem: "Há palavras/ feitas p'ra voar" (There are words/ made to fly). The twenty-five lines of the poem are distributed over twelve alternate pages, while the facing pages each contain a delicate illustration that uses the technique of paper cutting. By refusing the conventional graphic disposition of poetry, wings are given to the words which appear all over the page, justifying the title, which means kite. The kite that Mésseder offers readers of all ages is made of words. Not until the final page do readers discover that the words on the previous pages constitute a poem. The delicate monochromatic illustrations by Luís are paper cutouts that share the white space of the page with the few words of text. The minimal text and the small pictures leave a great deal of blank space, encouraging readers of all ages to fill it with their imagination.

The publication of modern poetry illustrated by established picturebook artists is currently a widespread trend. Junge's illustration of Jandl's poems in Germany and Luís's illustration of Mésseder's poem in Portugal demonstrate that this is not limited to the English-speaking world. While it was not a common occurrence in the past, this form of crossover is not an entirely new phenomenon. The whimsical poems in T. S. Eliot's *Old Possum's Book of Practical Cats* were written to amuse his godchildren and friends, but they were originally published for adults in 1939. The cat poems, which became a children's classic, were illustrated in 1940 by Nicolas Bentley and then in 1982 by Edward Gorey's famous pen-and-ink drawings. Andrew Lloyd Webber's brilliant musical *Cats*, based on the beloved poems, had the same crossover appeal. Although the content of some of Ogden Nash's comic poetry is quite adult, much of it has wide appeal with young readers whether it was written for them or not. The cover illustrations for some of his books were done by Maurice Sendak. *Crow: From the Life and Songs of the Crow* (1970), one of the best-known works by the English poet and children's writer Ted Hughes, was published for adults, although he once claimed to have begun it as a children's story.[66] The illustrations are by the American sculptor and artist Leonard Baskin, who illustrated books for both children and adults. Hughes began the work at Baskin's suggestion, as the artist wanted a text to accompany some of his bird drawings. The *Crow* poems have been dramatized and set to music many times and are familiar to a juvenile audience as well as adults. When a children's illustrator offers a visual interpretation of an adult poet, it is generally for a children's edition, although that is not always the case. Even when the book is aimed at children, the text and the quality of the illustrations often gives it adult appeal as well.

In a similar manner to poetry, songs for adults also find their way into picturebooks for children. *Mi laberinto* (My labyrinth), a Spanish picturebook published by Kókinos in 2003, is based on the words of a song by Pablo Guerrero. Illustrated with simple colour pictures by the well-known picture-book artist Emilio Urberuaga, *Mi laberinto* is a more conventional picturebook than those previously mentioned. A doublespread accompanies each line of the song:

> If I am a taxi driver I take you to the sea in my taxi
> If I am a pianist I sing to the rhythm of your heart.
> . . . .
> And as I am only a child I give you the key to my labyrinth.

Urberuaga gives new dimensions to the text by applying it fondly and humorously to the inner world of a child's thoughts, feelings, and imagination. The child in the story becomes, in turn, a taxi driver, a pilot, a tramp, a bricklayer, a writer, and so forth. This is a picturebook that can be read, told, or sung by/to all ages.

The works discussed in this section demonstrate that texts originally written for adults can be appreciated by very young children when published in picturebook format. At the same time, the majority of these books are not published only for young readers. Many of these adult-to-child crossover texts are picturebooks for all ages. The literary texts and sophisticated illustrations of these works extend the picturebook market to a very diverse audience of young and old alike.

Adult-to-child crossover is an important, if neglected, aspect of the cross-over phenomenon. Although children's literature that crosses over to an adult audience has been getting all the attention and hype in the current crossover craze, adult fiction has been crossing in the other direction ever since books were first published with an adult-only audience in mind. In the past few years, publishers seem to have rediscovered the potential of this crossover market. There is now a more concerted effort on the part of publishers in many countries to deliberately publish and/or market adult fiction for a younger readership.

Chapter Two
Rewriting for Another Audience

The gibberish is finished. This is my true style aimed at twelve-year-old children. And so much the better if it appeals to adults. The first *Friday* was a rough draft, the second is the good copy.

Michel Tournier, *L'Événement du jeudi*

A number of authors have crossed over by rewriting works for a different readership. The rewriting of adult texts for a young audience is the more common practice, although even it is a relatively rare phenomenon. Sometimes a prize-winning adult novel is rewritten to make a culturally important text accessible to children. The decision to rewrite the adult novel may be the initiative of the author or the publisher. Occasionally, a text is rewritten in a different genre for another audience. Generally such works are not, strictly speaking, crossover fiction, since different texts are addressed to children and to adults, even though the two works are often quite similar. In a few unique cases, however, the resulting work is not reserved for a single readership, but reaches a crossover audience. Rewriting children's fiction for adults is much rarer, and apparently more difficult, as a number of authors who have conceived such projects have never carried them through to completion. When an author rewrites a text for another audience, the revisions offer insights into the border zone where children's fiction and adult fiction meet and overlap.

Rewriting Mythical and Historical Fiction for Children

A number of authors have retold for young readers mythical, legendary, or historical stories originally published for adults. The first story from *Oriental Tales* that Marguerite Yourcenar published for children was a rewriting of the tale "How Wang-Fo Was Saved." The picturebook appeared, under the same title, in Gallimard's Enfantimages series in 1979. It is not certain whether Yourcenar rewrote the tale of her own accord or was urged to do so by her publisher. However, the process of rewriting played an essential part in

Yourcenar's craft, reflecting her constantly evolving conception of her role as a writer. In keeping with her desire to reach an ever-wider audience, Yourcenar may have undertaken the rewriting of "How Wang-Fo Was Saved" toward the end of her life in order to add children to her extensive adult readership. Rewriting one of her texts for children adds a new dimension to her status as a writer, a dimension that was generally ignored even by Yourcenar scholars, who admitted at the International Yourcenar Conference held in Mendoza in 1994 that they did not realize that the author had reworked the text to adapt it for young readers. The meticulous rewriting is proof of the author's desire to reach this new public.

In an attempt to discover whether the idea to rewrite the tale had been the author's or the publisher's, I wrote to Georges Lemoine, who illustrated the children's editions of both oriental tales, and his reply, on January 21, 2003, revealed the important role of Pierre Marchand, who suggested that Lemoine illustrate the two tales. Lemoine accepted with great joy, confessing to me in the same letter that, with the exception of illustrating Le Clézio, it was the most determining point in his career. This is a very great homage, indeed, as Lemoine is one of France's greatest contemporary illustrators and he has illustrated hundreds of authors. The correspondence between Yourcenar and Lemoine suggests that, at least in the case of *Comment Wang-Fô fut sauvé*, Gallimard was literally correct in claiming that in the Enfantimages series "the great writers meet the best illustrators." In the majority of cases, when adult texts cross over as picturebooks, the illustrator "meets" the author only through his or her text.

The rewriting of "How Wang-Fo Was Saved" dates from the period when Yourcenar came back to *Oriental Tales* for the 1978 reprinting and then the definitive version of 1982. Over the years, the work had evolved in the author's mind from a collection of oriental *nouvelles* to a collection of oriental *contes*. Seeing her stories as tales, a genre that has particular appeal to children, explains why the author came to feel that "How Wang-Fo Was Saved" and "Our-Lady-of-the-Swallows" were appropriate for children as well as adults. From the very beginning, however, Yourcenar nuances the meaning of the term *nouvelle* by adding the qualifier *orientale*, a word that is immediately associated with the archetypal tale of the *Arabian Nights*. Yourcenar had always had a predilection for the genre of the tale, and not long after *Oriental Tales* she published *La Petite Sirène* (1942), a retelling for adults of Andersen's *The Little Mermaid*.

Like Tournier, Yourcenar often takes as her starting point a historical, mythical, or legendary subject. In the postscript written for the reprinting of *Oriental Tales*, Yourcenar evokes the four stories that are "retranscriptions" developed more or less freely from "authentic fables or legends," including "How Wang-Fo Was Saved," inspired by a Taoist apologue from ancient China.[1] The success of the picturebook edition with young readers can no doubt be explained by the same mythological dimension to which Tournier attributes the success of some of his crossover texts. He explains that the wonderful thing about mythology is that it can be pushed "in the direction of the children's tale just as in the direction of metaphysical abstraction."[2] The myth that underlies "How Wang-Fo Was Saved," described by the author as the myth of the artist saved by his profession, stands out with more relief in the children's version, where it is pushed "in the direction of the children's tale." It is significant that the author barely touches the ending of the original story, which was already steeped in a fairy-tale atmosphere. In the so-called children's version, the entire story now bathes in that generic tradition.

When Yourcenar rewrote "How Wang-Fo Was Saved" for young readers, the story was reduced by approximately fifty per cent. While entire paragraphs of the original version are retained, others are completely eliminated. The flashback to the youth of the devoted disciple Ling and his meeting with the old painter who would become his master is removed, thus simplifying the chronology. Abstract metaphysical reflections are eliminated, although the text retains an important philosophical message. The children's version nonetheless also contains a certain number of additions, which are often of a somewhat didactic nature. These usually address the cultural difficulties that the story is likely to engender for the young Western reader, as in the case of the explanation concerning the Han Dynasty at the beginning of the story.

Fantasy and the supernatural are given more prominence in the retelling, where concrete examples of the old painter's extraordinary gift are multiplied. The very first page offers a striking example not included in the version for adults: the narrator explains that when Wang-Fo painted a horse he had to render it "attached to a post or held by a bridle, without which the horse would escape at full gallop from the painting never to return" (4). The style of the children's version is simpler, clearer, and more concrete, but Yourcenar refuses to impoverish the vocabulary, so that some descriptions are retained almost intact in spite of the lexical difficulty. Not all of the changes reflect the author's attempt to adapt the text to young readers; some are the result of a desire to simply improve the story. Her retelling for children is not an impoverished and watered down version of the original. By aiming for an ideal of concision and clarity in the rewriting of her *nouvelle* for a young readership, Yourcenar offers all readers a text in which the mythical quality is distilled and purified, bringing it closer to the crossover tales of great masters like Andersen.

The self-censorship that Yourcenar practises, especially with regard to sexuality, in adapting "How Wang-Fo Was Saved" to a young audience provides a striking contrast to "Our-Lady-of-the-Swallows." This time the references to prostitution are eliminated. The themes of death, cruelty, and violence, so essential to "How Wang-Fo Was Saved" and the genre of the oriental tale in general, are mitigated in the children's version. The author eliminates, for example, the troubling passage in which Ling's young wife hangs herself in the plum tree. Neither Yourcenar or Lemoine hesitate, however, to paint the colours of death that are so admired by the old painter, including Ling's decapitation. Interestingly, the striking image that likens Ling's detached head to "a cut flower" is eliminated by the author, but retained by the illustrator in two small symmetrical and complementary illustrations of an iris petal and a decapitated head.

An adult's reading of the shorter version cannot help but be coloured by his or her reading of the adult version of "How Wang-Fo Was Saved." Adults will be tempted to put the two texts side by side to compare them, reading one in the margin of the other. Lemoine read the two versions of Yourcenar's story, first the one for adults and later the rewriting for children, but he does not remember which comments marked his sensibility and inspired his illustrations. By unconsciously retaining elements of the Emperor's description that were eliminated by the author when she rewrote it, Lemoine brings to his illustrations of the children's version reminiscences of his reading of the adult version, in a process that Gérard Genette calls "a palimpsest of reading."[3] Only adults familiar with the first version will appreciate the intertextual dimension introduced by Lemoine's illustrations. "How Wang-Fo Was Saved" has been a highly successful crossover text. In 1990, Gallimard also published the tale in the popular Folio Cadet series, where it has subsequently been reissued.

Like Marguerite Yourcenar and Michel Tournier, the Mexican author Carmen Boullosa has rewritten an adult work that itself was a rewriting of a pre-existing text. As in the case of Tournier, Boullosa's second rewriting resulted in a crossover text that is read by both children and adults. The hypotext of Boullosa's two novels is *The Buccaneers of America*, the memoirs of the former pirate Alexandre Olivier Exquemelin, originally published in Amsterdam in 1678. It is widely claimed that perhaps no other seventeenth-century book in any language inspired as many works of fiction, both for adults and for children. Boullosa adds two innovative novels to the long list of hypertexts. In 1991, Boullosa rewrote Exquemelin's memoirs in a bestselling adult novel, *Son vacas, somos puercos*; the English translation, *They're Cows, We're Pigs*, marked her successful American debut in 1997. A rewriting of the adult novel, or more precisely a second rewriting of the hypotext, entitled *El médico de los piratas: bucaneros y filibusteros en el Caribe* (The pirates' doctor: buccaneers and free-booters in the Caribbean, 1992), was published a year after the adult novel, offering another variation on the hypotext. Although Boullosa's retellings remain relatively faithful to the events in Exquemelin's work, there are notable differences, some of which place them clearly in the recent trend in contemporary Latin American literature that has been called the "new" historical novel. Among the additions or "amplifications," to use Gérard Genette's terminology, are a number of new characters, notably women and the Black healer Negro Miel. In Boullosa's retellings, women, African slaves, and the indigenous peoples have a much stronger presence and some play an extremely important role.

The two novels are set in the pirate world of the seventeenth-century Caribbean, which is vividly evoked by Boullosa. They tell the story of Jean Smeeks, who was kidnapped and sent from his native Flanders on a slave ship to the West Indies at the age of thirteen. As a slave, the boy is initiated into medicine by an African healer and then apprenticed to a French-born surgeon, both of whom are mysteriously murdered. To gain his freedom, Smeeks joins a group of pillaging pirates or "pigs," The Brethren of the Coast, who view the law-abiding colonials as cattle. The protagonist never manages to reconcile his dual existence as a doctor and a pirate. *They're Cows, We're Pigs* has been praised for its blend of the picaresque and the postmodern in a subversive retelling of the original memoirs. Anna Forné claims, however, that Boullosa does not present a subversive or alternative version to Exquemelin's memoirs, but rather a complementary one, in which the image of the pirate and the pirates' brotherhood is, according to Genette's terminology, "transvalorized" in constructive terms.[4] Critics generally agree that Boullosa's fascinating story, which is dark, bloody, and macabre, as well as humorous and satiric, is for sophisticated readers.

El médico de los piratas offers a simpler version of the story, which is accessible to young readers as well. The adult novel is narrated in the first person by an old man looking back on his life and whose subjective presence colours the novel. As is often the case when an adult novel is rewritten with a younger audience in mind, *El médico de los piratas* has a more objective narrator. The author compares the two novels in the following manner: "the same characters, the same story, but two very different narratives." In the e-mail message she sent me on January 16, 2007, the author told me she wanted to tell the same story in a different "style." The result was the crossover novel *El médico de los piratas*, which was published by the Spanish publisher Siruela in a series for all ages that will be examined in chapter six. It is noteworthy that the rewritten version is listed on the author's website under the heading "novels" rather than with the "children's books."

The majority of rewritings of adult texts for children seem to involve realistic novels rather than tales of myth or legend, probably because the multilayered nature of myth makes such stories more accessible to young readers in their original form. The successful children's novel *Ballet Shoes*, by the British author Noel Streatfeild, was essentially a rewriting of her first adult novel *The Whicharts*, published in 1931. Her knowledge of the world of the theatre, gained from her years as an actress, grounds *Ballet Shoes* firmly in reality. When Mabel Carey, the children's editor for J. M. Dent & Sons proposed that Streatfeild write a children's novel about the theatre, the author had already published four adult novels, all of which featured children, as well as a collection of children's plays. The new audience was indicated in the original subtitle, *A Children's Novel of the Theatre*, but the subtitle was later changed to *A Story of Three Children on the Stage*. Although Streatfeild agreed to write the children's novel, she seems to have seen herself as an adult novelist and was not really interested in writing for children. Perhaps this explains why she used the earlier adult novel as the starting point. Like *The Whicharts*, *Ballet Shoes* tells the story of three girls who embark on stage careers as children. The opening of the two novels is strikingly similar, but *Ballet Shoes* is not a simple adaptation of the adult novel for a young audience. While the setting and characters are borrowed from the earlier novel (the two sets of sisters live in the same part of London), the children's novel is focused solely on the girls' childhood. The adult novel follows the girls into adulthood, but the children's novel ends at their adolescence.

In keeping with the code of children's books at that time, the cynicism of the adult novel is replaced by a more optimistic view of the world, and the tone of the children's novel is generally much more positive. For example, the Fossil girls have more genuine talent than the Whicharts and their future looks brighter at the end. In addition, the seamier side of life in the theatre is eliminated. In the children's novel, the girls receive a more presentable past: the Whicharts are all born out of wedlock, but the Fossils are orphans with rather exotic origins. *Ballet Shoes* was received with great acclaim by critics and the first edition sold out quickly. In 1936, it was a runner up for the inaugural Carnegie Medal, won by Arthur Ransome for *Pigeon Post*. *Ballet Shoes* is connected to a number of other Streatfeild books and short stories, where the main characters or secondary characters reappear.

The prolific Quebecois author Cécile Gagnon is especially known as a children's author and illustrator, but she has also written novels for adults. She rewrote the adult novel *Le chemin Kénogami* (The Kenogami Path) for young readers, under the title *C'est ici, mon pays* (My home is here). Six years of research went into *Le chemin Kénogami*, a historical novel about the pioneers who developed the Lac Saint-Jean region in the nineteenth century. It is the setting made famous by Louis Hémon's *Maria Chapdelaine*. Initially, Gagnon began writing *Le chemin Kénogami* for young readers, but as the project advanced she felt that it was addressed more to an adult audience. In 1994, the novel was published by Québec/Amérique, a well-known Montreal publisher specializing in books for adults.

The author never abandoned the idea of telling this story for young readers, however, as she felt that they did not know their own history very well. In her contract with Québec/Amérique, Gagnon even included a clause concerning a possible version for adolescents. She spent a year and a half writing the children's version, which was turned down by Québec/Amérique in 1997, supposedly due to their publishing timetable. In 1999, the novel was published in France in Flammarion's Castor Poche series for a readership of eleven years and up. The same year, a sequel to the adult novel, *Un arbre devant ma porte* (A tree in front of my door), was published by Québec/Amérique. It is narrated by Georgina's great-granddaughter, a historian who discovers a black notebook belonging to her ancestor in an old pine wardrobe. To date, no sequel has appeared for young readers, so children wishing to continue Georgina's story must turn to the adult novel. It is rather ironic that a novel written to introduce young Quebecois readers to their history was published in France and is not very well known in Quebec.

Both the adult and children's novels are narrated in the first person by Georgina, a twelve-year-old girl who experiences, with her family, the hardships of settling the Lac Saint-Jean area. The story follows Georgina from childhood through adolescence to adulthood and marriage. Like many authors rewriting adult novels for young readers, Gagnon uses a combination of the following techniques: deletion, addition, explanation, and simplification of the language. *Le chemin Kénogami* was reduced by a little over one-third in the version for children. The two-part adult novel has twenty-five chapters and 304 pages, whereas the children's novel has eighteen chapters and 192 pages. The deletions serve not only to reduce the length of the novel, but, more importantly, to increase the pace of the story. Often it is the reflections and descriptions that are eliminated, resulting in a more action-oriented story. Unlike some authors, for example Tournier when he rewrote *Friday*, Gagnon did not rewrite every single sentence, although in an interview she admitted wondering if that was a mistake. At the time, however, she was anxious to retain some passages in their entirety.[5]

Cécile Gagnon rewrote her adult novel to familiarize young Quebecois readers with their past history. A number of other adult novels have been rewritten in order to bring the injustices suffered by a minority culture to the attention of young people both within and outside that culture.

Rewriting Realistic Novels About Minority Issues for Children

The Canadian author Joy Kogawa was asked by Richard Telecky, her editor at Oxford University Press, to create a children's book based on her prize-winning adult novel *Obasan* (1981), which she had written to awaken public awareness to the treatment of Japanese Canadians during World War II. It was the first novel to trace the internment and dispersal of 20,000 Japanese Canadians from the West Coast following Pearl Harbor. The novel garnered several prizes, including the Books in Canada First Novel Award and the American Book Award from the Before Columbus Foundation. In addition, it had a significant political impact, as it was instrumental in the Canadian government's decision to compensate Japanese-Canadians. The story of Naomi Nakane is inspired by Kogawa's own experiences, as she and her family are sent from their Vancouver home to an internment camp in an interior British Columbia ghost town, and then after the war to a farm in southern Alberta. The effect of the war is seen through the eyes of a child, who grows up with suffering and prejudice without giving way to bitterness, despair, or anger. In the sequel, *Itsuka*, Naomi is an adult who, like Kogawa herself, becomes involved in the redress movement and comes to terms with the events of her childhood.

The rewritten version of *Obasan*, entitled *Naomi's Road* (1986), is the only story that Kogawa has targeted at young readers, although the ease with which she wrote it has caused the author to wonder if she should not do more children's books.[6] *Naomi's Road* was the first Canadian novel for young readers to deal with this painful page of the country's history. Initially Kogawa thought it was going to be more or less a case of doing captions to pictures for a simple book for very young children. As the rewriting progressed, the book was aimed at older and older children. The plot of *Obasan*, a complex and multilayered novel, was simplified, resulting in a much more direct story. Certain elements of the adult novel were completely eliminated, including the mother's death and the important character of Aunt Emily. Additions include Naomi's friendship with Mitzi and the dream sequence at the end that symbolizes the mother's death in Japan. As is generally the case in a rewriting for children, the language was simplified. The children's novel therefore has an entirely different tone and style, although reviewers praised the author's ability to preserve the same general effect. *Naomi's Road* was the object of a very successful, award-winning stage production by the Toronto Young People's Theatre (now the Lorraine Kimsa Theatre for Young People) in their 1991–92 season.

The rewriting of *Obasan* presents a particularly interesting case because a third version of the novel exists. Written at the request of a Japanese editor who did not want the author merely to translate *Naomi's Road*, *Naomi no michi* (1988) constitutes a unique example of a crossover text. Kogawa made a number of new additions, including the introduction of the grandfather and the grandmother, but she also eliminated certain elements. The new novel kept evolving as the Japanese editor made additional requests. Kogawa describes the Japanese novel as a combination of the two previous versions that addresses an intermediate audience of "junior high kids."[7] Although it was ultimately published in Japan for children in the ten-to-thirteen age category, the nature of the subject appeals to adult readers curious about the fate of Japanese-Canadians during and following World War II.

Another interesting Canadian example of a rewritten text is *In Search of April Raintree*, by the Métis writer Beatrice Culleton (later Mosionier). When the novel was published in 1983 as an adult novel by Pemmican Publishers in Manitoba, it met with immediate success. In the first nine years of publication, it sold over 82,000 copies. The historical period evoked is very similar to that of Kogawa's novel, but it deals with a different minority group in Canada, the Métis people, and the difficulties they faced in 1950s Manitoba. Culleton's novel has become part of the Canadian First Nations canon. Like *Obasan*, *In Search of April Raintree* addresses racism, displacement, and a search for self-identity within a minority that is often misunderstood by the dominant culture. It is one of the first works of fiction to examine the experiences of aboriginal children in the foster care system.

Like Kogawa's novel, *In Search of April Raintree* is partly autobiographical. The story is based very loosely on Culleton's own experiences as a foster child and the book is dedicated to her two sisters who committed suicide as adults. At the ages of six and four respectively, April Raintree and her sister Cheryl are removed from their alcoholic parents by the Children's Aid Society, first to a convent orphanage, and then to various foster homes. While April, whose complexion is paler, tries to pass as white and dreams of integrating into white society, the darker Cheryl is proud of her aboriginal identity and dreams of becoming a social worker and helping other children in similar situations. April marries into a wealthy white family, but eventually leaves the unhappy marriage in which she experiences prejudice, whereas Cheryl ends up becoming an alcoholic and a prostitute. When she returns home, April is abducted and brutally raped by men who mistake her for her sister. After Cheryl's suicide, April vows to raise her sister's son to be proud of his heritage. With gentleness and compassion, Culleton tells a powerful story of a Native people who have suffered greatly but are determined to regain a strong sense of self-identity and reclaim their unique place in Canadian society.

In Search of April Raintree has been the subject of censorship challenges in North America due to scenes of explicit sex and violence. In 1984, Pemmican published a "revised edition" of Culleton's novel, entitled simply *April Raintree*. The new version was requested, along with a teacher's guide, by the native education branch of Manitoba Education. The revisions were minor and the appearance of the book changes only in size and thickness. The novel did not undergo the extensive cuts that most adult texts do when they are rewritten for a young audience. The 228-page adult novel became a 187-page novel, for ages fifteen and up, with the larger format characteristic of young adult novels. In keeping with the goals of the second version, a paratextual document is added in the form of an introduction. The revised novel has been used as a teaching text in junior and senior high schools, while the adult version is included in university courses in literature, women's studies, and Native studies.

One of Australia's best-known Aboriginal writers and artists, Sally Morgan, has also rewritten an adult book about family heritage for young readers. Her autobiography, entitled *My Place*, was published for adults in 1987. The autobiography achieved immediate bestseller status and won several awards, including the inaugural Human Rights and Equal Opportunity Commission Humanitarian Award in 1987 and the Western Australia Week Literary Award for Non-Fiction (now called the Western Australian Premier's Book Award) in 1988. The autobiography has sold over half a million copies in Australia and has been published in many other countries. Just as Culleton's novel about the Métis is often taught in Canadian schools, Morgan's autobiography is widely studied in Australian secondary schools. In *My Place*, Morgan relates her quest to uncover her Aboriginality, a heritage that had been denied her for many years by her family's insistence that they were of Indian origin. The treatment of Aboriginal people by the white settlers of Western Australia has been a highly controversial subject in the country's history. Like Kogawa and Culleton, Morgan depicts the struggle, both individual and collective, of a minority people seeking its identity. This story is also set in the same time period, as Morgan grew up in suburban Perth in the 1950s and 1960s, but it traces her life and that of her family members for about three decades. *My Place* is a deeply moving account of the quest of three generations of the same family: Sally, her mother, her grandmother, and her great-uncle. A second adult novel, *Wanamurraganya: The Story of Jack McPhee* (1989), extends that family history by telling her grandfather's story. However, like Gagnon and Kogawa, Morgan has never rewritten the sequel for a young audience.

It was once again the publisher's decision to publish a version of Morgan's autobiography for young readers, largely in response to demand from the education sector, who felt that the adult edition was too long for use in schools. Clive Newman of Fremantle Press told me, in an e-mail message on February 5, 2007, that they had previously used the same strategy for A. B. Facey's bestselling 1981 novel *A Fortunate Life*, which they had licensed to Penguin. They accepted an offer from Reader's Digest Australia to publish a condensed version of *A Fortunate Life*, which was eventually published by Penguin under their Puffin imprint, and promoted for use in lower schools. The success of that rewriting encouraged them to repeat the process. Barbara Ker Wilson, who had edited *A Fortunate Life* for Reader's Digest, agreed to prepare a "condensed version" of *My Place*. However, she suggested that they consider three volumes rather than a single volume. As in the case of Kogawa, but in a very different manner, the rewriting of Morgan's novel resulted in more than one book for young readers. Contrary to general opinion, Morgan herself had no direct input into the rewriting, although she approved the project, reading the three manuscripts before they were published. By untangling the threads of the complex, intertwined stories of the autobiography, Barbara Ker Wilson rewrote Morgan's novel as a three-book version marketed as "*My Place* for Young Readers" in three parts. All three books were published simultaneously in 1990: *Sally's Story* (142 pages), *Arthur Corunna's Story* (109 pages), and *Mother and Daughter: The Story of Daisy and Gladys Corunna* (126 pages). Although the books are intended for readers nine to twelve, they are often read by older readers. The bold, vibrant Aboriginal cover art of both the adult and children's novels is by Morgan herself, who is also an internationally renowned artist. *My Place* has been hugely successful. Sales of the various editions in Australia are in excess of 500,000 copies, and it has been published in thirteen overseas territories.

Rewriting for a Different Audience Prior to Publication

In some cases, the original adult novel never gets published. The only work available to readers is the rewritten version ultimately published for a younger audience. This form of rewriting generally occurs at the suggestion of an editor or an agent, who feels that the work should be targeted at a different audience.

The British author Leslie Wilson originally intended to write her critically acclaimed novel about Nazi Germany, *Last Train from Kummersdorf* (2004), for adults. She had already written an adult novel based on her grandmother's life in Nazi Germany, titled *Mourning Is Not Permitted*. Her agent suggested that she should target *Last Train from Kummersdorf* more specifically at teenagers, so the author ended up reworking the novel and publishing it for that audience. At the time, Wilson was increasingly drawn to writing about adolescent girls and boys. This powerful, well-written novel evokes the horror of war through the eyes of two courageous teenagers, the streetwise adolescent girl Effi and the boy soldier Hanno, who witnessed the killing of his twin brother. As in many young adult novels, their growing love is an essential element of the story. *Last Train from Kummersdorf* was shortlisted for the 2004 *Guardian* Children's Fiction Prize and the 2005 Branford Boase Award, presented to an outstanding first-time novel for children.

In targeting the novel more specifically at teenagers, Wilson claims to have made significant changes to the work, mainly in terms of simplifying and condensing the material, strengthening the structure, and setting the story out in a clearer manner. The major modification was the ending. In the final version, Effi and Hanno manage to get across the Elbe and find their respective parents. Wilson was not at all certain this would happen when she wrote the adult version, in which they had been abandoned outside the train. In an e-mail message to me on April 12, 2006, the author admits that getting them across the Elbe with historical verisimiltude proved to be quite difficult, but the Imperial War Museum came to her rescue with some handwritten diaries. Like so many authors who publish for young readers, Wilson stresses the demands and challenges of writing for this audience. This view was not shared by all of her readers. One man asked the author why on earth she had written such a wonderful book for children, as if only adults are capable of appreciating a good book. Another person wanted to know if she was "happy" about writing for young adults, as if, as she puts it, she'd taken to walking the streets. Wilson enjoys "the rigor of writing for children, the necessity she feels to pare the story right down to the bone, making it as elegant and uncluttered as possible." She compares it with some adult writing that can "blather on for half an hour" about nothing, an accusation that is levelled at adult fiction by many other crossover writers as well.[8]

To illustrate her point during talks, Wilson sometimes distributes the first chapter of *Kummersdorf* both in the original unpublished adult version and its reworked form for young people, so that her audience can compare the two versions. Her comments about the superiority of the second text are very similar to Tournier's remarks concerning the second version of *Friday*, which will be examined below. It seems that Wilson's rewritten version is also really an improved novel that appeals to a crossover audience, as it was always intended to do. It merely crossed over in the opposite direction. The author claims to have seen *Last Train from Kummersdorf* as a crossover even when she was writing the adult version. Although critics do not specifically refer to the rewritten version as a crossover book, it has a large adult readership. In her e-mail message of April 12, 2006, Wilson told me she was working on a new novel about Nazi Germany for "young people—and adults who want to read it." This novel will not need to undergo the rewriting process, as it is targeted from the outset at a juvenile/crossover audience.

The American author Tamora Pierce made a name for herself with her quartet *The Song of the Lioness*, which follows the protagonist Alanna of

Trebond over the course of ten years, as she breaks ground by becoming a female knight. The quartet was originally conceived and written as a single-volume novel for adults, but it ended up being published as a four-volume series for teenagers. At the time Pierce was sending out the 732-page adult novel, *The Song of the Lioness*, she was a housemother in a group home for teenage girls. The girls would have liked to read the novel, but the director of the strict home felt that parts of the novel were inappropriate, so the author told the girls Alanna's story in a version "edited for teenagers." When Claire Smith, who would later become her first agent, recommended that Pierce turn the novel into four books for teenagers, the author had, in a sense, already done so. Jean Karl at Atheneum Books agreed to take Pierce on after the rewrites. Pierce spent much of the 1980s rewriting the adult novel. The first book, *Alanna: The First Adventure*, was published in hardcover by Atheneum in 1983 and the final novel, *Lioness Rampant*, appeared in 1988. In Pierce's case, the adult novel was never published and the author says it never will be. The original manuscript was cut up and pasted in around new material, and, once she had retyped clean pages, she got rid of all the fragments. She tells readers they have to accept her word that *The Song of the Lioness* quartet is better written than the original adult novel because she perfected her craft during the rewrite. After *The Song of the Lioness*, Pierce continued to write young adult novels that also appeal to adult readers. On her website, the author reassures readers who feel "they may be too old (16, 20, 34, 53, 80) to read [her] books," by telling them that one-third of her library consists of children's and young adult books, and that "the only thing that matters is that the reader enjoys the book, whatever her/his age."

Both Wilson and Pierce agree that the rewritten young adult work is superior to the original adult novel. Wilson kept the original manuscript and occasionally uses it to prove the point that the final work is an improved version. Pierce, on the other hand, destroyed the adult version once she had rewritten the work for young readers. In both cases, the result of rewriting an adult novel for young readers has been a crossover work that appeals to young and old alike.

From Adult Short Story to Children's Novel

When adult texts are rewritten for a young audience, the process almost always involves what Tournier calls "compression."[9] In addition to the texts examined thus far in this chapter, one could also mention the excerpt from Valentin Rasputin's "Downstream," which underwent a certain reduction to become the children's book *Na reke Angare* (On the Angara River). Similarly, the Russian writer Viktor Astaf'ev wrote a short children's book *Babushkin prazdnik* (Grandmother's celebration, 1983) based on the lengthy memoirs *Poslednii poklon* (The final bow) that he began publishing in 1968. One exception to the general "compression" rule is Roald Dahl's *Danny the Champion of the World*, which was, on the contrary, the result of an "expansion," to continue to borrow Tournier's terminology. Dahl had an international reputation as an author of short stories about the dark side of human nature before he began publishing for children in the 1960s. In 1959, Dahl published the short story "The Champion of the World" in his adult collection *Kiss Kiss*. Eventually, he rewrote and expanded the story, turning it into a children's novel that was published by Knopf in 1975.

Like most of Dahl's children's books, *Danny the Champion of the World* is rather unconventional. The subject of the story is poaching, and Danny's father, who maintains that poaching is "an art" rather than theft (30), is presented as "the most marvelous and exciting father any boy ever had" (173). Kay Webb, a former editor of Puffin Books, told Zohar Shavit that she questioned whether the novel should be published due to the "inappropriate" nature of the subject.[10] It is important to note that this is not just because the author was appropriating the subject of an adult book for a children's book. Dahl's other works for young readers were often considered vulgar and morally unsuitable for children. Because British publishers were uncomfortable with them, his children's books were first published in the United States. Although Shavit admits that "as a famous author, Dahl could afford to write on 'inappropriate' subjects and unusual relations between father and son," she argues that the generic change is explained by the author's need to "enlarge" the text in order to have the scope to make both the subject and characters acceptable within the children's code. She also mentions the possible commercial considerations, since "novels sell better."[11]

The adult short story begins in media res, has an open ending, and deliberately leaves gaps and creates ambiguity, but in the children's novel, the author felt obliged to fill in the gaps, providing explanations, motivations, and justifications. The 37-page short story for adults is turned into a 173-page novel for children. Whereas the adult story begins with the preparations for poaching, the children's story begins with a long, flattering buildup of Danny's father, who had to raise his son on his own after the sudden death of the boy's mother when he was only four months of age. When the dark secret of his father's poaching is finally revealed many pages later, the narrator seems to excuse his father by telling readers that they will learn as they get older that "no father is perfect" and "grown-ups are complicated creatures, full of quirks and secrets" (23). The children's novel is illustrated by small black and white pictures by Jill Bennett. The illustrations highlight the relationship between Danny and Dad. The first page shows a photo-like illustration of Danny as a four-month-old baby, when his father had to take charge of his upbringing. On the next page, he is portrayed as he appeared on his fifth birthday. In chapter two, we finally get a picture of his father. It is no doubt because Dahl's novel focuses on a father-son relationship that the claim is made that "this book is for the whole family." Although this billing by the publisher attempts to turn it into a crossover book, Dahl was addressing children when he rewrote the adult short story as a novel, and it is essentially a children's book, albeit a somewhat unconventional one.

Rewriting for All Ages: From Adult Novel to Children's Novel to Crossover Novel

Michel Tournier achieved instant renown in 1967 when he received the prestigious Grand Prix du Roman de l'Académie Française for his first novel, a retelling of Daniel Defoe's *Robinson Crusoe* titled *Vendredi ou les limbes du Pacifique* (Friday, or the limbo of the Pacific), which was translated into English as *Friday, or The Other Island* in Britain and simply as *Friday* in the United States. It is not fortuitous that Tournier, who would become a master crossover writer, made his debut with a retelling of a classic read by both children and adults. Almost immediately after the publication of his first novel, Tournier felt the need to rewrite his Robinsonnade "in a leaner, tauter form," but he claims to have been quite surprised to learn on the completion of *Vendredi ou La Vie sauvage* (Friday, or the savage life, 1971) that he had written a children's book.[12] The second surprise in store for the author, who was still basking in the glory of the two major literary awards garnered by his first two adult novels, was the fact that he could not find a publisher for his new book. At that time, Gallimard, who had brought out Tournier's two novels to date, had not yet launched its children's department and was not in the least interested in the condensed version of his award-winning adult novel. Several other publishers turned the author down before Flammarion reluctantly published the book in 1971, pessimistically predicting that it would not be a success.

A few years later, Pierre Marchand told the author that *Friday and Robinson* was one of the first books he wanted to publish in Gallimard Jeunesse's newly created children's paperback series, Folio Junior. Tournier delights in the fact that Gallimard has sold millions of copies of a book that it once refused, a book that is, in fact, a pirate edition, since a contract was never signed with the original publisher.[13] The so-called children's version has become one of France's bestselling children's books, surpassed only by Saint-Exupéry's *The Little Prince*. The book's popularity is indicated by the fact that in 1981 it was adapted for French television in a six-hour film directed by Gérard Vergez and starring Michael York as Robinson and Gene Antony Ray as Friday. A special edition of the work, published by Gallimard/Flammarion in 1981, is illustrated with photographs taken by Pat York during the filming of the movie. The popular novel has also been translated into many languages and has even been the subject of several pirate editions.

Knopf brought out the English translation in 1972, under the title *Friday and Robinson: Life on Speranza Island*. Tournier deplores the novel's singular lack of success in the United States and in the English-speaking market in general. He has blamed this on the fact that Knopf did not publish children's books at that time, which meant that *Friday and Robinson* was more of "an intellectual curiosity than a true children's book."[14] Yet, as we shall see, Tournier does not want it to be seen as a children's book. Further, he laments that the conservative laws governing the world of children's books prevented the novel from being co-published, by a British publisher and several other publishers throughout the world, with the innovative illustrations of a Czechoslovakian illustrator, Jan Kudláček. Although it has sold millions of copies in France, after a modest print run of two thousand copies in English, it was out of print until Walker Books reissued it in Britain in 2003 under the shortened title *Friday and Robinson*.

Over the years, Tournier's view concerning the status of *Friday and Robinson* has evolved significantly. Initially, he himself called the novel "the children's version" of the first *Friday* and an article published at the time of the book's launching was titled "When Michel Tournier rewrites his books for children." The rewriting of *Friday* reminds us of the long tradition of adaptations for young readers of novels such as *Robinson Crusoe*, adaptations that constituted a large part of the literature available for children when Tournier himself was growing up. The significant difference, of course, is that the adaptation is provided by the author. However, the rewriting process, as Tournier envisages it, is much more complex. The author describes another step that preceded the actual rewriting. An unformulated "children's version" of the novel had somehow pre-existed the adult version in his mind: "Translating *Friday* into *Friday and Robinson*, I had the distinct feeling I was taking a path already travelled in the opposite direction . . . in a sense, I was only able to derive a children's novel from an adult novel because the latter had itself in a way been taken from the former in the first place."[15] By the 1980s, Tournier regretted that his bestselling novel was classified as a "children's book," insisting that the shorter text is not an adaptation for children but rather a new and improved version. The author continues to maintain that there are merely two *Fridays*, and that the shorter one is the result of an evolution of his art toward a more perfect text that appeals to a crossover audience. He expresses this idea quite clearly in the quotation used as an epigraph to the present chapter, where he concludes that the first *Friday*, with all its "gibberish," was merely "a rough draft," whereas the second *Friday*, which represents his "true style aimed at twelve-year-old children," is "the good copy."[16] *Friday and Robinson* nonetheless continues to be marketed only as a children's book, even though many of the author's works are published in both adult and children's editions.

In spite of its status as a bestseller, *Friday and Robinson* has not attracted nearly as much critical attention as the version for adults. Unfortunately, this critical indifference to the children's books of even the most celebrated mainstream authors has been a common phenomenon in many countries. Despite the author's predilection for the shorter version, adults—publishers, critics, and readers alike—seem almost without exception to prefer the original novel. Gérard Genette, for example, refuses to consider *Friday and Robinson* as anything but a children's text in the pages he devotes to the novel in *Palimpsests*. It is nonetheless significant that Tournier's novel is the only "children's book" that the critic deigns to mention in his ground-breaking work on "transtextuality." The second *Friday* does indeed seem to transcend boundaries. Genette describes the "double 'reception'" that the text engenders, referring not to a dual reader-ship of children and adults, but rather to the reception on two levels by the intrusive adult reader "superimposed" upon the intended child addressee, in "a palimpsest of reading." In the author's view, however, the adult reader is not the unforeseen and importunate reader portrayed by Genette, but shares the same addressee status as the child reader.[17]

Tournier affectionately calls *Friday and Robinson* his "fetishist" book and considers it one of his best and most important works, superior to all his novels published for adults. Because Tournier judges the value of his books according to the minimum age of their readership, he feels that *Friday and Robinson*, which can only be read by nine-year-olds, is not quite as good as his two tales, "Pierrot, or The Secrets of the Night" and "Amandine, or The Two Gardens," which can be understood by six-year-old children and therefore constitute the summit of his literary achievement.[18] The author is convinced that his chance of being read by future generations lies with these two short tales and *Friday and Robinson*. In the 1990s, Gallimard made the ambitious claim that by the year 2000 *Friday and Robinson* would no doubt have been read by every living French person.[19]

From the "Rough Draft" to the "Good Copy"

It is revealing to consider briefly the changes that Tournier made to his adult novel in order to create a novel that is accessible to children. The most striking difference between the two works is once again the length. Although most of the original events are retained in the rewritten version, it is less than half as long as the first novel. Tournier rewrote his first *Friday* in order to make it less explicitly philosophical and abstract by weaving the metaphysical specu-lations into the fabric of the story. To this end, authorial commentary and philo-sophical meditation, including Robinson's logbook entries, were, for the most part, eliminated. *Friday and Robinson* was Tournier's first attempt at a narrative accessible to all ages, yet capable of conveying an important philosophical message. Although the original novel was reduced substantially, the author added many new scenes. In fact, according to Tournier, twenty-five percent of *Friday and Robinson* was new material involving games and inventions that appeal to the playful nature of young readers. These included the invention of theatre, music, poetry, and sign language. The author was so pleased with the result that some of these scenes were introduced into the revised adult paperback edition in 1972, notably the highly significant game of the effigies that Friday ingeniously invented for psychotherapeutic purposes. Tournier claims that these appropriations make it difficult to say whether the adult version or the children's version is really the original.[20]

The elimination of Robinson's logbook entries leaves only the voice of the third-person narrator, which some critics consider too intrusive. The shorter version also contains a number of alterations of a didactic or moralistic nature.

One of the most notable involves the scene in which Robinson rescues Friday when he first arrives on the island. In Tournier's adult novel, the rescue scene constitutes an ironic deviation from Defoe's. Robinson actually aims at Friday, thinking it is more prudent to side with the majority, but he misses and accidentally shoots the first of Friday's pursuers. In *Friday and Robinson*, Tournier self-censured the scene to make the hero more sympathetic and to give a more moralistic slant to the version targeted at children. Rather than attempting to kill Friday, Robinson aims at the first pursuer and ends up killing the second. The irony inherent in the profound gratitude that Friday feels toward Robinson is entirely lost.

A provocative author who tries to reach a public of all ages, Tournier often finds himself accused, on the one hand, of perversity by the mediators of children's books and, on the other hand, of bowdlerizing his own books by critics who disapprove of the self-censorship the author applies when he rewrites an adult novel for a young audience. Despite Tournier's bitter condemnation of the censorship of sexuality in children's books, the author himself eliminated several passages dealing with sex when he rewrote his first Robinsonnade. The fact that Defoe completely overlooked Crusoe's sexuality may now seem to be a rather glaring omission, but it certainly facilitated the appropriation of his novel by young readers. After redressing this oversight in his adult novel, Tournier eliminates from the children's version the scenes depicting Robinson and Vendredi's sexual relations with the island. Genette claims to be scandalized by the second *Friday*, "mutilated of its erotic dimension," and expresses his shock that the author himself would indulge in such an exercise.[21] Tournier, on the other hand, claims that sexuality has not been eliminated from the children's version, but has evolved in order to better conform to the needs of children and their diffuse, prepubescent sexuality. Many adults are shocked by the author's provocative statement, derived from Freud's theories, that children's literature should be "eroticized," perhaps even more than books for adults.[22] In his books published for children, the author attempts to respect the child's vague sense of sexuality that often blends with affectivity. Tournier points to the ambiguous scene, added in the children's Robinsonnade, of Friday's intimate relationship with the little she-goat Anda, with whom he sleeps. The absence of this passage in the adult *Friday* makes it the bowdlerized version, according to the author.[23]

The key to Tournier's ability to appeal to a crossover audience lies in the mythical pre-text which underlies all of his works. In his view, the vocation of every author is the renewal of myth. Robinson Crusoe is Tournier's favourite example of a "mythical hero," as he is "one of the basic constituents of the Western soul" and "the property of all mankind."[24] Defoe's hero quickly became the property of adults and children alike and a major figure in literature for all ages. Defining myth as *"a story that everybody already knows,"* Tournier describes it in terms of "a multistoried structure," with "a child's tale" as its "ground floor" and "a metaphysical summit." Tournier illustrates this by describing the pleasure and pride he felt when a technical afterword by Gilles Deleuze was being included in the paperback edition of the adult novel, "while the very same novel was simultaneously being brought out in a children's version and staged as a children's play by Antoine Vitez." Although Tournier refers to the two versions as if they were one, his concluding comment clearly indicates that in retelling Defoe's well-known story, the author sought to write a crossover work: "For me, the proof of the novel's success is the response that it was able to elicit from two readers at opposite poles of sophistication: a child at one end of the scale, a metaphysician at the other."[25]

From Rewriting Adult Novels to Writing Crossover Novels

When Tournier published his article on "rewrit[ing] his books for children" in 1971, the author had, in fact, written only two adult novels and rewritten only one of those for children. The use of the plural in the title of the article suggests that the author did not see *Friday and Robinson* as an isolated and unique phenomenon in his oeuvre. Shortly after unanimously winning the Prix Goncourt for *The Erl-King* in 1970, Tournier indicated his intention to rewrite the lengthy and difficult novel about Nazi Germany for children. Despite its award-winning status, *The Erl-King* is a second-rate novel in the author's eyes because it cannot be read by a juvenile audience. However, rewriting this novel for children would seem infeasible, and no doubt undesirable, to most adult readers familiar with the work. Although Tournier himself pronounced the undertaking hopeless in 1986, several years later he said that he still felt the novel could be rewritten for nine-year-olds. Convinced that extreme cruelty has an appropriate place in a children's book (he cites the example of Perrault's *Contes*), Tournier promised that "*The Erl-King* for children" would not be lacking in atrocities. It has been suggested that *Gilles et Jeanne* (1983) a short novel about Gilles de Rais and Joan of Arc, was the promised rewriting of *The Erl-King* even though it was published for adults, but Tournier does not see it in that light. The status of *Gilles et Jeanne* seems to pose a particular problem for the author. Although he has said that it is "a child's story" and that there is no reason why children the same age as the children in the story couldn't read it, he refused to send a copy of the gruesome story to his nine-year-old nephew.[26] A child may be able to read *Gilles et Jeanne*, but the censorship of adults prevents this book from finding its way into their hands.

At one point, Tournier had even envisaged a children's adaptation of his 1975 novel *Les météores* (translated as *Gemini* in 1981), his most ambitious and complex work. What prevented the author from recasting his other novels in a "purer, less cluttered and more chiselled form; in a word, so that even children could read them," was his conviction that he would never find a children's publisher willing to go out on a limb and take on such "non-standard" books nor an adult public willing to read these "children's stories."[27] It was more than ten years after the publication of *Friday and Robinson* before Tournier published another children's version of one of his adult novels, a rewriting of the story of the Magi, *Gaspard, Melchior et Balthazar*, published in 1980. The adult novel was translated into English as *The Four Wise Men* in 1982, but the children's version has never been translated. From the very beginning, Tournier had expressed his dissatisfaction with the adult novel: "I didn't go far enough, I didn't have enough talent or genius for the book to be accessible to ten-year-old children, but that is what one must strive toward."[28] Apparently the rewritten version, published in 1983, still didn't go far enough to suit the author because he readily admits his discontent with *Les Rois mages* (The Wise Men). Whereas *Friday* had been used as a kind of draft for a "new" book, in which Tournier claims not to have retained a single line, the adaptation of *The Four Wise Men* was not so much a rewriting as an abridgment. Apart from the exclusion of some philosophical or aesthetic meditations, and the reduction of the multiple narrative voices to a single, objective voice, the author was content, for the most part, to eliminate entire sections of the adult novel, while retaining the others more or less intact. The children's version contains only three of the original seven partially interwoven narratives, including that of the legendary fourth Wise Man, Taor, the Prince of Sugar.

At least one critic sees the rewriting of *The Four Wise Men* in a superior light to that of the first novel. He claims that Tournier transformed a highly sophisticated novel into a parable. This refinement of the art of rewriting is expressed in terms of the reception of Tournier's two rewritten novels by the adult reader: "When reading the second *Friday*, one has an awkward sensation of being alternately adult and child; when reading the second *Rois mages*, one feels that one is simultaneously adult and child."[29] Rather than considering *Friday and Robinson* and *Les Rois mages* as vulgarizations or more artless, watered-down versions of *Friday* and *The Four Wise Men*, these so-called children's versions should be seen in the light of an evolution towards a more concise and primal narrative that can be read by children as well as adults.

As we have seen, Tournier rejected very early on what he called the "gibberish" of his first adult novels and adopted a style targeted at twelve-year-old children. In his case, the rewriting of his works is part of a general evolution of his writing. The author expressed this to a group of high school students in the following terms: "When I write, one of three things occurs: in the exceptional case, I am brimming over with talent, with genius, . . . and I write straightaway a work so good that children can read it. Or, I don't carry it off and I write *Friday*, but I have the strength to begin again, and that produces *Friday and Robinson*, which is not at all a version for children but simply a better version. Or I don't pull it off, and the undertaking seems hopeless, beyond saving, and that results in *The Erl-King*." Tournier did not rewrite his later adult novels for children because he no longer felt the need to do so. Referring to *The Golden Droplet*, he says: "*Fabricando*, I learned to write. I believe it is so good that it could be read from ten years onward."[30] Henceforth, he aspires to write only novels that can be read by both children and adults.

Short Story Collections in Tandem

Just a few months apart in 1989, Tournier published two collections of short stories with strikingly similar titles, the first for adults and the second for children: *Le médianoche amoureux* (translated as *The Midnight Love Feast* in 1991) and *Les contes du médianoche* (Tales of the midnight feast). Although *Les contes du médianoche* could be considered the "children's version" of the adult collection, the relationship between the two texts is not at all the same as that shared by the two versions of *Friday*. The stories of the adult collection were not rewritten for children. Tournier insists that the second *Médianoche* cannot be compared to the complete rewriting *Friday* underwent, as he did not change a single line. The text for adults was not simply retitled and repackaged in a children's edition either, as the content of the two volumes is not identical. The children's collection contains a number of new texts—as yet unpublished for adults. Nor does the author try to claim that the shorter text is an improved, crossover version of the adult text.

The new title reflects the major difference between the two texts. *The Midnight Love Feast* is a collection of "*contes et nouvelles*," in which the fundamental difference between the two genres is essential to both the subject and the structure of the volume. In the children's version, Tournier eliminates all the *nouvelles*, in keeping with his belief that the *conte* is a genre more suitable for children because of its depth and mythic dimension. This generic selection process dictated the elimination of the initial story, "The Taciturn Lovers," which provides a unifying thread in the adult collection. "The Taciturn Lovers" tells the story of a couple who feel that they no longer have anything to say to one another and plan to announce their separation to their friends at the end of a *médianoche*, which is also to be a night of storytelling. The rest of the collection is made up of the nineteen stories told by the guests, first the *nouvelles*, "grimly realistic, pessimistic and demoralizing," which further separate the couple, then the *contes*, which seem to bring them back together and ultimately save their marriage because, at the end of the night, they decide not to separate (29). Although each narrative in the adult collection enjoys an independent status, the initial story also gives them a common context, creating a narrative in the storytelling tradition of the *Arabian Nights* or the *Decameron*. The elimination of "The Taciturn Lovers" from the children's version results in a much less structured collection of tales. With the exception of a few texts that are loosely related by common themes or generic characteristics, the tales have only an autonomous status. The adult reader may be surprised to note that Tournier also omitted one *conte* from the children's collection, and that it is precisely the one he considers his very best, "Pierrot, or The Secrets of the Night," published for the first time for adults in *The Midnight Love Feast*. "Pierrot" had already appeared for children in *Sept contes*, and the author claims that he did not want to include it in two collections, although he does not usually have any scruples about recycling his tales.

Les contes du médianoche is not the result only of a process of "compression," however, as the author also adds several completely new texts. The children's collection contains only four fewer narratives than the adult collection, but it is nonetheless about one-third the size. The new texts are generally quite short and several are fables reminiscent of La Fontaine, an author much admired by Tournier. In chapter one, we saw that Tournier's retelling of Hugo's epic poem "The Eagle on the Helmet" is followed by the hypotext in the children's collection. Tournier considers his "humble" retelling of Hugo's epic poem "the pièce de résistance" of his *Médianoche* for children, and it is this tale that inspires the illustration on the cover, whereas the jacket of the adult collection depicts a scene from "The Taciturn Lovers."

One of the tales included in both collections is a retelling of the story of the Magi entitled "Le Roi Faust" ("Faust I, King and Magus"). After retelling the famous Bible story in two novels that highlight the legendary fourth Wise Man, the author invents a fictional fifth Wise Man, King Faust I. By adding the numeral, the author is no doubt suggesting tongue in cheek that his Faust pre-dates Goethe's. In Tournier's highly original retelling, two great myths are superimposed to suggest the existence of a fifth Wise Man. Rewriting is an essential element of Tournier's craft and his rewriting always involves cross-writing children and adults.

Rewriting Children's Books for Adults

One of the rare examples of a children's text that was rewritten for an adult audience is T. H. White's fantasy classic *The Sword in the Stone*. Although it was originally published in 1938 as a stand-alone work, it eventually became the first book in a quartet, known collectively as *The Once and Future King*, an adaptation of Sir Thomas Malory's fifteenth-century romance, *Morte D'Arthur*. Whereas *The Sword in the Stone* is definitely a children's book, the other three novels, initially published between 1939 and 1958, are much more adult in nature and are really aimed at adults and teenagers. A fifth book, *The Book of Merlyn*, was published posthumously in 1977, turning the work into a pentalogy. From the outset, *The Sword in the Stone* was also popular with adults. In 1939, it was a Book-of-the-Month Club selection, giving White a very large popular audience. *The Sword in the Stone* was rewritten for the single-volume edition of *The Once and Future King* that White published in 1958. The tetralogy was the basis of Alan Jay Lerner and Frederick Loewe's very successful musical *Camelot*, which opened in 1960 and inspired a film in 1967, while *The Sword in the Stone* was made into Disney's animated film of the same name in 1963. *The Sword in the Stone* tells the story of Arthur's youth, a period that was not dealt with in Malory. During Arthur's education and training under the tutorship of Merlyn, the wizard transforms him into various animals, so that he can experience life from different perspectives. White's unique retelling of the Arthurian legend combines Malory with the image of Robin Hood's Merry

England (Arthur actually encounters the outlaw Robin Wood). Contrary to most retellings, the tone is quite humorous, although there are a few dark moments, especially during Arthur's transformation into an ant.

The version of *The Sword in the Stone* that appeared in the quartet underwent substantial revisions. No doubt White felt that his whimsical, humorous fantasy was inappropriate as the first part of a more serious retelling of the Arthurian legend. The first version was only loosely connected to the classical story of Arthur, although the limited material that White borrowed was faithful to Malory. While it is informed by White's extensive knowledge of medieval culture, the author was not concerned about historical accuracy and the story contains many anachronisms. White began rewriting *The Sword in the Stone* during World War II, which explains, at least in part, the darker mood of the second version. It certainly accounts for the addition of a pacifist passage in which Arthur is transformed into a bird that flies so high national boundaries are no longer visible. World War II colours White's retelling of the Arthurian legend throughout *The Once and Future King*, giving Arthur his world-weariness. The revised version of *The Sword in the Stone* contains numerous other new episodes, some of which were events and themes that White had originally intended to develop in a fifth volume, which was published after his death as *The Book of Merlyn*. A number of episodes from the original are also eliminated, including Merlyn's battle with Madam Mim, which was included in the Disney film. A significant number of critics felt that the revised version of *The Sword in the Stone* was actually inferior to the original, and some publishers continued to use the original version when the book was published independently of the tetralogy. In the case of T. H. White's classic *The Sword in the Stone*, both the original version and the rewritten version are read by a crossover audience.

In the 1990s, Tournier described several projects in progress that involved the rewriting for adults of texts originally addressed to children, thus completely reversing his previous rewriting practices. *La couleuvrine* (The culverin), a short children's novel or novella set in fifteenth-century France, was published in 1994, and later that year Tournier told me that he was enjoying himself immensely rewriting the novel for adults. He likes to compare the evolution of his art of rewriting, from *Friday and Robinson* to the present, to that of the sculptor César, who first created "compressions" and then "expansions." The adult version of *La couleuvrine* would be Tournier's first "expansion." When I pointed out that this rewriting project was counter to his proclaimed evolution toward texts like *The Golden Droplet*, which can be read by both adults and children, the author seemed to consider it more in terms of turning what is really a *nouvelle* into a "real novel." Tournier spoke at length about the genesis of the adult version and the "augmentations" that he was incorporating into *La couleuvrine* in order to turn it into an adult novel.[31] He was considering retaining the title *La couleuvrine*, in which case it would be the first time an identical title was used for the children's and adult versions of one of his texts.

His detailed comments about the rewriting led me to believe that the adult novel was well underway, but in 1996 he admitted that he had not really started writing the second version, and to date the novel has not appeared.

La couleuvrine was not the only expansion that Tournier was contemplating writing in the mid-1990s. He also mentioned a work in progress about the Paris subway, but a year later he had already decided that it would never make a children's story. From the beginning, the author had admitted that rewriting a children's book for adults was more difficult than the reverse exercise. In a manner of speaking, Tournier accomplished this feat rather in spite of himself with a "religious western" inspired by the story of Moses. In 1995, the author showed me the manuscript of *Éléazar ou la source et le buisson* (translated as *Eleazar, Exodus to the West* in 2002), which he intended to publish as an illustrated book for children before rewriting it for adults. The original version turned out to be too long and the subject too weighty for the children's journal *Je bouquine*, which had initially published *La couleuvrine*, so it was ultimately extended and published for adults in 1996. Thus Tournier did rewrite the work for an adult readership, but the original children's version was never published. In actual fact, however, the author considers *Eleazar, Exodus to the West*, like *The Golden Droplet*, to be a crossover text that does not require rewriting because the novel can be appreciated by young readers, such as the twelve-year-old girl, Coralie, to whom it is dedicated.

The rewriting of a text rarely has the purpose of deliberately turning an adult text or a children's text into a crossover work. More often a work is rewritten for a different age category, even when the end result is a crossover book. However, Tournier claims not to have rewritten *Friday* only for children and Carmen Boullosa's *El médico de los piratas* was first published in a series for all ages. Even the rewriting of T. H. White's *The Sword in the Stone* resulted in a crossover work that was read by adults and teenagers. When Wilson rewrote the manuscript of *Last Train from Kummersdorf* for a teenage audience, the result was a novel that appeals to adults as well. Even the second version of Culleton's *In Search of April Raintree* is read by adults as well as a young audience. Quite by accident, Joy Kogawa ended up with a Japanese version of her story that had crossover appeal. Perhaps even the two versions of works like Yourcenar's "How Wang-Fo Was Saved" and Sally Morgan's *My Place* can also be considered as crossover texts that take a slightly different form for the two readerships.

Chapter Three
Child-to-Adult Crossover Fiction

> The current Holy Grail for any children's author is to win the handle 'crossover.'
>
> **Julia Eccleshare, "Crossing Over"**

As we have seen in the first chapter, adult fiction has always crossed over to children, but until recently there was significantly less traffic in the other direction. It is widely believed, however, that the crossover phenomenon began with the enthusiastic adoption of the Harry Potter books by adults. In his 2006 article on the "re-branding" of adult fiction for young readers, the Canadian critic Andre Mayer acknowledges this widespread notion: "For many, the current crossover vogue began the other way around, with a YA title that cultivated an enormous adult following—namely J. K. Rowling's Harry Potter series."[1] The child-to-adult crossover trend has taken the literary world by storm, much to the surprise of most and the chagrin of some. To those who find it difficult to believe that a children's book could appeal to an adult, Dominique Demers, who writes books for children and for adults and has the same novels on bestselling lists for both audiences, responds: "From time immemorial young people have borrowed literature from adults. Why the devil should the reverse be surprising?"[2] Today, the fact that "We're all reading children's books" has become front-page news and is attracting a great deal of media attention.[3]

While child-to-adult crossover has become a market trend in recent years, it is far from a new phenomenon. In fact, since the creation of a literature specifically for young readers, adults have been reading children's books. Many critics have pointed out that children's literature has always had to appeal to adults: parents, reviewers, librarians, and educators, in other words, the many mediators who get the books into children's hands. For the most part, children's books are written, illustrated, published, and reviewed by adults. Young adult books aside, they are generally bought by adults as well. Most children's book awards are judged by adults and often go to literary children's books that appeal to adults rather than to the books most popular with children.[4] In *The Poetics of Children's Literature*, Zohar Shavit writes: "The children's writer is perhaps the only one who is asked to address one particular audience and at the same time appeal to another." Children's authors are described as "'walking the tightrope' between the official addressee (the child) and those who decide the character of [her] culture (the adults)." Shavit claims, however, that writers of children's literature either ignore adults completely or they try to appeal primarily to adults in "ambivalent" texts, many of which constitute the great classics of the children's canon.[5] However, the most enduring children's classics are not schizophrenic or Janus-like texts that have one part aimed at children and another directed over their heads at knowing adults. Rather, they are multi-levelled texts that appeal to readers of all ages. It is extremely important, as Hans-Heino Ewers pointed out in the 1980s, to distinguish carefully between the adult as "co-reader" and the adult as "reader" of a children's book.[6] Many of the great classics of children's literature are read by adults not only in their role as mediators, but also as consumers of literature reading for their own pleasure. In other words, such "children's books" are crossover fiction.

For some writers, critics, and readers, a children's book, at least a good one, must be a crossover book with appeal for adult readers. C. S. Lewis's well-known pronouncement on the subject was mentioned in the introduction. The author elaborated in another statement: "No book is really worth reading at the age of ten which is not equally (and often far more) worth reading at the age of fifty."[7] Writing about Lewis Carroll in 1962, W. H. Auden echoed Lewis's sentiment: "There are good books which are only for adults . . . but there are no good books which are only for children."[8] Views such as Auden's and Lewis's are not unique, nor are they limited to English-speaking writers. In 1958, Henri Bosco claimed that "the great children's books are those that touch childhood and maturity." His reflections on what constitutes a children's book seem to give greater importance to the adult addressee than to the child reader. In a journal entry, the French novelist wrote: "It is rare that good children's books aren't also—and perhaps especially—books for grown-ups."[9] The belief that a good children's book also appeals to adults is not restricted to the 1950s and 1960s, but persists even after children's literature has, in Maria Nikolajeva's words, "come of age."[10] In the 1970s, a French critic interviewing Michel Tournier questioned the existence of "children's literature" and suggested that only a very few rare exceptions among the authors writing for young readers— his examples are limited to Tournier and Bosco—could be considered " writers" of "children's literature," rather than merely "manufacturers of a functional, sterilized, and vaguely educational literature."[11]

In the twenty-first century, it is not unusual to hear similar views expressed, even by children's authors. On her website, the American author Tamora Pierce tells readers that "any decently written kids' book should be just as enjoyable for adult readers." The acclaimed Brazilian children's author Ana Maria Machado, who has written more than a dozen books for adults and received Brazil's main literary award for her body of work, sees "children's books as a bridge between adults and children." Although it may be possible "to build a weak bridge that can just provide an ideal crossing for a child but doesn't have to be strong enough to support the weight of an adult," such a bridge is unlikely to last and "should not be made available to children." Machado decries the fact that an engineer who built such a bridge would be punished, whereas an author may be lauded for doing so. As "a bridge between generations," children's books should not allow "only one-way crossing," she insists.[12] The child-to-adult crossover is predicated on the fact that a children's book can be enjoyed by adults. For many, however, a children's book not only can, but should, appeal to adults as readers in their own right. Without going so far as to make it a criteria of the genre, many authors who write for young readers have nonetheless expressed their belief that children's books are not just for children. Jostein Gaarder, who was a bestselling crossover author well before the genre became fashionable, has repeatedly stated his belief that "a children's book is not only for children."[13]

Some children's authors have nonetheless taken issue with the idea of cross-generational children's books. Commenting on the awarding of the Whitbread Book of the Year to Philip Pullman's children's book *The Amber Spyglass*, Anne Fine, the British Children's Laureate from 2001 to 2003, stated that "the definition of a children's book is one that is ideally met for the first time in childhood." In her view, "there is something strange about a book that is neither children's nor adults'" and the "barrier" should not be taken down.[14] Authors like Fine no doubt fear that the hype and huge advances in the crossover sphere will result in children's books that are addressed primarily at adults, neglecting their true readership. With all the attention focused recently on child-to-adult crossovers, it is easy to forget that children's books have always found an adult audience.

Crossovers in a Historical Context

It is extremely important to consider crossover texts in a historical context. The relationship between children's fiction and adult fiction or, for that matter, child and adult, can vary greatly between cultures and time periods. Although the tendency in Western countries since the mid-twentieth century has been to distinguish sharply between children's and adult literature, that has not always been the case, nor is it universally the case today. Often the borders are quite blurred or even non-existent. It would be appropriate, in some instances, to speak of a common literature for both. In many African countries, writers view their role as that of teacher of both adults and children.[15] Furthermore, throughout literary history, there have been authors who refused to make a distinction regardless of cultural conventions.

In the introduction to a study of children's and youth literature up to 1570, Theodor Brüggemann and Otto Brunken state that the early modern period offers numerous so-called children's books that are "not yet acquainted with the exclusive targeting of children and young people," but still address parts of the adult population as well.[16] Dagmar Grenz rightly questions whether even after

1570 one can generally speak of "a dichotomy between children's literature and adult literature." She provides the example of the Enlightenment, when children's literature and a great deal of adult literature shared similar didactic aims.[17] Most often critics point to the nineteenth century (or the Victorian era in the English-speaking world) as a period of significant blurring of children's and adult literature. At that time, books about children were still not assumed to be for children, or at least not for children only. The works of Charlotte Yonge or Evelyn Everett Green were widely read by women and girls, just as the adventure stories of R. M. Ballantyne and G. A. Henty were read by men and boys. As we have seen, Dickens's novels that focus on children were read by all ages, as were Mark Twain's.

In some countries, the divide between children's and adult fiction seems to reflect the general split between the popular and the academic audience, a split that became more pronounced as writers and critics abandoned Victorian and Romantic models of writing to adopt modernism. Bestselling crossover authors, such as Robert Louis Stevenson and Lucy Maude Montgomery, were viewed with increasing suspicion. Their appeal with a popular audience, and in particular with children, was seen as an indication of their inferiority. Critics refused to take them seriously, and appraisal was often patronizing, even hostile. Changes began to take place in the marketing of books, especially in the post-war economic boom. Books about children were often separated from adult books and marketed in a different manner. Many books read by a crossover audience were increasingly assumed to be primarily for children. For much of the twentieth century, Robert Louis Stevenson was viewed as a second-rate writer, relegated to children's literature or the popular horror genre.

British children's literature, in particular, has a rich tradition of crossover literature. Even works whose titles specify their implied reader have found an adult audience. Although written for children, Robert Louis Stevenson's *A Child's Garden of Verses*, published in 1885, was also popular with their parents. The collection of poetry includes such well-known favourites as "My Shadow" and "The Lamplighter." The subtitle, *A Story for Children*, certainly did not deter adult readers of *The Lion, the Witch and the Wardrobe*, the first volume of C. S. Lewis's famous crossover *The Chronicles of Narnia*. J. M. Barrie's goal was to appeal to both adults and children when he wrote the stage play, *Peter Pan, or The Boy Who Wouldn't Grow Up* in 1904. Since the nineteenth century, certain children's books have always been, in Emer O' Sullivan's words, "quotable and quoted" in British culture.[18] Literary critics have no qualms about citing authors such as J. M. Barrie, Lewis Carroll, and A. A. Milne. The tradition of child-to-adult crossover is not limited to British literature, however.

A notable nineteenth-century example from Germany is E. T. A. Hoffmann's children's fairy tale *Der Nußknacker und der Mausekönig* (*The Nutcracker and the Mouse-King*), which, since its publication in 1816, has been reissued frequently in many languages. Numerous critics feel Hoffmann's tale was not so much a story *for* children as a story *about* children, due to its complex structure and bleak view of humanity. However, Hoffmann himself responded to criticism that *The Nutcracker and the Mouse-King* was not very suitable for children with a tribute to the child reader and a warning to authors: "It is really astonishing, how rightly, and with what liveliness, [children] grasp many things that totally escape many an extremely bright Papa. Know this and have respect!"[19] *The Nutcracker and the Mouse-King* and *The Strange Child* are both children's fairy tales that also appeal to adults, as Dagmar Grenz has so persuasively demonstrated.[20] It is important to remember that the Romantic period viewed appropriate or inappropriate literature for children quite differently than we do today. However, as the Hoffmann case suggests, and as Hans Heino Ewers has convincingly argued, even in the Romantic period views already differed on this matter.[21] The enduring intergenerational appeal of Hoffmann's best-known work is nonetheless due not to the fairy tale, but to Tchaikovsky's balletic version, *The Nutcracker*, the most popular ballet in Western countries and an international favourite with all ages at Christmas time. Although his illustrations were based on the sets and costumes he designed for the Pacific Northwest Ballet's Christmas production of *Nutcracker*, Maurice Sendak brought Hoffmann's name back to the attention of a crossover audience with his 1984 picturebook edition, which is marketed on the Random House website as "a classic for all ages" in its own right.

Crossover works in Russia were strongly influenced by the political context during the Soviet era. Although he is not well known outside Russia, Alexander Grin's romantic novels, which are described by some critics as "adolescent fiction," are widely read by adults as well as young people in Russia. His most famous work is *Alye parusa* (*Scarlet Sails*), published in 1923, a powerful love story about a young girl who is told by a wizard that a beautiful ship with red sails will arrive and a noble prince will take her away to a new, happy life. After Nikita Khruschev's denunciation of Stalin's rule in 1956, Grin's work once again enjoyed widespread popularity and the novel was made into a movie in the Soviet Union in 1961. It has become a Russian classic. The beautiful edition of the novel published in 2000, with sumptuous painterly illustrations by Mikhail Bychkov, is a feast for the eyes for readers of all ages. The crossover appeal of the text is enhanced by the exceptional aesthetic quality of this book. It was the artist's personal project over many years and so escaped the commercial influence of commissioned works. The multi-layer painting technique of the doublespread illustrations are reminiscent of the seventeenth-century Dutch masters. Meticulous attention to detail went into every aspect of the design of the book, which incorporates the theme. For example, the text blocks take the form of wind-filled sails, giving an impression of movement to the reading process.

Some Russian authors owe their crossover appeal not to myth and fairy tale, but to more political and social topics. Since the 1930s, Sergey Mikhalkov has been one of Russia's most popular children's poets, and he was widely read throughout the Soviet Union. His most famous work, *Dyadya Stepa* (Uncle Stepa, 1936), whose very tall protagonist became a Soviet hero, was published in English under the title *Uncle Steeple* in 1974. Although Russian children claim him as their own, Mikhalkov also writes for adults. His witty, satirical fables are read by readers of all ages. The fact that Mikhalkov has written the lyrics of his country's national anthem three times over nearly a sixty-year period accounts in part for his broad crossover appeal. The Russian author Arkady Gaydar became famous when he published *Timur i ego komanda* (*Timur and His Squad*) in 1940, a children's story about an altruistic pioneer youth that gave birth to the mass Timur movement among Young Pioneers all over the Soviet Union. This and other works, such as *Golubaya chashka* (1936; *The Blue Cup*), which were inspired by his own experiences in the civil war, were read by both adults and children.

Crossover texts must be examined within their historical and social context. A work that attracts an audience of both children and adults in one country or one time period, may appeal to only one audience (either children or adults) in another. The question of context will be considered with regard to modern crossovers in a subsequent section.

From Children's Magazine to Crossover Novel

Robert Louis Stevenson is a much cited example of an author with wide crossover appeal. Like a significant number of nineteenth-century crossover novels, *Treasure Island*, his classic adventure story of piracy and buried treasure, was initially published in serialized format in a children's magazine. The story was begun as an entertainment for Stevenson's twelve-year-old stepson during a wet Scottish holiday. The author refers to the intended audience when he speaks of the story's genesis: "It was to be a story for boys; no need of psychology or fine writing; and I had a boy at hand to be a touchstone."[22] Under the pseudonym Captain George North, the story was serialized in seventeen weekly installments in the children's magazine *Young Folks; A Boys' and Girls' Paper of Instructive and Entertaining Literature* in 1881–82. Stevenson revised the periodical text for the first book edition, published by Cassell in 1883. Whereas the story was not particularly well received by the readers of *Young Folks*, it sold briskly in book form to a general audience and became Stevenson's first major success. In David Daiches's words, *Treasure Island* "transform[ed] the cliché-ridden Victorian boys' adventure story into a classic."[23] The many subsequent reprintings and illustrated editions demonstrate its popularity with generations of readers of all ages.

By the time his third and final serial, *Kidnapped*, appeared in *Young Folks* in 1886, Stevenson was an acclaimed author. *The Strange Case of Dr. Jekyll and Mr. Hyde* had been published earlier that year, captivating readers of all ages everywhere. The tremendous popularity of the frightening novella led one biographer to label it "a superseller."[24] In Britain, forty thousand copies were sold in the first six months and in America it was equally successful. *Kidnapped* appeared on the front page of the periodical for almost its entire run. Set in the Scottish Highlands, the story of David Balfour is a historical fiction adventure novel in the tradition of Sir Walter Scott and it likewise appeals to readers of all ages. The celebrity that Stevenson enjoyed during his lifetime declined with the advent of modern literature, but the many adaptations of his works in plays and films throughout the twentieth century attest to their continued popular appeal across generations.

In some regards, Stevenson's literary status is not unlike that of Jules Verne in France. Verne submitted the manuscript for his first science-fiction novel, *Cinq semaines en ballon* (*Five Weeks in a Balloon*, 1863), to Pierre-Jules Hetzel, one of the most important publishers in France at the time. The publisher, who also wrote books for young people under the pseudonym P.-J. Stahl, was just setting up the periodical *Le Magasin d'Éducation et de Récréation* (Education and entertainment magazine), a learning tool for parents and children that would include stories in serial form. Hetzel offered Verne a twenty-year contract to write two volumes a year, and *Cinq semaines en ballon* became the first volume in what would become the internationally renowned series Voyages extraordinaires (Extraordinary voyages). *Voyage au centre de la terre* (*Voyage to the Centre of the Earth*) was published in 1864, and the following year saw the publication of *De la terre à la lune* (*From the Earth to the Moon*), which had already enthralled the readers of the *Journal des débats*. Some critics feel that Verne's novels should have been published for adults, who have always widely read the visionary works of the father of science fiction. The author's best-known works, *Vingt mille lieues sous les mers* (*Twenty Thousand Leagues Under the Sea*) and *Le tour du monde en quatre-vingts jours* (*Around the World in Eighty Days*), published in 1869–70 and 1873 respectively, have, on numerous occasions, been made into movies for a general audience, including the 2004 Walt Disney adaptation of the latter starring Jackie Chan. Today, Jules Verne remains one of the most translated authors in the world.

Although, for a time, the literary establishment in France and Britain may have considered Verne and Stevenson as second-class writers, neither ever lost his popularity with a wide readership of both children and adults. Both writers are now receiving serious critical attention from literary scholars.

Classic Child-to-Adult Crossovers by Major Adult Authors

When authors who write for adults turn their hand to writing a "children's book," the result, in a significant number of cases, is a crossover book that is read by both adults and children. When Louisa May Alcott was asked by her publisher, Thomas Niles, to write a girls' book, she produced *Little Women* (1868), which achieved immediate commercial success and was hugely popular with adults as well as children. The book has never been out of print and is a long-established classic that has inspired several film adaptations. *Little*

Women's success brought demands for a sequel and Alcott complied, publishing part two the following spring. It is still one of the most popular American novels for young people. *Little Women* turned Alcott into a celebrated author and she would continue to write children's books because their sales supported her family. However, like a number of authors who achieved literary fame based on their children's books, Alcott seems to have considered her writing for children as a lesser art and to regret that her reputation did not come from her writing for adults, which is not nearly as well known. Ultimately, her reputation in the literary establishment suffered, like Stevenson's and Verne's, from the fact that her writing was too popular and appealed to children.

Whereas Alcott shifted almost entirely to writing children's books—as Roald Dahl and Robert Cormier would do in the twentieth century—until quite recently the majority of adult authors left only one or two children's titles in their literary oeuvre. Only in exceptional cases did these works capture a lasting crossover audience. Authors who have an established reputation in the sphere of adult fiction often attract the curiosity of adult readers when they publish children's books, but reputation alone is not enough to guarantee their success as crossover authors. Many such books do not even appeal to children because too many adult authors do not seem to realize that, to borrow the title of Tournier's article, "writing for children is no child's play." It takes a very talented writer to appeal equally to readers of all ages. The examples mentioned below are only a few of the remarkable crossover works written by major twentieth-century adult authors in the decades preceding the current crossover trend.

In 1934, the French author Marcel Aymé published the first four tales of *Les contes du chat perché* (The tales of the perched cat), one of the most popular French children's books of all time. The author claims to have written the first tales merely for his own pleasure, without a thought to his eventual audience, although he undoubtedly had his granddaughter Françoise in mind at the outset. Elsewhere, however, he has identified his readership as children "from four to seventy-five."[25] *Les contes du chat perché* was an immediate success with children and adults alike, and Aymé added to the popular tales for more than ten years, publishing the last in 1946. In the 1960s, Aymé's tales were adapted for television by Claude Santelli. Subsequent reprintings and new editions of the tales attest to their continued popularity in France. Unfortunately, they are not well known in the English-speaking world, even though the first volume to appear in translation, under the title *The Wonderful Farm*, was the first children's book illustrated by Maurice Sendak in 1951. In 1947, the popular poet Jacques Prévert published another French children's classic *Contes pour enfants pas sages* (Tales for naughty children), whose deceptively childlike stories, full of literary parody and witty social criticism, have always appealed to adults as well as children, naughty or otherwise. Like so many children's classics from other countries, Prévert's delightful tales have never been translated into English.

The Japanese author Kenji Miyazawa, known fondly by his first name Kenji, offers an interesting example of an author from the early twentieth century who is read by a wide crossover audience today. Kenji is now one of Japan's most widely read and best loved authors, although he was virtually unknown during his short lifetime. Strongly influenced by both Buddhist scripture and the new ideas in science and technology that were beginning to filter into the country-side a few decades after the opening of Japan to the outside world, Kenji was ahead of his time and his works were not well understood while he was alive. The centennial of his birth in 1996 was marked by unprecedented media attention, such as no Japanese literary figure had previously enjoyed. More than sixty years after his death, Kenji's spiritual and environmental messages had profound meaning for Japanese of all ages, caught up in the materialism of contemporary society. Despite his ever-increasing popularity in Japan, his writing remains little known in other countries. In an interview on The World of Kenji Miyazawa website, Roger Pulvers, one of Kenji's English translators, attributes this to the author's earlier lack of status in the Japanese literary establishment: he did not "fit into the mould of respectability and so-called high literary style" and his works were "labelled 'children's literature' and hence not taken very seriously." As we have seen, this problem is certainly not limited to Japanese literature.

Kenji began his literary career as a poet, but he is best known for his tales, which are read by both children and adults. In 1924, at his own expense, the author published the only two volumes to appear before his death, a collection of poetry and a collection of tales entitled *Chūmon no Ōi Ryōriten* (The Restaurant of Many Orders). The title tale and "Donguri to yamaneko" (Wildcat and the acorns) are two of Kenji's most famous stories. Many of the prolific author's works were published posthumously and researchers remain divided with regard to the target audience of his writing. His collection of tales is generally thought to have been published for children because the author seems to address young readers in the introduction, but he was not sure that all of the stories would be appreciated by children. In later editions of the tales, he claimed to use a literary style for older children and adolescents. His correspondence and other writing indicates that he often reflected on children and children's literature. Kenji also read the stories to his high school students and later to children of primary school age, whom he felt understood them. In the 1970s, they became part of the curriculum in Japan, where they are taught from primary school through university. Today, Japanese children begin reading Kenji's stories at a young age, and they return to them over and over as they grow up, discovering new levels of interpretation in the familiar stories. His tales are published in editions for both children and adults, frequently as illustrated books or picturebooks. In 2000, the International Foundation for the Promotion of Languages and Culture in Japan published a number of his stories in English in a series devoted entirely to the author, the Kenji Miyazawa Picture Book Series. Kenji is the most illustrated author in Japan. The

Japanese-Australian author-illustrator Junko Morimoto illustrated several of his tales for picturebooks published in English, including *The Night Hawk Star* (1991), a translation of the popular tale "Yodaka no hoshi."

Despite the simplicity of Kenji's beautiful prose, his philosophical tales are complex and multilayered. Undoubtedly his most famous work is the short novel *Ginga tetsudo no yoru*, which has been translated into English under several titles, including *Night Train to the Stars* and *Night on the Milky Way Train*. The unfinished novel first appeared in 1934 as part of the complete works of the author. In 1985, Gisaburo Sugii made it into an anime film, which was translated into English as *Night on the Galactic Railroad*. Critics cannot agree whether the challenging, multilevel novel, which is also a parable, is intended for children or not. However, the story of the two adolescents, Giovanni and his friend Campanella, whose voyage to the stars reflects the journey made by all children on the road to adulthood, is read by virtually every Japanese child. Before being translated in English-speaking countries, a number of Kenji's stories were published in English, in the 1970s and 1980s, by the Japanese publisher Kodansha. The covers and format of the books published in their pocket-sized paperback series, Kodansha English Library, appear to target children and the series is largely used by Japanese students of English, although many of the books published in the series are novels for adults. The series allows Japanese readers of all ages to read works by their own authors in English.

Kenji is not the only major twentieth-century Japanese author to have written successful child-to-adult crossovers. Morio Kita is the pen name of Sokichi Saito, a doctor and well-known Japanese novelist and essayist for adults. In 1960, he was awarded the Akutagawa Prize, Japan's most prestigious literary award, for *Yoru to kiri no sumi de* (In the corner of night and fog). He garnered widespread popular acclaim that same year with his adult bestseller *Dokutoru Manbo kokaiki*, which was translated as *Doctor Manbo at Sea* in the Kodansha English Library series. In 1962, Kita published a fantasy novel for young people, entitled *Funanori Kupukupu no boken*, which appeared, under the title *The Adventures of Kupukupu the Sailor*, in the Kodansha English Library series in 1985, two years before *Doctor Manbo at Sea*. Although it was targeted at a young audience, *The Adventures of Kupukupu the Sailor* seems to have been written with both children and adults in mind, and, since its publication, it has appealed widely to adults as well as young readers. In the 1960s, the story was particularly popular with university students.

The Finno-Swedish artist and author Tove Jansson, who won the Andersen Medal in 1966, claimed not to write for any particular audience, although she published books for both child and adult audiences. A national icon in Finland, Jansson became internationally renowned for her novels about the Moomins, which have been translated into thirty-five languages. Yet, she remains surprisingly little known by readers of any age in North America. The Moomin books have inspired a vast range of other works, including film, television, and theatrical adaptations; animated cartoons; comic books; and comic strips. It is rather ironic that the United States is almost the only place in the world that the highly commodified Moomins do not have "a Disney-like status" (there is even a theme park in Japan, where the books are hugely popular).[26] Jansson began her career as a comic-strip artist and the Moomintroll figure was originally used as a signature character in her political cartoons in the late 1930s. Her fame in England and much of the West was initially due to her Moomin comic strips, which were published daily in the *London Evening News* from 1954 to 1970, and read in the newspapers of forty countries, in sixty languages, at the height of their popularity.

Between 1945 and 1977, Jansson wrote and illustrated thirteen Moomin books that present a fantastic world of quirky, sometimes sinister, characters, with recognizable human traits. As well as being childhood favourites, they gained a certain cult status with adults. The strong adult appeal cannot be explained merely by nostalgia for their childhood, since many readers do not discover the novels until adulthood. All of the Moomin books offer levels that have deep resonance for adults as well, with *Trollvinter*, published in 1957 (translated as *Moominland Midwinter* in 1958), this became more pronounced. Darker themes, such as death, are introduced, and the tone is more pensive, almost brooding. The characters become more complex, and the protagonist, Moomintroll, begins the journey from childhood to adulthood. While many critics have questioned whether the later novels—in particular *Pappan och havet* (1965; *Moominpappa at Sea*, 1966) and *Sent i November* (1970; *Moominvalley in November*, 1971)—are appropriate for children, I would agree with those who prefer to see them as exemplary crossover works. W. Glynn Jones calls the later Moomin books "disguised adult literature," but Harju rightly argues that they should not be seen as being out of reach for children, because "grappling with existential questions is a challenge humans of all ages must face throughout their life-stages."[27]

Jansson never claimed that the Moomin books were for children. She began publishing adult prose while she was still writing the Moomin books and after their completion wrote only adult fiction. She did not distinguish between writing for children and writing for adults, but she had a publisher that brought out books in both spheres. The similarities between the Moomin books and her works issued for adults are striking. In all of her writing, the setting is the same, as are the often complex themes: identity, isolation, relationships with others and the environment, natural disaster, time, and death. Jansson's first novel for adults, *Sommerboken* (1972), translated as *The Summer Book* in 1975, is read by older children and young adults, who are drawn in by the apparent simplicity of the prose and the touching story of the relationship between a young girl and her grandmother. When the new edition of *The Summer Book* came out in Britain in 2003, the novel also captured a young audience in the English-speaking world. There is no reason, in fact, why young readers could not enjoy much of Jansson's adult prose. Harju wonders if one reason *The Summer Book* was marketed for adults is due to "the frank discussions that Sophia and

Grandmother have about 'taboo' issues like death and dying," but she points out that Jansson does not avoid such subjects in her children's books either.[28] Young and old alike appreciate the important psychological and metaphysical issues that are explored in all of her work. Because Jansson resists the child/adult dichotomy in her writing, her books naturally transcend age boundaries and appeal to readers of all ages.

The American author Russell Hoban is equally renowned for his children's books and his adult fiction, but he is best known for his children's novel *The Mouse and His Child*. This fable-like tale about a windup toy mouse and his son has had a very mixed reception from the reading public ever since its release in 1967. While many readers view it as a great children's classic, others feel it is a nihilistic book that is far too dark for young readers. Yet others consider Hoban's novel to be one of the great works of modern philosophy. The dark, philosophical tale is a profound examination of existentialism, best demonstrated by the scene in which the child mouse, who is rusting away at the bottom of a pond, is determined to see "the last visible dog" on the disintegrating label of a dog food can. The label replicates ad infinitum the scene of a chef-dog holding a tray upon which is a can of dog food. Like Tournier's philosophical texts for children, *The Mouse and His Child* can be read as a children's story or as an ontological treatise. Christine Wilkie-Stibbs calls it a "watershed book between Hoban's children's and his adult fictions" and points out that "although publishing pragmatics neatly classify Hoban's writing as either 'for adults' or 'for children,' there is more that unites than separates the two bodies of work."[29] The same could be said about the works of many authors who were published for both audiences throughout their careers.

Christine Nöstlinger is a popular and highly acclaimed Austrian children's author, but this winner of the most prestigious of children's awards (the Hans Christian Andersen Medal in 1984 and the first Astrid Lindgren Memorial Award in 2003) has also published for adults. It is generally said that her books are written for children of all ages. Despite her international reputation, Nöstlinger has not been very successful in English-speaking countries. Few of her translated works are in print in English, and many of her later works have never been translated. *Andreas oder Die unteren sieben Achtel des Eisberges: Familienroman aus der Wiederaufbauzeit* (Andreas or The lower seven-eighth of the iceberg: Family novel from the period of reconstruction), published in 1978, is, as the generic indication in the subtitle clearly suggests, a "family novel" intended for all ages. However, the subtitle was dropped when the novel was reissued by the same publisher in 1985, and a 1992 paperback edition came out in a series specifically for children, Gulliver für Kinder (Gulliver for children). Between 1978 and 1992, a family novel had been turned into a children's book.

Nöstlinger's German-language readers, both young and old, are extremely loyal. Many adults read all her books, regardless of the intended audience. Adults appreciate the distinctive, irreverent humour that characterizes her entire oeuvre and therefore enjoy her children's books as well. A prime example is the Gretchen Sackmeier trilogy (1981–88), which is subtitled "Eine Familiengeschichte" (A family story). It describes the coming of age of a typical teenage girl, whose mother is simultaneously becoming emancipated. One of Nöstlinger's masterpieces is the 1975 novel *Konrad oder Das Kind aus der Konservenbüchse*, published in English the following year as *Conrad: The Factory-Made Boy*. Mocking traditional methods of child-rearing, Nöstlinger tells a hilarious story in which an eccentric middle-aged woman receives an exemplary, mass-produced seven-year-old boy in a tin from a mail-order catalogue.

The subject of another realistic fantasy by Nöstlinger, *Hugo, das Kind in den besten Jahren* (Hugo, a child in the prime of life, 1983), explains its crossover appeal. The novel was written, as the subtitle "Phantastischer Roman nach Bildern von Jörg Wollmann" (Fantastic novel after pictures by Jörg Wollmann) suggests, after the author saw the fantastic graphics of the Austrian artist. Hugo is a fifty-year-old child in the prime of his life, who fights to defend the rights and improve the life of "old children" in society. He bears no resemblance whatsoever to Dav Pilkey's popular superhero Captain Underpants, who, after shedding his adult façade (clothing, toupee) and donning a red curtain/cape and a large pair of underwear, looks and acts somewhat like an overgrown baby. Nöstlinger presents a protagonist who is at once adult and child, and whose age, as Eva-Maria Metcalf rightly points out, "transcends all accepted categorization of adults and children." Traditional age categories are blurred. The people who inspire confidence in *Hugo* are generally either grown-up children or childlike adults. What Nöstlinger calls "the prime of life" can occur at any age, when the perfect blend of childlike and adult qualities exists. In her 1988 article, Metcalf describes "the blend of traditionally childlike and traditionally adult qualities" which, for Nöstlinger, make up "the ideal preteen, teen, and the ideal adult in today's fast-paced society." She contrasts this "child-adult ideal," characterized by "critical thought and active involvement in life and community," with "the narcissistic, hedonistic, and disinterested child-adult" observed by Christopher Lasch and Neil Postman.[30] Likewise, Nöstlinger's child-adult ideal would not coincide, a generation later, with the kidults or adultescents who are considered by some to be the driving force behind the crossover vogue.

Thus far all the works considered in this section have been novels. Michel Tournier considers his best work to be the tale "Pierrot ou les secrets de la nuit" ("Pierrot, or The Secrets of the Night"), which was published as a picturebook in 1979, with illustrations by Danièle Bour. In 1981, it won the prize for best foreign children's book at the Leipzig Book Fair. Ten years after its publication as a picturebook, the tale appeared in a short story collection for adults, *The Midnight Love Feast*, as well as in a collection for children, *Les contes du médianoche* (1989). *Pierrot* followed a similar path to *Angus*, which was published as a picturebook in 1988 before being included in both *Médianoche*. In the first chapter of this study, we saw that adult short stories often cross over for children in picturebook form. *Pierrot* and *Angus* demonstrate that, although much rarer, the opposite phenomenon also exists.

Pierrot is a simple story, based on the eternal love triangle, which places three characters from the Italian *commedia dell'arte* in a French village setting. It is a philosophical tale that has been described by its author both as "an onthological treatise that has all the appearance of a children's tale" and as "metaphysics for ten-year-olds."[31] In an article on how to write for children, Tournier explains that through the "little dolls" from Italian theatre, two metaphysical worldviews clash: "Great echoes resound in these childish spokespersons. It's Goethe and Newton divided on the theory of colours, it's Parmenide versus Heraclite. . . . The child, of course, doesn't know that. But he senses it, and he understands it in his own manner." Tournier places *Pierrot* at the pinnacle of his art precisely because it appeals to readers at both ends of the spectrum, young children as well as cultured adults. The author goes so far as to claim that he would gladly give up all his other works for these few pages.[32]

This section offers only a very small sampling of major authors whose "children's books" have become classic crossover works that are cherished by readers of all ages. Some of the authors discussed in the following section also fall into this category.

Allegories for All Ages

A number of children's books that cross over to an adult audience are allegories, often of a political nature. The fact that children's literature has generally had a rather low status and has not been considered a serious genre worthy of attention can make it a very useful tool under repressive regimes. Many writers have avoided, or attempted to avoid, ideological censorship by publishing political allegories in the guise of simple children's stories. This is sometimes the only manner in which authors dare to express social and political criticism in non-democratic regimes. In some cases, the genre may be strictly a pretext for a text that targets chiefly adults. However, the works that interest us here are bona fide children's texts even though they also address adults. In an essay in *Transcending Boundaries*, Larissa Tumanov describes the use of what came to be known in Russian as "Ezopov iazyk" (Aesopian language), that is, a "language of hidden meanings and deceptive means [used] to criticize . . . national life, politics and society."[33] Although Tumanov points out that the phenomenon existed during the tsarist era as well, she considers only the context of the former Soviet Union.

Aesopian children's literature was intended for enlightened and insightful adult readers capable of decoding the subtext, as well as for child readers who would appreciate it on another level. At the same time, the author was conscious of the possibility of a third category of adult reader: the censor, who would hopefully "read more like a child and not perceive (or even attempt to perceive) any subversive Aesopian subtext."[34] Lev Loseff uses the term "quasi-children's literature" to refer to the genre practised by those writing children's literature to convey subversive material.[35] The term is not entirely appropriate in the case of some authors, whose writing for children was not merely a pretext for reaching an adult audience. The works addressed to children by Kornei Chukovsky, Mikhail Zoshchenko, and Daniil Kharms, the authors examined by Tumanov, truly appealed to a young audience.

The well-known literary critic and translator Kornei Chukovsky began writing for children early in his career and played a major role in the development of Russian children's literature in the twentieth century. He earnestly sought to appeal to a child readership in his lyrical children's tales or *skazki*. In certain works, however, he sought simultaneously to address the adult reader. His verse tale "Mukhatsokotukha" (The chatterbox fly, 1924), about a fly who is attacked by a spider, is widely believed to have "a deeper level of social and political comment."[36] Unlike Chukovsky, Mikhail Zoshchenko began writing for children quite late in his career. Tumanov argues that his cycle of children's stories *Rasskazy o Lenine* (Stories about Lenin), first published in 1939 and 1940, could be interpreted as didactic or propagandistic literature for young Soviet readers—designed to present a hagiographic image of Lenin—or, on the contrary, as a satire of the Soviet deification of leaders.[37] "Prikliucheniia obez'iany" (The adventures of a monkey), a tale about a boy raising a monkey, was seen by the Secretary of the Central Committee of the Communist Party as "a vulgar lampoon on Soviet life and on Soviet people [in which] Zoshchenko's malicious, hooliganlike depiction of our way of life is accompanied by anti-Soviet attacks."[38] This tale and one of the Lenin stories seem to have provoked the ban of all of Zoshchenko's works that lasted until the 1950s.

As a member of the avant-garde literary group OBERIU, Daniil Kharms's writing for adults was childlike and playful. For that reason, Samuil Marshak encouraged Kharms to write for children in 1928, and he would continue to do so until 1941. In 1931, he was arrested as a member of a group of "anti-Soviet children's writers." Viewing the avant-garde in general with increasing suspicion, Soviet authorities considered Kharms's writing for children as anti-Soviet because of its absurd logic and its refusal to inculcate socialist values. When Kharms returned from exile, he found a refuge in children's literature, but some of his children's works also addressed the adult reader. The most obvious example is undoubtedly his poem "Iz doma vyshel chelovek" (A man left home), written in 1937, in which a man completely disappears after leaving home one day. The Aesopian language of this particular poem, poignantly premonitory, did not deceive the censor. After Kharms's death, his work was hidden by friends until the 1960s, at which time his children's writing was widely published. Many of his poems and short stories for children are considered classics in Russia, where they continue to be very popular with children today. His writing for adults remained virtually unknown until the 1970s, and was not published officially in Russia until glasnost. Kharms's writing for children and his writing for adults constitute a single oeuvre that is characterized by its playfulness and absurd logic.

Another striking example of child-to-adult crossover from the former Soviet Union is Yury Olesha, who is considered one of the greatest Russian novelists of the twentieth century and one of the few to have managed to produce lasting works during this period of stifling censorship. In literary histories, critics first discuss his landmark adult novel *Zavist* (1927; *Envy*) for which he is best known in English-speaking countries, followed immediately by the children's novel *Tri tolstyaka* (Three fat men), which is his most popular work in Russia. One critic even views the adult novel as a sequel to the children's fairy tale, depicting what happened after the revolution.[39] Written in 1924 and published in 1928, it has been called the first revolutionary fairy tale in Soviet literature. However, some critics feel the proletarian fairy-tale novel has a subversive subtext that makes it a masterpiece in the genre of political allegory and satire used to comment on non-democratic governments. In Olesha's fairy tale, the circus stars Tibul and Suok lead the ordinary people in overthrowing the repressive authority of the three fat, rich men. The depiction of revolution as a festive circus performance was highly unexpected, but for Olesha revolution shares with the circus (as well as art and fairy tale) the ability to transform the world and turn ordinary people into heroes.

The work and its author enjoyed an initial period of favour with the post-revolutionary Stalinist government. *Three Fat Men* quickly became very popular with readers of all ages. Olesha's children's novel was written as a large feuilleton and constitutes an outstanding example of literary avant-garde of the 1920s. The 1928 luxury edition, with illustrations done in Paris by the Russian-Lithuanian artist Mstislav Dobuzhinsky, was a major event in the publishing world. Some years later, an adult edition was published with striking woodcuts by the famous Russian Soviet avant-garde artist Vladimir Kozlinsky. *Three Fat Men* was made into a play in 1930 (performed by Stanislavsky at the Moscow Art Theatre), and an opera in 1935. It was also adapted as a ballet, a puppet show, and a radio drama. The novel's depiction of the revolution is somewhat ambivalent. Olesha was disillusioned with certain developments in post-revolutionary Russia, defending the need for freedom in creative activity. As Soviet policy became more rigid, authorities realized the dangerous nature of Olesha's social satire, and the author and his books disappeared from the Soviet literary scene until the Khrushchev "Thaw" in the 1950s. Since that time, Olesha's novel has continued to inspire numerous works in a variety of media. Natalia Sats, the founder of children's musical theatre in Moscow, turned it into a successful children's musical that was performed in Berlin in 1973. It was also made into a popular animation in 1963, and an even more successful feature film, by the director Aleksei Batalov, in 1967. It wasn't until the 1960s that the work became available in the West, where it was translated into numerous languages; the first English translation appeared in 1964. Today, *Three Fat Men* is still widely read and very popular with readers of all ages in Russia.

Not all crossover allegories of a political nature are written in non-democratic regimes or in periods of political repression. The Polish-Jewish author Janusz Korczak, the penname for Henryk Goldszmit, also chose the form of a children's book to express his disenchantment with the political and social situation in the newly created Polish Republic. In 1923, Korczak published *Król Macíus Pierwszy*, which was translated as *Matthew, the Young King* in 1945 and as *King Matt the First* in 1986. The sad parable tells the story of an orphan child king whose attempt to reform his kingdom fails and ends in exile on a desert island. Korczak recounts the young king's exile in a sequel, *Król Macíus na wyspie bezludnej* (King Matt on the desert island), which was also published in 1923, but never translated into English. Like the first book, this story does not have a happy ending, but concludes with the tragic death of the disillusioned Matt.

In Korczak's children's books, the social and political criticism was meant to be understood by children, although some of the deep philosophical and psychological reflections are only accessible to adults. With their multiple layers of meaning for readers of all ages, Korczak's novels are intended for, and appeal to, both children and adults. They not only deal with "adult" issues previously unknown in children's literature, but the author uses innovative formal techniques from modern adult literature, such as genre blending and polyfocalization.[40] Much of their crossover appeal can be attributed to the dual adult-child perspective: the naive perspective of the child protagonist contrasts with the irony of the adult narrator. This dual perspective is particularly striking in Korczak's 1925 novel *Kiedy znów będę mały* (translated as *When I Am Little Again* in 1992), which is narrated by an adult turned child again, that is, an adult-child. Dual perspective provides crossover authors with a highly effective strategy for creating intergenerational appeal.

The German author Erich Kästner was well known as an author for adults before he began writing for children, and he continued over the years to publish for both. In fact, he was convinced that authors should write for both readerships. Kästner won major awards for his writing in both spheres, notably the Georg Büchner Preis (the most important German literary prize) in 1957 and the Andersen Medal in 1960. Kästner's first and most famous children's book, *Emil and the Detectives*, was an immediate hit when it was published in Germany in 1929. It soon became an international bestseller, translated into more than twenty-seven languages. Because of his critical and satirical works, Kästner's books, with the exception of *Emil and the Detectives*, were banned and burned in public after Hitler came to power in 1933. The work that interests us here was not written under Nazism, however, but rather in the wake of World War II.

Kästner wrote his fable *Die Konferenz der Tiere* (translated into English as *The Animals' Conference*) in 1949 as a call for world peace. It is a moralistic tale in which the animals organize a conference because meetings of the heads of state have proved fruitless and the world is being destroyed by humans. Kästner depicts animals and children as being more responsible for the future of the world than adults. The humorous, satiric novel has always appealed to adults as well as children. In 1969, the book was also made into an animated film. The enduring crossover popularity of *The Animals' Conference* was demonstrated during the Kästner centenary in 1999, at which time the book was reprinted and a theatrical version was performed at festivals in Germany and Austria.

Salman Rushdie's only children's book, *Haroun and the Sea of Stories*, was published in 1990, one year after the controversial *The Satanic Verses*. The fact that the acclaimed adult author, who had received the Booker for *Midnight Children* in 1981, chose to write a children's tale at that particular point in time was generally seen to be highly significant. *Haroun* was considered by some as an avatar of the earlier work and an allegory of the author's personal situation following its publication, and, as such, a work that could only be understood by adults. For others, the novel is a true children's book targeted at young readers. Rushdie himself claims to have written it to fulfill a promise to his son Zafar that the next book he wrote "would be one he might enjoy reading" (Zafar's name appears in the acrostic poem that serves as a dedication to the novel).[41] Some critics felt that Rushdie had turned to the rather harmless genre of children's literature as a refuge from political and religious controversy. While *Haroun* escaped condemnation and censorship, the so-called Rushdie Affair undoubtedly explains, at least in part, why *Haroun* seems to be read by adults more than children and is rarely found in the children's section of bookstores, in spite of its appeal with young readers.

Haroun is an initiatory tale in which the child protagonist journeys to the realm of the Sea of Stories with his father, Rachid, who has lost his storytelling gift. It is difficult not to equate Khattam-Shud with Ayatollah Khomeini, whose death sentence attempted to silence Rushdie forever. *Haroun* can obviously be read as a socio-political allegory about freedom of speech and repressive regimes, but it is a multifaceted tale that can be read on many levels. Rushdie questions the conventional child–adult dichotomy by subverting conventional child and adult roles. The young protagonist rescues his father and saves stories, showing how the child and, by extension, the individual can influence global events. *Haroun* is a fable about the art of storytelling, which is highly self-reflexive and whose many intertextual allusions, ranging from the Sanskrit *Kathâsaritisâgara* to Carroll's Alice books, challenge even the most cultured adult reader. For this reason, Jean-Pierre Durix claims that "the reader is invited to consider the novel as belonging to the sub-genre of the children's story which only adults can really understand."[42] Like most tales, however, it explores complex moral and philosophical issues in a simple manner that can be understood by children.

In the tradition of the *Arabian Nights*, to which there are numerous allusions, *Haroun* is a crossover tale that is enjoyed by all ages. Part of the crossover appeal is due to the nonsensical language play, which is reminiscent of *Alice in Wonderland*. In the chapter "An Iff and a Butt," the usual parental response to a child's questioning of authority (no ifs or buts) is embodied in the narrative by the two characters Iff the Water Genie and Butt the Hoopoe, and Haroun's father tells him to quit all "this Iffing and Butting."(18) Even this apparently nonsensical wordplay has a serious message for all readers. Catherine Cundy interprets the role that ifs and buts play in a child's perception of reality on two levels: "They not only contest adult opinion on the primacy of their own view of the world, but (and here we move into one of the adult 'gears' of the text) also assert the validity of questioning and dissent on a wider scale within society."[43] Rushdie himself has indicated clearly that *Haroun* was intended for both children and adults. In a presentation of *The Wizard of Oz*, one of his favourite films, the author explains: "When I first saw *The Wizard of Oz* it made a writer of me. Many years later, I began to devise the yarn that eventually became *Haroun and the Sea of Stories*, and felt strongly that if I could strike the right note it should be possible to write the tale in such a way as to make it of interest to adults as well as children: or, to use the phrase beloved of blurbists, to 'children from seven to seventy.'"[44] The reception of *Haroun* by readers of all ages attests to Rushdie's success as a crosswriter.

None of the texts examined in this section can be considered mere political allegories principally for adults. They are also beloved children's works in their own right. The majority are first and foremost crossover works that appeal to readers of all ages. They examine important political, moral, and philosophical issues that concern young and old alike.

Children's Books With an Adult Cult Following

Some books written for children find a cult following among adults. This may happen immediately after the book's publication or it may develop more slowly over several decades. In a sense, *Alice in Wonderland* could be considered such a book. It has an uncontested place in the Western canon of children's literature but, in actual fact, it is seldom read, at least in its integral form, by today's children. The enthusiastic fans of the *Alice* books tend nowadays to be adults. The twentieth century offers a number of striking examples of books with adult cult followings.

The British author A. A. Milne was an established writer before he turned his hand to writing for children at the request of a friend, and he resented the fact that the immense success of his children's books overshadowed his other work. However, Milne insisted that he wrote the Pooh books "for grownups, and more particularly for two grownups. My wife and myself."[45] The stories were influenced by Kenneth Grahame's popular crossover animal fantasy *The Wind in the Willows* (1908), a work that Milne greatly admired. Between 1923 and 1928, the author wrote four Pooh books, which have never been out of print and have sold more than twenty million copies in England alone. The most famous book in the quartet is *Winnie-the-Pooh*, published in 1926, but *The House at Pooh Corner*, also illustrated by E. H. Shepard, is very popular as well. Since the 1960s, Walt Disney Productions has adapted the Pooh stories into a series of animated shorts that are one of the company's most successful franchises worldwide. Milne's characters have become cultural icons as well as cultural commodities. Their adult cult status is demonstrated by Frederick C. Crews's satire of literary criticism, *The Pooh Perplex: A Freshman Casebook. In Which It is Discovered that the True Meaning of the Pooh Stories is Not as Simple as is Usually Believed, But for Proper Elucidation Requires the Combined Efforts of Several Academicians of Varying Critical Persuasions*, which was published in 1963, and followed, almost four decades later, in 2001, with *Postmodern Pooh*. The success of these collections of parodies of critical literary theories is due, to a large extent, to the immense popularity of Milne's tale with adults. "*Winnie-the-Pooh* is, as practically everyone knows, one of the greatest books ever written, but it is also one of the most controversial," states Crews.[46] In the year it was published, *Winnie-the-Pooh* sold more than one million copies and it seems at first to have been even more popular with adults than children. Milne's American publisher describes the initial reception of the book in the following terms: "Adults loved him first . . . Every intellectual knew the books by heart. It was easily a year and a half before any children saw the books."[47]

The Pooh books have been translated into more than twenty-five languages. Another indication of *Winnie-the-Pooh*'s adult cult status is the success of Alexander Lenard's 1958 Latin translation, which became the first foreign-language book to be featured on the *New York Times* bestseller list in 1960 (the only book in Latin to ever make the list). Few readers of the Latin edition would have been children. *Winnie-the-Pooh*'s enduring appeal with adults and young adults is acknowledged by Emer O'Sullivan: "To the present day the book enjoys an almost cult-status amongst young adults in America and, together with *Alice in Wonderland*, is one of the most quoted children's books in British culture."[48] Milne's children's classic did not enjoy the same crossover appeal in every country. Its lack of success in Germany when it was translated in 1928, is attributed by O'Sullivan to a translation in which the dual addressee is lost. A poor translation can prevent crossover fiction from successfully crossing over as such into another culture. O'Sullivan shows how aspects of Milne's text, which target and appeal to adult readers (in particular the irony), are lost in the original translation, but restored in a 1987 translation by Harry Rowohlt, who tends to translate authors likely to attract a cult following. Rowohlt's translation proved to have more appeal for adults than the original translation, a fact that can no doubt be ascribed in part to the translator's reputation. However, O'Sullivan also feels that it was only when the status of children's literature began to change in Germany that a translation of *Winnie-the-Pooh* with adult appeal could appear and succeed on the German market.[49]

The Pulitzer Prize-winning American author E. B. White wrote three children's stories which are all considered classics of the genre. The first was *Stuart Little* (1945), the story of a two-inch-tall boy who looks like a mouse. Although White's tongue-in-cheek humour is appreciated by adults, the story did not gain adult cult status until Columbia Pictures adapted the work in a 1999 film. The success of the film, which combined computer-animated characters with a cast of live actors (Michael J. Fox was Stuart's voice), took everyone completely by surprise. It grossed $140 million, in large part due to the many adults who flocked to theatres without any kids in tow, perhaps out of nostalgia for the childhood classic. Without losing any of its appeal with children, the film contained material that was geared to the adult audience. Although the film modified the original story, it generated new book sales, as well as two film sequels and other spin-offs. White's most popular book was *Charlotte's Web*, published in 1952 with illustrations by Garth Williams, who had also illustrated *Stuart Little*. White's classic about a wise spider named Charlotte and the young pig Wilbur, whom she saves from slaughter, is a story about friendship and death that resonates with young and old alike. The novel very quickly became a bestseller and, according to the list published by *Publishers Weekly* in 2001, it was the bestselling children's paperback of all time.[50] Sales of *Charlotte's Web*, which has been translated into twenty-three languages, are in excess of forty-five million worldwide. The live-action/computer-animated feature film adaptation released by Paramount in 2006 was generally reviewed as a movie that, like the book, appealed to all ages.

True to C. S. Lewis's own definition of a good children's book, his seven-volume classic fantasy series, *The Chronicles of Narnia*, has always been appreciated by adults as well as children. Lewis did not begin writing for children until he was fifty, but his Narnia books are his best-known and best-loved works. The series was published, with illustrations by Pauline Baynes, between 1950 and 1956. The first volume, *The Lion, the Witch and the Wardrobe: A Story for Children*, is his most famous. Prior to *Harry Potter*, *The Chronicles of Narnia* was the world's bestselling fantasy series, with over one hundred million copies in print in more than forty languages. The books continue to sell over a million copies a year. The Narnia books are read by college students and other adults as well as by children and adolescents. While some adults read the books as allegorical Christian fiction, children mainly appreciate the novels as exciting fantasies. References to the Narnia books are common in popular culture, and one or more of the books have been adapted several times for radio, television, stage, and cinema. New interest in the books by readers of all ages was sparked by the 2005 Disney film adaptation of *The Lion, the Witch and the Wardrobe*, which grossed $745,000,000 worldwide. Movies based on a sequel, *Prince Caspian*, and on Lewis's most popular adult work, *The Screwtape Letters* (1942), are both due to be released in 2008. The enduring popularity of *The Lion, the Witch and the Wardrobe* among adults was clearly demonstrated when it placed ninth in the BBC's 2003 Big Read, the largest survey of popular fiction ever conducted among adults, with the goal of finding Britain's "Best-Loved Book." The fact that Lewis's children's book appeared in the top ten proves that his fantasy stories appeal to a wide audience of adults.

J. R. R. Tolkien, known as the father of modern fantasy fiction, was instrumental in establishing fantasy as a popular literary genre that straddles the divide between children's and adult literature. Although few of his works were written specifically for children, the majority are accessible to young readers, and teenagers constitute the largest percentage of his readership. *The Hobbit,* which Tolkien had written for his own children, was published in 1937 with black-and-white drawings by the author. The novel became an immediate success with adults as well as children. Its enduring cult status with adults is indicated by the collectors' market, where the first printing of the first English language edition rarely sells for less than $10,000 and clean copies may sell in excess of $100,000. Tolkien undertook *The Lord of the Rings* when the publisher asked him to write a sequel following *The Hobbit's* surprising success. Intended initially to be a children's tale in the style of *The Hobbit, The Lord of the Rings* developed into a darker and highly complex novel that addressed an older audience. Although it deals with serious political and moral issues of the twentieth century, it can also be enjoyed simply as an elaborate adventure story set in a fantastic world. Completed in 1949, *The Lord of the Rings* was published in 1954 and 1955 in three individually titled volumes, despite the fact that the author had intended it to be a single volume. The hardback edition sold well, but the work's immense popularity dates from its publication in paperback in the 1960s, when it became a cult book among college students.

The Lord of the Rings subsequently attracted immense mainstream popularity with young and old alike. It ranks as one of the most popular works of the twentieth century, according to both sales and reader surveys. In a 1999 poll conducted by Amazon.com, *The Lord of the Rings* was found to be the greatest book of the millennium.[51] It also topped the list in the "Big Read" survey in Britain in 2003 and was declared the "Nation's Best-Loved Book." Tolkien's enormous popularity is not limited only to the English-speaking world, but constitutes a global phenomenon. Inspired by Britain's "Big Read" initiative, a similar poll was conducted in Germany in 2004, where *The Lord of the Rings* was also found to be the favourite literary work.[52] The epic novel has been translated into more than forty languages. Nearly all subsequent fantasy writers, for both children and adults, have in some way been indebted to Tolkien, whose works have had a profound and enduring influence on the genre. *The Lord of the Rings* is deeply ingrained in popular culture, where it has inspired video games, musical works, and a multitude of spin-offs. Over the years, numerous adaptations have been made for a wide range of media. Peter Jackson's widely acclaimed three-part live-action film, released between 2001 and 2003, prompted a new surge of interest among readers of all ages. The final film was the second film, after *Titanic,* to break the one billion dollar barrier, and it also won eleven Oscars. *The Lord of the Rings* has now sold 150 million copies, one-third of those since the release of the Jackson films. Tolkien's crossover masterpiece has had a huge cultural impact around the globe.

Like a number of other exceedingly popular crossovers, *The Lord of the Rings* occupies a very ambivalent position in twentieth-century fiction because it challenges modern literature. After its publication, the work received very mixed reviews, ranging from scathingly unfavourable to ravingly positive. Some of the opinions expressed are curiously similar to those found in reviews of the Harry Potter books. In 1961, the British writer and journalist Philip Toynbee hoped fervently that the Tolkien craze had passed into "a merciful oblivion." At the other end of the spectrum, a reviewer for the London *Sunday Times* stated that "the English-speaking world is divided into those who have read *The Lord of the Rings* and *The Hobbit* and those who are going to read them."[53] Tolkien's work revived, indeed reinvented, the fantasy genre and filled a vacuum left by the formal innovations of twentieth-century fiction, creating a new publishing market with a longing for grand magical narratives. The immense popularity of *The Lord of the Rings* greatly extended the demand for fantasy fiction, leading the way for the creation of new works, such as Ursula Le Guin's Earthsea trilogy, and the rediscovery of earlier works, like Mervyn Peake's Gormenghast trilogy. The runaway success of the Harry Potter books is a contemporary manifestation of the same phenomenon.

Watership Down, published in 1972 by the British author Richard Adams, has been called one of the first contemporary crossover hits. The story was originally told to his two daughters, who, according to the author, had a great deal of input in the story. *Watership Down* became Adams's first novel and his best-known work. He went on to write adult literary fiction, although he has also published a few children's books. In response to public demand, Adams published a follow-up novel many years later, but *Tales from Watership Down* (1996) was not very well received by fans, who had expected a more conventional sequel. *Watership Down* is a heroic fantasy about rabbits that was inspired by Joseph Campbell's *The Hero with a Thousand Faces*, as was George Lucas's *Star Wars*, another crossover phenomenon of the 1970s. *Watership Down* appealed to the same taste for mythic narrative as Tolkien and, later, Pullman and Rowling. The rabbits' epic adventure is reminiscent of the adventures of Odysseus or Aeneas, and the novel is full of sophisticated allusions to Homer, Virgil, Greek tragedy, the Bible, Shakespeare, and so forth. Further, the chapter epigraphs are taken from a wide range of great works of world literature. According to Adams, the novel was turned down by numerous publishers, essentially for the same reason: "older children wouldn't like it because it's about rabbits; younger children wouldn't like it because it's written in far too adult a style." The author has always maintained that "Watership Down is not a book for children . . . it's a book, and anyone who wants to read it can read it." Adams supports his view by the fact that he has received fan letters from young children to octogenarians.[54] Most reviewers agreed that the novel was for older children and adults alike.

Adams's novel proved to be both a commercial and a critical success. *Watership Down* won Britain's oldest and most prestigious children's literary award, the Carnegie Medal, as well as the *Guardian* Award for Children's Fiction in 1972. The modest print run of 2,500 copies, issued by the small publisher Rex Collings, sold out almost immediately. *Watership Down* was already labelled a classic before the novel was published in the United States, where it became an instant bestseller. Within a month, it reached number one on *Publishers Weekly*'s bestseller list, and remained there for over three months. Since its publication, it has never been out of print and today it still sells half a million copies every year. It has sold over fifty million copies worldwide and holds the distinction of being Penguin Books' bestselling novel of all time. In 1978, it was made into a feature film that took off slowly (the blood and brutality did not appeal to all) but eventually climbed to number six in the U.K. box office for 1978, in part thanks to adult fans who attended late-night screenings. Conversely, older fans were disappointed with the television series that aired in 1999 and 2000. *Watership Down* has been rightly described as "one of the original popular culture crossovers: a book that hooked adults and children on such a vast scale that it made publishing history."[55]

The German author Michael Ende considered himself first and foremost a playwright, but his most successful work is the children's book *Das unendliche Geschichte*, published in 1979 and translated into English as *The Neverending Story* in 1983. Its release caused quite a sensation in Germany, where it soon became a bestseller. It held the top spot on *Der Spiegel*'s bestseller list, Germany's most important top ten list, for 113 weeks, and it remained on the list for 332 weeks. Very quickly, Ende's novel became a cult book, especially with young adults. The fantasy novel won at least ten international prizes within the first four years of its publication and it has been selling well ever since. The fact that *The Neverending Story* was relatively expensive—Ende initially rejected paperback editions because he wanted his book to replicate the book the protagonist steals—did not seem to deter readers or affect sales. Approximately 200,000 copies were sold in the first year. More than three million copies have now been sold in Germany and close to eight million copies worldwide. Although *The Neverending Story*, which has been translated into thirty-six languages, has been very successful in several countries, notably Japan, it has not been widely read in the English-speaking world, where it is best known by a film version that was so unfaithful to the book that the author took legal action against it.

Ende's cult status is perhaps best indicated by the fact that, a generation after its publication, the German publisher Droemer Knaur could commission several of the country's best-known authors of fantasy to write novels inspired by *The Neverending Story*. In 2003–04, five such novels were published by Droemer Knaur in the series Die Legenden von Phantasien (The legends of Fantastica), including one by Ralf Isau, who has been heralded in Germany as Ende's successor. The series was initiated by Roman Hocke, who was Michael Ende's editor at Thienemann Verlag for many years and is now Ralf Isau's agent. In Germany, *The Neverending Story* seems to appeal especially to readers between the ages of eighteen and thirty-five.[56] Many critics question whether Ende's complex, metafictional novel is a children's book at all. While the intricate metafictional structure and the philosophical content "intrigue the cognoscenti," Dieter Petzold acknowledges "the long, if not neverending, success of *The Neverending Story* among readers of all ages."[57]

It is noteworthy that many of the novels dealt with in this section were illustrated. In the tradition of earlier great crossover works like *Alice in Wonderland*, this did not automatically eliminate an adult readership. The crossover novels examined here have not only attracted a large adult cult following, but they enjoy a widespread, for the most part global, mainstream popularity among readers of all ages. These novels are not necessarily "cult" books in the usual sense of the term. Their fans are passionate and loyal, but they also span all the ages from young children to the elderly.

A Pre-Potter Crossover Hit: *Sophie's World*

Jostein Gaarder's international bestseller *Sophies verden* (*Sophie's World*) was published in Norway by Aschehoug in 1991, six years before the first Harry Potter book. It is the bestselling Norwegian book of all time and it remained Norway's number one bestseller for three years. When it finally appeared in the United States in 1994, it was already an international phenomenon. Its international reputation was established in Germany, where it climbed to the top of *Der Spiegel's* bestseller list and remained there for most of the year. In 1995, *Sophie's World* sold more copies than any other novel in the world. To date, sales are in excess of thirty million copies and the book has been translated into fifty-three languages. Gaarder's novel was a highly unlikely international success, as suggested in two reviews that are cited in the U. S. paperback edition. *New York Newsday* called it "Europe's oddball literary sensation of the decade" and *Time* described it as an "improbable international bestseller . . . a runaway hit." In the guise of a whimsical mystery novel, *Sophie's World* explores three millennia of Western philosophy through the eyes of a fourteen-year-old girl. It was mocked by some critics, including one British reviewer in *The Times*, who called it "a potted philosophy primer masquerading as a novel of ideas."[58] When the novel was released in France, a reviewer for *Le Monde* described it as "a story for children that is none other than the history of thought, from the Greeks to us." This endorsement by the compatriots of Descartes and Sartre impressed American reviewers, one of whom wrote: "It is heartening to know that a book subtitled 'A Novel About the History of Philosophy' was not only a bestseller in France, but for a while Europe's hottest novel."[59] Gaarder accomplished the rare achievement of gaining both commercial success and the approbation of the literary establishment with a book for young readers, a feat that would be repeated a few years later by Philip Pullman.

All of Gaarder's novels, whether published for an adult or a juvenile audience, deal with difficult metaphysical questions. For this reason, his work has been seen as highly innovative in children's literature. However, Gaarder's philosophical child-to-adult crossover has many precursors, including such classics as *Alice in Wonderland, At the Back of the North Wind, Le Petit Prince*, and *The Mouse and His Child*. Gaarder has frequently been compared to Lewis Carroll and *Sophie's World* has been called "an Alice in Wonderland for the 90s."[60] The playful, philosophical novel, like all of his books, is intended to make readers wonder at the mystery of the universe. Determined "never to become a grown-up who took the world for granted," Gaarder began to write, "first for adults and then for children as well," in order "to try to make people stop and take note of this extraordinary adventure we pass through all too fleetingly— the great mystery of life." The fantasy genre helps us "to wipe the dust from reality so that we may again experience the world as clearly as when we were children." That is why, in Gaarder's mind, "adults also need children's books."[61] His use of realistic fantasy to explore moral and philosophical issues evokes Philip Pullman, even though their worldviews are very different.

After the success of *Sophie's World*, adults started reading Gaarder's other books. His literary breakthrough had actually come with *Kabalmysteriet* (*The Solitaire Mystery*) which was published for young readers in 1990, one year before *Sophie's World*. It was awarded the Norwegian Literary Critics Award and the Ministry of Cultural and Scientific Affairs Literary Prize. Released in English in 1996, *The Solitaire Mystery* was described by one American reviewer as a "bedtime story for grown-ups in the proud tradition of 'Alice in Wonderland.'"[62] The story traces the mysterious quest of a precocious twelve-year-old boy, who sets out with his father on a journey to Greece in search of his mother. Like *Sophie's World*, it blends mystery and fantasy in a complex story that involves sophisticated intertextual and metafictional play. The unusual format of the novel reflects the content: the book is presented as a deck of cards which gradually reveals the mystery that is hidden in a game of solitaire. Although it was published for a juvenile audience, it has been a highly successful crossover, and the author suggested in an e-mail message on July 24, 2007, that it may be read by even more adults than young people.

The year after *Sophie's World*, Gaarder published *Julemysteriet* (1992), which was translated into English as *The Christmas Mystery* in 1998. Constructed around the Advent calendar, the story is developed as the windows of the calendar are opened, and the protagonist and the reader are taken on a journey through European and church history. Gaarder's novels often present what appears to be a fantastic story within a realistic frame story, but the two worlds ultimately converge. In 1993, he published *I et speil, I en gåte* (translated as *Through a Glass, Darkly* in 1996), the title of which refers to St. Paul's first epistle to the Corinthians. The novel deals with humanity's inadequate knowledge of life and death, in a moving story that describes the last few months in the life of a twelve-year-old girl who is dying of cancer and converses with an angel about heaven and earth, life and death. *Appelsinpiken* (2003), published in English as *The Orange Girl* in 2004, is another modern fairy tale that captivates both young readers and adults. Part of the intergenerational appeal is due to the dialogue that takes place between fifteen-year-old Georg and the dead father he can scarcely remember, when the boy discovers the letter his dying father intended him to read when he came of age. The protagonist is called upon to take up his father's quest and discover the identity of the elusive "orange girl," who turns out to be Georg's own mother. In all of his novels, Gaarder inspires young and old alike to reflect on and ask penetrating questions about themselves and the world they live in.

All of these novels, like *Sophie's World*, were published by Aschehoug for a juvenile audience, but they are popular with adults as well. They are perhaps more widely read by adults than the novels the author has published specifically for an adult audience, *Vita Brevis* (1996), *Maya* (1999), and *Sirkusdirektørends datter* (*The Ringmaster's Daughter*, 2001). Critics often question the target audience of Gaarder's novels. His books for children and young adults are sophisticated, baffling, ingeniously contrived, and open to a broad range of interpretations. They are widely read by adults, but they appeal equally to the young readers for whom they are published, defying strict lines of demarcation between children's and adult books. They have been, as the author himself put it in an e-mail message on July 24, 2007, "successful as crossovers (for both juveniles and adults, or for 'the whole family')." The metaphysical questions they address are of interest to young and old alike. Feeling the acute need for more intergenerational communication and dialogue, Gaarder gives the readers of his novels a shared ground where they can begin to discuss the challenging questions that concern human beings of all ages.

The Harry Potter Phenomenon

The Harry Potter books have been called "the first megalevel juvenile-to-adult crossover hit."[63] *Harry Potter and the Philosopher's Stone*, published in the United States as *Harry Potter and the Sorcerer's Stone*, is repeatedly referred to as "the book that changed everything." Thanks to J. K. Rowling's books, "adults became aware of children's books in a way they never had been," says the editorial director of Bloomsbury USA Children's Books.[64] According to the industry analysts Book Marketing, nearly fifty per cent of the Harry Potter books were bought for adults in 2001, compared with twenty-nine per cent only two years earlier. NDP Group marketing statistics showed that half of the readers are over age thirty-five and a quarter are over fifty-five.[65] Despite the statistics, a few critics nonetheless persist in believing that Harry Potter is just another "kids' craze," like *Goosebumps* or *Pokémon*.[66] In fact, Rowling is largely responsible for the current crossover vogue that has made children's literature so fashionable with adults.

Rowling was writing a novel for adults when the idea for Harry came to her during a train trip in 1990. The author claims that she did not consciously set out to write for children and, like so many children's authors, she insists that she writes for herself. However, *Harry Potter and the Philosopher's Stone* was accepted by Bloomsbury Children's Books and it appeared in Britain as a juvenile fiction title in 1997. People tend to forget that, in the beginning, the first book in the series was a "real" children's book, published for eight- to twelve-year-old children, with no attempt whatsoever to attract a crossover audience. The first edition was a paperback original with a modest print run of 500, a standard print run for a debut children's novel, and it arrived almost unnoticed in bookstores in 1997. When it quickly soared to the top of the adult bestseller lists, Bloomsbury did not delay in getting out an edition for this unexpected public. In 1998, the book was published for a juvenile audience in the United States, where a similar phenomenon occurred. It has been said that *Harry Potter and the Sorcerer's Stone* became the first children's book to occupy the number one position on the *New York Times* bestseller list since E. B. White's *Charlotte's Web* in 1952, but, in fact, the latter never made it past the thirteenth position. Further, *Charlotte's Web* spent only three weeks on the list in December 1952, whereas Rowling's blockbuster stayed near the top of the list for most of 1999 and 2000.

The first Harry Potter book did not win the major children's literature awards chosen by adults in Britain. Although *Harry Potter and the Philosopher's Stone* was shortlisted for the Carnegie Medal and the *Guardian* Children's Fiction Prize, it did not win either. In the past, children's books that had wide appeal were often viewed suspiciously, in the belief that their popularity with so many children was a sign that they were too easy and of inferior literary quality. Works that won critical acclaim were generally read by a minority of readers, much as award-winning literary novels for adults are rarely read by the masses. Prior to Rowling, the two most popular children's authors in the English-speaking world were Enid Blyton and Roald Dahl, both of whom were rejected by the literary establishment. Rowling was hailed as "the next Roald Dahl," the long-awaited successor to the incredibly popular children's author who had continued to dominate bestseller lists after his death. Like Dahl, Rowling overwhelmingly won the prizes voted on by children. The first Harry Potter book won the Nestlé Smarties Book Prize Gold Award in 1997 by an easy margin, beating out Philip Pullman's *Clockwork, or All Wound Up* and attracting significant media atten-tion. In 1998, the novel won all the important British children's book awards that were selected by children. Rowling also received two awards given by the publishing industry in recognition of the book's commercial success, Children's Book of the Year at the prestigious British Book Awards (called "the Oscars of the Book Trade" and known throughout the trade as the "Nibbies") and the Booksellers Association/*The Bookseller* Author of the Year. The following year, the novel also won the American Booksellers Book of the Year (ABBY) Award. Initially, Rowling's success was entirely due to her immense popularity with a loyal and passionate following of young readers.

When *Harry Potter and the Chamber of Secrets* was released in 1998, Rowling already had an enormous readership. She became the first author to win the

British Book Awards Children's Book of the Year two years in a row. The novel was number one in the overall adult hardback bestseller charts for a month after publication in Britain. However, it was not until *Harry Potter and the Prisoner of Azkaban* that records started to be broken and Pottermania set in. Rowling was no longer merely a successful author but an international celebrity. The third book became the top-selling title on the bestseller list at Amazon.com nearly two months before going on sale. No previous title had made it to number one on pre-orders so far ahead of publication. At the same time, *Harry Potter and the Sorcerer's Stone* and *Harry Potter and the Chamber of Secrets* occupied the second and third spots respectively. Each of Rowling's first three books held the number one position on the *New York Times* list of hardcover bestsellers. For sixteen weeks beginning September 26, 1999, they took over the top three rungs of the list. Adult authors further down the list, who felt they had been denied bestseller status by Rowling's books, claimed that they had been "Pottered." The Harry Potter books' domination of the top spots sparked a huge controversy about whether children's bestsellers should be on the regular fiction bestselling list. Many publishers, other than Scholastic, were complaining, because it cut down on their chances of putting the lucrative "New York Times #1 Bestseller" label on the jacket of their books. The result was the creation of a separate list for children's bestsellers, but on the last day of the old list (July 16, 2000), all three books were still in positions two, three, and four. The new list was strategically timed to coincide with the release of the fourth novel in the series, preventing it from joining the others on the regular list.

A similar debate over the status of children's literature occurred with regard to the 1999 Whitbread Book of the Year award in Britain when the third Harry Potter book lost out, by one vote, to Nobel laureate Seamus Heaney's translation of *Beowulf*, the poetry winner. The Whitbread is the British book world's second highest honour after the Man Booker prize. One judge, author Anthony Holden, created quite an uproar in the press by threatening to resign in protest if *Harry Potter* won. He viewed the selection of a children's book over Heaney's epic work as a "national humiliation" that would send the wrong message about a serious literary competition. For several years, the children's book winner had not been forwarded to the final round of judging for the overall award. The rule seems to have been abandoned that year in the belief that Harry Potter was so popular that a children's book might finally be recognized with an adult prize. The chair of the 1998 Whitbread jury had admitted that two of the books on the children's shortlist, both *Harry Potter and the Chamber of Secrets* and David Almond's *Skellig*, could have made the adult prize list. In February 2000, Rowling became the first children's author to win the British Book Awards Author of the Year.

The fourth book in the series, *Harry Potter and the Goblet of Fire*, was a blockbuster of unprecedented proportions. The initial print run of 5.3 million copies (1.5 million hardback copies in the United Kingdom and 3.8 million in the United States), the largest in publishing history, was sold within a matter of days. The release of the book was surrounded by more hype than any other book in recent times. Pottermania reached extraordinary heights around the globe. *The Goblet of Fire* was the fastest-selling book in history. Within days, the book was sold out, netting Rowling an estimated £11 million in one week. It remained on the *New York Times* newly created children's bestseller list for 115 weeks. Guiness World Book of Records proclaimed her reading at Skydome Stadium (Toronto) in October 2000, to an audience of more than twenty thousand, to be the world's largest author reading. The BBC cleared eight hours of air time on December 26, 2000 to broadcast *Harry Potter and the Philosopher's Stone* in its entirety, an unprecedented action that had been done previously only for newsbreaking stories such as the death of Princess Diana. Rowling had accomplished what would previously have been seen as an impossible feat: a children's author had become the most popular writer on the planet and spawned a mega-million dollar industry.

The next two books in the series, *Harry Potter and the Order of the Phoenix* (2003) and *Harry Potter and the Half-Blood Prince* (2005), which sold over two million copies in Britain alone on the first day of its release, carried the phenomenon to new heights, as did the grand finale. It is important to remember that these sales figures include adult versions of the novels, making the Harry Potter books the fastest-selling adult hardbacks as well. Rowling has been the bestselling fiction author in both adult and children's fiction since 1998. The seventh and final book, *Harry Potter and the Deathly Hallows*, released on July 21, 2007, ten years after the first, reached the top spot on both the Amazon.com and Barnes and Noble bestseller lists just a few hours after the release date was announced on February 1, 2007. It was the largest pre-ordered book in history. Scholastic announced a record-breaking initial print run of twelve million copies. The weekend the seventh book went on sale, it grossed more than any Hollywood movie. This would seem to suggest that reading a book is now the quintessential form of entertainment. As of the beginning of August 2007, the Harry Potter series had sold over 350 million copies worldwide in two hundred countries and had been translated into sixty-five languages, ranging from Albanian to Zulu, and including Ancient Greek, Latin, Irish, and Welsh.

Much ink has been spilled trying to account for the success of the Harry Potter books with such a diverse readership of all ages. Part of it can perhaps be explained by the fact that Harry grows up throughout the seven volumes of the series: the protagonist is ten years old in the first volume and goes through adolescence to enter adulthood in the last. All readers appreciate Rowling's complex plotting, attention to detail, and humour. While the broad slapstick appeals especially to children, adults particularly enjoy the parody, pastiche, and satire. Many of the intertextual references to mythology, folk and fairy tales, and classic fantasy may only be decoded by adults. Certain details, such as the steam train to Hogwarts and the Ford Anglia car, evoke the nostalgia of adult readers. The subtle wordplay may only be fully appreciated by adults, but, unlike similar techniques in Carroll's *Alice* books, they do not go entirely over the heads of her young readers. Rowling's series offers something for readers of all ages.

Rowling's rapid rise from an unknown to a bestselling author with her first novel was a rare achievement. It has paved the way for other debut children's authors. Although not on the same scale, the feat has since been repeated by a number of crossover authors, a striking American example being Christopher Paolini. Rowling's Harry Potter books continued to accomplish feats that would have been exceptional even for an adult book, but seemed inconceivable for a children's book. In September 1999, Harry Potter appeared on the cover of *Time*; in December 1999, *People* voted J. K. Rowling one of "the 25 most intriguing people of '99"; in 2007, she became the only British woman on the exclusive Forbes list of the world's U.S. dollar billionaires. A book for children became a global cultural phenomenon and its author an international media superstar whose status was recognized far beyond the children's book sphere, or even the literary world. Rowling had the status of a pop star, a movie star, or a top athlete, unlike anything any author, either for adults or children, had ever known. Her celebrity has given all writers, and children's writers in particular, a new status in contemporary society.

The significance of Rowling's achievement in the age of multimedia is formulated in the following terms by Julia Eccleshare in her book on the Harry Potter novels: "For the first time since the arrival of other mass media a series of children's books is holding a cultural position that is a match for a series such as *Friends* or *Neighbours*, something that had seemed unimaginable in an era in which reading, and children's reading in particular, is not especially highly valued beyond the level of a functional literacy."[67] The old-fashioned recreation of reading was suddenly in vogue with readers of all ages. It is precisely for that reason that, in November 2006, the Europe edition of *Time* magazine included her, along with names like Mother Theresa and Nelson Mandela, in their special issue "60 Years of Heroes," devoted to people who have made the world a better place since 1946. Jumana Farouky, who works in the magazine's London bureau, justified the author's inclusion in the following terms: "In a time when everything comes to us in bits and bytes, Rowling has made storytelling cool again. And that is something truly magical."[68] It has been pointed out by many writers, critics, educators, and readers that Rowling has singlehandedly lowered the illiteracy rate worldwide.

The success of the first Harry Potter novels led to speculations about the "next J. K. Rowling." Harry Potter clones and knock-offs were produced in an attempt to repeat her success. The Artemis Fowl books by Irish author Eoin Colfer and the Karmidee series by Scottish author Charlotte Haptie, which began with *Otto and the Flying Twins* in 2002, were both seen in this light. Publishers and major retailers everywhere began promoting new books by positioning them in relationship to Harry Potter. Reviewers and librarians created "If You Like Harry Potter" lists. Ironically, Rowling's books have spawned significant competition for the Potter industry. Writers and publishers all aspire to repeat her phenomenal success story. As the series neared completion, the search for Rowling's successor was stepped up. However, the thriving field of crossover literature, which owes much to the Potter effect, is proof that there is no need of a single successor. There are now a remarkable number and diversity of authors worldwide who are publishing books that appeal to the huge crossover market generated by Rowling's extraordinary success. Some of these authors were already publishing excellent crossover books when the first Harry Potter novel hit the bookstores.

Crossovers Gain Literary Respectability: *His Dark Materials*

Some critics claim that what has been called "the Harry Potter phenomenon" actually began a couple of years earlier with the publication, in October 1995, of Philip Pullman's *Northern Lights*. Jane Nissen, a former children's editor at Penguin, contends that "Philip Pullman's trilogy heralded the rise of quality fiction and led the way for Harry Potter."[69] Although Pullman has had a lower profile than Rowling, he has also played a major role in the crossover phenomenon. The author of *His Dark Materials* has always maintained that it is intended for all ages, and it was not the first of his works to attract an adult audience. The author's first novel was written for adults, but the successful children's series known as the Sally Lockhart quartet is also read by adults. A series of historical thrillers set in Victorian England, the Sally Lockhart novels combine the clichéd devices of the traditional detective story, in the tradition of Conan Doyle, with modern elements drawn from popular film and fiction. The first novel in the series, *Ruby in the Smoke*, was published in 1985, but it was originally written as a school play to entertain pupils and their parents. Like Harry Potter, the young protagonist of the Sally Lockhart series ages. Sally begins *Ruby in the Smoke* as a sixteen-year-old orphan, but she is a successful businesswoman in *The Shadow in the North* (1987) and an unwed mother in *The Tiger in the Well* (1991). The fourth novel in the series, *The Tin Princess* (1994), is not about Sally herself, but involves three other characters from the previous novels. The serious issues that Pullman addresses in this series, including a young woman's attempt to build a career in a man's world, the opium trade, and the struggles of immigrant Jews in East End London, explain much of its popularity with teenagers and adults.

The first novel of *His Dark Materials, Northern Lights*, was released in Great Britain in 1995 as a children's book, but when it was published in the United States by Knopf, under the title *The Golden Compass*, it was marketed for both children and adults. It was only after the novel's release in the United States, where it received oustanding reviews (it was a *Publishers Weekly* Best Book of the Year), that it began attracting an adult readership in Britain. The author confesses that it was a fortunate combination of circumstances, as the novel's reception in the United States was a "big boost" for the book in Britain, where "it hadn't sold particularly well before that." About one month after its

American release, *Northern Lights* won the Carnegie Medal in Britain. Pullman's "deliberately provocative" acceptance speech, which, as he puts it, "insulted all the grown-up novelists," was a very effective publicity ploy, as it created quite a stir in the media.[70] It was at that point that the adult readership in Britain began to increase significantly. The second book, *The Subtle Knife*, garnered some very glowing reviews, including that of Amanda Craig, the British novelist and children's book editor of the *Times*, who said Pullman's novel would "outlast any Booker contender with ease."[71] The final volume, *The Amber Spyglass*, had an unprecedentedly positive reception in Britain, with full-page reviews in major newspapers, Germaine Greer interviewing Pullman on Radio 4, television interviews as part of the evening news, and so forth. S. F. Said called Pullman's trilogy "clearly the most ambitious, thrilling literary undertaking of our time."[72] *The Amber Spyglass* spent months on bestseller lists not far behind *Harry Potter*.

His Dark Materials is for a slightly older age group than *Harry Potter*. Many critics feel that Pullman's work can better lay claim to the crossover label because it is much more sophisticated, complex, and multilayered. The tone is much darker and there are many deaths throughout the trilogy, whereas Rowling's series did not turn particularly dark until the fourth novel. The success of Pullman's trilogy was largely dependent on word of mouth and there was no hype whatsoever surrounding the publication of any of the novels. Prior to winning the Whitbread, Pullman had remained relatively unknown, except to an enthusiastic and loyal readership that had been steadily growing. In the 2003 "Big Read" survey, however, *His Dark Materials* placed third, while the top Harry Potter novel, *Harry Potter and the Goblet of Fire* (the fifth had not yet been released), placed fifth. It has sold over twelve million copies worldwide and been translated into thirty-seven languages. Although Pullman's extraordinary success has been somewhat overshadowed by Rowling's, it took decades for authors like C. S. Lewis and J. R. R. Tolkien to build up comparable sales. In spite of Rowling's domination of the children's book market, there have been times when Pullman's U.K. sales figures for *His Dark Materials* have surpassed those of *Harry Potter*, notably during the three-year hiatus between volumes four and five. However, the figures are perhaps somewhat misleading, in that the three volumes of Pullman's *His Dark Materials* are considered as one title, whereas Rowling's novels are considered individually.[73] The release of the mega-budget film adaptation of the first novel in December 2007 created a new surge in book sales. The first omnibus edition was published for old and new fans in April 2007, in preparation for the film debut.

The final volume in Pullman's trilogy achieved what the third *Harry Potter* had failed to do two years earlier. *The Amber Spyglass* overwhelmingly won the 2001 Whitbread Book of the Year award, bringing Pullman, his trilogy, and children's literature in general to the attention of the literary establishment and marking another milestone in children's literature's journey toward respectability. It was an achievement that had been inconceivable for many people.

However, a few commentators had already begun to speculate on the possibility of a children's book winning the prestigious Booker Prize in the near future. In 1999, a British journalist wrote: "The real barrier to overcome is not one of the possibilities of the genre but the judges' reluctance to value something that could also be valued by a child, believing that if a child could like it, it must be childish for an adult to like it."[74] Pullman had been a catalyst for change in the Whitbread rules, causing some embarrassment to the Whitbread company and the judges when he protested about the entry of the first two novels in the series because they were ineligible for the overall prize. He was also annoyed that the children's category winner received less money. The author wanted nothing to do with a prize that considered children's literature as second-class. Betting on Pullman, who was initially a 7–1 second favourite, was so heavy that the bookmakers William Hill closed their book on the Whitbread prize several days before the announcement of the winner. Normally few people bet on literary prizes and the stakes are small, but the heavy betting led to rumours that the result had been leaked in advance. After receiving the Book of the Year award, Pullman stated: "I have always believed that children's books belong with the rest, in the general field, and general marketplace and general conversation about books."[75]

With regards to the target audience of his trilogy, Pullman has said: "I wanted to reach everyone and the best way I could do that was to write for children . . . and hope that they'd tell their parents . . . which is what happened." He is pleased that both adults and children are reading the trilogy but insists neither was intended to be "the sole readership."[76] Pullman often claims that his series was conceived as a fantasy epic in the tradition of Tolkien and not as a children's story, irrespective of how it was marketed. He insists that he never targets a particular audience, because, as he told me in an e-mail message on May 5, 2000, the best way to increase the size of one's audience "is to take no notice of it whatsoever and write only for yourself." He feels that the only difference between writing for adults and for children is that the author cannot expect the latter to have as much knowledge. In his mind, it does not matter in the least whether children understand the references to the Bible, mythology, or Milton. Pullman describes *His Dark Materials* as "*Paradise Lost* for teenagers." If the trilogy inspires someone to read *Paradise Lost*, the author thinks that is great, but, as he puts it: "I don't require them to submit a reading list at the door before they're allowed into the first page!" If the story is told correctly, the meaning is implicit, as it is in fairy tales. He uses the example of "Little Red Riding Hood" to illustrate how children and adults discover different meanings in the same text.[77] Some critics, particularly in the United States, feel that Pullman writes more for adults because his sophisticated, multilayered books require a certain knowledge of religion, metaphysics, physics, psychology, and politics. However, it has been rightly pointed out that "adults read J. K. Rowling because she is not complicated; children read Philip Pullman because he is."[78]

Pullman's highly successful children's books, like those of Rowling, shook up conventional attitudes toward children's and adult fiction, questioning the demarcation lines established by publishers, canons, and bestseller lists. They prompted discussions about the status of children's literature and even the appropriateness of such a generic category. Pullman's winning of the Whitbread convinced even the literary establishment that books published for children are literary works worthy of the attention of adults.

Realistic Crossovers

Although contemporary crossover fiction is often equated with fantasy,[79] in fact, a wide variety of genres cross over. Many are realistic novels that deal with serious, topical issues of interest to adults as well as young readers. In this section, the term "realism" is used in a very general sense to distinguish from crossover fantasy. For our purposes, it includes social realism as well as historical fiction. In any case, crossover authors commonly cross genre boundaries as well as age boundaries, so it is often difficult to classify their novels according to conventional generic categories.

The category of young adult fiction, which is a relatively new addition to children's literature, was originally associated chiefly with realistic fiction. Authors who were popular in the late 1960s and 1970s include Judy Blume and S. E. Hinton. Novels depicted the experiences and emotions of teenagers, and commonly dealt with issues such as racism, bullying, juvenile delinquency, teenage rebellion, gender, sexuality, and dysfunctional families. Authors interested in literary quality led a reaction to the problem novel, which often neglected form. As young adult fiction developed and moved away from the problem novel in the late 1970s and 1980s, both content and form became more adult. In addition to mature subject matter, exciting literary experimentation marked works like Aidan Chambers's innovative novel *Breaktime* (1978), the first in his young adult Dance Sequence of six novels. The starkly realistic and controversial novels of Robert Cormier revolutionized the young adult genre in the 1970s. His pessimistic novel *The Chocolate War*, which was published in 1974, launched Cormier's career as a young adult author and has become a classic of the genre. Cormier pursued this dark path in his next two novels, *I Am the Cheese* (1977) and *After the First Death* (1979). In 1985, he published a sequel to the first novel, entitled *Beyond the Chocolate War*. In an interview on the teenreads.com website, Cormier says his adult audience steadily increased with the years. He speculated that this was partly because the teenagers who read *The Chocolate War* and *I Am the Cheese* back in the 1970s were then in their thirties and, "like so many readers, are loyal to the writers they like." The realistic trend continued throughout the 1980s and early 1990s, with the works of authors like Anne Fine and Melvin Burgess. The rather bleak narratives are generally issue-driven and often deal with taboo subjects.

Even with the rise of fantasy in the late 1990s, stark realism continued to find a market. Burgess is sometimes considered a crossover writer, but it is doubtful he would appreciate the label. His gritty, controversial novels, such as *Junk* (1996), *Smack* (1999), *Lady: My Life as a Bitch* (2001), and *Doing It* (2003), treat young readers like adults by dealing with difficult subjects such as drugs and sex. *Doing It* was shortlisted for the first Booktrust Teenage Prize in 2003. Most young adult novels of this nature appeal only to their target audience of teenagers and are not meant to attract adult readers. This is not true, however, of the sophisticated works of authors like Aidan Chambers, whose Carnegie Medal-winning novel *Postcards from No Man's Land* (1999) indicates the extent to which the "literary novel" has been gaining a foothold in young adult fiction. The novel was recommended for sophisticated teenage readers and adults. Like many other young adult novels, *Postcards from No Man's Land* could have been published for the adult market. In fact, a few years ago, it is unlikely that novels such as Chambers's *This Is All: The Pillow Book of Cordelia Kenn* (2005) or M. T. Anderson's *The Astonishing Life of Octavian Nothing, Traitor to the Nation* (2006), which won the National Book Award in the Young People's Literature category, would have been published as young adult novels. The same trend can be seen in the Nordic countries, in novels such as *Nøgen* (Naked, 1995) and *Den kløvede mand* (The split man, 1999) by the Danish author Louis Jensen. In his young adult novel *Nøgen*, the author offers a unique view of adolescence. Whereas children are deeply perceptive but powerless, adults are all-powerful but without understanding. Between the two is a time when the individual can perceive everything and discover love. The young adult novel is being redefined in the current crossover trend. The success of *Harry Potter* and *His Dark Materials* made publishers realize "how lucrative the market could be if it grew beyond its problem novel origins to include genre fiction and literary fiction." Jonathan Hunt argues that "young adult literature has matured into something virtually indistinguishable from the best adult literary fiction."[80] The move away from the hyperrealism that dominated the genre in the 1980s and early 1990s has thus been accelerated in recent years, but realism is still very much alive in young adult fiction. It is not all of a dark and disturbing nature, however, and can often be light-hearted, quirky, and humorous.

Before Rowling, young adult success stories were the exception rather than the rule, even though some critics had long been claiming that the best writing was going on in that arena. The majority of young adult novels did not receive the attention they deserved. Today young adult fiction is very much in vogue, and not only with young readers. A large number of young adult novels win the crossover label, which is sometimes used to refer exclusively to books of that genre that cross over to adults. To a large extent, there is simply a new awareness of books that span the gap between children's and adult fiction. The amorphous category of young adult fiction is a literature of transition from childhood to adulthood and the lines are particularly blurry. Authors such as Francesa Lia Block and Tanith Lee, who are best known as young adult authors, have a faithful adult following who read all their books, regardless of the target audience. However, young adult literature still has a rather low status in some countries. In the Netherlands, upper level high school students are not allowed to read novels published for young adults. An anthology of fiction about adolescence, entitled *De perfecte puber* (The perfect adolescent), was published in the Netherlands for a young adult audience in 1991, but all of the one hundred extracts were taken from adult fiction about adolescents. In the introduction, Jaap Goedegebuure, a professor of Dutch language and literature, justifies the selection of texts and explains why excerpts from young adult novels were not included, by suggesting that they are inferior. An entirely different view is expressed by Helma van Lierop-Debrauwer and Neel Bastiaansen-Harks, in their 2005 study, where they compare adolescent novels published as juvenile literature (books about adolescents for adolescents) with adolescent novels published as adult novels (books about adolescence). They make the case that young adult books should be used in the education system in the Netherlands because there are only very minimal differences in structure and style.[81] An increasing number of books being published as young adult titles could just as easily be published for adults, and vice versa.

Realistic child/young adult-to-adult crossovers are a global phenomenon, and they seem to have a longer tradition in some northern European countries than in the English-speaking world. Some of the most striking earlier examples are from Nordic countries. The Norwegian author Tormod Haugen has repeatedly denied the division of literature into children's and adult books, claiming to write for everyone who wants to read his books. From the outset of his career, his novels were radically different from most traditional children's books being written in the 1970s and 1980s. Although they won international acclaim and have been translated into at least twenty-four languages, only two early novels have appeared in English, *Nattfuglene* (1975), translated as *The Night Birds* in 1982, and *Zeppelin* (1976), published in Britain as *Zeppelin* in 1991 and in the United States as *Keeping Secrets* in 1994, almost two decades after its release in Norway.

Haugen constantly reminds adults, as he does in the opening of his acceptance speech at the 1990 Hans Christian Andersen Award presentation ceremony, that all of us were once children. The awareness of childhood in all of its complexity is of vital importance to young and old alike. This theme is central to all of Haugen's works, which examine the complex relationships between children and adults. In *Skriket fra jungelen* (The cry from the jungle, 1989), the river goddess attributes all of the misery in the modern world to the fact that people have forgotten the child and fail to see that the child and the adult are one. Haugen's books stress the continuum between childhood and adulthood, so it is not surprising that his novels cannot be said to be for children only. His young readers identify with the pain and hopes of the child characters, but adult readers remember their own childhood. While Haugen takes the child's point of view, exploring the psychological problems of children, his books constitute a warning to adults that children are very vulnerable and easily destroyed. When he won the Andersen Medal, the importance of his work was seen in crossover terms: "His writing erases age categories."[82] However, very early in Haugen's career, Norwegian critics pointed to the intergenerational nature of his writing. In 1986, one critic already considered this to be the great achievement of his novels for children and young people: "He transcends age limits. His books are not only for children. Nor are they only for young people. And certainly not only for grown-ups. He reaches his readers, regardless of age."[83] *Vinterstedet* (The Winter Place), is the story of seventeen-year-old Andreas Sandervik, a hypersensitive teenager who goes to Eden, the family summer holiday house by the sea, in the winter with the intention of committing suicide two days after his birthday. In addition to the difficult topic of suicide, Haugen introduces erotic elements into the story, which was published for a juvenile audience in 1984. That year, one critic claimed the novel was "addressed to old and young readers although published as a young people's book."[84]

Haugen's novels are also formally innovative and often written in a postmodern style. *Vinterstedet* breaks up traditional narrative continuity, presenting the protagonist's troubled thoughts in a disorderly stream of consciousness. Some of his novels combine realism and fantasy. *Skriket fra jungelen*, which is subtitled "a film novel," parodies several different genres, including fantasy, realism, mystery, spy thriller, and science fiction. The overall story is a science fiction plot about a technical invention to amputate children's imaginations and use them for evil purposes. All of Haugen's novels are characterized by their literary quality and masterly craftmanship. His simple, but elusive prose, in which the silence is almost as eloquent as the words, hovers between prose and poetry. The minimalist trilogy about Georg and Gloria, which began with *Georg og Gloria (og Edvard)* in 1996, is cleverly written into a tradition of well-known generic patterns from romance literature. With its elegant, poetic style and sophisticated use of intertextuality, one would expect it to appeal mostly to adults, but it is also appreciated by young readers. Although the Andersen Medal consecrated Haugen's oeuvre "for children" in 1990, he has nonetheless continued to write works that appeal to a crossover audience.

Dutch language fiction also offers a rich selection of realistic crossovers, especially beginning in the 1990s. A volume of avant-garde, nonsense stories with the awkward title *Verse Bekken! Of Hoe Heel Kort zich in een kip vergiste, uit het wc-raam hing, het op een sluipen zette an andere avonturen van de rat* (Fresh beaks! About How Very Short was mistaken about a chicken, hung from the WC window, made a sneak for it, and other adventures of the rat), by the Dutch children's author Anne Vegter, was the first children's book to be nominated for the prestigious AKO Literatuurprijs in 1990. Although it was published for young children, it was mostly read by adults. The novels of the Flemish author Anne Provoost are written for young people, but they are equally appealing to adults and she reaches a very wide audience. Her second novel, *Vallen (Falling)*, published in 1994, won several major Dutch-language awards, including the

Woutertje Pieterse Prize, as well as a number of international awards. Provoost deals with xenophobia and racism, moral choice and personal responsibility, and love and forgiveness in this compelling coming-of-age story that traces the rapid moral, mental, and emotional decline of Lucas Beigne following the revelation of dark family secrets. The widely acclaimed novel has been translated into twelve languages, and, in 2001, it was made into an English-language feature film, starring Jill Clayburgh, that brought the novel to the attention of a wider crossover audience.

Provoost's much-acclaimed novel *De Arkvaarders* (The Ark-builders) was brought out by the important Dutch publisher Querido in 2001. The novel's launch in English in 2004, under the title *In the Shadow of the Ark*, was a much talked about literary event throughout the English-speaking world. It was immediately categorized as "a YA/adult crossover."[85] Provoost retells the well-known Bible story of Noah and the Ark through the eyes of a teenage girl who is not among the chosen few to be saved from the Flood. The lengthy novel, narrated in the first person by the young girl Re Jana, questions the motives and morals of the Old Testament story. Some of the religious and philosophical background of the complex tale may be difficult for young readers. The novel also contains subtle portrayals of sexual scenes: the forbidden love affair between Re Jana and Ham leaves her pregnant, a relationship develops between Re Jana and Ham's wife, and Re Jana is repeatedly raped by Ham's brothers. In 2002, the novel was awarded the Gouden Zoen (Golden Kiss), the major award for young adult literature in The Netherlands and Belgium. It was also longlisted for the 2006 International IMPAC Dublin Literary Award, a rarity for a young adult novel. Provoost's novel has been likened to Anita Diamant's 1997 bestselling adult novel *The Red Tent*, which retells the episode from Genesis that is generally known as the "Rape of Dinah." A review in *Booklist* sums up the critical reception of *In the Shadow of the Ark* in the following terms: "This is a YA novel only in the broadest sense; no one would blink if it appeared on an adult list."[86]

When John Nieuwenhuizen, the English translator of Provoost's *Falling*, was awarded the 2005 New South Wales Premier's Translation Prize and Pen Medallion for the major role he has played in introducing novels written in Dutch to the English-speaking world, he was praised not only for the high literary quality of the books he has chosen to translate, but for "venturing into the field of fiction for young adults." It seems that children's and young adult literature also suffers from a status problem in the world of translation. The jury pointed out that two of Nieuwenhuizen's major successes, the young adult novels *Falling*, by Provoost, and *The Baboon King* (*De bavianenkoning*, 1982), by Anton Quintana, have both been "read and praised as books for the adult market."[87] *The Baboon King* is the story of a young African hunter who becomes the king of a baboon troop when his mixed Kikuyu and Masai blood makes him an outsider with both tribes. The novel has been compared to survival classics such as *Lord of the Flies*. It has been translated into several languages, including

English, but the latter did not appear until 1998. Nieuwenhuizen has trans-lated a number of other Dutch works that are read by a crossover audience, including Imme Dros's *Ongelukkig verliefd* (Unhappily in love, 1995), Peter van Gestel's *Nachtogen* (Night eyes, 1996), and Ted van Lieshout's *Gebr.*, 1996 (*Brothers*, 2001). Van Lieshout's novel, which tells the story of a young man coming to terms with the death of his younger brother, won the Deutscher Jugendliteraturpreis in 1999 and was translated into English in 2001.

The novels of the well-known German children's author Mirjam Pressler are also read by young people and adults alike. The author, who won the Deutscher Bücherpreis (German Book Award) for her lifetime achievement in children's literature in 2004, also publishes adult fiction. Pressler is best known for her work revising the diaries of Anne Frank, and a number of her young adult novels deal with Holocaust survival. Her earlier novels, such as *Novemberkatzen* (Novembercats, 1982), have not been translated into English. It was not until the late 1990s that a few of her works began to appear in an English edition. *Wenn das Glück kommt, muß man ihm einen Stuhl hinstellen* (When good fortune comes, you have to offer it a chair) was published in 1994 and won the Deutscher Jugendliteraturpreis in 1995. Translated into English as *Halinka* in 1998, the novel gets its original title from one of the sayings that the twelve-year-old protagonist writes in her secret book of thoughts: "When good fortune comes, you have to offer it a chair." Halinka writes in the book in her secret hiding spot in the German home for neglected and troubled girls where she lives, shortly after World War II. The young girl attempts to hide her Jewish heritage by claiming to be a gypsy. Based on a true story, *Malka Mai* (2001), translated simply as *Malka* in 2002, is the poignant story of a young Jewish girl who, during World War II, has to fend for herself when her mother, Dr. Hannah Mai, is forced to leave the sick child with strangers as she flees from Poland with her two daughters. The young girl is miraculously reunited with her mother when the latter, torn by guilt, returns to look for her. The alternating perspectives of the girl and the mother explain the cross-generational appeal of this powerful story. In 1999, Pressler published the successful crossover novel *Shylocks Tochter* (*Shylock's Daughter*, 2001), set in sixteenth-century Venice, which addresses the haunting question of Shylock's motivation in demanding a pound of Antonio's flesh in Shakespeare's famous play.

The English-speaking world has many notable realistic crossovers. *Sisterland*, published in 2003 by Linda Newbery, is another novel about dark family secrets. Shortlisted for the Carnegie Medal, it tells the story of a young girl who discovers secrets buried deep in the past when her sick grandmother comes to live with the family. In Britain, *Sisterland* was considered "one of this year's most compelling 'crossover' reads for teenagers and adults."[88] The previous year, Newbery had published *The Shell House*, a novel about two very different gay relationships, one in the present and one in the past. Although it was shortlisted for both the Carnegie Medal and the *Guardian* Children's Fiction Prize, it was also seen as a crossover novel. Newbery does not think of her "older novels, such as *The Shell House* and *Sisterland*, as 'teen fiction,'" a term that she dislikes. "I simply think of them as novels in which the main character happens to be seventeen, eighteen or whatever," she clarified in an interview posted on the Wordmavericks website. In 2006, the year in which the prestigious Whitbread became the Costa, Newbery won the 2006 Costa Children's Book of the Year Award for *Set in Stone*, inspired by the Victorian Gothic novel. Some people were surprised that the novel won a children's prize because the main characters are in their twenties. On her website, the author carefully identifies the novel as "young adults' fiction," rather than children's fiction. The author describes it as "a young adult book, or a novel of adolescence, likely to be enjoyed by capable readers of fourteen up to and including adults." When an interviewer remarked that he was "pleasantly surprised by the intellect assumed of *Set in Stone*'s young readers" (the novel deals with the subject of incest), the author replied that she simply writes the best book possible. Like so many other crossover authors, she insists that she does not try "to aim at any imagined readership," but assumes that if she writes "a good story" that pleases her, there will be readers who will enjoy it as well.[89]

The Irish-American author Jennifer Donnelly also skilfully weaves past and present together in books that appeal to a diverse audience. Her first young adult novel, *A Northern Light*, was published in 2003 in the United States, where it was also very popular with adult readers and was considered an outstanding crossover title. Published in Britain by Bloomsbury, under the title *A Gathering Light*, it won the CILIP Carnegie Medal. The press release on April 4, 2004, posted on the CILIP website, to announce the 2003 shortlist, indicates the growing acknowledgement of crossover fiction. The Chair of the Judges, Colin Brabazon, stated that all six of the books on the 2003 shortlist "will appeal not just to children and young people, but to the whole family." In fact, he went so far as to say: "This year's shortlist showcases writing that is as enjoyable for adults as it is for children and young people. . . . All six books . . . are as intense and illuminating as the best adult fiction can be." In the press release of July 9, 2004 that announced the winner, also posted on the CILIP website, Brabazon once again commented on the "incredibly strong and diverse short-list," which included Whitbread Book of the Year winner, Mark Haddon, Whitbread Children's Book of the Year winner, David Almond, and Children's Laureate Michael Morpurgo, but said that Donnelly's "compelling novel swept all before it." In her review in the *Guardian*, novelist Adèle Geras wrote: "If ever a novel for teenagers deserved a crossover audience, this is it."[90] Donnelly blends murder mystery, romance, and historical fiction in this coming-of-age story inspired by an infamous murder case that gripped America in the early 1900s and has been described as "the O. J. Simpson case of its time." It involved the mysterious drowning, in 1906, of Grace Brown, an unwed pregnant nineteen-year-old, whose boyfriend was found guilty and executed in 1908. In Donnelly's novel, the heroine, Mattie Gokey, is given a secret bundle of letters to burn by a guest in the hotel where she works. The author had read Theodore Dreiser's fictionalized account of the murder, *An American Tragedy*, which was made into a film in the 1930s and again in 1951, as *A Place in the Sun*, starring Elizabeth Taylor. Donnelly was pleased that adult readers were enjoying the novel, but says she wrote it with an audience of young women Mattie's age in mind.[91]

Donnelly actually became an overnight success as a writer for both young adults and adults. Just prior to *A Northern Light*, Donnelly published *The Tea Rose* (2002), a historical novel for adults set in London's East End in the late nineteenth century, which introduced a trilogy that continued in *The Winter Rose* (2007). Donnelly admits she was consciously writing for two different audiences in *A Northern Light* and *The Tea Rose*. She explains the difference in the following manner: "I basically write for young adults to give them a glimpse into the complicated adult world they'll soon be entering, and I write for adults to give them a way out of that world." However, she dislikes the idea that "teenagers will only read about teenagers, and forty year olds about forty year olds." In an e-mail message on April 30, 2007, she told me, "good stories should transcend age, race, gender." Some of the young adult readers of *A Northern Light* also read her adult series and vice versa. Donnelly is a relatively rare example of an author who began her career writing books for all age groups and continues to move easily from one to the other. Between *The Tea Rose* and *A Northern Light* she published a picturebook, entitled *Humble Pie* (2002). She is currently working on the final novel of her adult trilogy, *The Wild Rose*, while at the same time writing her next young adult novel, set in late eighteenth-century Paris.

The historical novel *The Queen's Soprano*, by the American author Carol Dines, was published in 2006 by Harcourt for ages fourteen and up, but the book has a very adult look. The novel is based on the true story of Angelica Voglia, sometimes called Angelica Quadretti, who becomes Queen Christina's soprano in seventeenth-century Rome, where Pope Innocent XI has forbidden women to sing in public. Caught up in the deadly power struggle between the Pope and the Queen, Angelica is the victim of sexual assault by a bishop, resulting in her flight from Rome and the loss of the French artist she loves. Dines fell in love with the story after reading about Queen Christina and she wanted it to be "accessible to teens on up." The novel was thus conceived as a crossover book, but, like Donnelly, the author felt the story was especially relevant to teenagers. Most reviewers seem to consider it clearly young adult fiction, but the author told me in an e-mail message on May 19, 2006 that most of her fan mail has been from adults who have enjoyed the novel. The gripping narrative and the rich, historical detail make Dines's novel a pleasurable read for both adolescents and adults.

Anglo-Indian author Jamila Gavin has written many children's books that reflect today's multicultural society, in particular the Indian and British experience. She feels that children's literature should be taken as seriously as fiction for adults and her complex novels are rather difficult to categorize. Her acclaimed novel *Coram Boy*, a dark and skilfully crafted historical novel set in eighteenth-century England, won the 2000 Whitbread Children's Book Award. It deals with difficult subjects such as class prejudice, racism, and child trafficking. Its crossover appeal is indicated by the fact that the National Theatre in London adapted it for their Christmas season, following the hugely successful adaption of Pullman's *His Dark Materials*. Gavin insists that "children shouldn't be ghettoised," in literature or in any other art form. With regard to the National Theatre's production of *Coram Boy*, the author said: "[Children are] completely entitled to mainstream theatre. This production is as much for your mainstream audience as it is for children."[92] Gavin has published other crossover novels, including *The Blood Stone*, a historical novel set in the seventeenth century. Shortlisted for the 2003 Carnegie Medal, *The Blood Stone* tells the disturbing story of a young Venetian who travels to the Hindu Kush to ransom his father, a jeweller, from the bandits holding him in Afghanistan. Gavin's sophisticated novels, with their strong plots and mature themes, appeal to adults as well as children.

Michael Morpurgo, who became Britain's third Children's Laureate in 2003, does not like the crossover tag and makes no attempt to write children's books that appeal to adults. Julia Eccleshare, children's book editor of the *Guardian*, says that "children can easily tell that he respects them as readers and writes for them alone, rather than searching for that now so fashionable 'crossover' market."[93] Morpurgo's serious and gripping historical narratives nonetheless appeal to adult audiences as well. The year that Rowling won the Whitbread Children's Book Award for *Harry Potter and the Prisoner of Azkaban*, Morpurgo was shortlisted for *Kensuke's Kingdom* (1999), a novel about the aftermath of the bombing of Nagasaki. In 2004, he was shortlisted for the same award for *Private Peaceful* (2003), the story of a soldier in World War I. Many critics and readers agree that these and other titles, such as *The Last Wolf* and *Out of the Ashes*, are crossover novels. Although Morpurgo has published almost one hundred titles and won numerous prizes, his name was not well known by the general public, even in Britain, before he became Children's Laureate. Morpurgo himself feels that the children's writers who are known are either "the ones who are dead" or those "who have done what is called 'crossover.'" In his view, the purpose of the Children's Laureate is to try to draw attention to those "who write wonderful stories but not necessarily crossover books."[94] This Children's Laureate has nonetheless written wonderful stories that *are* crossover books.

The British freelance investigative journalist-turned-novelist Clare Sambrook published her debut novel *Hide & Seek* to much acclaim in 2005. The rights to the novel were bought in fourteen countries and the film rights were sold to BBC Films. Narrated by a nine-year-old boy whose younger brother disappears during a school field trip, the suspenseful novel traces the disintegration of normal family life after the brother goes missing. Like many crossover novels, *Hide & Seek* is difficult to classify. It has been compared to *The Curious Incident of the Dog in the Night-Time*, whose author offered a review in the *Observer*.

Some critics consider Sambrook's novel more of an adult read than a children's book, due to the dark and disturbing look at adult grief. However, everything is seen and described, often with a great deal of humour, from the perspective of the nine-year-old narrator, who feels responsible for the tragedy. With regard to her target audience, Sambrook herself says: "I don't really draw a distinction between children's literature and adults'. I wrote it with adults in mind, but aware that bright children of 12 or 13 might read it."[95] She suggests that parents should decide whether or not it is suitable for their children.

South African children's literature has also produced a number of striking crossover novels, both in English and in Afrikaans. The Scottish-born South African author Lesley Beake's youth novels, which address the plight of the children of certain tribes in southern Africa, attract an adult audience. The poignant stories are told in a polished, poetic prose that captures young and old alike. *A Cageful of Butterflies*, published in 1989, is the story of a deaf-mute Zulu boy who is brought from his village to live with a white family. In 1991, it won the M-Net Book Prize, the most important literary award in South Africa. The prize was established in 1991 by the Electronic Media Network, a commercial television station, to encourage the writing of quality novels which could be adapted for the screen. The sponsors conceived this award originally to be open to both adult and children's books, so that young adult fiction was judged against adult works. It was the first time that a children's/young adult book had achieved that kind of recognition in South Africa. The following year, the award once again went to a teen novel, T. Spencer-Smith's *The Man Who Snarled at Flowers*; the subtitle, *A Fantasy for Children*, clearly indicated its target audience. Winning this particular award indicates that these two teenage novels were widely read by adults as well. In 1991, Beake published her much-acclaimed novel, *Song of Be*, which tells the coming-of-age story of an adolescent San girl within the political context of the newly independent Namibia. The story is told in flashbacks as the girl dies from a self-inflicted, poisoned-arrow wound. *Song of Be* has been published in ten other countries and has received a number of awards, including being selected as a 1994 Best Book for Young Adults by the American Library Association.

Dianne Hofmeyr is another well-known South African author for children and young adults. Her business card says she is a "children's author," but her novels are widely read by adults. Her books have garnered awards for both youth literature and general fiction. In 1994, *Boikie You Better Believe It* won the Sanlam Gold Award for Youth Literature. As Dee Nash, convener of the panel of judges for the Sanlam prize pointed out in a press release posted on the website of the University of South Africa's Children's Literature Research Unit, Hofmeyr deals with important issues without the least trace of "writing down" to her audience. The mature issues examined in her juvenile novels include violence and erotic fantasies. A terrorist attack on a pub, in which the fourteen-year-old narrator's father is one of the victims, is described quite vividly. It is the manner in which Hofmeyr deals with these topics combined with her well-crafted prose that makes her popular with adults as well as children. In 1995, the same novel was awarded the prestigious M-Net Book Prize for popular fiction. The calibre of the competition is indicated by the fact that the other novels shortlisted for the M-Net that year included J. M. Coetzee's *Master of Petersburg* and Mike Nichol's *Horseman*. Nobel Laureate Nadine Gordimer was also nominated, but withdrew. In an e-mail message on April 3, 2006, Hofmeyr told me she thinks *Boikie You Better Believe It* won because the novel was timely and captured what was happening in the "new" South Africa just prior to Nelson Mandela coming to power: it had "a certain edgy energy people were looking for." For a time following Hofmeyr's win, the sponsors no longer considered children's titles for the M-Net Prize. In 2005, the award was re-christened the M-Net Literary Awards and children's novels were once again allowed to compete. The judging criteria include literary merit and strong narrative content as well as accessibility to a broad reading public. Those criteria certainly apply to the best crossover books.

Adults often hear about Hofmeyr's novels through daytime radio interviews that are aimed at adults. *Boikie You Better Believe It* (1994) was read in its entirety by a professional actor on the Morning Novel slot on National Radio at 10:00 a.m., a time when all South African children are at school and only adults are listening. In her e-mail message, the author expressed her view that, with a new reading culture developing in South Africa, there is scope for the shorter novel or novella, including the "teen novel, which is more accessible and perhaps less complex in plot." Hofmeyr received great acclaim for her novel *The Waterbearer*, a mystical coming-of-age story set in fourteenth-century Africa, that was published in 2001. Although her earlier novels are also read by adults, Hofmeyr says that *Fish Notes and Star Songs*, published in 2005, is the first of her books that she has seen displayed in the adult section of bookstores. It is a short, poetic, and haunting novel that begins in a realistic mode but slides into the spirit world of rock art. Hofmeyr's gritty yet mystical writing has been compared with the best of David Almond.

One of the best examples of a South African book with crossover appeal is Riana Scheepers's *Blinde Sambok* (Blind whip), published in 2001. Contrary to Marita van der Vyver's *Childish Things*, *Blinde Sambok* was not intended to be a crossover novel. Scheepers, who had previously published only for adults, wrote the novel for children/young adults because there was a lack of good books for young readers, whom she felt were being given nothing but problem novels. However, she does not believe in having a specific age group in mind when writing, saying that she read adult literature when she was very young and still reads children's literature today. Scheepers's motto as a writer is: "Do not underestimate a child's intelligence." The novel posed a problem for the publisher, who did not know where to pitch the book. In the end, it was marketed for children ten to twelve years of age. The author did not have very young readers in mind when she wrote the novel, although the protagonist begins the story as a baby and is only six or seven at the end. It is the story of Gideonette, who, from the moment she is born as a frail premature girl and sees her father's disappointment, is determined to be a boy and so fears the family curse or the "blinde sambok." The literal translation of "blinde sambok" is "blind whip," but it is an Afrikaans saying, of Zulu origin, meaning a bolt that strikes out of the blue as a form of justice for a wrongdoing. In Scheepers's novel, the protagonist fears the family curse passed down through the male line because she has assumed the identity of a boy. In an e-mail message on June 19, 2007, Scheepers says she wrote the novel for herself and readers "from 2–102 years old," who still enjoy "a beautiful story." The book was hugely popular with adults, many of whom read it in reading clubs, but it was equally popular with children, winning the ATKV Kinderboekprys, the only children's choice award in South Africa. When it was translated into Dutch—as *Scorpioenkind* (Scorpiongirl) due to the difficulty in translating the proverb—it was shortlisted for Die Vlaamse Kinderjurie-prys, a Flemish youth prize determined by a jury of twenty children. The overwhelmingly positive reviewers of *Blinde sambok* repeatedly referred to its appeal to readers of all ages.

In the past few years, there have been an increasing number of crossover books in South Africa, reflecting the general worldwide trend. In 2006, Scheepers published *Die avonture van wilde Willemientjie* (The adventures of wild Wilhelmina), which is written in rhyme and "aimed at 'children' of all ages." A theatrical adaptation, staged at the largest art festival in South Africa, received the Kanna Prize for children's theatre. However, it was mostly attended by grown-ups, who identify with the wild baby's loveable grandparents. Like Scheepers, Anoeschka von Meck was an author for adults prior to publishing her first award-winning young adult novel *Vaselinetjie* (Vaseline) in 2004. It is the story of a young protagonist who gets her unusual name from her shiny skin, which is the result of her grandparents rubbing it with Vaseline in the winter. The novel won awards for both young adult and adult books. In 2005, Von Meck won the MER Prize for Youth Literature, which is awarded to the best South African young adult book published in English or Afrikaans. However, it is widely felt that the author did not intend the novel to be for young adults.

Some novels cross over in part because of their appeal to readers of all ages in a specific cultural community. Victor Martinez won the 1996 National Book Award for Young People's Fiction with his debut novel, *Parrot in the Oven: mi vida*. Set in Fresno, California, it is the story of a fourteen-year-old Mexican-American boy's coming of age within a poor, dysfunctional family. In this Bildungsroman, Martinez brings the experimental form that characterizes Chicano literature for adults to the sphere of young adult literature. The novel won the National Book Award in 1996, the year that The Young People's Literature category was added. Although *Parrot in the Oven* was marketed for young adults, its literary sophistication is on a par with Chicano adult novels that have crossed over to younger readers, including Cisneros's *House on Mango Street* and Anaya's *Bless Me, Ultima* (1972). Manny's first-person narrative offers a portrait of barrio life that has cross-generational appeal not only for the Chicano population. Like many crossovers about a minority culture, *Parrot in the Oven* is used in American schools, especially within those communities.

A number of novels appeal to a crossover audience in the Asian-American community and are also taught in schools. *Shizuko's Daughter,* published in 1993 by the Japanese-American novelist and poet Kyoko Mori, is a remarkable coming-of-age story that transcends cultural barriers. A semi-autobiographical novel, it is the story of Yuki, an adolescent in 1970s Japan who lives with an unfeeling father and a cruel stepmother after her mother's suicide. Mori presents a detailed portrait of the life of a Japanese family whose traditional customs stifle a young girl. Narrated in beautiful, poetic prose, the bleak, sometimes grim, yet hopeful, story is very adult in tone. Like the best realistic Japanese fiction, Mori's prose is a delicate blend of candidness and restraint. *Shizuko's Daughter* was a *New York Times* Notable Book in 1993 and an American Library Association Best Books for Young Adults in 1994. Mori now publishes for adults as well as young adults. A second young adult novel, *One Bird* (1995), the story of a fifteen-year-old girl in 1970s Japan, was followed by her first novel for adults, *Stone Field, True Arrow* (2000), about a Japanese-American artist. Mori's novels for both audiences are written in the same evocative prose and deal with the same themes, notably relationships between daughters and parents, but the protagonist of her adult novel is thirty-five, whereas those of her young adult novels are adolescents who are coming of age.

The Long Season of Rain (1996) was the debut novel by Seattle writer Helen Kim. The novel presents a fascinating portrait of life and traditions in late 1960s Korea. It was a finalist for the National Book Award for Young People's Literature the year that *Parrot in the Oven* won the award. Through the lives of the female members of a very unhappy Korean family, Kim shows the plight of the oppressed female in a traditional Asian society. While the novel is a sensitive portrayal of the life of eleven-year-old Junehee, it is also the story of her mother. Although a few reviewers feel that the emphasis on marital issues will bore many children, the focus on the two generations explains much of the cross-generational appeal. The reviewer of an anthology of Korean–American fiction, published in 2001, regrets that it does not contain excerpts from Kim's novel "or any of several other excellent novels whose fate it is to have been marketed for young adults."[96] In addition to addressing concerns of a particular community, these multicultural crossovers provide American readers in general with a window into the lives and way of life of other cultures. They demonstrate the diversity of crossover literature in the English language.

Parallel to the trend of comic fantasy crossovers, there have also been a significant number of comic realist crossovers. *Martyn Pig* (2002), by the British author Kevin Brooks, is a dark and comical tale of accidental murder and betrayal. In 2003, it won the Branford Boase Award for a debut novel against stiff competition, including Nicky Singer's *Feather Boy*. He was the first ever debut author to be shortlisted for the CILIP Carnegie Medal in 2002 for *Martyn*

Pig, while his second novel, *Lucas*, a love story between a young girl and a stranger falsely accused of sexual assault by ignorant island residents, was shortlisted for the *Guardian* Children's Fiction Prize as well as the new Book Trust Teenage Fiction prize in 2003. Brooks continues to write books that, as the Barnes and Noble website puts it, "both adolescents and their elders can relate to." *Kissing the Rain* (2004) is the story of an overweight, shy teenager who witnesses a crime, and *Candy* (2005) is a love story about Joe and Candy, the heroin-addicted prostitute he falls in love with. In an interview with Joseph Pike for the Jubilee Books website, Brooks claims to dislike "the idea of writing for a particular market," and says he writes for himself in the hope that it "strikes a chord with the readers."

The darkly humorous novel *Holes*, by the American author Louis Sachar, won numerous awards, including the National Book Award for Young People's Literature in 1998 and the Newbery Medal in 1999, but adults began reading it after Disney released a screen version starring Sigourney Weaver and Jon Voigt. When the protagonist, Stanley Yelnats, is falsely accused of stealing a pair of shoes (further evidence of the family's bad luck that is attributed to a curse on a distant relative), the boy is given the choice of going to jail or going to camp. Camp Green Lake turns out to be a hellish detention camp in what was once the largest lake in Texas, but it is now a scorching desert wasteland dotted with the countless holes dug by the boys sent there. In this coming-of-age story, Stanley discovers himself, as well as the treasure the warden is looking for, that of Kissing Kate Barlow, an infamous outlaw of the Wild West. The American novel took Britain by storm, where it was published by Bloomsbury in 2002. It was widely read by both children and adults, and was voted one of the BBC Big Read's Top 100.

Realistic crossovers have not received nearly the same level of hype and media attention as fantasy crossovers, but they constitute an exciting and thriving dimension of the genre in many parts of the world. In a number of countries, the current crossover trend seems to have had its origins in realistic fiction, for example the work of Tormod Haugen in Norway or Bart Moeyaert in Belgium. Child-to-adult crossovers exist in other genres as well. Although it may seem to be an unlikely candidate, even children's and young adult poetry crosses over to an adult audience. We have already seen the example of Robert Louis Stevenson's *A Child's Garden of Verses*. Lewis Carroll's famous nonsense poem "Jabberwocky" is probably the world's best-known crossover poem. An interesting modern example of crossover poetry is *Who Look at Me*, the first book published by the African American author June Jordan, who defied all borders. The sophisticated poem about race was originally written for a book of images by black and white visual artists that was marketed for children in 1969, at a time when black children's literature was receiving its greatest recognition.[97] The poem has since been reprinted for adults, without the images that it was originally meant to accompany, at the beginning of Jordan's two volumes of selected poems. Many contemporary poets published for a juvenile audience are read by adult poetry enthusiasts, including the Guyanese-British poet Grace Nichols, the Palestinian-American poet Naomi Shihab Nye, and the Flemish poets André Sollie and Daniel Billiet.

Over the past decade, millions of adult readers are discovering or rediscovering the pleasure of reading children's books, a joy that some adults had always known. What seems to have been the well-kept secret of a relatively small number of adults, suddenly became popular knowledge around the globe. The crossover phenomenon has brought about a dramatic juvenile book renaissance. While child-to-adult crossovers can be found in most genres, the super crossovers that have garnered most of the public and critical attention have been fantasy titles.

Chapter Four
All Ages Fantasy

"Fantasy is . . . uni-age—it is the great cross-over genre."
Terry Pratchett, Interview in the *New Zealand Herald*

The fantasy genre is undergoing an exciting revival thanks to the crossover phenomenon. *Harry Potter* and the renewed interest in *The Lord of the Rings* gave the genre a huge boost on a global scale. According to Whitaker BookTrack, one out of every thirty novels sold in British bookshops is a fantasy novel. Fantasy has become less marginalized or ghettoized in the literary establishment. In 2002, Terry Pratchett claimed: "fantasy and science fiction have just entered the mainstream even if only unofficially."[1] Publishers and literary agents everywhere have been inundated with manuscripts from aspiring fantasy authors. "I get a lot of letters beginning, 'I'm writing a fantasy trilogy,'" says Sophie Hicks, a literary agent whose clients include Eoin Colfer.[2] Everyone seems to be tapping the fantasy market for all ages since the release of the first Harry Potter books. The awareness of fantasy has been raised to a new level in the mainstream today and its crossover appeal has surged. Fantasy has always been appreciated by a broad spectrum of readers, but all ages fantasy is now a widespread global trend. In Germany, the anglicized term "All-Age-Fantasy" is used to designate this category of crossover fiction. In the minds of many, crossover literature is synonymous with fantasy.

Acknowledging that "the crossover thing has been led by fantasy," Melvin Burgess claims that "fantasy shelves are the only part of the bookshop which is browsed freely by kids, teenagers, adults."[3] Fantasy is a very flexible genre that easily bridges the young adult and adult markets, and, in many cases, includes younger children as well, as the Harry Potter books clearly demonstrated. Since the debut of Rowling's series, the top children's sellers are often fantasy books that appeal to both children and adults. Fantasy readers tend to be very loyal fans and children who become addicted to the genre at a young age often remain fantasy readers as adults. Fantasy authors who publish for both the children's and adult markets or who write crossover books therefore retain their readers from childhood through adolescence to adulthood. "Readers of fantasy are notoriously uninterested in the adult-child divide," writes Farah Mendlesohn in her book on Diana Wynne Jones.[4] The same could be said of most fantasy writers. Although Ursula Le Guin's fantasy writing is generally considered her children's literature, it is often suitable for all ages and the author herself claims that "fantasy is the great age-equalizer."[5] In the quotation used as an epigraph to this chapter, Terry Pratchett similarly describes fantasy as "uni-age" and "the great cross-over genre."[6]

Although it now has a much higher profile in the literary world, fantasy is a long-established genre in children's literature. Many major classics in the children's literature canon are fantasies: *Alice's Adventures in Wonderland*, *The Wizard of Oz*, *Peter Pan*, and *The Chronicles of Narnia*, to name only a few. A number of twentieth-century, pre-Potter children's authors have excelled in the arena of deeply intelligent fantasy fiction for young adults. Philip Pullman is a great fan of the British author Alan Garner, who published his first fantasy novels in the 1960s. His debut novel, *The Weirdstone of Brisingamen*, published in 1960, has become a children's classic. The sequels, *The Moon of Gomrath* (1963) and *Elidor* (1965), are also children's favourites. Garner's fourth book, *The Owl Service* (1967), brought him wide acclaim when it won two major literary prizes, the *Guardian* Award and the Carnegie Medal, in 1968. In the years that followed, Garner's writing became increasingly sophisticated, ambiguous, and poetic. Works like *Red Shift* (1973), a haunting novel that spans over a thousand years around the same hill in Cheshire, garnered a growing adult audience. Garner has always insisted that he does not write for children, but for himself. However, he recognizes that his most passionate readership is made up of adolescents between the ages of ten and eighteen.[7] Another fantasy writer of the same period is the British-American author Susan Cooper, whose works have been compared to Lewis and Tolkien. She is best known for her five-book Dark Is Rising high fantasy sequence, which was written for older children and young adults between 1965 and 1977. The fourth novel, *The Grey King*, won the Newbery Medal in 1976.

Even when social realism was in vogue in the 1970s and 1980s, fantasy still had a loyal following. Other British writers joined Garner and Cooper, notably Diana Wynne Jones, who published the first three novels of her Dalemark quartet in the 1970s. The first novel in her hugely popular Chrestomanci series, *Charmed Life*, was commended for the Carnegie Medal and won the *Guardian* Award in 1977. Almost thirty years after the publication of the first novel, the author added two more books to the Chrestomanci series, *Conrad's Fate* in 2005 and *The Pinhoe Egg* in 2006. To date, Jones has published over forty books for children and adults. Although she is generally considered a fantasy writer, like many fantasy and science fiction authors, Jones transcends the very permeable borders between the two genres. Her readers are quick to point out that she systematically stretches the limits and defies the conventions of genre. Initially rejected by perplexed publishers, she now has a cult following of adults and children and is one of Britain's most respected fantasy writers. In 2004, Studio Ghibli in Japan adapted *Howl's Moving Castle*, a novel especially for younger readers, into an anime film, *Hauru no ugoku shiro*, that was hugely successful with a general audience. The film, directed by the celebrated anime artist Hayao Miyazaki, set a Japanese box office record and went straight to the top of the Japanese film charts when it was released in 2004. After its release in North America, where it also enthralled young and old alike, one critic insisted that Miyazaki had created "not a kiddie movie that appeals to adults, but an adult movie that appeals to kids."[8] Although less famous than either Philip Pullman or J. K. Rowling, Jones is nonetheless credited with laying the foundations for them. Like these celebrated successors, Jones grounds her fantasy firmly in real life. She says she does not write for a specific audience, but admits she started writing when her husband was attempting to read books aloud at bedtime to their children and kept falling asleep. She vowed then to write books that would have appeal for adults as well as children. The author of the article devoted to Jones in the "Books" section of the *Guardian* website goes so far as to claim that Jones "pioneered the craft of 'crossover' writing."

Another fantasy author who contributed greatly to the trend in the final decades of the twentieth century is the British author Brian Jacques. He began publishing his phenomenally successful Redwall animal fantasy series in the 1980s. The first book, entitled simply *Redwall*, was published in 1986. As of fall 2007, Jacques had published nineteen books in the series. Published in twenty-eight languages, the books have sold more than twenty million copies worldwide. Although the novels are aimed at young readers, with whom they are hugely popular, they have found adult readers, in spite of their formulaic nature. In paperback, the novels are published by an adult imprint, Berkley Books. Like a number of other prose authors who have published successful crossover series, Jacques recently crossed over into the graphic novel genre. In October 2007, Philomel published *Redwall: The Graphic Novel*, which is based closely on the first book in the series. Stuart Moore, the writer responsible for adapting *Redwall* into graphic novel form, feels he was chosen in part for the project because of his interest in "bringing comics to a general audience."[9] The graphic novel is expected to appeal to fans and newcomers of all ages.

Without being unique, *Harry Potter* broke with the type of realistic children's book that was seen as popular and successful at the time. It also brought fantasy to the attention of a wide audience of adults. In the past decade, fantasy has become an increasingly popular genre with adults as well as children. Although it has often been said that adults are hindered, when it comes to fantasy, by their inability to suspend belief and by their rational enquiry, that certainly does not seem to be an obstacle for the many adults reading crossover fantasy today. Furthermore, fantasy has never been a genre exclusively for young readers. Maria Nikolajeva points to the example of George MacDonald's *Phantastes*, which was not intended for children and never adopted by them.[10] As we saw in the previous chapter, fantasies for a crossover audience of children and adults are not a new or rare phenomenon. *Harry Potter* has many illustrious ancestors, including *Alice's Adventures in Wonderland, The Lord of the Rings, The Chronicles of Narnia,* and *Watership Down.*

Philip Pullman proved conclusively to a new generation that the best fantasy writing transcends the category of children's literature. The author of *His Dark Materials* has been hailed as the new Tolkien. *The Lord of the Rings* constitutes a benchmark for the fantasy genre, and Tolkien has been at once inspiring and daunting for his successors, whose works are inevitably compared to his masterpiece. Pullman's trilogy was no exception, but, in his case, comparisons were universally favourable. *His Dark Materials* was described by Amanda Craig as "the most ambitious work since *Lord of the Rings,*" and by William Waldegrave as "a tour de force of cosmic adventure, far outstripping the many modern imitators of Tolkien, and matching the quality of the master himself."[11] Pullman has said repeatedly that the work is "not a fantasy," but rather "stark realism." The author claims not to read fantasy, although he admits he has read Tolkien. He dislikes *The Lord of the Rings* and its particular brand of fantasy, finding that it lacks psychological interest.[12] The fantasy elements in Pullman's own trilogy allow him to explore human psychology. *His Dark Materials* has led a move toward more realistic fantasy or fantasy realism, in which other worlds help us better understand our own, and the characters seem quite real and have very human thoughts and emotions. The fantasy universes of both Pullman and Rowling are evoked in staggeringly precise detail.

Another highly successful British crossover author is Jonathan Stroud, who had written several books for young adults before he shot to fame with *The Amulet of Samarkand,* book one of the bestselling Bartimaeus trilogy. Stroud had a crossover audience in mind when he wrote *The Amulet of Samarkand,* as his goal was "to write a book that he would have loved as a kid and would also enjoy reading as an adult."[13] Stroud's rather sophisticated novel and its sequels are sometimes catalogued in the children's, rather than the young adult section of libraries, although they also appear in the adult section of some libraries. The novel has a complex structure, as there are two interwoven narrative strands and two narrators. In turn, chapters are devoted to the third-person story of Nathaniel, an ambitious apprentice magician who begins the series as a young boy, and the first-person narrative of Bartimaeus, a 5,000-year-old wisecracking djinni. The first novel was followed by the equally successful sequels *The Golem's Eye* (2004) and *Ptolemy's Gate* (2005).

Stroud offers an original take on the fantasy genre, with which he, like Pullman, has an ambiguous relationship. As a child, he got fed-up with the many "sub-Tolkien rip-offs" that offered nothing new and lacked rigour. In his mind, fantasy must have frameworks, parameters, rules, and structures. He claims to write "a fantasy that's almost for people who don't normally like fantasy," by adding a "grubby," realistic dimension. Fantasy is combined with politics in this thrilling story set in a mythical England ruled by power-hungry magicians. The political element is a literary device for the author, who uses it as "an antidote" to the fantasy dimension. Stroud's approach to fantasy is at once dark and humorous. The Bartimaeus Trilogy, especially the final novel, is much darker than most children's fantasy. The author's trademark humour, especially in the extensive footnotes, has had particular appeal for adults. By using humour to navigate the tricky portrayal of teenage romance when Nathaniel falls in love in book three, Stroud manages to avoid the "yuckiness" that Rowling was accused of in book six of *Harry Potter*.[14] The series has been hugely successful, with over 2.5 million copies sold worldwide and rights sold to more than thirty-five countries. It has also won a number of important awards, including the 2006 Mythopoeic Fantasy Award for Children's Literature and the Grand Prix de l'Imaginaire 2007. A big-budget movie by Miramax Films, a subsidiary of The Walt Disney Company, announced when the first book was published, is scheduled to appear in 2009.

The British author and screenwriter William Nicholson, who co-wrote the screenplay for the award-winning film *Gladiator*, gained renown as a novelist with his popular crossover The Wind on Fire trilogy, a fantasy dystopia published for older children. The first novel of the trilogy, *The Wind Singer* (2000), won the Smarties Gold Medal in 2000 and the Blue Peter Book Award in 2001, both of which are judged by children as well as adults. Nicholson's trilogy, completed by *Slaves of the Mastery* (2001) and *Firesong* (2002), is, in the manner of Philip Pullman and Garth Nix, epic fantasy that deals with real threats and very human issues, such as sacrifice, displacement of populations, and maintaining one's individualism in a totalitarian state. Like Pullman, Nicholson also uses intertextual references from a wide range of literary sources. Allusions to Exodus, Homer, and Bunyan reinforce the theme of the dangerous quest for a better place. His publisher, Egmont, suggests an age range of "10–15" for *The Wind Song*, but raises it to "10–19 and over" for the sequels, pitching the latter more directly to an older audience following the first novel's crossover success. Nicholson's fiction for children was not a one-time foray into the field. In 2005, he published *Seeker*, the first novel in The Noble Warriors Trilogy, which was completed by *Jango* in 2006 and *Noman* in 2007, all hefty novels of several hundred pages.

Kevin Crossley-Holland, a well-known poet who translated *Beowulf* from Anglo-Saxon, published his first novel, *The Seeing Stone*, to universal acclaim in 2000. The author did not set out to write specifically for children, but rather to find a new way of passing on the ancient Arthurian legends. Crossley-Holland's retelling of Arthurian legend is blended with a realistic view of rural medieval life at the time of the Crusades. It is the story of a thirteenth-century boy named Arthur, whose life becomes entwined with that of his namesake when his father's friend Merlin gives him a shining piece of obsidian. An unexpected success, the novel won the *Guardian* Children's Fiction Prize and was shortlisted for the Whitbread in 2001. The critical acclaim was worldwide, and the series has been translated into twenty-three languages and has sold well over a million copies. The first novel in the Arthur trilogy, *The Seeing Stone*, was followed by

At the Crossing-Places and *King of the Middle March*, published in 2001 and 2003 respectively. The meticulously researched books are full of period detail and the language is marked by Crossley-Holland's knowledge of Old English. The spare, direct language is not an attempt to be accessible to children but simply a lesson the author learned from Old English: "you don't need long words when you can use good, clean, short ones." The same can be said with regard to the conciseness of the one hundred chapters. Each chapter is "sharp and distinct and beautifully shaped, so the effect is almost like looking at a book of hours rather than reading a modern novel."[15] It is not surprising that adults as well as children are drawn to the Arthur trilogy. In 2006, Orion released it for adults in their Phoenix imprint.

Another example of a crossover series that blends fantasy with historical fact in a meticulously researched and carefully crafted narrative is the British author Mary Hoffman's Stravaganza series, set in Talia, an alternative Italy, in the sixteenth century. In an e-mail message on April 25, 2006, Hoffman spoke about the crossover appeal of her series. The author receives mail from readers ranging in age from nine to seniors, but she thinks that her typical reader is a fourteen-year-old girl and she feels that a substantial minority of [her] readers are in the eighteen-to-twenty-five age group, which is well known for its attachment to fantasy literature (although she admits Stravaganza does not fully fit that category). Hoffman thought of the books in her series as crossover fiction in the planning and writing. This was in part because she wanted to have "relationships between older adults in the series as well as just teenage romance." It also allowed her "to make the plots, structure and language as complex as . . . the stories needed them to be."

Critics often tend to focus on the large number of authors writing crossover fantasy in Britain, disregarding the many examples from other parts of the world. Pointing to Madeleine L'Engle's *A Wrinkle in Time*, a reviewer of Michael Chabon's *Summerland* states that some American authors have written "all-ages fantasies almost as good as the Brits have, yet lack the same fanatical following among grown-ups." Tongue in cheek, he puts forward the following hypothesis: "Maybe it's just that when British readers put away childish things, they're better than some self-consciously mature Americans at remembering where they put them."[16] The United Kingdom and the United States do not have a monopoly on all ages fantasy. Crossover fantasy is thriving in many countries and constitutes a global phenomenon.

Beyond British and American Crossover Fantasy

Australia has produced some very exciting all ages fantasy. One of the most popular young adult/crossover fantasy writers in Australia today is Garth Nix. He has been hailed by some as the successor to Philip Pullman, although, in fact, he published his first novel, *Sabriel*, in 1995, the same year as *Northern Lights*. *Sabriel* took the world by storm, earning wide critical acclaim, including that of Pullman himself, and immediately finding a crossover audience. *Sabriel* was published the same year in which the Aurealis Awards for Excellence in Australian Speculative Fiction were created. According to their website, the judges declared that "1995 was arguably the strongest year to date for Australian fantasy." Recognizing "the strong crossover interest" of the genre, both the adult and young adult categories were considered for the fantasy award. As a result, *Sabriel* won the first Aurealis Award in both the adult and the young adult categories. *Sabriel* is the first novel in The Old Kingdom series (known in the United States as The Abhorsen Trilogy), which was completed, after a significant hiatus, by *Lirael* (2001) and *Abhorsen* (2003). Both the sequels repeated the feat of winning the Aurealis Award for fantasy in both the adult and young adult categories. Like Pullman, Nix believes that "all the best fantasy is very firmly grounded in reality," as he stated in an interview on the Harper Teen website. The tone of the novels in The Old Kingdom series is dark and, as in *His Dark Materials*, the struggle between good and evil is complex, explaining the books' appeal with an older audience. In an interview on the Phantastik-Couch website, Nix states that it is difficult to differentiate between adult and young adult books, which he feels are really "a subset of adult books." He is convinced that "whether an adult story gets labeled as a young adult story or not is basically a marketing decision."

Nix's readers come from a very broad cross-section of ages. This is due, in part, to the fact that his books are published for a variety of age groups. In 2000 and 2001, the six volumes of The Seventh Tower series were released in quick succession for a younger audience. While this series has an entry reading level of about nine or ten, Nix points out that the books have no upper age limit. "Many children's books are enjoyed by people of all ages and I think that's the ultimate aim, to write a book that escapes all boundaries of category and genre and reading age," he told Carol Fitzgerald during an interview for KidsReads website on April 14, 2004. Although most of Nix's other books, which are longer and somewhat more complex, are "for an older audience, what is known as 'young adult crossovers,'" he insists, in an interview on the Scholastic website, that essentially there is very little difference. His latest young adult fantasy series is the seven-part Keys to the Kingdom, which began with *Mister Monday* in 2003 and is supposed to end with *Lord Sunday* in 2009. Although the novels in this series are published as young adult fiction and read by a crossover audience, they address a slightly younger audience than his first fantasy series and they are read by even younger readers than intended by the author and publisher. *Drowned Wednesday* won an Aurealis Award in 2005, not in the young adult category as one might expect, but in the children's (8–12 years) long fiction category. As of 2006, Nix's young adult fantasy books had sold close to four million copies internationally and had been translated into more than thirty languages.

Another successful Australian fantasy author is Kate Constable, whose debut young adult novel, *The Singer of All Songs* (2002), is the first book in the

Chanters of Tremaris trilogy. It was followed by *The Waterless Sea* in 2004 and *The Tenth Power* in 2005. Constable gives a very original twist to the story that forms the basis of fantasy works from Tolkien to Rowling, that is, the quest of a small group of young people trying to prevent an evil, power-hungry sorcerer from ruling the world through the mastery of magic. Although she was not thinking of a specific age group when she wrote the books, she had just finished reading Le Guin's Earthsea trilogy and admits that her aim was no doubt to write a book for young people that could also be enjoyed by adults. As the writing process went on, she forgot that she was supposed to be writing for a young audience and just wrote for herself, she told me in an e-mail message on April 27, 2006. The protagonist, a young priestess by the name of Calwyn, is only seventeen, but she is very much a woman, and the story includes what seems to be a star-crossed romance, a common trait of many successful crossover series, including Jonathan Stroud's Bartamaeus Trilogy and Lian Hearn's Tales of the Otori. Although marketed as young adult fiction, Constable's trilogy successfully reaches the adult market, as testified by the fan mail she often receives from adult readers.

While it has a strong mythic and epic adventure dimension, Lian Hearn's The Tales of the Otori trilogy is a very different kind of fantasy. Like Hoffman's Stravaganza series, it represents a new facet of the fantasy genre that has much in common with historical fiction. In order to write the trilogy, which is set in a mythical feudal Japan, the author immersed herself in Japanese history, culture, and language. When the first novel in the series, *Across the Nightingale Floor*, was published in 2002, the sixteen-year-old orphan protagonist, Takeo, very quickly became known as the "Oriental Harry Potter." This rites-of-passage tale is also a love story with very adult sensuality but told with restraint; the author does not dwell unnecessarily on either the sex or the violence, although there are scenes of graphic bloodshed. She incorporates the graceful violence of the Martial arts, which have been exploited in movies like *Crouching Tiger, Hidden Dragon*, as well as the sensual beauty of landscapes and art. Hearn acknowledges the influence of classics like *The Tale of Genji* and the films of Akira Kurosawa, in an interview entitled "The Tale of Genji for the Potter Generation."[17] The Australian author is able to play with Japanese history and culture, using some of the familiar motifs, such as samurai, ninja, and shogun, without being taken to task by historians. Myth and history are also combined in Dianne Hofmeyr's *The Waterbearer*, which was published for young adults in 2001, but is also read by adults. Set against the fourteenth-century dhow trade in Persia, Mogadishu, Zanzibar, and Kilwa, Hofmeyr's novel, like Hearn's series, is a story of good versus evil, a rich tapestry interwoven with myth and painted in very luminous, evocative prose.

In her home country, Cornelia Funke is called "the German J. K. Rowling" and her books are to German readers what the Harry Potter books are to English-language readers. Her international breakthrough came with *Herr der Diebe*, which appeared in Germany in 2000. It is a novel that examines the theme of crossover, as it involves a magical carousel that can turn children into adults, and vice versa. The English translation, *The Thief Lord*, marked Funke's brilliant debut in the English-language market in 2002. After the novel's huge success in Germany, the author decided to have it translated into English at her own expense, so that it could be marketed to English-language publishers. Funke is published in the United States by Scholastic, the same publisher as Rowling, with whom she has been so favourably compared. Furthermore, her British publisher, The Chicken House, was founded in the United Kingdom by Barry Cunningham, who discovered Rowling and, with the same insight, bought the worldwide English rights for Funke's *The Thief Lord*. Funke became one of the most successful first-time children's authors in the United States, where *The Thief Lord* had a 75,000-copy printing and was a *New York Times* bestseller for twenty-five weeks, climbing to the number two position. The intricate narrative blends magical fantasy and real-life adventures to tell the story of a gang of misfits living in a deserted cinema in contemporary Venice. A successful film version, rated PG for language and thematic elements, was released in Germany in 2006.

In 2003, Funke published the bestseller *Tintenherz*, released the same year in English as *Inkheart*. The first novel in the Inkheart trilogy tells the story of Meggie, whose bookbinder father brings fictional characters to life when he reads aloud. Like Rowling's later novels, it is very long (almost 600 pages), even though it targets readers from ten years of age and up. The novel became an instant success and was on the *New York Times* bestseller list for twenty-one weeks. The sequel *Tintenblut*, released in English as *Inkspell*, was published in Germany in 2005. It was the first of Funke's novels to be released in hardcover in English. The final novel in the trilogy, *Tintentod*, with the English title *Inkdeath*, was released in Germany in Fall 2007. The trilogy is to be adapted to the screen by New Line, the makers of *The Lord of the Rings* trilogy. Funke was by no means a newcomer to children's literature when she published *The Thief Lord*, so she has a long backlist that can be exploited by publishers in other countries. Along with *The Thief Lord*, Cunningham bought the rights to the earlier fantastic adventure novel *Drachenreiter*, which had appeared in Germany in 1997. The novel became a breakaway bestseller when it was brought out in English as *Dragon Rider* in 2004. It hit number one on the *New York Times* bestseller list in less than a month and remained on the list for seventy-eight weeks, becoming the longest-running number one bestseller since Harry Potter. To date, there are more than five million copies of her books in print in the United States. More than four million copies of her books have been sold in the German-speaking countries alone. The German author's books are now available in forty-two countries and twenty-eight languages. In 2005, *Time* magazine put Funke on its "Time 100" list of "the world's most influential people." It is to be hoped that Funke's success in the English-speaking market will encourage publishers to bring out English translations of more foreign crossover authors in the future.

Another fantasy author who is extremely popular in Germany is Ralf Isau. Unfortunately, Isau has not had the same breakthrough in the English-language market as Funke. Although his books have been translated into almost fifteen languages and have been extremely successful in Japan, none have been translated into English. He is a particularly interesting example of a crossover author because his books cross over in both directions. His Neschan trilogy (1995–96), which begins with *Die Träume des Jonathan Jabbok* (Jonathan Jabbok's dream), is similar in style to Michael Ende's *Neverending Story*, so it is not surprising that it is very popular with readers of all ages. Although the trilogy was written for an entry age of twelve, the author told me, in an e-mail message on May 21, 2007, that he has "many enthusiastic adult readers, some of whom are about eighty years old." Isau won the coveted Buxtehuder Bulle award, in 1997, for his young adult novel *Das Museum der gestohlenen Erinnerungen* (The museum of stolen memories, 1997), in which people start losing their memories when stone figures suddenly come to life and prowl around a dark museum. In 2003, Isau published his first novel for adults, a thriller and fantasy entitled *Der silberne Sinn* (The silver sense), about an anthropologist who finds a tribe with the ability to read and manipulate human emotions in the jungle of Guyana. Isau saw this novel as an important milestone in his career as an author. However, unlike Mark Haddon, it was not the fulfilment of a desire to be acknowledged as an author for adults, but merely the opportunity to reach across arbitrary age categories to adult readers who would not otherwise discover his books. Furthermore, the 768-page novel is recommended for sixteen years and up, so, in fact, it is also marketed for a crossover audience of young adults and adults. The author says all of his "adult novels" are read by young readers as well.

The same year as his first adult novel was released, Isau published *Die geheime Bibliothek des Thaddäus Tillmann Trutz* (The secret library of Thaddäus Tillmann Trutz), based on one of the never told stories mentioned in Ende's novel. It recounts the story of Karl Konrad Koreander's first journey into Phantásia and how the old antique dealer gets the book *The Neverending Story*. In 2003, Droemer Knaur launched Isau's novel in what is called the "general line" (allgemeine Reihe) in Germany, that is, general fiction intended chiefly for adults. Two years later, Arena, a publisher specializing in books for children and young adults, released an edition for young readers. Because German booksellers consider Ende's novel to be a juvenile book and shelve it in the children's section, they automatically view all other novels set in the world of Phantásia as juvenile books. In an e-mail message on May 22, 2007, Isau described his novel as an "All-Age-Titel for readers from about 13 to 130."

Although Isau feels all of his writing crosses over, the work that best embodies crossover literature, in his mind, is his four-part fantasy series *Der Kreis der Dämmerung* (The Circle of the Dawn), which was published (for readers from fourteen years of age) between 1999 and 2001, that is, over the turn of the millennium. It is "a century saga," about a "century child"—born on January 1,

1900—whose destiny is to save humankind. The fact that the first public reading of part four of the series took place on September 12, 2001, and that it contains a paragraph about Osama bin Laden gave the work particular interest for adults. A few years after *Der Kreis der Dämmerung* was brought out by Thienemann, which is a publisher of books for children and young people, Bastei Lübbe published a paperback version for adults. The same situation occurred with Isau's novel *Pala und die seltsame Verflüchtigung der Worte* (Pala and the strange evaporation of words), which was published by Thienemann in 2002 and Bastei Lübbe in 2005. More recently, Isau wrote the series *Die Chroniken von Mirad* (The chronicles of Mirad, 2005–06), a pure fantasy which the author describes, in an e-mail message on May 22, 2007, as "juvenile literature for readers from 12 to 120."

In Japan, Isau has a very large adult readership. The author had a signing in Tokyo at Libro Books, the largest Japanese bookstore, and ninety-eight percent of those attending were adults. When Isau asked some of them if they wanted him to sign the book for their children, they told him it was for themselves. On a much less impressive scale, a similar phenomenon exists in Germany, where, according to the author, thirty to forty percent of his readers are above the age of twenty. Isau agrees that one of the reasons so many adults are reading his books for young people is because they are what he calls "phantagons." On his website, he defines the term he coined in the following manner:

> 1. (math.) a polygon whose number of sides is determined by the beholder's imagination. 2. a novel in which every reader sees a different mixture of literary forms or genres.

This conception of fiction explains its broad appeal, as all readers, regardless of age, are intended to construct the multilayered novel differently. None of Isau's books fit neatly into a category. While many young people read them for the adventure and fantasy, it is not only older readers who discover the deeper meanings. Isau points out that a large number of his young readers re-read the books repeatedly (as many as twenty times), so that they necessarily discover new and more profound meanings with each reading. For this reason, young people may actually have a better understanding of a crossover book than adults, who are much less likely to re-read a work multiple times.

Crossover fantasy is also flourishing in the Latin American market. The best-known example is the Chilean author Isabel Allende, who will be considered in the next chapter. The Argentinian author Liliana Bodoc is also quite successful throughout the Latin American world, but, unlike Allende, she has not managed to break into the English-language market yet. When Bodoc finished writing her first novel, she went to Buenos Aires looking for a publisher for *Los días del Venado* (The days of the stag). The author did not feel she had written a juvenile novel, but rather an epic saga. It was only after her novel had been published by the children's division of Grupo Editorial Norma in 2000 that

Bodoc realized how much appeal it had for young readers and how enthusiastically it would be received by that audience.[18] Although it arrived virtually unnoticed in bookstores, the novel soon found an enthusiastic readership of all ages. Bodoc's debut novel met with wide critical acclaim and won several awards.

Los días del Venado became the first volume in the highly original trilogy La saga de los confines (The saga of the lands at the end of the world), which also includes *Los días de la Sombra* (The days of darkness, 2002) and *Los días del fuego* (The days of fire, 2004). It is a magical epic story in the tradition of Tolkien or Le Guin, but inspired by the native legends of Latin America. This story of the clash of two worlds, the people of the "Fertile Lands" and the invaders led by the Son of Death, is also that of the conquest of the Americas, which explains part of the series' appeal with adults. Bodoc's novels are exquisitely written and quite lengthy, ranging from 322 to 468 pages. Reviewers urged adults, as well as children, to read these stimulating books that address important moral issues of our time. Considered one of the rising stars of Argentinian literature, Bodoc has given new life to heroic fantasy in Latin America.

Comic Fantasy Crossovers

There is a thriving crossover market for fantasy that is primarily humorous in intent and tone. Terry Pratchett has been called "Britain's most universally popular author."[19] He has been completely ignored by the literary establishment, but he has a huge cult following among both adults and young readers. His particular brand of fantasy is quite unique. He began by spoofing the conventions of the fantasy genre, but his work evolved into an increasingly satirical commentary on almost every aspect of today's world. In a fantastic, surreal setting, he humorously examines real-world questions. Some critics feel that Rowling learned a great deal from Pratchett. His hugely successful comic/fantasy Discworld series, a humorous and often satirical fantasy that now contains more than forty books, is aimed chiefly at adults, although four of them have been marketed for older children or young adults. Pratchett's fantasy has the same trademark wit, which depends heavily on intertextuality and metafiction, whether he is writing for children or adults. He also uses what has been called "stealth philosophy," slipping philosophical issues subtly into his books.

Newly released Discworld novels regularly top the *Sunday Times* bestseller lists. Although he has now been surpassed by Rowling, Pratchett was Britain's bestselling author of the 1990s. According to the 2005 Booksellers' Pocket Yearbook, in 2003 Pratchett's U.K. sales amounted to 3.4 percent of the fiction market by hardback sales and 3.8 percent by value, putting him in second place behind J. K. Rowling (6 percent and 5.6 percent respectively), while in the paperback sales list Pratchett came fifth. Pratchett also has the distinction of being the most shoplifted author in Britain.[20] In the BBC's Big Read, four of

Pratchett's novels placed in the top 100 and fourteen were in the top 200. The first Discworld novel, *The Colour of Magic*, published in 1983, placed ninety-third. Although he may not have the same cult status in other countries, Pratchett's popularity is not limited to Britain. He has sold almost fifty million books worldwide.

Discworld books have won awards for both adult and children's fiction. *Pyramids* won the British Fantasy Award in 1989 and *Night Watch* was awarded the 2003 Prometheus Award by the Libertarian Futurist Society for the best libertarian science fiction novel of the year. *The Amazing Maurice and His Educated Rodents*, a retelling of the tale of the Pied Piper, was the first Discworld novel to be classified as young adult and it received the prestigious Carnegie Medal in 2001. Critics generally agreed that Pratchett's novel was for all ages, but some felt that marketing it as a juvenile novel would prevent the work from reaching the adult audience that could appreciate much more of the humour. However, all of the Discworld books published for children are read by adults, just as those for adults are read by young people. The Discworld style is essentially the same whether the books are published for children or adults, and all of the books, regardless of target audience, appeal across a very wide age range. The author himself does not draw a distinction between writing for children and writing for adults. Explaining why only a few of his books have chapter divisions, Pratchett says his editor forced him to use them in the "putative YA books."[21] The author has often claimed that the Discworld series was never intended for children, but aiming a few of the books at a younger audience allowed him to explore new paths. Pratchett's popular crossover series has spawned related books, maps, short stories, even music. The first live action adaptation for television, *Hogfather*, was broadcast at Christmas 2006, traditionally a time for "family" entertainment. A film adaptation of *The Wee Free Men* (2003), another young adult Discworld book, is currently in development.

In Germany, Walter Moers has the same kind of enthusiastic crossover audience as Pratchett. Like the British author, Moers writes for both audiences and his adult books are also read by a young audience. He is one of the most popular and commercially successful present-day German authors. His fantastic fairy tales and rather risqué comics appeal to a very broad audience. In 1988, he created his character Käpt'n Blaubär, who has become very popular in Germany and elsewhere, in comics, books, and films. The film was released in 1999. *Die 13½ Leben des Käptn Blaubär* (*The 13½ Lives of Captain Bluebear*), published in 1999, is the first book in the Zamonia series. The novel is hugely popular in Germany, where it appeals to both children and adults. Moers is also a cartoonist and he illustrated the novel himself. In *The 13½ Lives of Captain Bluebear*, which bears the unwieldy subtitle *Being the Demibiography of a Seagoing Bear, with Numerous Illustrations and Excerpts from the "Encyclopedia of the Marvels, Life Forms and Other Phenomena of Zamonia and its Environs" by Professor Abdullah Nightingale*, the blue bear with twenty-seven lives uses up half of them. Although it has been compared to the fantasy of *The Lord of the Rings* and *The Neverending Story*, the comical and satirical treatment of fantasy motifs is more reminiscent of Pratchett. In 2004, Moers published *Die Stadt der Träumenden Bücher* (*The City of Dreaming Books*), his third novel set in Zamonia. It is a zany story featuring Optimus Yarnspinner (Hildegood von Mythmason in the German edition), a Lindworm, that is, a dinosaur, and writer who sets out on a quest to find the anonymous author of the most perfect story ever written. In Bookholm, a city of authors, publishers, antiquarian book-sellers, literary agents, and critics, he falls into the clutches of Pfistomel Smyke, a literary scholar, who treacherously abandons him in the terrifying underworld below the book-obsessed city, where reading books can be truly dangerous. Like his other novels, *The City of Dreaming Books* offers a fast-paced, hilarious plot, thrilling adventures, savvy beasts and monsters, and witty allusions. It is a clever parody of the literary world, poking fun at critics and publishers. Dennis Wright's review on the Newsvine website warns this book isn't really for children because much of it will be lost on those "who do not have a knowledge of and interest in books, literature, literary forms, literary devices, authors or the world of publishing," but obviously readers of all ages are interested in books. Like Pratchett, Moers offers a witty and satiric reflection on contemporary society in his novels, but his style is unique. *A Wild Ride through the Night* (2003) is a fantastical tale inspired by twenty-one engravings by the famous nineteenth-century illustrator Gustave Doré. The book follows the comic adventures of Captain Gustave, a twelve-year-old boy, who dreams of one day becoming a great artist, but before he can do so, he must undergo a series of difficult tests. Doré's engravings of monsters, damsels, and dragons are reproduced throughout the book. Moers brings the fairy tale into the twenty-first century. While children will enjoy the book as a modern fairy tale, older readers will appreciate the tale as an allegory of the hopes and dreams of youth.

In 2001, the Irish author Eoin Colfer, a teacher-turned-author, shot to fame with *Artemis Fowl*, a comic fantasy somewhat in the Pratchett tradition. It is the story of a twelve-year-old criminal mastermind who, as the last heir in a legendary Irish crime family, sets out to replenish their dwindling fortune. Colfer adopts the partnership quest pattern of *The Lord of the Rings* but gives it a twist: rather than fighting evil, Artemis Fowl and his side-kicks are plotting to steal the legendary fairy gold. *Artemis Fowl* sparked the inevitable comparisons with *Harry Potter*. As in Rowling's series, the protagonist's name figures in each of the titles, and it is difficult to say whether Colfer was imitating or challenging *Harry Potter*. His eponymous protagonist is an anti-hero who is at once evil and attractive. The Artemis Fowl novels, of which there are currently five (a sixth and final novel is to be released in 2008), have been an international crossover hit, selling to publishers in forty countries. Miramax Films bought the movie rights, but a dispute has delayed production of the film, which will be based on the first two novels in the series.

Colfer's publisher, Penguin, jointly with Hyperion Books for Children, promoted his novels to Harry Potter fans of all ages. It was generally felt that Artemis Fowl would perhaps do for fairies what Harry Potter had done for wizards and witches. Like the Harry Potter books, the Artemis Fowl series has special appeal for reluctant readers, especially teenage boys. The first novel was described by the author and his publisher as "*Die Hard* with fairies." Using an action-film formula, Colfer blends folklore, fantasy, crime, and technology in a fantasy novel where the fairies, goblins, trolls, and dwarfs carry high-tech weapons. The Artemis Fowl books are not literary works of art: the style is simple, the characters are two-dimensional, the emphasis is on action, and there is a lack of depth and atmosphere. The series is nonetheless popular with an adult audience. There are numerous references to James Bond (the wisecraking centaur gadget wizard Foaly is reminiscent of James Bond's Q), as well as to many other intertexts from both literature and popular culture. The allusions to television, cinema, video games, and the Internet explain much of Colfer's appeal to a hip audience of both adults and young readers. *Artemis Fowl: The Graphic Novel*, a full-length comic version of the first book that was released in Fall 2007, also appeals to the same diverse age range. It was adapted by Eoin Colfer and the graphic novelist Andrew Donkin, with striking artwork by Giovanni Rigano. On his website, the author says he feels that the word "comic" doesn't really do it justice, and that it "will stand proud beside any work of art on the bookshelves." Before the series was completed, Colfer had already begun to diversify. In 2004, he published the futuristic thriller *The Supernaturalist*. The story about fourteen-year-old Cosmo Hill, who escapes from Clarissa Frayne's Institute for Parentally Challenged Boys, is described in a jacket review from *The Times* as "the *Matrix* crossed with *Oliver Twist*." The fast-paced science fiction novel contains all the trademark qualities that have earned Colfer so many fans of all ages.

Fantasy/Science Fiction Crossovers

Often it is difficult to distinguish clearly between fantasy and science fiction, as writers in these spheres often ignore genre boundaries. Like fantasy, science fiction tends to attract very loyal fans who often remain sci-fi readers throughout their lives. However, science fiction does not share the same long-established place in children's literature as fantasy and therefore tends to be more marginalized. Many authors cross effortlessly between fantasy and science fiction, as well as between adult and child audiences, as in the case of Ursula Le Guin.

One author who crossed between these two audiences and genres, but who is best known as a crossover writer for her young adult science fiction, is Jan Mark. Although the British author was a rare two-time winner of the prestigious Carnegie Medal—for her first novel, *Thunder and Lightnings* in 1976 and for *Handles* in 1983 (she was shortlisted for her third after her sudden death in 2006 but did not win)—Mark is not as widely known as she deserves, largely because much of her children's writing is unusually difficult and sophisticated. "Mark stretches the range of children's books," declared the American author Jane Langton in 1985. In her review of *Handles*, Langton elaborates: "She provides for young people the combination of fine prose and strong realism generally reserved for adults."[22] Mark admitted that her novels for older readers are "deliberately written to discourage an unsophisticated reader" and "to make the reader work hard." Although she published books for both young people and adults, the author stated categorically: "I do not write specifically for children, any more than I write for adults. I tend rather to write about children."[23] Unlike many children's authors, Mark often presents a dark, bleak view of the world, especially in her science fiction novels for older readers, *The Ennead* (1978), *Divide and Rule* (1979), *Aquarius* (1982), *The Eclipse of the Century* (1999), *Useful Idiots* (2004), and *Riding Tycho* (2005). These complex, disturbing stories, which do not fit the typical science fiction mould, appealed to adults as well as young readers. Mark is particularly popular with a crossover audience in Belgium, where a website is maintained by her Flemish fans.

John Marsden's *Tomorrow, When the War Began*, published in 1993, has been called the most powerful novel for teenagers ever published in Australia, but it is also considered one of the most celebrated and widely recognized books of Australian literature in general. It has been translated into several languages, received numerous awards, and enjoyed unprecedented reprints. This landmark novel of Australian young adult fiction was the first in the critically acclaimed seven-book Tomorrow series, which smashed sales records and captured the hearts and imaginations of young readers, gaining a cult-like following. In 2006, publisher Pan Macmillan presented author Marsden with an award in recognition of the fact that his series had sold two million copies and become the highest selling series of books for teenagers in the history of Australian publishing. The fast-paced action/adventure novels recount the invasion and occupation of Australia by a foreign power. The novels are told in first-person perspective by a teenage girl named Ellie Linton, who is a member of a small band of teenagers waging a guerrilla war on the enemy garrison. The hugely successful novels were written for teenagers, but they are widely read by adults as well, and have appeared in an adult edition. In a poll conducted in 1997, three of Marsden's works were voted onto a list of Australia's 100 most loved books of all time.

The first sequel, *The Dead of the Night* (1994), met with the same wildly enthusiastic response in Australia, winning the Talking Book Of the Year Award, and competing fiercely with *Tomorrow, When the War Began* for awards judged by the young. Expectations for the third novel in the series, *The Third Day, the Frost* (1995; published in the United States as *A Killing Frost*), were so great that twenty thousand hardbacks were printed—an unprecedented print run in pre-Potter years. It was still insufficient and two more reprints were needed in the first three months of the book's release. In October 1996, Pan

Macmillan Australia published what was supposed to be the final volume in the Tomorrow series, *Darkness, Be My Friend*. The hardcover volume broke all sales records for the series and remained on bestseller lists all over the country for weeks. Marsden was inundated with letters and e-mail messages from fans mourning the end of what was the most popular series for young adults ever written in Australia. That year Marsden's books took up the top six spots on the teenage fiction bestseller lists for Australia. In October 1997, book five, *Burning for Revenge*, was added to the series that had become a legend in its own time. The fifth novel was considered by many to be the most exciting and action-packed book of the series. In a field of nominees that included such illustrious names as Peter Carey, Steve Biddulph, Tim Winton, and Richard Flannagan, Marsden won the Australian Booksellers Association's Book Of the Year award in July 1998 for *Burning for Revenge*. Although it is not the first time that an author for young people won a national open award anywhere in the world, as has been claimed, it was nonetheless a remarkable achievement. The seventh and final book in the Tomorrow series was released in 1999. In 2003, Marsden began publishing a follow-up series, entitled The Ellie Chronicles, which deals with the aftermath of the war and Ellie's attempts to regain a normal level of functioning after the psychological damage sustained during the war.

In spite of the unprecedented success of the Tomorrow series in Australia and the fact that he was nominated for the prestigious Astrid Lindgren Award in 2007, Marsden and his work are largely unknown in North America. Reviewing the books for the SF Site in 1998, Georges T. Dodds laments the fact that Marsden's books were "leftovers in the SF reviewer bin, and none of the major bookstores in Montreal stock them or know of them." The term "crossover" had not yet become a popular label, but the Canadian reviewer emphasized the cross-generational appeal of the series by putting it in very personal terms: "These books are for young adults, but are so well written that even edging 40, I ignored my wife and children and read the last two non-stop until 5:30 a.m. . . . So, I don't care if you're a teenager or a middle-aged businessman, these books transcend age barriers."

The Craving for Crossover Continuations

For many people, the crossover phenomenon seems to be synonymous with fantasy trilogies. Although this is an extremely limited view of crossover fiction, it is certainly true that the publishing of series of varying lengths—not only trilogies—for the crossover market has been the hottest ticket in the book world in recent years. In 2002, the journalist Damian Kelleher wrote in *The Times Educational Supplement*: "One of the unwritten rules for crossover novels is that one book isn't enough."[24] In his discussion of the Harry Potter books in *Sticks and Stones*, Jack Zipes views this as a widespread cultural trend: "In keeping with the tendency in Western popular culture, one story is never enough, especially if it sells well and sits well with audiences."[25] The emphasis on trilogies is somewhat surprising, since the benchmark is Rowling's septet. Many other authors also offer their readers longer series, including Michelle Paver's Chronicles of Ancient Darkness and Eoin Colfer's Artemis Fowl series, each with six books. To date, Diana Wynne Jones's Chrestomanci series consists of seven books.

Many earlier sequences, like Jones's that began with *Charmed Life* in 1977, are often loosely linked and easily stand alone. In fact, one of the novels, *Conrad's Fate*, which was not published until 2005, contains a brief note in which Jones assures readers that the world in which it takes place is the only one relevant to the story. There is no need to read the novels in order or even to read previous novels of the series, although it obviously adds to the enjoyment. On the other hand, Maria Nikolajeva points out the importance of viewing Tove Jansson's Moomin books as a sequential work, rather than dealing with each book individually as many scholars do, because the series is structured like a Bildungsroman, tracing the development from childhood to adulthood.[26]

Contrary to the works of Jones or Jansson, the books in contemporary crossover series generally tend to be more closely linked. In some cases, it appears that a publisher has deliberately spread a single story over several books in order to force readers to buy them all to find out how it ends. Peter Dickinson's *The Kin*, a quartet of novels for older children, may seem to be such a story, at least in the United States. It is really a novel in four parts, told from the perspectives of four different characters, all children of the Moonhawk Kin. The author interspersed the Kin's mythical creation stories, called "Oldtales," between the chapters. An American editor who had enjoyed Dickinson's earlier novel about prehistoric people, *A Bone from a Dry Sea* (1992), asked his British agent if the author would be interested in writing three shorter books for younger children on a similar theme. The three books quickly became four books. The story was first published in the United States in 1998 as four linked novels, *Suth's Story, Noli's Story, Po's Story* (which became *Ko's Story* in Britain), and *Mana's Story*. The British publisher, Macmillan, decided to publish *The Kin* in a single lavishly produced volume of 640 pages, and only later to issue the four separate sections as paperbacks. Although Dickinson was initially opposed to Macmillan's plan, he later blamed the four-volume format, at least in part, for the initial complete lack of success in the United States of a novel that was shortlisted for the Carnegie Medal in the United Kingdom. It was later reissued in the United States, to more acclaim, as a single volume. In Britain, where both formats are readily available, children tend to read the four-volume edition, while young adults and adults generally opt for the omnibus edition.

Some authors seem to think naturally in terms of large ensembles. This is by no means a new phenomenon. Balzac's monumental *La Comédie Humaine* offers an excellent example in the adult sphere. In some cases, such groupings may include novels for both children and adults. Henri Bosco's five-book Pascalet cycle and the Hyacinthe trilogy are both part of a larger sequence of ten novels, written over a space of thirty-five years. Although only three books were published before the author's untimely death, Mervyn Peake's Gormenghast books, which are often erroneously referred to as a trilogy, were the beginning of what Peake envisaged as a lengthy cycle that would follow his protagonist Titus Groan from birth to death. The work of the British author Sean Wright offers a striking contemporary example of an ambitiously conceived sequence. *Jesse Jameson and the Golden Glow*, published in 2003, is the first novel in the Jesse Jameson Alpha to Omega series. It has been recommended for fans of the Harry Potter books, with which it shares a number of similarities. Like Rowling's books, each novel in Wright's series includes in the title the protagonist's name—in this case, a twelve-year-old girl who can shape-shift into any creature imaginable. Targeted at a similar readership of eight years and up, the Jesse Jameson series is planned as a twenty-six novel series, a project that could understandably meet with reluctance on the part of major publishers.

Intratextual allusions may link an author's stand-alone novels to another work or a series, sometimes written for an entirely different audience. Hyperion's promotion of children's books written by established adult novelists included Michael Dorris's 1997 novel *The Window*, which takes a character from his bestselling novel for adults, *A Yellow Raft on Blue Water*, published ten years earlier. Sean Wright's standalones for the teenage-adult crossover market, for example *Dark Tales of Time and Space* (2005), include references to his other works. *The Twisted Root of Jaarfindor*, his first "teenage-adult crossover," hinted at a sequel. Two years later, in 2006, it was followed by *Jaarfindor Remade*, his first novel exclusively for adults. That same year, Wright published a debut short story collection entitled *Love Under Jaarfindor Spires*. The author continually weaves narrative elements from previous works into his new ones. *Wicked or What?* (2005) merges and blurs Jaarfindorian settings with places that are familiar to readers of the Jesse Jameson books. A number of crossover authors thus weave their narrative strands together on a very large canvas that contains elements for readers of all ages.

Series always pose a challenge for the author, who must close each book in a satisfying manner while leaving the ending open enough to drive the narrative into the sequel. In the works of the best authors, each novel in a series, particularly a longer series, can still be read as a stand-alone work. Rowling, Pullman, and Nicholson, for example, are careful to ensure that each novel in their series affords readers a pleasurable and satisfactory reading experience on its own. The novels in Paver's series have also been praised for this quality. This is not always the case, however. Clive Barker's *Abarat*, published in 2002, was criticized for trailing off without providing readers with a satisfying ending to the first book of his much-hyped quartet The Books of Abarat, but at least he did not leave them on a huge cliffhanger. Obviously, all of these novels are much more satisfying when read in the context of the series, and few readers would deprive themselves of the enjoyment of reading all of the books. Sequels tend to have the reputation of being inferior to the original work. Some critics believe that the last few volumes in Colfer's Artemis Fowl series have not equalled the standards of the series opener. On the other hand, John Marsden's sequel to *Tomorrow, When the War Began, The Dead of the Night*, was so successful that many readers felt it broke the inferior sequel rule.

Rowling planned her entire seven-book series prior to the publication of *Harry Potter and the Philosopher's Stone.* The overall plan and the writing of the first novel took place over a five-year period. Thus, contrary to many works, the sequels were not an afterthought to take advantage of the unexpected success of the first novel. While most authors give their series a separate title, Rowling merely retained the protagonist's name in the title of each of the books, so that they are referred to simply as the "Harry Potter books." For that reason, there is a tendency to view the series as a single work. In actual fact, there has been significantly more evolution throughout the books than is generally the case within a series. The difference is particularly striking between books three and four. While *Harry Potter and the Prisoner of Azkaban* was slightly darker in tone, the first three novels are nonetheless similar in length, level, tone, and target audience. *Harry Potter and the Goblet of Fire* and the successive novels were markedly different, in both look and content, and many critics feel this was due to the author's growing success with adults and the pressure to give more consideration to this increasing readership. At the same time, her original child readers, like Harry himself, were growing up. Rowling may therefore have felt that she could put greater demands on her young readers as well. The later novels are much longer and much darker, more sophisticated and more complex. They also contain more episodes likely to appeal to adults, such as the parodic treatment of the media in the caustic caricature of Rita Skeeter and the romance between Hagrid and Madame Maxime in volume four.[27] On her website, Rowling stated that the final book relates so closely to the previous book in the series that it is "almost as though they are two halves of the same novel."

Diana Wynne Jones, on the other hand, does not plan a series; continuations always take her by surprise. Although she has written many one-off works, she is best known for her series. The first three novels in the Dalemark series appeared in the 1970s and it was not until the publication of *Crown of Dalemark* in 1993 that the perceived trilogy became a quartet. Although her official website designates the Dalemark series as a quartet, it seems risky to give such specific designations to the series of an author who makes a habit of continuing them at intervals of a decade or more. T. H. White's *The Sword in the Stone* was published as a stand-alone work, but in its rewritten form it became the first book in a quartet that became a pentalogy when *The Book of Merlyn* was released posthumously, almost two decades later. Pre-planned series have become more common since the success of the first Harry Potter books. Although not to the same extent as Rowling, Eoin Colfer also planned his successful Artemis Fowl series. Unlike Rowling, he did not know that there would be six books in the series, but three of the books were "planned fairly comprehensively" when he began writing. Each book in the Artemis Fowl series ends with an allusion to the adventures that will follow in the sequel. In an interview with Joni Rendon on

May 16, 2005, posted on the KidsRead website, Colfer claimed he deliberately leaves "vague hints," which he has to follow up on in the later novels, in order to spark his imagination by making it "as difficult for [himself] as possible." Although Pullman did not plan *His Dark Materials* in the same manner as Rowling, he knew from the beginning that there would be three books and twelve hundred pages.

Not all works that are published in three novels are necessarily viewed by their authors as trilogies. Tolkien saw *The Lord of the Rings* as a single work (he intended it to be published in one volume). In a somewhat similar manner, Pullman thinks of his trilogy as "one story in three books" rather than "three separate stories."[28] It was not until 2007, however, that the three books were finally published together in an omnibus edition. Although Lian Hearn's Tales of the Otori seemed to fall naturally into three parts, the author claimed, in an interview posted on the BookBrowse website, to have written it "without a break as one overarching story." Originally she intended to write only one book, but well before completing the first novel she knew that her story could not be contained in a single volume. Over a two-year period, the entire story was written out longhand in four large notebooks before it was rewritten on the computer. It was only after all three books were written that the author showed the story to anyone.

Sequences of two books tend, to an even greater extent, to tell a single story in two volumes. They may result from an author's decision to split a work into two separate books. Examples can be found not only in the sphere of fantasy, but also in historical fiction. In 2000, Celia Rees published the historical novel *Witch Child*, written in diary form. *Sorceress*, released in 2002, is a follow-up that tells the rest of Mary Newbury's story and provides other background information. The Scottish author Julie Bertagna devoted two critically acclaimed novels, *Exodus* (2002) and *Zenith* (2007), to her futuristic environmental story of global warming, in which the young girl Mara must leave her island and find a new home. Although it was intended to be a two-part series, the author is currently working on the third novel, *Aurora*, of what she now calls the Savage Earth saga. Tamora Pierce writes mostly in quartets, the first of which was The Song of the Lioness quartet, published in the 1980s. However, in 2003 and 2004, she published the duology *Daughter of the Lioness*, also known as the Trickster books, which tells the story of Alianna, the daughter of the legendary Lady Sir Alanna of the first quartet.

The fact that all three volumes of Hearn's series were written before the first was published explains, in part, the intense excitement of the publishing and film industries. There would not be the long wait between instalments that generally characterizes a series and its film adaptations. *Across the Nightingale Floor* was published in 2002 and the sequels, *Grass for His Pillow* and *Brilliance of the Moon*, in 2003 and 2004 respectively. The first three novels in Dickinson's The Kin series appeared in the United States in 1998 and the fourth in 1999, so readers did not have to wait too long to read the entire narrative. The first four Harry Potter novels were brought out annually between 1997 and 2000, but there was a hiatus of three years between volumes four and five, and two years between volumes five and six, and six and seven. The three volumes of Pullman's *His Dark Materials* were published over a period of five years. The much-hyped first novel in Clive Barker's Abarat quartet was published in 2002 and the second appeared in 2004. The third book was for sale on Amazon.com in March 2006, even though it will not be released until August 2008. The wait was long indeed for the readers of Garth Nix's Abhorsen trilogy, as six years separated *Sabriel* from the second volume, *Lirael*, although the third volume, *Abhorsen*, appeared only two years after the second. This was due largely to the fact that the author originally thought that *Sabriel* was a stand-alone book. A further delay resulted from the fact that *Lirael* and *Abhorsen* were initially written as a single book, but Nix's editor felt it should be two books and the author eventually agreed. Publishers are understandably delighted when the books can be brought out quickly in order to give desperate readers their next fix while interest is high.

Many authors are reluctant to adopt a term that limits a series to a specific number of books and precludes, at least in theory, the addition of further titles. In some cases, what was originally announced as a trilogy turns into a longer sequence. P. B. Kerr's initial three-book contract with Scholastic for The Children of the Lamp series did not prevent the author from adding a fourth book in 2007. The same is true of Michael Hoeye, whose Hermux Tantamoq Adventures did not end with his three-book contract with G. P. Putnam's. When G. P. Taylor published *Wormwood* in 2004, he considered it the second title in a thematic trilogy that began with *Shadowmancer*, although the characters and plot are original. The following year saw the release of the third novel in the so-called trilogy, *Tersias* (2005), which is the story of a young boy who, after losing his sight, is overcome by a dark creature that allows him to the see the future. However, in 2006, Taylor published a true sequel to *Shadowmancer*, entitled *The Curse of Salamander Street*, which follows on where the first novel left off. While the series is widely referred to now as The Shadowmancer Quartet, some consider *Wormwood* and *Tersias* to be stand-alone novels and *The Curse of Salamander Street* to be the second book in the Shadowmancer series. When Cornelia Funke started writing *Inkheart* it was intended to be a stand-alone book, but the story evolved into a lengthy trilogy.

The flexibility of some "trilogies" is well demonstrated by Mary Hoffman's Stravaganza sequence, set in the country of Talia, an alternative Italy, in the sixteenth century. The series began in 2002 with *City of Masks*, about a parallel Venice called Bellezza. The first novel was followed by *City of Stars*, about Sienna (2003), and *City of Flowers*, about Florence (2005). Meticulously researched and carefully crafted in rich and sensuous prose, the novels blend fantasy with historical fact. They can be read as stand-alone titles, but Hoffman's fans are unlikely to want to miss a single volume. In an e-mail message on April 25, 2006, Hoffman told me that she thought of the books in her Stravaganza series as crossover fiction in the planning and writing. This was in part for thematic reasons, as she wanted to have "relationships between older adults in the series as well as just teenage romance." It also allowed her "to make the plots, structure and language as complex as . . . the stories needed them to be." Before the third novel was completed, Hoffman admitted the possibility of extending the series, since there are twelve city-states in Talia, each with its own story. She suggested that the stories would be in groups of three, which would allow for three more trilogies. We now know for certain that the series will extend beyond the original trilogy because the fourth novel, *City of Secrets*, will appear as a paperback original in 2008. While favourite characters will return, it will also introduce new characters.

Although Pullman's and Hearn's series have been referred to as trilogies, this has not prevented the authors from writing further books. Pullman has said that there will be no direct sequels to *His Dark Materials*, but at the Whitbread awards ceremony he revealed his plans to add another book to the series, a prequel called *The Book of Dust*, which would focus on secondary characters. Since that time, the work has apparently evolved in a different direction, as Pullman stated at the Oxford Literary Festival in 2007 (quoted on the *His Dark Materials* website) that the main character will be an older Lyra. However, he maintained that it is "not really a sequel." *The Book of Dust* is expected to include a continuation of the short story about Lyra that was published in *Lyra's Oxford*, but Pullman readers who have been anxiously awaiting the companion volume since the Whitbread ceremony are losing patience. After completing Book Three of The Tales of the Otori, which was seen as the conclusion, Hearn said that she was writing a prequel about Shigeru and Lady Maruyama, the tragic lovers who died in the first book of her trilogy. She also expressed her intention of writing a final book that would tie things up. In 2006, *The Harsh Cry of the Heron* was published as "The Last Tale of the Otori" or Book Four of Tales of the Otori. It takes up Takeo's story fifteen years after the conclusion of the third novel. The promised prequel was published in 2007, under the title *Heaven's Net is Wide*, as "The First Tale of the Otori." In 2006, Crossley-Holland published a follow-up to his popular Arthur trilogy, entitled *Gatty's Tale*, a medieval pilgrimage tale told through the eyes of Gatty, a young girl from the trilogy. Despite a great deal of speculation, Rowling has insisted there will not be an eighth book in her series but, as we have seen, such statements do not necessarily prevent an author from adding some form of follow-up to a series.

Fans are often given pieces of new material to keep them tantalizingly entertained between the novels of a series or to prolong the pleasure afterward. Sometimes this takes the form of small bits of additional information in a new edition of the work. This may be just enough to make the new publication indispensable as a "collectible" to those who have already read the novels. A deluxe edition of Christopher Paolino's *Eragon* contained an exclusive fold-out map, new art by the author, an expanded language guide, and an excerpt of the sequel *Eldest*. In the 2007 omnibus edition of Philip Pullman's *His Dark*

Materials, each book ends with two pages of new vignettes that the author wrote expressly for this edition. The publication of Pullman's omnibus edition and Paolini's deluxe edition of *Eragon* were strategically timed to coincide with the release of the film adaptation of the first novel in each series. Another common strategy is spin-offs or companion volumes that are tangential to the series. Rowling has written three spin-offs from the Harry Potter series, but in her case they were done for charity. In 2001, *Fantastic Beasts and Where to Find Them* was published to benefit the British charity Comic Relief. It purports to be a reproduction of a copy of a textbook owned by Harry Potter and written by Newt Scamander, a famous magizoologist. The same year, Rowling published a companion volume, *Quidditch through the Ages*, by Kennilworthy Whisp, another Hogwarts schoolbook. According to Comic Relief, sales from these books have raised more than £15 million. In 2007, Rowling completed *The Tales of Beedle the Bard*, mentioned in the final Harry Potter book. There are only seven copies of the handwritten tales; the first was auctioned for the author's charity, The Children's Voice, and the others were to be given away by the author to people she wished to thank for their role in the series.

Often companion volumes contain short stories about the series' characters, either the protagonist or secondary characters, as well as other peripheral material. Eoin Colfer wrote the short story "Artemis Fowl: The Seventh Dwarf" for World Book Day 2004. The same year it also appeared in *The Artemis Fowl Files*, a companion book to the series that includes another short story, interviews with the characters and the author, and various miscellaneous pieces, such as a Gnommish alphabet table, a spotter's guide to fairies, a guide to Foaly's inventions, and Artemis Fowl's report card. In 2005, Nix published *Across the Wall: Stories of the Old Kingdom and Beyond* (U.S. title: *Across the Wall: A Tale of the Abhorsen and Other Stories*), which is considered a companion book to The Old Kingdom series and is listed on his website with the books of the trilogy. In fact, the only story linked to the series is the one that opens the book, the 2005 World Book Day novella "Nicholas Sayre and the Creature in the Case," whose crossover appeal was demonstrated by the fact that it won the Aurealis Award for best young adult short story, as well as the overall Golden Aurealis Short Story Award in 2005. Pullman's *Lyra's Oxford* (2003), a small, sumptuous cloth-bound book with illustrations by master engraver and illustrator John Lawrence, packages together a short story, entitled "Lyra and the Birds," and other assorted materials, including a fold-out map of the alternate-reality city of Oxford. According to the author's introduction, these "might be connected with the story, or they might not; they might be connected to stories that haven't appeared yet." Authors of adult-to-child crossovers engage in similar projects, although not as frequently as children's authors. In 2006, Susanna Clarke published *The Ladies of Grace Adieu*, a collection of short stories, described as "fairytales." One of the stories concerns two characters from *Jonathan Strange & Mr Norrell* and was written while the novel was in progress. Clarke claims to be working on another book set in the same world as

Jonathan Strange & Mr Norrell. According to the book's website, the author does not think the follow-up will be "a sequel in the strictest sense," but she expects it to begin a few years after the end of the first novel and to include familiar characters as well as new ones.

Although many authors produce spin-off books related to a series, Daniel Handler, alias Lemony Snicket, has turned it into an art. According to an article in *Psychology Today* magazine, A Series of Unfortunate Events contains "just enough disheartening warnings—and mature overtones—to give the best-selling children's series crossover appeal."[29] The first such book was the highly self-conscious *Lemony Snicket: The Unauthorized Autobiography* (2002), which is composed largely of facsimile documents, such as scraps of half-burned manuscripts, letters, blurry photographs, and old newspaper clippings. While the book helps elucidate some of the loose ends from the series, it also raises many new questions. Shortly before the thirteenth and final instalment of A Series of Unfortunate Events, Handler published *The Beatrice Letters*, which, according to the cover, is "suspiciously linked to Book the Thirteenth" (2006). Both of these companion books are read by the same crossover audience as the series. Other spin-offs have little or no appeal to an adult audience, including *The Pessimistic Posters* (2004), a movie poster book; *The Puzzling Puzzles* (2006), a paperback of puzzles and games; and two blank journals for kids to write in, *The Blank Book* (2004) and *The Notorious Notations* (2006), the latter of which contains illustrations and quotes on most pages. There have also been a number of very short materials. *The Dismal Dinner* was four mini stories, set before *The Bad Beginning*, on fold-out cards attached to Oscar Mayer Lunchables (Kraft Bologna and American Cheese boxes) just before the movie came out in 2005. The nine-page booklet *13 Shocking Secrets You'll Wish You Never Knew About Lemony Snicket* was published by HarperCollins in 2006 to prepare readers for *The End*. Another book published under the Snicket name is *Horseradish: Bitter Truths You Can't Avoid* (2007), a volume of witty observations, including quotes from the series and selections from his unpublished papers.

Sequels are a common phenomenon in children's literature and much has been said about the profound pleasure that young readers get from the continuation of a well-loved story. However, it would seem that adults take equal delight in reading series. Writing across several titles and building up a series is a process associated with popular fiction, but in the case of much crossover literature that popularity has been translated into more literary works. When there isn't a sequel, readers look at the author's previous titles. Often publishers reprint titles from an author's backlist with new covers and other paratextual material that draws on the author's success. This strategy was particularly effective after Cornelia Funke's debut in the English-speaking world, as her lengthy backlist was unfamiliar to that market. The same trend exists in adult literature. After the huge success of Dan Brown's blockbuster *The Da Vinci Code* (2003), his earlier novel *Angels & Demons* (2000) also became a bestseller. Since it offered the same protagonist, it was like reading a prequel for the majority of readers, which included a large number of young adults. Two of Brown's earlier novels, which are quite different, also hit the bestselling list in the wake of *The Da Vinci Code*. At one point, all four novels occupied the top four spots on the *New York Times* bestseller list.

Although sequences are still extremely popular with readers, writers, and publishers, there is a noticeable move away from the trend of putting everything into a series and a return to one-off novels. Apparently publishers feel less need to put everything into a series to increase sales, realizing that good novels can sell on their own merits, provided they are well marketed.

A much wider range of publishers are now bringing out fantasy. In fact, few publishing houses don't have at least one fantasy title on their list. Not only is innovative new fantasy being written, but earlier books are being redis-covered. Established writers like Ursula Le Guin, Diana Wynne Jones, and Tanith Lee are gaining a wider crossover audience. Publishers are reissuing and repackaging fantasy novels from their backlists. Jones's most popular books, the Chrestomanci series, the first of which were published in the 1970s, were reissued by Collins in striking new editions in 2000. In addition, a two-volume work of four Chrestomanci stories, entitled *The Chronicles of Chrestomanci*, was published by HarperCollins in 2001. There have also been stunning new paperback editions of Jones's Dalemark quartet, designed for crossover appeal to adult fantasy readers as well as young Harry Potter fans.

Some publishers have even established new series and imprints devoted to fantasy fiction. Liliana Bodoc's unique talent prompted the Argentine publisher Grupo Editorial Norma to create a new series, entitled Otros mundos (Other worlds), in which to publish her trilogy La saga de los confines in 2000. To date, no other books have appeared in the series, suggesting the unique nature of her fantasy novels. In 2002, Time Warner created the Teen Fiction imprint Atom, in recognition of the huge fantasy crossover market. Atom's editor, Ben Sharpe, believes that the one reason kids would want to turn to books in a world where there is a plethora of media from which to choose our entertainment is for "imaginative fictions." Despite the fact that the most consistently success-ful franchises with teens have "a strong imaginative grounding" (*Star Wars* and *The Lord of the Rings* in movies, *Lara Croft* and *Final Fantasy* in gaming, and *Buffy* and *Smallville* on television) and "despite the enduring popularity of authors like C. S. Lewis and the recent high-profile success of J. K. Rowling and Philip Pullman, there has been no imprint solely devoted to producing such imaginative material in books."[30] Among the first books brought out by Atom were Francesca Lia Block's Dangerous Angels series.

Other publishers quickly jumped on the bandwagon. In 2003, Del Rey launched its Imagine program to offer the best in classic fantasy and science fiction for readers twelve and up, reissuing titles from its illustrious backlist. Del Rey Books began as an imprint of Ballantine Books in 1977 with Terry Brooks's bestselling *The Sword of Shannara*. The new line's inaugural releases were the three volumes of Brooks's trilogy, followed by Robert A. Heinlein's

Have Space Suit, Will Travel, first published in 1955. Among the fantasy reprints for Tor's Starscape, launched in 2003, are Ursula Le Guin's *The Eye of the Heron* and Tanith Lee's *Red Unicorn*. Tor was not the only publisher to reissue Tanith Lee, who has entertained fantasy enthusiasts of all ages with more than fifty books. The same year, Penguin Young Readers Group also brought out *The Claidi Collection*, the first three novels in Lee's popular Claidi Journals series, in a hardcover three-in-one omnibus volume, which includes *Wolf Tower*, *Wolf Star*, and *Wolf Queen*. By creating these imprints, publishers acknowledged the prominence of crossover fantasy in the current and future literary scene. Parallel to this publishing trend is the adaptation of earlier fantasy films for the screen. In 2005, following the successful motion picture adaptations of other fantasy classics, it was announced that Susan Cooper's *The Dark is Rising* was being developed as a major motion picture. The first film, *The Seeker*, was released in Fall 2007.

Despite the fact that Tolkien pushed fantasy into the mainstream, many fantasy writers, including Terry Pratchett and David Gemmel, feel that fantasy still tends to be ghettoized. Although that may be true for the literary establishment, Philip Pullman's *His Dark Materials* did much to change the attitude of even the most sceptical critics. Certainly, a very diverse audience of readers of all ages have universally adopted the fantasy genre. The most successful commercial franchises in the book and entertainment worlds over the past decade have been *The Lord of the Rings* and *Harry Potter*. Fantasy was the driving force behind the current crossover phenomenon and it has become the darling of the literary marketplace.

Chapter Five
Authors Crossing Over

With more adult authors writing for kids, the children's book market comes of age.

Judith Rosen, "Growing Up"

The Move from Adult Books to Children's/Crossover Books

As critics are constantly pointing out, almost all children's literature is written by adults. In recent years, an increasing number of children's books are written by adult "adult authors." In the wake of the extraordinary success of authors like J. K. Rowling and Philip Pullman, many writers not associated with juvenile fiction are now making the transition from adult books to children's and young adult books. Although the current commercial success of children's books— especially those that win the coveted "crossover" handle—has made this trend seem like an exodus, there has always been some movement in this direction. We have already seen a number of earlier examples, which include authors as different as Louisa May Alcott, Roald Dahl, and Daniil Kharms.

The recent trend of writers for adults moving to children's books is not unique to English-speaking countries. Even though crossover literature has not received a great deal of attention in Denmark, the trend of authors of adult fiction writing for children began there more than a decade ago. Louis Jensen began writing for children a decade before that trend began. In some cases, acclaimed adult authors are being asked to write for children and are doing so to much praise. The majority of these authors have contributed to a series published by Dansklærerforeningens Forlag, a publishing house owned by the Danish teachers' organization, which encouraged them to write for children. A notable example is Christina Hesselholdt, one of Denmark's most respected adult authors. She made her literary debut in 1991 with the short novel *Køkkenet gravkammeret & landskabet* (Kitchen, burial chamber & landscape), a singular story about a boy who loses first his mother and then his father, which became the first novel in a highly unusual trilogy for adults. In 1998, Hesselholdt published her first children's book, as well as another adult novel, and she continues to write books for both audiences. Pia Juul is an innovative Danish poet and novelist who has also begun writing for children. Her first novel for young adults, *Lidt ligesom mig* (A bit like me), was published in 2004. The successful Danish poet Katrine Marie Guldager began writing "Easy Readers" for children, but now has a wide range of children's books. Like Hesselholdt, both Juul and Guldager continue to publish for both readerships. Other well-known Danish authors who have been turning their hand to writing for children include Pablo Henrik Llabías, Henrik Nordbrandt, and Jens Smærup Sørensen.

In English-speaking countries, as in Denmark, this marked move from adult to children's fiction began in earnest in the late 1990s. In 1997, the American publisher Hyperion was actively promoting children's books written by established adult novelists. That fall, Hyperion launched children's books by both Alice Hoffman and Rudolfo Anaya. In 1998, the British author David Almond, who had previously written short stories for adults, published his first children's novel, *Skellig*, to widespread acclaim. The author claims to have felt quite liberated when he realized, on writing the first page of *Skellig*, that it was a book "aimed principally at young people." At the same time, Almond is quick to point out that a "good writer doesn't start writing with a sense of how it's going to be classified," but just has to write "the very best story" possible.[1] The haunting story about the strange creature a boy discovers in the garage of their rundown new house won the 1998 Whitbread Children's Book Award, for which Rowling's second *Harry Potter* had also been nominated. However, according to the president of the jury, Almond's novel could have competed in the adult category. Almond has continued to write highly successful crossover novels that are published for young readers but read by adults as well. Some critics felt that his *Heaven Eyes*, a children's story about waifs in an abandoned dock, should have won the Whitbread Book of the Year in 2000, but, as John Ezard put it: "Not a literary novel so, with the usual mindset of judges and literary commentators, barely a dog's chance of winning."[2] The very next year Pullman won the award for *The Amber Spyglass*. Almond's *The Fire-Eaters*, which tells the story of a child coming of age in England during the Cuban Missile Crisis, also received the Whitbread Children's Book Award in 2003, putting him once again in the running for the overall prize, which was won by Mark Haddon's *The Curious Incident of the Dog in the Night-Time*. Grounded in reality, Almond's novels also have a characteristic mystical overtone that appeals to readers of all ages. His much-acclaimed children's books are now translated into more than twenty languages.

The large number of authors trying their hand at children's fiction since 2000 is undoubtedly due, in part, to the financial attraction. Children's books, particularly those with crossover potential, have suddenly become a very lucrative business. Many bestselling adult authors with international reputations have crossed over in recent years. Apparently a number of them did so in the belief that they were doing something entirely original. Julia Alvarez compares the rush of adult authors writing for young people to "one of those embarrassing high school fashion moments": "You go out and buy an outfit [and] you think you're being so original. Go to school and everyone's wearing it."[3] It does seem to have become the latest literary fashion.

The award-winning Chilean author Isabel Allende, whose acclaimed adult novels have been translated into more than twenty-five languages and top bestseller lists in many countries, published her first children's book in 2002. The hefty fantasy novel *La Cuidad de las Bestias* was published in English, one month after its Spanish release, as *City of the Beasts*. The first book in what has been called the Jaguar and Eagle trilogy was seen as a kind of Latin American *Harry Potter*. Like the first Rowling novels, instalments of Allende's trilogy were brought out yearly. The second novel, *El Reino del Dragón de Oro* (*Kingdom of the Golden Dragon*) was published in Spanish in 2003, and the final novel, *El Bosque de los Pigmeos* (*Forest of the Pygmies*), in 2004, with the English translations appearing within a few months. The fast-paced novels are eco-thrillers that blend magical realism with grim reality, and high adventure with a spiritual dimension. The fifteen-year-old protagonist, whose mother is battling cancer, accompanies his adventuresome grandmother, a magazine reporter with *International Geographic*, to several remote areas of the world. The simple, spare style is not, as it might first appear, a case of talking down to young readers. Allende continues to write adult novels as well, some of which have crossover appeal in the other direction, notably *Zorro* (2005), a swashbuckling story of the legendary hero's formative years.

Lemony Snicket is the pseudonym of the American author Daniel Handler, who had written two adult novels prior to his hugely successful foray into children's literature with A Series of Unfortunate Events. One of the many publishers who turned down his first adult novel, *The Basic Eight*, published in1998, told Handler they were interested in him writing a story for children. The author planned an unlucky thirteen books in the series, which began with *The Bad Beginning* in 1999 and ended with *The End* in 2006 (fittingly released on Friday the thirteenth of October). In his saga of the Baudelaire orphans, who go from disaster to disaster after the death of their wealthy parents in a fire, Snicket/Handler pokes fun at the cheerful, positive tone of much traditional children's literature. Misery and bad luck pervade the series and are emphasized in the paratext and the publicity of the books. The metafictional comments and the irony of the intrusive narrator, who plays a mysterious role in the novels, are appreciated by older readers in particular, but his playful sense of the subversive appeals to readers of all ages. Although he undoubtedly owes something to Edward Gorey, Handler invents an entirely original genre: dark, comic Gothic novels for children that are a hit with adults as well. Skilfully crafted and literary, the books are also irreverent and funny.

Since 1999, the books have spent more than a combined six hundred weeks on the *New York Times* bestseller list. When the eleventh volume, *The Grim*

Grotto, was released in 2004, it topped a number of American bestseller lists, in some cases besting even Stephen King. "To see *The Grim Grotto* top bestsellers lists in publications like *The Wall Street Journal*, *USA Today* and the *Boston Globe*, where adult and children's books are ranked against one another, is a sign that readers of all ages are embracing Lemony Snicket," said Susan Katz, HarperCollins Children's Books president and publisher. The publisher's goal for Snicket's titles at the time was that of "reaching more adult readers," and Katz claimed the numbers indicated that they were "definitely making strides toward that goal."[4] Perhaps they were responding to complaints such as the one voiced by a reviewer in 2002, who accuses HarperCollins of hiding the books from adults by tucking them away in the kids' section in the back corners of bookstores. "We adult readers . . . should immediately take up our pitchforks and torches and storm the nearest bookstore, demanding Equal Humor Rights," he writes tongue in cheek.[5] Many adults had already discovered Snicket's very funny books without the publisher's help. According to the Amazon.com website, customers who bought his books in 2002 were also buying adult novels such as Ian McEwan's *Atonement*. The Series of Unfortunate Events books are no strangers to bestseller lists around the globe either. Translated into forty-one languages, the books have sold more than fifty million copies worldwide.

The *New York Times* bestselling series spawned the inevitable crossover film in 2004. Unlike the adaptation of *Harry Potter*, however, *Lemony Snicket's A Series of Unfortunate Incidents* was based, not on a single novel, but on the first three books in the series. Although the film did not do very well in cinemas, it was hugely successful on DVD, and there is interest in producing a sequel, which would be based on the next few books. Fans are so keen for a sequel that thousands signed an online petition to be sent to the author and filmmakers. A video game, released in 2004, is based largely on the film rather than the books. *The Tragic Treasury: Songs from A Series of Unfortunate Events*, a collection of the thirteen songs by The Gothic Archies that originally appeared on one of the corresponding thirteen audiobooks of the series, was released in 2006. The songs are written and performed by Stephin Merritt, who leads the band The Magnetic Fields, with whom Handler plays the accordion part time. Handler's adult fans, especially those in their twenties and thirties, also follow his alternate life as a musician with the popular New York band.

Publishers naturally exploit an author's success in the sphere of adult fiction when marketing his or her children's books. Neil Gaiman's *Coraline* was billed in the HarperCollins Fall 2002 catalogue as "a chilling and charming children's debut from a *New York Times* bestselling author." Prior to writing *Coraline*, all of Gaiman's adult novels had been bestsellers, including *American Gods*, which was published the previous year. *Coraline* was the second children's book by Gaiman, whose novels, graphic novels, and short fiction appeal to a hip audience which includes a large number of teenagers. His eerie children's novel about a girl who discovers a parallel world of evil button-eyed beings behind a door in her new house was a bigger hit with adults than children when it first came out. It landed in the top ten of the *New York Times* children's books bestseller list after its release in summer 2002, but the fans that attended the author's initial readings of *Coraline* were mostly adults. Gaiman admits that in the first week or so, it was probably chiefly adults who were buying the novel, but he is quick to point out that younger readers soon started steering their parents toward the novel. He claims to have thought up the idea for the novel in 1991 for his then five-year-old daughter, because "there was nothing around that had, for example, the Lemony Snicket quality." In his eyes, there were only two kinds of children's books at that time: "terribly nice" and "very, very safe" books or books "that had that quality of real life about 7-year-olds shooting up heroin."[6] Contrary to the types of children's books Gaiman describes, *Coraline* and Handler's books manage to appeal to adults as well as children.

The American author Michael Chabon was catapulted to literary celebrity when his debut novel, *The Mysteries of Pittsburgh* (written as his master's thesis), became a bestseller in 1988. In 2001, he won the Pulitzer Prize for *The Amazing Adventures of Kavalier & Clay* (2000), a coming-of-age story about two boys who invent a comic-book hero during World War II. The following year, Chabon published his first children's book, *Summerland* (2002), in which a boy who hates baseball and is the worst player on his Little League team is recruited to head a team being formed by a race of fairy folk to play games that will determine the fate of the world. His debut children's book had a first printing of 250,000 copies, which is huge for an adult novel, let alone a children's novel. The novel appeared on the *New York Times* and Book Sense bestseller lists, "though relegated to . . . their children's lists," as *Locus Magazine* put it when they posted their online bestsellers' chart for the week of September 29, 2002. *Summerland* was hailed as a "novel for all ages," "a crossbreed" with "the body of a grown-up novel [it is 492 pages] and the head of a prodigiously gifted children's book." Chabon's goal in writing the novel was supposedly "to transplant the hitherto primarily British tradition of all-ages fantasy to America." In the words of one critic, "the happy product of that ambition now mounts a lofty shelf just shy of Tolkien, Rowling and C. S. Lewis."[7] *Summerland* won the 2003 Mythopoeic Fantasy Award for Children's Literature. The novel was received with less enthusiasm in Britain, where some critics felt that it did not export well. Boyd Tonkin suggested that its "all-American landscape of baseball lore and Indian legend" was an indication that "today's isolationist current in the U.S. has swept even into the fairylands of 'kid lit' fiction—a sign of how much grown-up money is at stake."[8] In fact, Chabon's novel offers much to readers of all ages everywhere: Native American folklore and American fables are combined with Norse and Greek mythology; intertextual allusions refer to works as varied as Homer, Gabriel Garcia Marquez, *Close Encounters of the Third Kind*, Tex Avery cartoons, and *Charlie Brown's All-Stars*; and there are reminiscences of universal fantasy favourites such as Tolkien and C. S. Lewis.

The same year that Chabon published *Summerland*, the bestselling American author Carl Hiaasen brought out his first young adult novel, *Hoot* (2002). The offbeat, environmental mystery/adventure tells the story of three boys in Florida who trick adults into saving a colony of endangered burrowing owls from being destroyed by a large company. Known for his satirical black humour, Hiaasen seemed an unlikely children's author, as he himself is the first to admit. *Hoot* deals with the same signature environmental themes as his adult novels, including greedy developers and corrupt politicians, themes that are not common in children's literature. However, the novel was highly successful with its target audience, perhaps because Hiaasen wrote it for his stepson, nieces, and nephew, who were all in the ten- to fourteen-year-old age group. The 2003 Newbery Honor Book also appealed to adult readers, and reviewers insisted that you did not have to be a young adult to enjoy *Hoot*. As is generally the case, Hiaasen's reputation as an adult author ensured that the novel received a great deal of attention in the press. In spite of the novel's success, the movie version was released in 2006 to rather disappointing reviews. Hiaasen has continued to write for adults, publishing his bestseller *Skinny Dip* in 2004, before writing a second children's novel. Released in 2005, *Flush*, another pro-environmental story set in Florida, has had a similar reception to *Hoot*. Hiaasen has said that he would like to write one more children's novel, so he does not seem to see himself as a long-term children's author.

The British author Michelle Paver had published four historical novels for adults before she wrote *Wolf Brother*, the first book in her six-volume crossover children's sequence, the Chronicles of Ancient Darkness. None of Paver's adult novels have received nearly as much attention as her debut children's novel, which had its origins in a discarded story about a boy and a wolf begun years earlier at university. The success of the Harry Potter series may have encouraged Paver to re-work it as a children's book. *Wolf Brother*, published in 2004, generated record-breaking interest in publishing houses around the world. Paver's initial £1.5 million advance was believed to be the highest ever paid for a debut British children's book. The film rights to the novel and the sequels were bought by Fox film studio for more than £2 million. Set 6,000 years ago in the Stone Age, it is the story of a twelve-year-old orphan, Torak, whose father was murdered by a demon-haunted bear, and who must survive and defeat the bear with the help of an orphaned wolf cub. The story is told from the perspective of both Torak and the wolf. As in *Harry Potter*, Torak, Wolf, and his friend Renn, a girl from another clan, age with each book. The idea for the children's series had come to the author in the middle of a three-book contract for her popular Daughters of Eden series. In 2005, she published the final novel in the adult series as well as the second novel in the children's series, *Spirit Walker*. The latter was followed by *Soul Eater* in 2006 and *Outcast* in 2007; the fifth novel, *Oath Breaker*, has been announced for 2008. The books, which are exquisitely illustrated (by Geoff Taylor) and produced, have been highly successful with both children and adults, due to their excellent plotting, vivid characterization, meticulous research, and deep sensitivity to the natural world. They have been sold into every major publishing market worldwide.

P. B. Kerr was already well known, under the name Philip Kerr, as a highly successful British author of adult thrillers before publishing his debut children's book, *The Akhenaten Adventure*, the first novel in his popular Children of the Lamp sequence. The novel was actually written specifically for his own children, in an attempt to encourage his eldest son to read. It is the story of twelve-year-old twins who have an extraordinary gift for making other people's wishes come true. Intending to have the book privately printed, Kerr commissioned an illustrator to add some pictures. The author mentioned the work to his agent in Los Angeles, who had a son about the same age, and suddenly found himself publishing a children's book. It was brought out in 2004 by Scholastic, who published *Harry Potter* in the United States and Pullman's *His Dark Materials* in Britain. When the novel was released in the United States, it quickly made the *New York Times* bestseller list. The big advances and film deals Kerr had been obtaining in the adult sphere crossed over with him into children's literature. Scholastic UK and Scholastic US reportedly paid about $1.8 million for three books and DreamWorks bought the film rights. The author says writing for children did not really seem like a change, and he feels that one or two of his adult books would make "pretty good children's books" if he edited them somewhat. On the Scholastic website, he even goes so far as to call thrillers "children's books for grown ups." Kerr has obviously enjoyed writing for children, as he did not stop after publishing the contracted sequels, *The Blue Djinn of Babylon* (2005) and *The Cobra King of Kathmandu* (2006), but went on to write a fourth novel, *The Day of the Djinn Warriors* (2008).

The British author Louisa Young wrote adult novels—a series of fast-paced romantic thrillers featuring an ex-belly dancing single mother, referred to unofficially as the Evangeline Gower trilogy—before publishing the novel *Lionboy* in 2004 with her daughter Isabel Adomakoh Young, who was eight when they began writing under the joint pseudonym Zizou Corder. It was the first novel in the Lionboy trilogy, which continued with *Lionboy: The Chase* (2004) and *Lionboy: The Truth* (2005). The action-packed trilogy tells the story of a boy who acquired the gift of "catspeak" when he was scratched by a leopard as a baby. The mother-daughter team was reportedly paid close to one million pounds for the publishing rights to *Lionboy* and DreamWorks bought the film rights. It proved to be a popular trilogy that sold quite well despite some critical reservations. As the story progressed, the style improved and matured.

Nicky Singer had written four critically acclaimed adult novels before she made an impressive debut as a children's author with *Feather Boy* in 2001. The British author received $100,000 for the U.S. rights to the novel, which has been published in twenty-four countries. The novel, about a boy haunted by dreams that seem to tell the future as well as the past, won the Blue Peter Book I Couldn't Put Down Award, as well as the overall Blue Peter Book of the Year Award in 2002. *Feather Boy* was adapted by the BBC into a children's series that won the British Academy Award (BAFTA) for Best Children's Drama in 2004 and into a musical that was performed at the National Theatre in London in July

2006. Singer's second book for young readers, *Doll* (2003), a story about dysfunctional parents and new love, was aimed at older teenagers. The novel was shortlisted for the first-ever Booktrust Teenage Prize, created to recognize the best book for teenagers. The award was won that year by Mark Haddon's acclaimed crossover novel *The Curious Incident of the Dog in the Night-Time.* In 2005, Singer published *The Innocent's Story*, a challenging post-9/11 story, in which terrorist events are seen from the perspective of both victim and terrorist. The unusual novel is narrated from beyond the grave by the thirteen-year-old victim of a suicide bomber. Although popular with young readers, Singer's novels have not had the same degree of crossover success as those by authors such as David Almond.

Julie Burchill's *Sugar Rush* was published as a young adult novel in 2004. Before Macmillan released it again the following year, they were promoting the teenage novel as a crossover title. This was due largely to the reputation of the author, Britain's most controversial journalist, whose adult novel *Ambition* was an international bestseller in 1989. The subject of the novel is targeted directly at a young adult audience, as it tells the story of a teenager who has to leave her posh school for a notorious comprehensive school, where she is rescued by "Sugar—queen of the Ravers." The novel has been turned into a television drama series which first aired in 2005. The lesbian theme has put the book on lists of crossover works that appeal to the gay community.

Many of the authors discussed in this section seem to have turned their attention entirely to writing books for young readers, at least for the time being, but some continue to publish adult fiction as well. While crossing over into children's literature may have a lucrative side, it would be unfair to think that these authors are all making the shift for commercial reasons. Many of these authors are receiving much larger advances than most children's authors, but some, including Chabon and Hiaasen, reap even greater sums for their adult novels. At the beginning of the twenty-first century, children's literature has become such an exciting field that adults want to be involved, both as writers and as readers.

The huge success of crossover literature now seems to be spawning a trend in the opposite direction. Writers who have had sensational literary debuts with child-to-adult crossover hits and established their reputations as crossover authors are turning their hand to writing adult novels and are now publishing bestselling adult novels as well. Between two successful children's trilogies, William Nicholson launched his career as an author for adults, publishing two novels for that market in 2004 and 2005, the first being the acclaimed existential novel *The Society of Others.* Yet other authors were well established as children's authors before a popular crossover novel brought them to the attention of adult readers and encouraged them to write for adults. The examples of Mark Haddon and Dominique Demers will be considered in subsequent chapters. The British author and illustrator Colin Thompson, perhaps best known for his picturebooks, published his first adult novel, *Laughing for Beginners*, in 2002 following the release of his crossover science fiction *Future Eden*. In the wake of the crossover success of his young adult series *Der Kreis der Dämmerung*, Ralf Isau published his first novel for adults in 2003. Now that the Harry Potter series is finished, perhaps J. K. Rowling will publish one of the adult novels she had written prior to falling under the spell of the young magician. If so, this particular children's author is unlikely to have any difficulty finding a publisher for her adult books.

Crossover/Adult Novels by Young Authors

A few critics and publishers have pointed to a very different contemporary trend, that of children or teenagers writing adult novels. Toward the end of 2005, Petro Matskevych and Kseniya Sladkevych, co-founders of MSBrand Corporation that works closely with Calvaria Publishing House in the Ukraine, noted this European trend, citing the examples of Melissa Panarello (better known as Melissa P.) in Italy, Anne-Sophie Brasme in France, Miroslav Nahach in Poland, Anna Vikovich in Serbia, and Ljubko Deresh in the Ukraine.[9] As teenagers, these authors all wrote national bestsellers that were read by adults. Brasme was seventeen in 2001 when she published *Respire* (*Breathe*), a dark novel about an absolute friendship that ends in prison. Panarello was seventeen when her diaries about the sexual adventures of a Sicilian schoolgirl, entitled *Cien colpi di spazzola prima di andare a dormire* (*100 Strokes of the Brush Before Bed*), became an international bestseller in 2003. The novel has sold more than two million copies and been translated into more than thirty languages. In 2005, it was made into a film. However, young authors writing for adults is not a new phenomenon, as the works published by Juvenilia Press clearly indicate. Founded by Juliet McMaster, a professor at the University of Alberta in Canada, and relocated to the University of New South Wales in Australia in 2002, Juvenilia Press publishes "'adults' literature' by children." Juvenilia is literature *by* children, but not necessarily *for* children. In fact, McMaster is convinced that these works are written by child writers essentially for an adult audience. She points out that they use themes such as love and sex, in spite of the expectations of adults, who would find this degree of knowledge troubling.[10] Their works are often quite humorous and surprisingly sophisticated. Juvenilia Press has published more than thirty volumes of early works, from the eighteenth through the twentieth centuries, by known authors such as Jane Austen, Louisa May Alcott, Charlotte Brontë, George Eliot, Margaret Atwood, Margaret Laurence, and Malcolm Lowry. These young authors were headed for stellar careers.

Perhaps the best example of a child author writing adult fiction is Jane Austen, who was a very skilled writer at age thirteen. According to McMaster, Austen wrote *The Beautiful Cassandra* at twelve, *Jack and Alice* at thirteen, and *Love and Freindship* at fourteen.[11] McMaster claims to have reflected a great deal on the audience for Austen's juvenilia because she has long entertained the idea of producing an illustrated version of one of the novels for an audience of children. She has been encouraged in her enterprise of "returning Austen's *Juvenilia* to the hands of children," but even though she would like to produce a children's edition, she feels that children are not their target audience.[12] Austen's early work is an interesting example of a teenager writing adult fiction that has crossed over to young adults. One could also cite Mary Shelley, who completed *Frankenstein* when she was nineteen and published it anonymously the following year.

Daisy Ashford's highly successful *The Young Visiters*, written when she was nine, offers an exceptional example of juvenilia. Ashford never intended to be an author; writing stories was a source of entertainment for her and her sisters. She began writing at the age of four when she dictated *The Life of Father McSwiney* to her father, and her precocious "career" ended at the age of fourteen with *The Hangman's Daughter*. *The Young Visiters*, written in 1890, was her best work. The novella parodies upper-class society in nineteenth-century England. When Ashford and her sisters discovered *The Young Visiters* while clearing their mother's house after her death, they found it so amusing Daisy sent it to a sick friend to cheer her up. The friend gave it to Frank Swinnerton, a novelist and reader for Chatto and Windus, who thought it could be successfully published. What ensued would seem today to be a clever marketing strategy, but, in fact, was quite unintentional. When the book was published in 1919 with a preface by J. M. Barrie, astounded readers were unable to accept that a nine-year-old could possibly have written it and assumed that Barrie was the real author. The immense publicity that this produced, in both Britain and the United States, turned *The Young Visiters* into an immediate bestseller. Ashford was obliged to give readings in London to prove that she was indeed the author. While Ashford's other stories have also been published, none has been as popular as *The Young Visiters*, which has remained in print for almost a century.

While some contemporary authors who begin their literary careers as teenage prodigies are published for adults, many are published for young adults, although they are often read by adults as well. Bart Moeyaert gained immediate fame in 1983, at the age of nineteen, when he made his debut with *Duet met valse noten* (Off-key duet), an autobiographical novel for young adults. Written between the ages of fourteen and sixteen, the novel grew out of the diary he had kept from the age of thirteen, and it is known in Belgium as "that teenage love-story written by a teenager in love." Chosen as the Best Book of the Year in 1984 by the Flemish Children and Youth Jury, the highly successful novel was reprinted eleven times in the first ten years and became what the author calls a "longseller."[13] Although the novel has been translated into several languages, including Catalan and Japanese, it has never appeared in English. The crossover appeal of *Duet met valse noten* is indicated by the fact that it was made into a play and a successful musical that ran for three consecutive seasons in the late 1980s.

Since his precocious debut, Moeyaert has continued to write young adult novels that appeal widely to adults. In 1998, he became the youngest author ever to be nominated for the Hans Christian Andersen Award. His novels, which are often described as "filmic," are characterized by a concise, poetic style; controversial, melancholic subjects; and an emotionally charged, often oppressive, atmosphere. In the hands of this skilled storyteller, simple stories become subtle, haunting portrayals of the complexity of adult-child relationships. These thought-provoking narratives are told in such limpid and poetic prose that they remain accessible to children while also appealing to adults. The versatile author, who also writes television scripts, plays, and poetry, is hugely popular with a broad crossover audience in Flanders. His poems have appeared on calendars, subway billboards, and even the façade of a public building (The Palace theatre) in Antwerp, where, in 2006, he became the city poet for a two-year period. Moeyaert has given many talks and written numerous articles in newspapers and magazines on the border traffic between adult and child audiences, and the role of juvenile literature in a contemporary cultural context.

The Australian author Sonya Hartnett published her first book, *Trouble All the Way*, in 1984, when she was just fifteen years of age. In both 2001 and 2003, she was named one of the *Sydney Morning Herald* Best Young Novelists of the Year, an award for Australian novelists under the age of thirty-five. When she won the award for the second time, Hartnett had published eleven novels and was already "a young veteran," as one critic put it in an article entitled "Writers Coming of Age."[14] Although Hartnett is generally classified as a young adult writer, she finds the label inaccurate and denies that she writes young adult novels in the conventional sense of the term. Her novels published for young adults often cross over and are enjoyed by adults. They include, among others, *Wilful Blue* (1994), which was also produced as a play, and *Thursday's Child* (2002), for which she won the *Guardian* Children's Fiction Prize in 2002. With regard to her target audience, the author claims: "I write only for me, and for the few people I hope to please, and I write for the story."[15] Critics have often suggested that her books are too grown-up for their usual target market. Some of her later novels, such as *Of a Boy* (2002) and *Surrender* (2005), are treated more as adult novels and have been nominated for adult fiction awards. *Surrender*, for example, was shortlisted for the 2006 Commonwealth Writers Prize. Perhaps there is a sense in the literary establishment that the author has indeed "come of age," and that her novels can be considered adult novels. In 2006, Hartnett published *Landscape with Animals*, a book with numerous explicit sex scenes, under the pseudonym Cameron S. Redfern. The author denied that it was a publicity stunt or an attempt to avoid responsibility for the work, claiming that she and her publisher wanted to prevent the book being mistakenly shelved with her books for young readers in libraries and bookstores. Perhaps Hartnett just felt the need, for once, to completely escape the "children's author" label.

The phenomenon of teenage writers publishing crossover or adult literature is widespread in Europe and it is not just a trend of the past few years. A number of these books have been national bestsellers and some have found success in other countries as well. Germany has had a significant number of writers with precocious debuts. Jutta Richter, one of Germany's most celebrated children's authors, writes for children, young adults, and adults. She wrote her first novel, *Popcorn und Sternenbanner*, at the age of sixteen. Despite her success in her own country, her first book to be translated into English was *Hechtsommer*, published in Germany in 2004 and in English, as *The Summer of the Pike*, in 2006. It was followed closely by a translation of *Die Katze oder Wie ich die Ewigkeit verloren habe* (2006), in 2007, under the title *The Cat, or How I Lost Eternity*. Although the modern fable, beautifully illustrated by Rotraud Susanne Berner, was published for readers eight and up, it is a story meant to be shared by children and adults. In a rather repressive atmosphere that evokes the 1950s for adult readers, Christine is torn between the demands of her parents and teachers and the anarchic ideas of a philosophical, talking alley cat. Richter was awarded the Deutscher Jugendliteraturpreis in 2001 and the Herman Hesse Prize for her complete works in 2004.

The German author Alexa Hennig von Lange won the NDR Schreibwettbewerb "Kinder schreiben für Kinder" (Children write for children) at the age of thirteen. However, the "Spice Girl of Literature," as she has been called, did not publish her debut novel, *Relax*, until the age of twenty-three.[16] *Relax*, an extremely funny story about drugs, love, and sex, was a huge success with adults as well as young adults. The antiheroine from *Relax* reappears in Hennig von Lange's second novel, *Ich bin's* (I am, 2000), as well as in her third, *Ich habe einfach Glück* (I am simply lucky, 2001), which won the Deutscher Jugendliteraturpreis in 2002. Published by Rogner und Bernhard, which is not a traditional publisher of young adult fiction, these novels are intended for both adults and young adults. In 1999, the author's first play, *Flashback*, was performed. Hennig von Lange has continued to publish a steady stream of novels in a similar vein. *Woher ich komme* (Where I come from, 2003), *Erste Liebe* (First love, 2004), and *Warum so traurig?* (Why so sad?, 2005) appeared with the publisher Rowohlt Berlin, which is well known for its adult fiction. Hennig von Lange has also written books for young readers. Although she has been one of the most successful authors of her generation in Germany, none of her novels have been translated into English.

Benjamin Lebert was hailed as a literary wunderkind when he published his first novel *Crazy* in Germany in 1999, at the age of sixteen. This autobiographical debut novel was a runaway bestseller and an international publishing phenomenon, selling in more than thirty countries. *Crazy* was adapted as a successful film in Germany by Hans-Christian Schmid in 2000. This funny, poignant, modern coming-of-age novel tells the story of a maladjusted teenager, paralyzed on one side from birth, who lives, in company with a number of other misfits in a new boarding school, the "crazy life" that he feels is the only way to deal with a crazy world. The novel revolves around the clichés of adolescent life, but it is narrated with warmth, wit, and self-irony. Like *Catcher in the Rye*, it appeals to teenagers and former teenagers of all ages. *Crazy* was published by

Kiepenheuer & Witsch, who do not publish juvenile fiction, and the English edition was released by Knopf in 2000. It nonetheless won a spot on the Young Adult Library Services Association's list of Best Books for Young Adults in 2001. *Crazy* was followed by a number of humorous, edgy novels. The only other novel that has been translated into English is *Der Vogel ist ein Rabe* (*The Bird Is a Raven*), which, unlike *Crazy*, was published as general fiction in Germany in 2003, and also brought out for adults by Knopf in 2005. It is the story of two young men who, in a sleeping compartment on a night train from Munich to Berlin, share stories and secrets of their journey from the innocence of childhood to a still-new adult life. The success of *Der Vogel ist ein Rabe* continued to convince critics that Lebert had begun what promised to be a stellar career.

Ljubko Deresh has been called the new "wunderkind of Ukrainian literature." He wrote his first novel, *Культ* (Cult, 2002), at the age of fifteen. Some of the minor characters in this novel became central characters in his next novel, *Поклоніння ящірці* (Worshipping the lizard), published in 2004. His first three novels were originally published, beginning in 2001, in the literary journal *Chetver* (Thursday), which Petro Matskevych told me in an e-mail message on November, 24, 2007, has become "a cult journal for students and a laboratory of contemporary Ukrainian prose." Most well-known contemporary Ukrainian prose authors were first published in *Chetver*. Deresh has now published four novels, all of which have been bestsellers, and he has gained a kind of cult status in the Ukraine. Recently, he has achieved a breakthrough in several countries, notably in Germany where he has been published by the renowned publisher Suhrkamp. His work, which is surprisingly mature, is characterized by a cinematographic description of events, psychological details, and an ironic sense of humour. Deresh has become the leader of a new literary generation in the Ukraine and receives a great deal of media attention. Another rising star of Ukrainian literature is the rock singer Irena Karpa, who published her first novel, *Znes Palenogo*, in 2000 at the age of nineteen. The chick lit sensation and rising literary star has continued to publish controversial novels with provocative sexual content, including *Freud Would Weep* (2006) and *Bitches Get Everything* (2007). At a conference in the Ukraine in 2007, Matskevych and Sladkevych described a new trend in the Ukraine, that of "another" generation of young writers, aged sixteen to twenty-six, who began writing literature for adults as young adults, including Kseniya Kharchenko, Tetjana Vynokurova-Sadychenko, and Halyna Lohinova. They believe this fiction, which has been referred to as "alternative" or "subculture," is not only a literary phenomenon, but the reflection of a much deeper cultural trend. They wonder if this phenomenon is limited to the Ukraine or if it is a European tendency.[17] It would seem that it may even be somewhat of a global trend.

The Canadian author Ken Oppel was also a literary child prodigy, writing his first children's book when he was fifteen. A family friend sent *Colin's Fantastic Video Adventure* to one of Oppel's favourite authors, Roald Dahl, who recommended it to his own agent. The author was eighteen when it was published in 1985. Oppel is best known for his award-winning Silverwing trilogy, a modern animal epic saga about Shade, a silverwing bat. *Silverwing*, which was published by Simon & Schuster in 1997 and has been translated into many languages, was followed by *Sunwing* (2000) and *Firewing* (2003). The books have sold more than a million copies worldwide. The trilogy was adapted as an animated film series that began airing in Fall 2003. Trilogy may once again be a misnomer, as a fourth novel in the series, a prequel entitled *Darkwing*, appeared in 2007. In 2004, Oppel won the Governor General's Award in the Children's Literature category for his novel *Airborn* (2004), a thrilling, Jules Verne-style adventure set in an alternate past, where air travel has developed in the direction of zeppelins rather than jet planes. The nature of the protagonist's wide appeal is indicated by the fact that critics often describe him as a young Indiana Jones. Due to its huge popularity with a family audience, an eighteen-episode abridged reading of *Airborn* was broadcast in Summer 2005 on CBC's popular program *Between the Covers*, which features contemporary fiction read in fifteen-minute instalments. This general audience appeal is also demonstrated by the fact that a film adaptation of *Airborn* is being produced by Universal Pictures. A bestselling sequel, *Skybreaker*, was published in 2005, and the author is currently working on a third novel in the popular series.

The British author David Lee Stone began imagining the fantasy world depicted in The Illmoor Chronicles at the age of ten. One day he got very frustrated and threw his work in the garbage, but his mother salvaged it and, without David's knowledge, sent it to a publisher. It became his first book, *The Ratastrophe Catastrophe*, which was published by Hodder in the United Kingdom in 2003 and Hyperion Books in the United States in 2004. It has been published in at least seventeen countries worldwide. The author signed a six-figure deal with Hodder for the first three novels. There are now six volumes in the series, which the Hackwriters website refers to as "Narnia for the Tarantino generation...." The series is aimed at a young adult/crossover market, but it has not captured a significant adult audience. The claim on the cover of book six, *The Coldstone Conflict*, that its author is "the natural heir to Terry Pratchett," is not yet proven with regard to crossover appeal. Stone's first non-Illmoor book, *Davey Swag*, a pirate adventure set in the seventeenth century, was published for the same market in 2008, under the pen name David Grimstone.

The most successful young American prodigy is Christopher Paolini, who was catapulted into the literary limelight when his debut novel *Eragon*, the first novel in the fantasy Inheritance Trilogy, became a bestseller in the United States when he was still a teenager. Paolini began writing the novel when he graduated from high school at the age of fifteen (he was home-schooled in Montana). By the age of nineteen, Paolini was a *New York Times* bestselling author. *Eragon* is an epic fantasy novel that appeals to *Lord of the Rings* fans. It tells the story of a fifteen-year-old boy who learns that his destiny is to be a Dragon Rider and save the Empire from an evil king. More than two million copies of *Eragon* were in print in the United States when the sequel came out in 2005. *Eldest* was the most anticipated young adult book of the year in the United States and sales for the first week broke Random House's record for the greatest single-week sales of any children's book. It quickly displaced *Harry Potter and the Half-Blood Prince* on Amazon.com's list of bestselling children's books. A mega-budget 20th Century Fox movie adaptation of *Eragon* was released worldwide in December 2006.

The current crossover trend is encouraging authors to explore new markets and more diverse audiences. The status of authors is increasingly flexible. It is now more accepted that authors write for a wide range of audiences or for a single cross-generational audience. While adult authors are being drawn to the world of children's and young adult fiction, teenage authors are attracting a wide adult audience. With established adult authors as well as budding young authors, crossover books are currently the hot ticket in the literary world.

Chapter Six
Publishers and the Marketplace

This was previously a no man's area of publishing which has now hit both the financial jackpot with Harry Potter, and the critical jackpot with *The Amber Spyglass.*

Clive Barnes, *Books for Keeps*

Until recent years, adult books and children's books had belonged to very different worlds, largely due to the pragmatics of the publishing world. Everything about the books was different: appearance, price, marketing, reviews. Although crossover books are not a new phenomenon, the crossover market as such was virtually non-existent until the late 1990s. "The idea that books written for children or teenagers might also appeal to adults would have seemed ridiculous to publishers a decade ago," wrote a British journalist in 2002.[1] The same year, David Fickling, publisher of Philip Pullman's *His Dark Materials*, said: "Ten years ago no-one wanted to publish children's fiction. In the 1980s it was all picture books and Walker [Britain's leading independent children's publisher]."[2] What a difference a decade can make in the world of books. Publishers tend to be quite fashion-conscious. Crossover literature had always existed, but suddenly it had become highly fashionable, thanks to Harry Potter. As Nicholas Clee points out, "every publishing phenomenon is the result of one outstanding success, which finds an enthusiasm that publishers hadn't previously tapped." He uses the example of *Bridget Jones's Diary*, which created a market for chick-lit.[3] Several decades earlier, Tolkien's *Lord of the Rings* did the same for fantasy. These publishing trends reflect socio-cultural changes. By the mid-1990s, it was widely assumed in the publishing world that there was no longer a market for the imaginative fiction of writers like Tolkien and Le Guin. In fact, "reading itself was believed to be in its last throes," as S. F. Said rightly points out, adding: "But that was to reckon without a new generation of writers, electrified by the idea of books for everyone."[4] By the late 1990s, children's fiction was entering another golden age thanks to a newfound market of adult readers for the imaginative fiction of this new generation of writers.

The publishing world was not long in realizing the potential of crossover books after the unexpected success of Rowling's young wizard. Harry Potter's appeal to both children and adults was a dream come true for publishing houses. In the 2002 article "Once Upon a Time in the Marketing Department ...," Boyd Tonkin claims that "cynical publishers are pushing 'kid lit' as a crossover phenomenon."[5] It is important to remember, however, that the crossover trend was not initially publisher-driven. It took more than marketing magic to turn crossover fiction into the Holy Grail of the publishing world and one of the most striking phenomenons of contemporary culture.

Much has been made of the hot new market of kidults, but they do not constitute the only coveted new audience. Publishers have begun pitching to the adults of all ages who are avidly reading children's books, as well as to the children and young adults who are reading adult books. They are trying to attract a larger section of the market for their authors and to sell the same book in two spheres. While some publishers are now marketing adult books for children and young adults, the book industry has seen the crossover phenomenon essentially as children's books or young adult books crossing over to adults. The following statement from the *Children's Writers' and Artists' Yearbook 2006*, posted on the Allen & Unwin website, is typical: "We talk a great deal these days of the 'crossover' book where an adult market has been identified for a children's book, a phenomenon which started with Harry Potter."[6] Although crossover fiction did not "start" with Rowling's books, they did bring it to the attention of the publishing world.

The Potter effect has had a monumental impact on the publishing and marketing of major children's titles with crossover potential. "Historically, there have been books published for children that crossed over," says Scholastic president Barbara Marcus. "What happened after 'Harry Potter' is that this became the rule rather than the exception."[7] Publishers are now implementing strategies for marketing children's books to an adult audience, across what has been perceived as the great divide. "Crossover" is now a category recognized by writers, readers, critics, and publishers. Writers, as well as publishers, deliberately market books as crossover fiction. Many authors have been categorizing their works in this manner on their websites since the late 1990s. Ian Bone's 2000 novel *The Song of an Innocent Bystander*, a powerful story of a young woman haunted by the choices she made ten years earlier—at the age of nine—to survive a restaurant siege, was listed on his website from the outset as a "young adult/adult crossover novel."

Publishing, especially children's book publishing, has not traditionally been seen to be driven solely by the bottom line. Children's books have had an intrinsic value in terms of a cultural artifact. Perhaps some highly successful adult authors carried a more commercial attitude over into the world of children's books. Michel Tournier perfected the art of crosswriting child and adult in part for commercial reasons, admitting unapologetically that he writes to be published, sold, and read as widely as possible. By publishing the same text in different contexts for new audiences, Tournier and his publisher, Gallimard, were undoubtedly able to sell more books. Since the Potter phenomenon, children's books, particularly those read by adults, have become very big business.

Publishers are anxious to repeat Rowling's success with other books that have wide appeal to a diverse audience. There has been a great deal of look-alike publishing, as everyone eagerly sought the next J. K. Rowling or the next Philip Pullman. Some critics believe authors and publishers are directing all their energies into books that transcend boundaries rather than those written specifically for children. Julia Eccleshare, for example, warns against using children "as a leg-up to a bigger market."[8] Publishers deny, however, that this has become an obsession. When Philippa Dickinson, who runs Random House Children's Books (their crossover authors include Terry Pratchett, Jonathan Stroud, Christopher Paolini, Mark Haddon and Philip Pullman), was asked if their editors are constantly on the lookout for crossover fiction, she categorically denied it. "Everyone talks about 'crossover' fiction, but really you can only make it work if you have a very special book," she claimed.[9] Some publishers, such as Penguin and Faber, are adamant about not determining for the market which books should be crossovers. Mike Bryan, senior vice-president of sales at Penguin International, does not think it is either possible or ethical to do so. He stresses: "We will only market it as a very good children's book. It's for the public—not the publisher—to decide."[10] This has been the case for the best crossover books, according to Andre Mayer, who writes: "If there's a pattern to the most successful crossover titles, it's that none were officially announced as such."[11] While that may have been true in the early years of the phenomenon, as crossover fiction establishes itself as an official literary category and carves its place in the literary market, publishers are not always so willing to leave the decision to the public. The publishers of Mark Haddon's *The Curious Incident of the Dog in the Night-Time* and Lian Hearn's *Across the Nightingale Floor* had no qualms about making the decision for readers.

The Publisher's Role in Determining an Author's Status and/or a Book's Audience

Acknowledging how absurd it sounded, John Rowe Townsend claimed, in 1971, that "the only practical definition of a children's book" was "a book which appears on the children's list of a publisher."[12] Many authors claim that they write only for themselves and that they write children's literature completely by accident. Mark Haddon explains why he considered *The Curious Incident of the Dog in the Night-Time* to be an adult novel: "Like most writers, I wrote for myself and as a 41-year-old I saw it as an adult book."[13] His publisher ultimately decided that the novel should be published for both children and adults. In recent years, the Harry Potter factor has forced publishing houses to rethink their marketing strategies, and their impact on the current crossover trend is enormous. However, the major role that publishers play in blurring the distinctions between adult and children's fiction is not only a contemporary phenomenon. Publishers have long determined the ultimate status of many writers whose works fall into the crossover category. Jules Verne is a famous example from the nineteenth century. As we saw in chapter three, it was the French publisher Pierre-Jules Hetzel who decided that Verne's first novel should be published for a young audience. The twenty-year contract Hetzel offered the author ensured that his subsequent works would appear for the same readership. Although Verne is one of the most translated authors in the world, he has served as a warning to French authors who wish to avoid being categorized as "children's authors" and his name is often cited by contemporary crossover authors hoping to avoid his fate.

A large number of authors have had the experience of writing a novel with a particular target audience in mind and being told by a publisher that they had in fact written for an entirely different audience. In some cases, they think they have written a book for children and are informed that it is, in fact, a book for adults. Dominique Demers, who has had this experience herself, feels that it is much more frequent than the reverse situation.[14] The Swedish author Harry Kullman expressed his astonishment when his publisher declared that *Natthämtaren* (The nightfetcher, 1962), a novel intended for teenagers, was going to be published for adults. He addresses the subject in an article entitled ironically "Writing Too Well."[15] This editorial decision nonetheless seems to have encouraged Kullman to write deliberately for adults because, in the years immediately preceding his death in 1982, he wrote two thrillers for adults, the first in what was intended to be a ten-book series. In the post-Potter period, there seems to have been a shift to a more flexible attitude on the part of many publishers. When Neil Gaiman submitted his initial draft of the eerie novel *Coraline* to his editor, she told him: "You can't publish this for kids. This is obviously an adult novel." Gaiman asked her to read the book to her six- and nine-year-old daughters, who loved it, and *Coraline* was published for children in 2002.[16]

Whether or not Demers's claim is correct, the cases that generally get reported seem far more often to be those of authors who, like Jules Verne, are told by a publisher that the book they thought they had written for adults is really more appropriate for a juvenile audience. The Swedish author Gunnel Beckman, who had already written two detective novels for adults with her husband under the pseudonym Luis Bank, sent a manuscript for a book penned on her own to a publisher in the late 1950s. An editor wrote back and told her that if she cut the detective plot entirely and rewrote it slightly, it would make a fine children's book. Although she was initially angry and put the manuscript away in a drawer, she eventually complied and *Medan katten var borta* (While the cat was lost) was published in 1960. Beckman even published a sequel the following year. Subsequently, she wrote many novels for adolescents on subjects that were quite shocking in the 1960s: suicide, fatal illness, pregnancy, divorce, unhappy mothers, and so forth. Her only "crossover" work is an "easy read" book, titled *Varför just Eva?* (Why exactly Eva?), which was published in 1978 for adults with literacy problems and/or mental disabilities, but used subsequently in schools. This is obviously a rather special type of crossover text because it was intended for a limited and very specific adult audience. Another Swedish author to have had a similar experience is Peter Pohl. His much-acclaimed 1985 novel *Janne, min vän* (*Johnny My Friend*) was intended for adults, but the publisher decided otherwise and it was published for a young adult audience.

When the popular British children's poet Michael Rosen sent his first collection of poems, *Mind Your Own Business*, to a publisher, he did not think it was children's poetry. He was, as he puts it, "arrogant enough" to believe that, influenced by James Joyce's *Portrait of the Artist as a Young Man*, he had used "the voice of the child" to write poetry that would interest adults. After sending the manuscript to several publishers, someone finally suggested that it might be a children's book. He was joined up with the well-known illustrator Quentin Blake, and the collection *Mind Your Own Business* came out in 1974. When Rosen made the connection between poetry and performance the following year, resulting in an anecdotal style that combines poetry and prose, some critics felt that he had defiled the field of poetry. There was little hope of him moving back into adult poetry at that stage, although it is highly unlikely that the successful children's poet would have wanted to make that shift. Rosen claims to operate in a "borderland territory" that is quite liberating. However, many of his works are now out of print, a fact that he attributes to the influence of schools on publishers. He laments the fact that his volume *The Hypnotiser*, released in 1988, coincided with a new age in education in Britain, when literature was replaced by literacy, and a collection of children's poetry now had to have a theme to interest educators. Having become a children's poet at the whim of an editor, Rosen feels that schools and publishers are now making it difficult for him to reach his young public, and he fears he may now end up writing for one adult: himself.[17]

Authors generally choose their publisher according to the nature of their project, although that is becoming increasingly complex with the blurring of borders between genres and audiences. Denis Côté set out to write for adults so, in 1983, he submitted his first manuscript to Hurtubise-HMH, a Quebec publisher chiefly known for adult literature. The publisher felt, however, that *Les parallèles célestes* (The celestial parallels) would fit well in a series for adolescents. Although it was published in 1983 as a children's book, the following year it won two literary awards that are not reserved for children's fiction, the Grand Prix de la science-fiction et du fantastique québécois (Quebec science fiction and fantasy award) and the Prix Boréal (Boreal Prize). As in the case of Rosen and so many others, this initial editorial decision determined the writer's future path and Côté is now a successful children's author. His only publications for adults have been a few short stories in journals or collective volumes. Although

Côté does not regret becoming a children's author, he told me in an e-mail message on November 24, 2000, that he often dreams of writing a novel for adults, but says taking time out to do so is too great a risk since he makes his living from his writing.

Until very recently, writers classified at the outset of their career as "children's authors" frequently remained confined to the field of children's literature, even though their texts had a rather ambivalent status. In the 1970s, the first book by Tormod Haugen was published in Norway for children, but a number of critics remain puzzled as to why the sophisticated writer was launched as a children's author. Unlike Côté's later works, which are indisputably targeted at young readers, Haugen's books continued to be quite complex and to appeal to a crossover audience. The well-known Norwegian publishing house Gyldendal Norsk Forlag, who puts out Haugen's books, recognizes that the author's works offer a good example of border literature, but told me in a letter dated May 8, 2000, that none of his books has ever been published for adults in any country. In actual fact, *Romanen om Merkel Hanssen og Donna Winter og den store flukten* (The story of Merkel Hanssen and Donna Winter and the great escape) first appeared, in 1986, as the book of the month of Bokklubben Nye Boker, the largest book club for adult fiction in Norway. The publisher's Book Club Magazine presented Haugen's novel as "allalderslitteratur," the newly coined Norwegian term for literature for all ages. One reviewer considered the publication of the novel on Bokklubben Nye Boker as "a happy step toward literary equality for youth publishing."[18] Two years earlier, Anne Born had stated that the novel *Vinterstedet* (The winter residence, 1984) was addressed to readers of all ages, even though it had been published for a juvenile audience.[19] Whereas certain literary critics claimed that Haugen had established a reputation as a writer for adults with *Romanen om Merkel Hanssen og Donna Winter*, the majority of readers and critics considered it uniquely as young adult fiction, since the market had definitively catalogued Haugen as a children's author. In 1987, the novel was awarded the Pier Paolo Vergerio European Prize for Children's Literature. A few critics once again questioned the status of the complex, postmodern novel *Skriket fra jungelen* (The cry from the jungle), which was published for a juvenile audience in 1989. In the succeeding years, Haugen continued to write long, complicated fantasy novels, more or less in the tradition of *Skriket fra jungelen*. Books such as *Tsarens juveler* (The tsar's jewels, 1992) and *I lyset fra fullmånen* (In the light of the full moon, 2001) are read chiefly by adults, apparently finding few readers among children and adolescents, even though they are published for young readers.

Bart Moeyaert, who is considered one of the most important and popular contemporary Flemish writers—in the Netherlands as well as in his native Belgium—finds himself in a somewhat similar position to Haugen. The three-time nominee for the Hans Christian Andersen Award is generally seen as a children's author, but he has constantly fought against such classifications, insisting that literature must rid itself of labels like "children's book," "adolescent novel," or "adult book." The affinity between the two highly successful young adult/crossover authors is illustrated by the fact that Moeyaert's popular novel *Kus me* (Kiss me, 1991)—adapted into a play and a short television film—was translated into Norwegian by Haugen in 1994. Almost all of Moeyaert's books are published by the Dutch publishing house Querido, which plays a very important role in the crossover phenomenon in Dutch-speaking countries.

Although Moeyaert's first two books were primarily hailed by the children's literary world, his third work caught the attention of literary critics in general. Since that time, all his books have been major literary events and the author has enjoyed unceasing interest from the media. His books, which have become increasingly unconventional over the years, are extremely difficult to label. The novel *Suzanne Dantine*, in which Moeyaert blends the first seven years in the life of the protagonist with one day seven years later, was published in 1989 to much acclaim. After a revised edition appeared under the more evocative title *Wespennest (Hornet's Nest)* in 1997, it was published in English, in 2000, by Front Street, an American publisher whose goal is "to expose young readers to the best literature in other countries, cultures, and languages." Front Street had already published an English edition of *Blote handen* (1995), *Bare Hands*, the first of Moeyaert's novels to appear in English in 1998. It is a gripping story of revenge, narrated in the first person, in which a boys' prank has tragic consequences. One of Moeyaert's most talked about novels is *Het is de liefde die we niet begrijpen* (1999), which was translated quite literally into English, in 2001, as *It's Love We Don't Understand*. Through the eyes of a fifteen-year-old girl, readers witness the intimate life of a very dysfunctional family. The novel is structured around three simple scenes, each depicting an aspect of what we call "love." *It's Love We Don't Understand* was marketed by Moeyaert's publisher for both children and adults.

In recent years, publishers seem to be much more flexible when it comes to the initial positioning of a book. However, it is still quite common for authors to disagree with the manner in which their publishers categorize and/or market their books. *Future Eden: A Brief History of Next Time* (1999), by the British author Colin Thompson, is a case in point. The imaginative, satirical science fiction novel is a pioneering work in the developing field of the Internet novel, notably those that are published online prior to publication in conventional book format as a trade paperback. It was Thompson's intention from the outset to publish *Future Eden* on the Internet, and he began designing the website at the same time he started writing the story. According to the author, "the subject matter of *Future Eden*, the world in the 23rd century, . . . made publishing it on the Internet, the major communications system of the future, seem like a logical thing to do." The first draft of the novel was published on the Internet in daily episodes, beginning in January 1999. An online novel posted in daily episodes brings the tradition of serialized novels into the technological age. Writing a book online represents a great deal of extra work and poses new challenges for the author because the reader follows the creative process on a daily basis. Thompson kept getting new ideas as the work progressed. When the story was well advanced, the author came up with a new character he liked so much that he was introduced much earlier when the story was rewritten. The challenges of this new media explain the surprisingly few successful crossover novels published online to date. The sequel to *Future Eden, Space: The Final Effrontery*, did not appear online before it was released in print in 2005.

As an online novel, no target audience was specified for *Future Eden*. For the most part, Thompson's readers are science fiction and fantasy fans of all ages, and notably those who seek their entertainment on the Internet. This audience is not limited to older children and young adults, but includes many adults, especially in their twenties and thirties. The genre blending of *Future Eden* appealed to a wide audience of all ages. Thompson admits there is a strong fantasy element in his science fiction novel. Denying that he put Merlin and Camelot into the story "to attract readers who are into all that legend stuff," he claims, on Amazon.co.uk, to have "felt deeply that it was time that all the false myths about the whole King Arthur thing were laid to rest and that Merlin and his lot were shown up for the extraterrestrial aliens that they really are." Thompson prefers to think of the Internet version "as a first draft," since the "finished book," which was published by Simon & Schuster in 1999, was "completely edited and re-written twice." The author insists that *Future Eden* was written for adults, the same audience as Douglas Adams's *Hitchhiker's Guide to the Galaxy*. Thompson told me in an e-mail message on June 14, 2007, that he was very upset when Simon & Schuster put the novel on their children's list, because, according to him, that "meant almost no adults read it." Despite the contrary evidence of current reading trends, Thompson believes that "kids will read adult books, but seldom vice versa." *Future Eden* is now out of print in English, but the entire book can be downloaded free of charge from Thompson's website. Although the author had initially wanted to do five books in the series, his publisher's handling of the first book caused him to lose interest in the series, and he has since moved on to other projects, notably his zany series *The Floods*, about a family of very unusual wizards and witches.

It is undoubtedly true, as many children's authors claim, that well-established mainstream authors are often able to get their books published even when they ignore the norms and codes of the publishing world. That seems to have been the case for Neil Gaiman's *Coraline*. However, even eminent adult authors often disagree with their publishers concerning the target audience of a particular manuscript. Since Michel Tournier now measures the success of all of his books according to their reception by a twelve-year-old child, he and his publisher do not always see eye to eye on the subject of audience. An excellent example is *Eleazar, Exodus to the West*, which was supposedly first written for children, but ultimately appeared in Gallimard's Collection blanche for adults with a dedication to a twelve-year-old girl who represents the ideal reader in the author's eyes. Although an author may strive for a readership that includes both young people and adults, it is often the publisher who ultimately determines his or her readership.

Capitalizing on Bestselling Authors

The large number of well-known adult authors who have written texts that address a crossover audience is due, to a large extent, to publishing houses who capitalize on their stable of bestselling authors, encouraging them to write for children or marketing their adult fiction for a young audience. It is very often at the publisher's initiative that texts written for adults subsequently appear for children, having undergone only paratextual changes.

The post-war economic boom marked a period of significant changes in the marketing of books, as children's books became an increasingly separate sphere from adult books. Paradoxically, however, the borders between the two were being blurred by some of these very same children's publishers. The widespread phenomenon of crosswriting child and adult in France can be traced back to the end of World War II, when prestigious publishing houses finally began to take a serious interest in young readers. Gallimard's reasons for launching La Bibliothèque blanche series in 1953 provide an indication of the status of both the children's author and the child reader in 1950s France. The creation of the series stemmed from the belief that "a great number of writers, and some of the most renowned, have often had the spontaneous urge to write for young readers." The series had a laudable "crossover" goal, that of providing children with a library that would parallel their parents', a library composed of works of "indisputable literary value" that would not be abandoned as the child grew up, but would withstand the test of time and continue to find a place on the adult's library shelves.[20]

Gallimard deliberately chose not to turn to "specialists of children's literature" (they were quick to add that they did not wish to imply that there were not some "excellent" ones), but rather to call upon "writers 'for grown-ups,'" "authors of serious books."[21] The "renowned" authors approached by Gallimard for the new children's collection naturally included writers who had won prestigious literary prizes for their adult fiction. One of the first three authors to appear in the important series was Henri Bosco, who had received the Prix Théophraste Renaudot for *Le Mas Théotime* (*The Farm Theotime*) in 1945, the very year in which he also published *The Boy and the River*. In the 1950s, four sequels to *The Boy and the River* were published in the children's series, as well as an earlier novel, *L'Âne Culotte* (The donkey Culotte, 1937). These "books for children," some of which had already been published for adults, offered very few concessions to the young reader. They had more or less the same format as the novels in Gallimard's prestigious Collection blanche for adults, apparently all the better to find their place in the library of the child become adult. The text contained no illustrations other than the small vignette on the cover. In seeking to justify the presentation of the series by claiming that its purpose was to instil in the child the habit of the effort required of the "*true* reader," that of "seeing and imagining for himself what he is reading," Lemarchand further illustrates the lack of status attributed to the child reader in the 1950s.[22]

The terms used by Gallimard, a decade later, to describe the goal of the newly dressed Bibliothèque blanche series, in which Bosco's *The Boy and the River* was reissued in 1966, indicates that the status accorded both children's authors and children's books by publishing houses such as Gallimard remained extremely low. The books are meant to offer young readers "texts written by *real* writers," so that they "acquire from the outset a taste for *good* literature."[23] This attitude is echoed by journalists and critics writing in the late 1960s and early 1970s. A journalist interviewing Michel Tournier in 1971 concludes that if children's literature exists, it is made up of the texts dedicated to children by a few rare authors like Bosco and Tournier.[24] In the minds of many such critics, as for C. S. Lewis, the only *true* children's literature was crossover literature.

Like many other publishing houses in the West, Gallimard did not officially create a children's department until the 1970s. Similarly, Beltz & Gelberg was established in 1971 as the children's book division of the prestigious German publisher Beltz Verlag. Like Gallimard Jeunesse, many of their titles are by authors who also write for adults, including Klaus Kordon and Christine Nöstlinger. In the case of Gallimard, a certain number of titles and series for children had been published regularly since the 1930s, but no formal structure had existed to develop this area before 1972. In a history of children's literature published in 1993, Gallimard recognized the absolute necessity of this internal reorganization, as "the rules of children's literature are totally different from those of general literature."[25] Yet the children's division of Gallimard would continue to publish many works by well-known adult authors. When Gallimard Jeunesse launched the popular 1000 Soleils series at the end of 1972, two of the first publications were Bosco's *The Boy and the River* and Ernest Hemingway's *The Old Man and the Sea*. It was often at the initiative of Pierre Marchand, founder of Gallimard Jeunesse, that many important French authors gained, almost in spite of themselves, a readership of children and young adults. J. M. G. Le Clézio admits that he became a "children's author" by the intermediary of Marchand, who suggested that certain stories from *Mondo* be published in a paperback edition for young readers. As we saw in chapter one, collections of short fiction for adults often provide publishers with material that is easily repackaged for children. The majority of Le Clézio's and Tournier's "children's books" are taken from short story collections for adults that were published in the years following Gallimard's creation of their children's department. Unlike Le Clézio, Tournier tends to downplay Gallimard's role in the recycling of his fiction for multiple audiences. Although he has undoubtedly taken a much more active role in this process than Le Clézio, Gallimard have nonetheless been instrumental in making Tournier's texts accessible to a crossover audience, often in a variety of formats. On one occasion, Tournier stated that he thought the editor was absolutely right to publish *Barbedor* in its different children's series, indicating that Gallimard's role in addressing his texts to different readerships is, in fact, greater than the author generally cares to admit.[26]

Gallimard are certainly not unique in encouraging bestselling adult authors to write for children and, in the process, creating crossover authors. Italo Calvino's *Il barone rampante* (*The Baron in the Trees*), the second novel of Calvino's trilogy I nostri antenati (Our Ancestors) is often directed at children and young adults. Published in 1957, it appeared two years later in an illustrated edition and then, in 1965, as an annotated school edition. The novel is a very self-reflexive text with a great deal of intertextual play that young readers will not recognize or appreciate fully.[27] In 1966, the important German publisher Gertraud Middelhauve published a collection of stories entitled *Dichter erzählen Kindern* (Writers tell stories to children). The German word *Dichter* is used to refer only to writers for adults and does not include children's authors. The collection, which was widely read by adults, contains stories for children written by thirty-six well-known German-language writers, including Heinrich Böll and Peter Bichsel. The Swiss author Peter Bichsel, who won the prestigious Gruppe 47 prize in 1965, contributed the story "Ein Tisch ist ein Tisch" (A table is a table) to the collection. In 1969, the story was published in his own collection, *Kindergeschichten* (Children's stories), which won literary prizes in the adult sector. In 1995, a picturebook edition, with sophisticated graphics by Angela von Roehl, was published in Germany. According to the publisher's insert, the picturebook was intended "for children, young people, and adults." The story of a lonely, bored old man who invents his own language might seem little apt to appeal to children, but it has been popular with young and old alike. The success of the stories in Middelhauve's collection encouraged some of the authors to continue writing for children. In 1972, Middelhauve edited a second collection, *Dichter Europas erzählen Kindern* (European writers tell stories to children), which contains forty-six stories by writers from seventeen European countries.

There are many examples of the influential role that publishers have played in the crossover of authors in other countries as well. It was Herman Schein of Parnassus Press who convinced Ursula Le Guin to write something for young adult readers. The result was *A Wizard of Earthsea*, published in 1968.[28] In the 1980s, the intervention of two publishers eventually resulted in a crossover work for Joy Kogawa. When the author's Canadian editor asked her to rewrite *Obasan* for children, the resulting work, *Naomi's Road*, ultimately led to the Japanese version, *Naomi no michi*, which is read by adults as well as children in Japan. This crossover version owes its existence to the Japanese editor, who did not want a mere translation and kept requesting additional changes.

In the late 1990s, publishers began encouraging adult authors to write for a young audience with an eye to the new crossover trend. Hyperion/Disney's vice-president and associate publisher, Ken Geist, confessed, in 1997, that "for some crossover titles, he tries to place an adult author's work in a children's book format or encourages an adult author to write a book for kids." In subsequent years, adult authors have required little encouragement from publishers to write for children, as we saw in the previous chapter. The recent trend of adult authors turning their hand to children's and young adult novels, a trend that is particularly striking at present in the United States, has some industry insiders worried that well-known newcomers may edge out true children's authors. "Young-Adult Books Are No Longer Child's Play for Bestselling Authors" is the title of an article in the *Boston Globe* that cites a few of the "respected" authors suddenly putting out "kiddie novels" in 2002. American children's book publishers are signing up authors like Pulitzer Prize-winner Michael Chabon, *New York Times* bestseller Neil Gaiman, and other notable authors such as Julia Alvarez and Carl Hiaasen. Lois Lowry, two-time winner of the Newbery Medal, is sceptical about how successful most adult authors will be writing for kids, but she fears that even the bad books will be published because of "the reputation of the writers."[29] The big names from the adult publishing world are producing far larger numbers than the majority of young adult authors could ever hope to achieve. Chabon's *Summerland*, for example, had a first printing of 250,000, whereas an average children's novel in the United States has a first print run of ten to twelve thousand. It is no mystery why so many publishers are jumping on the bandwagon and signing up authors "who can straddle the literary divide." The bottom line clearly explains this trend. In a quote in the *Boston Globe* article, Roger Sutton, editor of *The Horn Book Magazine*, describes the dilemma facing today's publishers who are "looking for big money." When given the choice of a Richard Peck or a John Updike, he says that it no longer matters that the former is a better writer for young people. Writers and editors in the children's publishing industry suspect that children do not even know who these big-name authors are, but that seems to be of little importance. Parents and booksellers know, points out Nancy Siscoe, executive editor of Knopf and Crown Books for Young Readers. She worked with Carl Hiaasen on *Hoot*, which was already in its third printing a week before its publication date. In the past, many adult authors found a young audience without any help from a publisher. Now it seems that, as the author of the *Boston Globe* article puts it, "the search is on for modern-day equivalents to *The Catcher in the Rye, A Tree Grows in Brooklyn,* and *To Kill a Mockingbird*."[30]

Children's editions of adult fiction can be published at the initiative of the author, an illustrator, an editor, or even a translator. Most often, however, it is a publisher who is responsible for the decision that targets adult fiction at children or young adults, turning it into crossover fiction. It may be the children's division of the author's own publisher, as is generally the case with Gallimard's stable of authors, or it may be another children's publisher, as in the case of many of the authors published in Middelhauve's collections.

Although not as common, the opposite phenomenon also exists. Publishers have encouraged their best-known children's authors to write for adults. Dominique Demers is a children's author who has successfully crossed over from children's and young adult books to adult novels. She was urged to try writing for adults by her publisher, Québec/Amérique. Her first novel written expressly for adults, *Le Pari* (The bet), published in Quebec in 1999, was an unqualified success. Although she continues to publish books for children and adolescents with Québec/Amérique, her second adult novel, *Là où la mer commence* (There where the sea begins), inspired by *Beauty and the Beast*, came out with the French publisher Robert Laffont. Demers is considered more of an adult novelist in France because her popular young adult trilogy was published there in a single volume for adults. When journalists interviewed Demers about her first adult novel, they constantly asked her what was the biggest difference between writing for children and writing for adults, but they rarely reported her answer, that is, that "writing for children is much more difficult." The author attributes this to the fact that they did not believe her. Confronted with the success of Demers's bestseller for adults, "some critics were surprised that a children's author managed to appeal to so many adults."[31] This was the reaction of many critics and journalists to the Harry Potter books and so many other child-to-adult crossover works. Now that children's literature and children's authors are getting such a high profile, we are likely to see an increasing number of children's authors being encouraged by their publishers and agents to try their hand at writing for adults.

Crossovers Across Borders

Books published for a particular audience in one context sometimes appear for a different audience in another context, for example, in different time periods or cultures. In some instances, the dual addressee of the original is lost when the work is translated into another language.[32] Novels targeted at adults in one country have sometimes been marketed for a juvenile audience in another. An early example is *Tom Sawyer*, which became a children's book when it was translated into Dutch. William Golding's *Lord of the Flies* was not meant for children, but it was published in France in a series for young readers. The Swedish author Inger Edelfeldt wrote a novel for adults about teenagers, entitled *Brev till nattens drottning* (Letters to the queen of night), but when it was translated into German, it was published as a young adult novel and won the Deutscher Jugendliteraturpreis in the juvenile fiction category in 1987, even though one German critic warned readers that the book was far beyond young people and unsuitable reading material for them. The first novel in Peter Pohl's Rainbow series was published in Sweden as an adult novel in 1986, but it was generally released in other countries as a juvenile novel, as was the case, for example, with the Dutch translation published in 1995. Likewise, Sue Townsend's *The Secret Diary of Adrian Mole, Aged 13½* was published as a young adult novel in the Netherlands. Jostein Gaarder's *Maya* was published as a novel for adults in Norway and in most other countries, but in Germany it was presented on the list of books for juveniles. More recently, *The Book Thief,* by the Australian author Markus Zusak, was published to wide acclaim in Australia, where it was positioned as his adult debut. However, in the United States, Random House chose to publish it as a young adult novel.

The reverse phenomenon of young adult novels being marketed for adults when they are translated into another language is much more common. A notable example is Richard Adams's *Watership Down*, which was published in England in 1972 as a children's book, but appeared in Sweden in 1975 as a novel for adults. In the 1990s, this phenomenon began to attract attention when a number of international bestsellers that had appeared for a juvenile audience at home were published for adults in one or more countries abroad. Jostein Gaarder's bestseller *Sophie's World*, published in 1991, is an excellent recent example of this type of crossover. It was published in Norway—and subsequently in most European countries—as a book for young adults, as the author intended it to be. In France, it was released in an adult edition in 1995 by Seuil, who nonetheless marketed it that year at the Seuil Jeunesse stall at the French children's book fair in Montreuil. The crowd that lined up waiting for the author to sign their copy of the very adult-looking book was composed almost entirely of adults. Furthermore, it was later reissued, as were several of his other novels, in Seuil's Points series, which is intended for adults but has nonetheless published a number of children's books with great success. When *Sophie's World* crossed the Atlantic, it was marketed in the United States as a novel for adults. One wonders if it was the subject of philosophy or the length of the 523-page novel that the American publisher considered unsuitable for young readers. In a number of European countries, for example England and Germany, *Sophie's World* appeared for both children and adults, and remained number one on the bestseller lists there for many months. However, it did not enjoy the same success in North America, where it was never published in a children's edition.

Four years after *Sophie's World*, in 1995, Pullman's *Northern Lights* was published for young people in Britain, but in Sweden it came out as a novel for adults. The first novel in *His Dark Materials* appeared as a children's book in Britain because Scholastic UK publishes uniquely for children. The trilogy continued to be published there exclusively as children's books for children twelve and over, although the marketing strategy changed somewhat with the second novel when they realized that the books were also attracting an adult audience. In contrast, Pullman's American publisher, Knopf, was able to easily sell in both sectors as they have a very large adult division in addition to the children's division that brought out the novel. Knopf had just undergone major restructuring about the time they acquired Pullman's *The Golden Compass*, which became the object of one of the most successful young adult promotion campaigns to date. Pullman attributes the advance of $150,000 he received for the trilogy, a much larger amount than for previous books, to the fact that they already felt it could be marketed differently. According to Kerry McManus, marketing manager of Knopf and Crown Books for Young Readers, the editors involved thought, from the outset, that the novel had "a significant appeal to the adult market," and this belief spawned "all subsequent marketing efforts . . . , therefore creating the entire *Golden Compass* 'crossover' campaign." The result was that many stores sold *The Golden Compass* "as a book, not a kids' book."[33] The paperback rights to the entire trilogy were sold to Del Rey, so that *His Dark Materials* followed a path already blazed by Brian Jacques's Redwall fantasy series, which was also published in paperback by an adult house, Berkley Books.

Pullman's crossover success in the United States was due to the same publisher that Tournier blames for the failure of the American edition of *Friday and Robinson* twenty-five years earlier, but in the interim, Knopf had established their children's division, Knopf Books for Young Readers. Although Pullman was very glad that *Northern Lights* could be marketed to a dual readership in some countries, including Denmark and Germany, he told me in an e-mail message on May 5, 2000 that it was not due to any decision on his part. He rightly points out that a book's audience can be determined by very small things, citing the example of publishers' sales representatives. If they have only sold children's books, as was the case for Scholastic's sales representatives in Britain, they know all the children's bookshops and the children's buyers in general bookshops, but they do not necessarily know the people who look after adult fiction. Generally content has much less to do with where a book is shelved in bookstores than the imprint or division, adult or children's, that happens to publish it.

Whereas Isabel Allende's *City of the Beasts* was published for young readers in Spain and the United States, in Germany it was one of the rare books to appear in that country in two editions, one for young readers and one for adults, each with a different cover. The adult edition was published by the prestigious publishing house Suhrkamp in 2002 and the children's edition appeared with Hanser the following year. Like the Harry Potter books in Britain, the adult paperback of *City of the Beasts* is more expensive than the children's paperback.

Yet another example of this kind of recontextualization is the publication in a crossover edition of a book originally published for children or for adults. That is the case for many books reissued in Siruela's Las Tres Edades series that will be examined in the next section. On the other hand, some novels released deliberately for a crossover audience are published in other countries for a specific audience, most often for children. Carmen Martín Gaite's *Caperucita en Manhattan* (Little Red Riding Hood in Manhattan) was published in Spain in 1990 for readers of all ages. The Spanish edition is presented more like a novel for adults, with a large format and a rather sober cover design depicting Norman Rockwell's *Statue of Liberty*. Furthermore, the novel was later released in Siruela's adult paperback series, with an even more subtle cover, on which the familiar Rockwell rendition of the Statue of Liberty was replaced by a much darker silhouette. In other countries, however, most editions were targeted uniquely at a juvenile audience and made no attempt to attract adult readers.

In France, the choice of the series eliminated the possibility of a crossover audience, since the novel appeared in Flammarion's children's paperback series, Castor Poche, as a novel for readers aged eleven to twelve. The presentation of the French edition makes it clear that the novel is intended only for a young audience. The book has a much smaller format than the Spanish edition, and the cover illustration by Zaü is more colourful and draws its inspiration from caricature and comics. In light of the obvious desire to appeal to a young audience, it is rather paradoxical that the French edition eliminated the author's thirteen naive, black-and-white drawings, which are done in a style that resembles children's drawings. In Germany, Martín Gaite's novel was brought out, in 1994, by Suhrkamp in a new series for young readers, so it was initially received almost exclusively as a children's book. However, the novel appeared in Suhrkamp's paperback series for adults in 1998, this time with a very sober, grey cover illustration of the Statue of Liberty that contrasts with the brightly coloured and fanciful illustration of a car and a pink cake flying through the air above the statue on the children's edition. In Germany, Martín Gaite's fairy-tale novel was thus returned to its intended crossover audience, but in two separate editions.

It is not just in the crossing of geographical or cultural borders that the audience of a book can change. In some cases, a book published for children in one time period is released for adults in another, or vice versa. The shift of fantasy and science fiction into the mainstream toward the end of the twentieth century, largely thanks to Rowling and Pullman, has led to the reissuing of earlier young adult fiction in editions for adults. A rather striking example, which appeared in the millennial year, is a trilogy by the American science fiction author Sylvia Engdahl. Her trilogy, *This Star Shall Abide* (1972), *Beyond the Tomorrow Mountains* (1973), and *The Doors of the Universe* (1981), published in the 1970s and early 1980s as young adult books, were reissued in one volume, in the year 2000, as adult science fiction, under the title *Children of the Star*.

Some crossover books do not manage to cross borders at all, either as children's books or adult books. Crossover authors are more likely to encounter censorship problems than those who write only for a specific audience. This is especially true in the case of texts initially addressed to an adult readership and later published for children. Many authors and illustrators have had negative experiences with foreign publishers and markets. This applies particularly to certain continental European authors who attempt to break into the British and North American markets. None of J. M. G. Le Clézio's or Marguerite Yourcenar's "children's books" have been published in either Britain or the United States. One can imagine that Georges Lemoine's illustrations of nude women in Le Clézio's *Pawana* or Yourcenar's *Notre-Dame-des-Hirondelles*, for example, might encounter some disapproval on the part of more conservative publishers, critics, and readers in the English-speaking world, as they regularly do with students in my university classes. Agreeing with the critic who tells him that he writes "children's books which should not be put into all hands," Michel Tournier adds sarcastically: "Not to be put into the hands of all adults." The French novelist has often bitterly denounced the conservative children's editors, booksellers, and reviewers, whose censorship prevents many of his texts from reaching a wide juvenile audience. He is particularly critical of the United States, where, at least in the 1980s, he felt the world of children's books was dominated by what he called "the Walt Disney factory."[34]

Tournier's *Friday and Robinson* offers an interesting case in point. It has sold millions of copies in France and has been translated into many languages, including Estonian and Iraqi. "Sadam Hussein considered that the Iraqi children could no longer do without my *Vendredi*," joked the author in 1993.[35] However, the bestselling novel has met with a complete lack of success in the United States, where the very modest two thousand copies printed did not even sell. Although Tournier blames the novel's failure, in part, on the fact that it was published by Knopf rather than by a children's publisher, he acknowledges that the main reason for the lack of success of many of his crossover books in other countries is his refusal to avoid the subjects considered taboo in children's literature: money, politics, cruelty, and sex. Tournier has expressed his regret that he cannot even find a publisher abroad for his children's tale *Pierrot*, which he calls "a hymn to physical contact" and "a lesson in love."[36] The erotic suggestiveness of the ending of *Pierrot* shocked even adult readers in France. When Harlequin arrives at Pierrot's bakery, creating a kind of *ménage à trois*, the former rivals watch with fascination as Columbine greedily separates the breasts of her life-size brioche effigy and avidly plunges her nose and her tongue into "the mellow gold of the cleavage," before inviting them to join her in a kind of sensual Communion: "Taste, eat the good Columbine. Eat me" (32). The French novelist's view of children's literature is problematic for some foreign publishers not only because he believes that children's books should be "eroticised," but because he insists that an author should not hesitate to introduce extreme cruelty when necessary. The author considers "Tupick"—the story of a boy who castrates himself to escape the gender roles imposed by adults—his cruellest story, and yet he says that it was intended to be a tale for children.[37]

These problems are not, however, limited to authors who publish for a juvenile audience books written initially for an adult audience, but also affect authors like Dominique Demers, whose books follow the opposite path. In spite of the impressive number of prizes won by *Un hiver de tourmente* and the sequels, the Marie-Lune trilogy was never translated into English. It is more than likely that this is due to the sexuality in the novels. Even in Quebec they have been the object of repeated complaints by parents on school committees because the fourteen-year-old heroine makes love for the first time and becomes pregnant. *Maïna* has never found its way into English either, and, like the trilogy, it caused problems for the author in her native Quebec. A number of parents who had read the novel in the adult edition decided that it was not at all suitable for young readers. *Maïna* was withdrawn from libraries in one of the largest school boards in Quebec because it contains a scene in which the protagonist is the victim of an attempted rape and another in which cannibalism is practised. The author points out how ridiculous it is to apply concepts of rape and cannibalism to a story that takes place 3,500 years ago.[38]

The phenomenon of challenged books is not limited to the North American market, however. After the publication of *The Neverending Story*, Michael Ende came under attack from the extreme religious right, in much the same manner as J. K. Rowling and Philip Pullman in more recent years. While many challenged books—like those of Ende, Rowling, and Pullman—still manage to reach a crossover audience across geographical and cultural borders, some remain confined within a nation, a territory, or a single-language area. Books that cross age boundaries in one country do not necessarily do so when they cross geographical borders. And some crossover books never manage to cross cultural borders for any audience.

The Creation of Crossover Series and Imprints

An interesting publishing phenomenon of the 1990s, which pre-dates the publication of the first Harry Potter book, was the creation of series that openly and explicitly display the intent to address readers of all ages. This trend was in stark contrast to the contradictory tendency that dominated children's literature at the time, that is, the fragmentation of young readers into ever more specific age categories. This increasingly precise labelling of the target audience still exists in much of the children's publishing industry. In Sweden, the practice of putting age categories on books was largely abandoned for a time, but it is now returning. In most Western countries, publishers provide children's authors with ever more detailed criteria pertaining to number of pages, vocabulary, themes, narrative techniques, and so forth. Many authors, like Demers, feel that these categorizations are extremely arbitrary. In the publishing world and the marketplace, two contradictory trends thus currently co-exist: on the one hand, there is an ever more precise definition of readerships, while, on the other, there is the explicit recognition of a crossover audience that includes both children and adults.

In 1990, the major Spanish publishing house Siruela launched what is perhaps the most ambitious and significant series devoted to border literature. Las Tres Edades (The three ages) series for readers "from eight to eighty-eight" was created in the belief that "no clear boundary exists between titles for children and adults." The publisher's claim that it was "the first series for all ages" is certainly true for Spain, but it may even be true on a global scale. Michi Strausfeld, who had a major impact on children's literature in Spain in her position as director of Alfaguara's important children's collection, became director of Siruela's new series. Unlike Britain, Sweden, Italy, or even France, where there was a more open-minded attitude toward children's literature, in

Spain it was impossible, until well into the 1980s, to solicit a text for children from an eminent author for adults. Feeling that his or her merit as a writer was not being taken seriously, an author would have considered such a proposition as an insult. For that reason, Alfaguara published international children's literature, but the absence of Spanish authors was conspicuous. Over the years, Strausfeld set about, patiently but insistently, to convince authors that writing children's texts did not diminish their literary talent and that it was a common practice in Anglo-Saxon countries, where internationally renowned authors for adults also wrote for children.[39]

One of the first Spanish authors to take the leap was Juan José Millás, who successfully crossed over with *Papel mojado* (Wet paper) in 1983. Another well-known Spanish novelist who took up the challenge was José María Merino, who had gained widespread recognition in 1976 with his award-winning debut adult novel *Novela de Andrés Choz* (Novel about Andrés Choz). In the 1980s, he wrote a trilogy, *Crónica de las aventuras verdaderas de Miguel Villacé Yolotl* (Chronicle of the true adventures of Miguel Villacé Yolotl), which tells the story of the conquest of the Americas through the eyes of a fifteen-year-old boy, the son of one of Cortes's men and an Indian woman. Merino offers an interesting example of an adult author who creates a crossover work when he turns to writing juvenile fiction. When the three novels—*El oro de los sueños* (The gold of dreams, 1986), *La tierra del tiempo perdido* (The land of lost time, 1987), and *Las lágrimas del sol* (The tears of the sun, 1989)—were published together in a single volume in 1992, under the title *Las crónicas mestizas* (The mestiza chronicles), it was marketed for readers of all ages ("toda clase de lectores"). Although the works of both Millás and Merino were published for children by Alfaguara (while Strausfeld was director), the content is fairly adult. In Spain, this was a period of tremendous change in the field of children's literature, just as it was in other aspects of culture and in society in general. By the mid-1980s, many Spanish authors for adults began considering writing for children as well. This was partly due to the fact that they began to realize, thanks to international examples like Roald Dahl in Britain and Michael Ende in Germany, that children's literature could be both literary and lucrative.

Siruela's Las Tres Edades series was created with the idea that "only good and bad literature exists," that age boundaries are very artificial, and that certain texts are suitable for everyone. This made it easier to approach writers, since the director of the new series was not asking them to write for children, but "to write for all ages." At the same time, Strausfeld warned them that, in her mind, this task was more challenging. Siruela was very anxious to launch the series with a Spanish writer. In the end, two of the first four titles to appear were by Spanish authors, only one of which had previously written for children.[40] The goal of the new series, that of convincing readers that "good literature knows no age," is curiously similar to that formulated by Gallimard forty years earlier when they created the Bibliothèque blanche children's series.[41] Like Gallimard, Siruela did not turn immediately to specialists of children's literature, but rather to authors who wrote chiefly for adults. Just as the French publishing house had chosen a novel by the winner of a prestigious literary award for adult fiction (Bosco's *The Boy and the River*) as one of its first titles, Siruela selected *Caperucita en Manhattan* by Carmen Martín Gaite, the first woman to win Spain's prestigious Premio Nacional de Literatura—for her novel *El cuarto de atrás* (*The Back Room*)—in 1978. Shortly before Martín Gaite mentioned her recently completed manuscript to Siruela's director, another prize-winning novelist, Alejandro Gándara, had offered them the novel *El final del cielo* (The end of the sky), which is a modern epic that recounts the adventures of two children following an airplane crash. Gándara's novel became the first book and Martín Gaite's the third in Las Tres Edades series when it was launched in 1990.

Caperucita en Manhattan, a retelling of the story of Little Red Riding Hood in novel form, with thirteen illustrations by Martín Gaite, is one of the most successful books published in Las Tres Edades. Strausfeld feels that this novel illustrates, better than any other title, the series' goal, that is, "to interest readers of all ages" and "to permit Literature to be free" of rigid, arbitrary age categories.[42] Much of the novel's crossover appeal is explained by the fact that the framework of the familiar fairy tale is used to tell an initiatory story about the passage from childhood to adulthood. Although Martín Gaite had already published two books for a young audience, *El castillo de las tres murallas* (The three-walled castle, 1981) and *El pastel del diablo* (The devil's cake, 1985), she never had the intention of writing children's books. Like Tournier and so many other *grantécrivains* who have been published with equal success for adults and children, Martín Gaite resists attempts to draw a distinct boundary between the two readerships. She points out that *Cuentos completos* (Complete tales), a collection of short stories for adults, appeals to twelve-year-old children, while, conversely, her "children's book" *El castillo de las tres murallas*, is appreciated by an adult readership and considered by certain critics as her best work. In the early 1990s, the author expressed her regret that the prejudices against children's literature in Spain prevented "an excellent novel" from being considered as anything but a minor work by a major novelist asked to write for children. Martín Gaite did not want *Caperucita en Manhattan* to share the fate of the two earlier books, which she felt were destined to remain essentially children's books.[43] The aesthetic innovation, as well as the universal theme, of *Caperucita en Manhattan* attracted international attention in the publishing world. In 1993, it was the first of Martín Gaite's novels to appear in Italy, where critics expressed their surprise at the "discovery" of an author who was so renowned in her own country. They even compared her to their own Italo Calvino. The novel appeared immediately on the bestseller list of *Tuttolibri*, the literary supplement of Turin's newspaper *La Stampa*.[44] In spite of its huge success with a crossover audience in a number of countries, *Caperucita en Manhattan* has never appeared in English.

The other two titles published when Las Tres Edades was launched in 1990 were by foreign authors. They confirm the perspicacity with which Strausfeld has always chosen the titles for the crossover series. *The Hounds of the Morrigan,* the first novel by the Irish author Pat O'Shea, is a fantasy set in Ireland, in which a boy unwittingly frees an ancient evil force from an old manuscript in a bookshop, setting in motion a battle between the forces of good and evil. Published in 1985, O'Shea's inventive and humorous fantasy, which blends magic and mythology, can be seen almost as an Irish forerunner of *Harry Potter.* The other title was *Erzähler der Nacht* (translated as *Damascus Nights* in 1993), first published in 1989 by the Syrian-German author Rafik Schami. A timeless story in the tradition of the oriental tale, like its predecessor, the *Arabian Nights,* it crosses cultural as well as age boundaries. Remarkably reminiscent of Rushdie's *Haroun and the Sea of Stories,* which was not published until the following year, *Damascus Nights* is also a tale about storytelling in which the storyteller loses his ability to tell tales, in this case literally losing his voice. Like Tournier's *The Midnight Love Feast,* written the same year, Schami's novel evokes the structure of the *Arabian Nights* and celebrates the power of storytelling. When Salim the Coachman, one of the most famous *hakawatis* (storytellers) in 1950s Damascus, becomes mute, seven old friends gather for seven nights to tell seven different stories in an attempt to restore his voice. Schami is generally considered a children's author and the novel was originally published by the well-known German children's publisher Beltz & Gelberg, but *Damascus Nights* is nonetheless marketed in English-speaking countries as an adult novel. In the West, Schami has found an enthusiastic audience of young and old alike for his tales inspired by the Arabic tradition of storytelling.

In the footsteps of Gándara and Martín Gaite, other Spanish authors for adults began contributing works to Siruela's highly regarded series. The very first book that the award-winning Spanish journalist Rosa Montero wrote for children, *El nido de los sueños* (The nest of dreams), came out in the series in 1991. In 1993, José María Merino won one of Spain's most important awards for children's literature, the Premio Nacional de Literatura Infantil y Juvenil, for *No soy un libro* (I am not a book), which had appeared in the series the preceding year. The science fiction novel is actually titled *Los trenes del verano* (The trains of summer), but the words "No soy un libro," which appear on the cover in uneven typography, became the accepted title. While this book, more than any of his others, appealed to a juvenile audience, the author insists it did not include children because of the rather sophisticated play with typography that is an integral part of the story. To an interviewer who admitted that he had not read the novel because he thought it was for children, Merino points out that it was published in a series for readers "from eight to eighty-eight." He regrets that a later edition in Siruela's Colección Escolar (Scholastic series) describes the novel as "stimulating for twelve-year-olds" and contains a pedagogical study that he dislikes intensely.[45] Many of the books published in Las Tres Edades were later brought out in the Colección Escolar with pedagogical paratexts. In doing so, Siruela seems to constrain once again the literature that, according to Strausfeld, they had "freed" with the creation of Las Tres Edades.

Although Siruela initially turned to authors for adults, they were convinced that children's authors could also contribute to Las Tres Edades. In the years following the creation of the series, an increasing number of children's authors, including the Catalan writer Álvaro del Amo, were added to the catalogue. Like Martín Gaite, the well-known Spanish author and illustrator Miguel Fernández-Pacheco contributed a novel based on a classic fairy tale, entitled *Los zapatos de Murano* (The shoes from Murano). Set in twelfth-century Venice, the 129-page novel tells the story of Angélica di Fiore, who would later be immortalized as Cinderella. *Los zapatos de Murano* was accepted by Las Tres Edades a couple of weeks before it was awarded Spain's most prestigious children's literature award, the Premio Lazarillo, in 1996. Many of the authors published in Siruela's series, whether Spanish or foreign, have written for both adults and young people, although some have only written for adults. One of the earlier titles was *The Robber Bridegroom*, a novella published for adults in 1942 by the Pulitzer Prize-winning American author Eudora Welty; the charming southern fairy tale relocates the Grimms' tale to the Natchez Trace area of Mississippi at the end of the eighteenth century. The Spanish author José Antonio Millán has two titles in the series, the most recent being "a digital adventure" inspired by modern technology, *Base y el generador misterioso (una aventura digital)* (Base and the mysterious generator (a digital adventure), 2002). Other notable crosswriters who appear in the series are Karel Čapek, Peter Härtling, Russell Hoban, George MacDonald, Yuri Olesha, and Ana Rossetti, to name only a few.

A number of works in Las Tres Edades are by authors who have never written specifically for children. One such novel is *El médico de los piratas* (The pirates' doctor), by the Mexican author Carmen Boullosa. First published in Las Tres Edades in 1992, her pirate story, set in the seventeenth-century Caribbean, was released in Siruela's adult pocketbook series Bolsillo in 2002. Other works in the series are written by authors who only publish for children or young adults, including *Blueprint: Blaupause* (1999), by the German author Charlotte Kerner. This fascinating examination of the ethical and scientific issues surrounding human cloning, in which the 22-year-old protagonist reflects bitterly on her relationship with her recently deceased "mother-twin," won the Deutscher Jugendliteraturpreis. Strausfeld feels that Scandinavian children's literature is "particularly rich and particularly seductive" for readers of all ages and nationalities. She cites Tove Jansson, whose novel *The Summer Book* was published in Las Tres Edades in 1996. She also mentions the title *Hunden som sprang mot en stjärna* (The dog that ran towards a star, 1990), a novel by Henning Mankell that was intended mainly for a juvenile audience. The internationally acclaimed Swedish author, whose crime novels featuring inspector Kurt Wallander have been published in thirty-three countries and consistently top the bestseller lists in Europe, actually has several titles in the series. A number of notable contemporary crossover titles appeared in Las Tres Edades, including several of Cornelia Funke's novels. Strausfeld was especially pleased to publish

Jostein Gaarder's *Sophie's World*, as the "600-page book on philosophy" was a very audacious editorial venture for Siruela.[46] The acquisition of Michael Ende's *The Neverending Story*, which had to be published in two colours, was a similarly daring feat while Strausfeld was at Alfaguara. Although both ventures were enormous risks for small publishing companies, the two crossover novels paid off significantly. Las Tres Edades, a series intended for all ages, is now Siruela's most popular series.

A number of other publishing houses in the Hispanic world offer series with titles that glide between young adult and adult literature, including Ediciones S. M.'s Gran Angular and Anaya's Espacio Abierto in Madrid, and Sudamericana's Sudamericana Joven in Buenos Aires. This phenomenon exists in other countries as well. There are a few new series in Germany that are supposed to close the gap between youth literature and literature for adults. A number of French-Canadian publishers, such as Vent d'Ouest in Ottawa, bring out books that are also situated in what Danielle Thaler calls the "grey zone" between adolescents and adults.[47] The most interesting of these initiatives was taken, in 1996, by La courte échelle, the leading children's publisher in Quebec, who established the series 16/96 for young adults as well as not so young adults. Until that time, La courte échelle had published only children's books. In contrast with Siruela's Las Tres Edades series, the first titles in La courte échelle's 16/96 series were signed by well-known children's authors, often those whose names were already associated with the publishing house. Chrystine Brouillet and Raymond Plante, who are among La courte échelle's most popular children's authors although they have written adult fiction as well, have contributed four novels each to the series. Brouillet's titles all fall into the detective novel category: *Le collectionneur* (The collector, 1995), *C'est pour mieux t'aimer, mon enfant* (All the better to love you, my child, 1996), *Les fiancées de l'enfer* (The fiancées from hell, 1999), and *Soins intensifs* (Intensive care, 2000). Plante's novels include an unusual thriller, *Baisers voyous* (Hoodlum kisses, 2001), and a diverse selection of titles that suggest the adult nature of the subjects dealt with in the series: *Projections privées* (Private showings, 1997) is a sensual, troubling novel about a man who must deal with the death of his beloved; *La nomade* (The nomad, 1999) traces fifty years of Quebec's evolution through the life of one of its many unsung heroes; and *Novembre, la nuit* (November, at night, 2000) is the story of a young woman dying of cancer who spends her last month writing letters to all the people who have marked her life.

While both Siruela's and La courte échelle's series were established to publish crossover literature, the nature of the two series is quite different. 16/96 publishes only Quebec authors and the novels are generally targeted at an older audience. Las Tres Edades, on the other hand, seeks to include as many international authors as possible, and its titles are more suitable for younger readers as well. Many are international bestselling crossovers, for example, the novels of Jostein Gaarder and Cornelia Funke. Siruela and La courte échelle established their crossover series prior to the publication of the first Harry

Potter book. As the publishing world began to realize the potential of crossover fiction, children's publishers everywhere started promoting titles that could be considered to fall into this category. On their website, the Italian publisher Adriano Salani informs customers that "the children's novels read by persons of all ages, and that opened the crossover season" are published outside their two main series for children.

The books of many genre publishers are widely read by teenagers although they are not necessarily targeted at that audience. An excellent example is Edge Books, Canada's largest genre publisher of science fiction and fantasy. Founded in 2000, Edge Books produce thought-provoking titles that appeal as much to young readers as to adults. Some large publishing companies began to create new imprints to capitalize on this "new" market. In 2002, no less than five new imprints were launched in Britain to target mixed age readers. Time Warner established Atom, a new Teen Fiction imprint run by the team that manages their adult fantasy imprint Orbit. According to Atom's editor, Ben Sharpe, they were looking for imaginative and sophisticated works "that would suit readers who grew up with Harry Potter." He points out that "teen interests have been driving strange and peculiar genres into the mainstream."[48] Publishers are quick to pick up on these trends. Some of the first titles to be launched in the new Atom imprint were Francesca Lia Block's Dangerous Angels series. Other imprints launched in Britain in 2002 included Collins Flamingo by HarperCollins, Definitions by Random House, Signature by Hodder, and Young Picador by Pan Macmillan. Similar imprints have been appearing in other countries, as publishers attempt to cash in on crossovers. One of the premier crossover genre imprints is Firebird, launched by the Penguin Group (USA) in January 2002. The new young adult science fiction and fantasy imprint was aimed specifically at a crossover market of teenagers and adults. Most of these imprints combine reprints of classics with new titles. Firebird's ambitious catalogue includes original hardcovers as well as paperback reprints that are drawn from the Penguin Group's children's imprints as well as their adult genre imprints (Ace and Roc). Their titles have won awards for both children's and adult fiction.

The Global Commercialization of Crossovers

Globalization has brought major changes in the publishing industry and the literary marketplace over the past few decades. The influence of globalization and consumerism has been particularly striking in the field of children's literature, which has become increasingly commercialized in recent years. Since the year 2000, a number of studies have dealt with this disturbing development. In *Sticks and Stones: The Troublesome Success of Children's Literature from Slovenly Peter to Harry Potter*, published in 2001, Jack Zipes examines the commodification of children's literature and childhood experience in the United States under the influence of market forces and the culture industry. He states that the children's book industry has become more interested in creating consumer products than in nurturing high quality books.[49] While the trend may be most noticeable in the United States, the concern about the impact of commercialization on quality children's literature is globe-encircling, and Harry Potter has borne more than his share of the blame. In 2002, Andrew Blake devoted an entire book, entitled *The Irresistible Rise of Harry Potter*, to the impact of the Potter phenomenon on the development of consumer capitalism. Rowling's lawyers forced the publisher, Verso, to withdraw the book from shops and do a new dust cover, claiming it gave the misleading impression that Blake's study was endorsed by the author of *Harry Potter*. According to Blake, "capitalism is, as the truism has it, global; certainly, the much-translated Harry has repeated his Bloomsbury trick for child-consumer capitalism the world over."[50] In recent years, children's books, notably those that cross over to an adult audience, have become very big business, and it is a business that extends well beyond the book itself.

In a paper entitled "Stories as Commodities," Dan Hade laments that the book is now seen merely as the vehicle or "container" of images and ideas, and that publishers no longer sell books, but ideas and access to ideas.[51] Today's publishers have become huge corporations that seem to have learned from the Disney empire the art of commercializing culture. They are promoting characters and their worlds, the most obvious example being Harry Potter and Hogwarts. Jostein Gaarder's *Sophie's World* spawned a large range of spin-offs, including a movie, a musical, a board game, and a CD-ROM, but their success did not extend to English-language markets. The range of products inspired by bestselling books is quite remarkable: dolls, action figures, CD cases, key chains, clothing, mugs, school supplies, backpacks, lunch boxes, candies, and a multitude of other items. Toy tie-ins are huge business with bookstores as well as children's book publishers. An article in the *Los Angeles Times* in 1998 revealed that even at that time certain bookstores already devoted up to thirty per cent of their space to book-related merchandise.[52]

Like any large company referring to its products, publishers now speak of books and their characters as "brands." The most successful crossover brand has obviously been that of Harry Potter, which is now a multi-billion dollar global brand. As part of her film deal, Rowling sold the worldwide merchandising rights to U.S.-based media giant Warner Brothers, who then granted licences to rival toy maker giants Mattel and Hasbro. Large film studios like Warner Brothers rely on merchandising to recoup some of the huge costs involved in making today's feature films. The range of product spin-offs for the Harry Potter books seems endless: t-shirts, sweatshirts, ornaments, lightning bolt icicle lights, electronics, a board game, a card game, stickers, notebooks, calendars, Lego, action toys, plush toys, toothbrushes, toothpaste, Bertie Bott's Every Flavour Beans, and Nimbus 2000 broomsticks, to name only a few. The merchandising is so extensive that Rowling's five per cent has been called "the Harry Potter tax on Christmas." In July 2000, the cover of *Maclean's* magazine depicted the boy magician on a corn broom, dressed in a pinstriped suit and dumping two boxes of money. The caption read: "Harry Potter Inc.: How a Young Wizard Turns Books into Gold." After the Harry Potter brand, the next most successful is the *Lord of the Rings* brand. However, many other crossover books have spawned important brands, including those of Philip Pullman, Lemony Snicket, and Eoin Colfer. Often characters are merchandised even before the book has become established in the market. Very often a book is only the first step of a story that is developed subsequently in a variety of other media. The "same" text can appear in print-based, audio, film, and television versions, as well as in the form of video games and popular music albums (for example, Tolkien Metal). Furthermore, a book may not be the only print-based version of a text. Many books are now being published as graphic novels or variations of that genre. G. P. Taylor coined the term "illustronovella" for the blend of prose and sequential art in *The Tizzle Sisters & Erik*, a book he published in 2006. It was released by Markosia Enterprises, a British publishing company that specializes "in sequential story-telling" and whose authors, according to their website, appeal to "a wide and varied readership." The art work for Taylor's illustronovella was done by Cliff Wright, creator of two of the Harry Potter book covers.

Print-based and audio versions of a text are generally followed by film adaptations. The first Harry Potter movie became the second highest grossing film of all time, after *Titanic*. When the meteoric sales of the latest *Harry Potter* started to slow down somewhat, the release of the next blockbuster film would spark sales again. Now that the final novel has been published, the release of the remaining films will continue to boost book sales until 2010. Film and television producers everywhere are looking for great children's books. As in the case of adult novels, children's book editors now consider the film potential before signing up an author. A new Television and Film Professionals Meeting Area was introduced to the Bologna Book Fair in 2002 to provide a base for movie people scouting for stories to adapt. A few publishers realized the potential well before the first Harry Potter film started a general trend. When rumours of a film based on *The Lord of the Rings* leaked out, HarperCollins bought Tolkien's publisher Unwin Hyman in 1990, and acquired exclusive world publishing rights for the adult market tie-in books to the movie trilogy. Michael Morpurgo claims that all the publicity has been focused on the advances and the big Hollywood movies rather than on children's literature itself.[53] Now that the Harry Potter and *Lord of the Rings* movies have demonstrated that a book franchise can translate into many years of commercial success for the film industry, Hollywood has taken notice. Film companies are paying big dollars for movie rights to crossover books. Film rights are now being snapped up by Hollywood even before books are published. In 2002, Disney paid eight million dollars for the film, merchandising, and theme-park rights to Clive Barker's *Abarat*—the first in a quartet of books that began with over three hundred oil paintings—before it was even in stores. *Abarat* seemed poised to become its own industry before the first book was even published, but the deal with Disney has since died and the work is back in the author's hands. The merchandising appeal of such a book is quite obvious, since Barker virtually provided the toy designs in his many illustrations. The first book had so much pre-publication hype that many people said they were tired of hearing about it before it was even released. However, many adults later admitted that, contrary to their expectations, they were very favourably impressed with the book and were looking forward to the sequels. Extremely lucrative film and television tie-ins have become the norm for successful crossover novels.

Although the Harry Potter and *Lord of the Rings* films are the most striking examples of major box office hits derived from crossover books, there have been many attempts to repeat the success. The mega-budget Twentieth Century Fox movie adaptation of Christopher Paolini's *Eragon* was released in seventy-six markets worldwide between December 13 and December 15, 2006. In light of the scope of the global launch, it is perhaps not surprising that *Eragon* was the number one film worldwide during its opening weekend, with over $30 million in revenue. Reviews were quite mixed, however, and movie-goers generally agreed that it was no *Lord of the Rings*. Film rights for Mark Haddon's *The Curious Incident of the Dog in the Night-Time* were bought by Heyday Films, the makers of the Harry Potter movies, and Plan B (a company set up by Brad Grey and Brad Pitt), but as yet the film has not been produced. The film rights to many crossover books are optioned, but not all actually make it to the big screen. Those that do get released are not necessarily successful.

The first film based on Philip Pullman's *His Dark Materials*, directed by Chris Weitz and produced by New Line Cinema, had a rather modest opening weekend, in December 2007, compared to other crossover fantasy December releases, such as *The Lord of the Rings* and *The Chronicles of Narnia*. Although the box office receipts for the first weekend in the United States did not meet industry expectations, *The Golden Compass* still pulled in over $26 million, and also took box office receipts of more than $55 million in the first few days in twenty-five other countries. The religious controversy surrounding the film as well as the "(Parents strongly cautioned)" that followed the PG-13 rating may have had a negative impact on attendance by young viewers. Publishers have also begun reaching out to game manufacturers and graphic novel publishers, as the book industry realizes, along with the other media, that this collaboration allows them to capitalize on existing entertainment brands and to reach new audiences. An action tie-in video game was launched in conjunction with *The Golden Compass* film. New Line signed a video game licensing deal with Sega giving them interactive rights to all three instalments of Pullman's trilogy. The game was developed for multiple platforms and shipped in time for Christmas 2007, just prior to the opening of the movie on December 7. It is common practice to release the game first in order to increase the buzz for the movie. Further, the movie is inevitably better than the game, so it is preferable that the game precede the movie to avoid disappointing gamers.

In the tradition of classics like *The Nutcracker* and *Peter Pan*, theatrical adaptations of contemporary crossover novels have become popular family entertainment, especially at Christmas time. In some cases, crossover books are making it onto the stage even before their debut on the screen. While the film and the video game were still in the planning stages, Pullman's *His Dark Materials* was produced as an epic two-part, six-hour performance for the Royal National Theatre in London, where it played at the Olivier Theatre from December 2003 through March 2004. It was adapted by Nicholas Wright, directed by Nicholas Hytner, and the ingenious dæmon puppets were designed by Michael Curry, who was the puppetmaster for *The Lion King*. The sophisticated, highly cinematic performance included artists from new technologies as well as old. According to the promotional material, the goal was "to create an experience as meaningful for 12 year olds as for adults." The enormously successful stage play was revived with a revised script for a second run in 2004–05. After the Whitbread awards, Mark Haddon said he had been asked if he was interested in a Broadway musical adaptation of *The Curious Incident of the Dog in the Night-Time*, but he turned it down. Parents take children to these theatrical adaptations, just as they take them to cinematic versions of children's novels, but today adults are no longer afraid to admit that they enjoy them. In fact, accompanying their kids is often only a pretext, and many adults attend with no kids in tow. The huge box office takings would not be possible from families and children alone.

In today's marketplace, there is extensive cross-promotion of cultural products, or what the business community refers to as synergy. As Dan Hade puts it, the movie constitutes a kind of "ninety-minute advertisement" for the book and the book is a "two-hundred-page advertisement" for the movie.[54] A kid wearing a Harry Potter or *Lord of the Rings* T-shirt becomes a walking advertisement for the book. A book, particularly a bestselling crossover novel, is now first and foremost a consumer product. Rowling's series constituted the literary jackpot of all time, and its huge commercial success extended well beyond the publishing world to the film, toy, and gaming industries, to name only a few industries to reap the profits of the wizard who "turns books into gold." It is no wonder that publishers and authors alike have been hoping for years to come up with the next *Harry Potter*.

In addition to the extensive publicity by publishing houses and film studios, crossover literature and films are getting a great deal of media coverage, which has a huge impact on the consumers of these products, as well as on the authors, illustrators, and filmmakers who create them. Some critics have speculated that media pressure diminished Rowling's creative freedom, preventing her from writing real books for children as the series progressed. Every aspect of the Harry Potter books' development was surrounded by intense commercial and media hype. The huge success and incredible sales of the super crossover books have had a major impact on media attention given to children's authors in general. This is particularly true of newcomers to the children's literature scene, who have sometimes been cast into the public eye even before their first books are released. In January 2002, Georgia Byng was given a full spread in the *Daily Telegraph*, several months before the publication of her first novel *Molly Moon's Incredible Book of Hypnotism*, while the *Times* devoted a full-page lead review in December 2001 to the still unknown British author Sally Prue, whose debut novel *Cold Tom* appeared that month. The rush to cover unknowns in the years following the release of *Harry Potter and the Philosopher's Stone* suggests that the media were afraid of missing out on the next J. K. Rowling. Established authors have also been receiving extensive media coverage. Following his historical Whitbread win, major features on Philip Pullman appeared in a number of British newspapers, including the *Times*, the *Guardian*, the *Sunday Telegraph*, and the *Independent*. However, even prior to that win, the *Observer* presented their review of *The Amber Spyglass* at the front of the section, "just as we might . . . any important adult writer," in the hope that it would help to have Pullman evaluated "as an important contemporary novelist who happens to write in a certain genre, a significant writer to be spoken of in the same breath as, say, Beryl Bainbridge, A. S. Byatt or Salman Rushdie."[55]

The publishing market, especially in North America, is now dominated by a few gigantic companies due to the numerous mergers that have taken place in recent decades. Large publishing houses have taken over many of the smaller ones, which then have a great deal of difficulty retaining their autonomy and diversity. Scholastic is a family-owned business, but it nonetheless groups numerous publishing houses and considers itself to be the largest publisher of children's books in the world. Although its books are targeted chiefly at schoolchildren, as the name of the company suggests, Scholastic is a major player in the crossover arena, as the American publisher of the Harry Potter books. The Rowling books caused Scholastic stock in the United States to soar in the late 1990s. At the end of 1999, ten per cent of the company's sales came from the first three Harry Potter books. By 2001, the Potter peak for the company, that figure had increased to thirty per cent. In the article "Harry Potter and the Vanishing Brand Magic," *Forbes Magazine* stated in July 2005, prior to the release of the sixth book, that poor financial performance had made Scholastic realize that it had "to look beyond young Mr. Potter's magic."[56] Since then, the series has accounted for a much smaller percentage of the company's revenue. In Britain, Scholastic UK also played a major role in the crossover scene, as the publisher of Philip Pullman's *His Dark Materials*.

The success of child-to-adult crossovers has resulted in major restructuring changes within publishing houses. In large conglomerates, such as Penguin and HarperCollins, children's division heads play an increasingly important role in company policy. HarperCollins Children's Books is one of the world's leading publishers of children's books, known for its tradition of publishing quality, award-winning books for young readers. It is home to such crossover classics as *Charlotte's Web* and *The Chronicles of Narnia*. In 2001, the children's division at HarperCollins was detached from the educational division and became part of

HarperCollins General Books. Publishers are now investing a much greater percentage of their capital on their children's divisions. Marketing budgets have been increased significantly. It is not surprising that publishing houses are now looking for children's publishers who are top-notch business people as well as excellent publishers.

The grouping of publishing houses that began in the United States, before spreading to Britain, is now occurring in other countries. The merger of Gallimard and Bayard in France made them the largest children's publisher in that country, with almost twenty-five per cent of the market. Obtaining the French rights for the Harry Potter books ensured that Gallimard Bayard Jeunesse would retain that status for some time to come. These huge publishing conglomerates, like any large corporation, are concerned chiefly with profit margins and market share. The bottom line for literature is that economic factors now have a huge impact on who reads what, when, and where. Small language areas, for example, Denmark, Finland, Norway, the Netherlands and Flanders, to name a few, are not able to compete on prevailing marketplace terms. Substantial subsidies are necessary for children's literature in areas such as these to allow publishers to continue to bring out quality books at competitive prices. In developing countries, the problem is considerably worse. Dianne Hofmeyr points out some of the obstacles faced by children's literature publishing in South Africa: small print-runs, no up-front payment, low literacy, and a poor book-buying public. Marketing and advertising are expensive when profits are so low. If books are not co-produced overseas, it is difficult for authors and illustrators to earn a living from writing.[57] Similar conditions exist in a large number of countries around the globe.

Along with the huge conglomerates, there are still a significant number of middle-size, small, and independent publishers who are offering author attention and focused marketing for crossover authors. These publishers often play a very important role in the publication and promotion of crossover fiction. The independent British publisher Bloomsbury, in particular, is a major player. The founding of Bloomsbury in the 1980s was counter to the reigning trend in British publishing, which was dominated at the time by the rise of large conglomerates. Bloomsbury is known for its commitment to literary quality and its special relationship with authors, as well as a rigorous commercial approach. Its founding principle was that of bringing quality to the mass market. The quality of the edition of the Harry Potter series was particularly high for a children's book. Since Bloomsbury set out to shun mass-market books, it is certainly ironic that much of their success is due to the most commercial books in the history of publishing. They had just started publishing children's books in 1994, only two years before they took on Rowling's first novel, a gamble that paid off on a monumental scale. The company's annual turnover increased from £13.5 million in 1996 to £70 million in 2002 and the company's share price sky-rocketed. Financial analysts estimated that Harry Potter accounts for more than half of Bloomsbury's sales and profits. That seems to be "a double edged sword," as an article in *Forbes Magazine* pointed out in 2007, prior to the release of the last instalment. Bloomsbury is facing a very difficult period due to the gap created by the end of the series and the fact that the franchise may be reaching "saturation point." According to the article, Bloomsbury stock had fallen forty-four per cent over the previous year.[58] Their situation is similar to that experienced slightly earlier by Harry Potter's American publisher. Bloomsbury nonetheless has an enviable position in the publishing industry, as one of the rare small companies to combine commercial success with literary prestige, while retaining its independence.

A number of other small publishing houses also play an important role in the crossover phenomenon. One notable example is Front Street Books in North Carolina, a publisher devoted entirely to children's literature, but whose modest list contains several award-winning crossover titles. In particular, Front Street Books is the publisher of the only English translations of Bart Moeyaert's novels. Raincoast Books, based in Vancouver and noted for using high amounts of recycled paper in their publications, is the Canadian publisher of the Harry Potter series. They acquired the Canadian rights after initially being told, in error, that Scholastic had bought them with the American rights. Raincoast Books have demonstrated that a small Canadian publisher can compete with large multinational houses. The Chicken House, founded by Barry Cunningham in 2000, has demonstrated that a small publisher can make an impact on a global scale, thanks to the worldwide success of Cornelia Funke. In both 2004 and 2005, it was shortlisted for Small Publisher of the Year at the British Book Awards. After a highly successful five-year partnership with Scholastic in the United States, Chicken House was acquired by the American company in 2005.

Canongate, the independent, Edinburgh-based publisher of Yann Martel's Booker Award-winning novel, *Life of Pi*, made literary history by becoming the first Scottish publishing house to sell one million copies of a novel in its first imprint. Canongate was voted Britain's Publisher of the Year after the phenomenal success of Martel's novel. Of all the Booker Prize winners, only Thomas Kenneally's *Schindler's Ark* sold more copies. Almost a year after the Booker win, Martel's novel remained the third bestselling paperback in Britain. *Life of Pi* helped the company's turnover to soar from £2.6 million in 2001 to an estimated £6–7 million for the 2003 financial year. Jamie Byng, the head of Canongate, admits that the tremendous success of Martel's book opened up exciting new opportunities for the small Scottish publishing house, which is now being sought out by agents (London publishing houses pay them more) and whose catalogue now gets much greater attention from book suppliers.[59]

Some critics have expressed the concern that quality publishing will soon rest solely in the hands of the smaller publishers. Although he acknowledges that the large publishing houses continue to publish some very good books, Dan Hade wonders if the smaller companies will become the principal source of "great literature," whereas the large corporations will produce the books that are the most profitable.[60] Oxford University Press's Publishing Director Fiona Kenshole admits: "The children's list used to be about prestige publishing, now it's about profitability."[61] Often the most profitable books are those published as part of a merchandising package.

Within the big companies, there are some exceptional small editorial-led lists, a notable example being David Fickling's imprint. Fickling was Philip Pullman's editor at Scholastic UK and he encouraged the author to write *His Dark Materials*. In 1999, he formed his own imprint, David Fickling Books, in Oxford. Publishing only about a dozen titles a year, it is one of five hardback imprints of Random House Children's Books, which is part of the Random House Group that merged with Transworld Children's Books in 2001. David Fickling Books became the first bi-continental children's publisher, publishing books simultaneously in the United States and the United Kingdom. In 2004, Fickling was voted the Editor of the Year at the British Book Awards. The imprint, which offers fine-looking books that are scrupulously edited, is, as the David Fickling Books page on the Random House website states, "a tiny publisher . . . with some GIANT books." Among the Fickling titles are numerous highly successful crossover novels, including Mark Haddon's *The Curious Incident of the Dog in the Night-Time*, Jan Mark's *Eclipse of the Century*, Robin McKinley's *Beauty*, and Linda Newbery's 2007 Costa Award-winning *Set in Stone*. He also brought out Pullman's *Lyra's Oxford* in 2003. Fickling has a flair for quality children's books that also appeal to adults, as well as an uncanny sense of timing. When Adèle Geras approached publishers with her idea for *Troy*, a love story set during the Trojan War, historical fiction was out of fashion and a hard sell. While other publishers showed no interest, David Fickling took on the young adult novel, which would be shortlisted for the Whitbread Children's Book of the Year Award in 2000. When the events of September 11, 2001 occurred shortly after the novel was published in the United States, the subject of the sacking of a city suddenly became very relevant and the novel attracted an adult audience as well. Pullman had written *Paradise Lost* for teenagers for Fickling; Geras gave him the *Iliad* and the *Odyssey* for teenagers (*Ithaka*, a follow-up about Penelope's wait for Odysseus, was published in 2005).

Although a great deal of emphasis has been put on the commercialization of children's literature since the beginning of the crossover phenomenon, some of the most remarkable crossover hits have been highly uncommercial endeavours. It is true, however, that these tend to be brought out by small, independent publishers. Both Jostein Gaarder's *Sophie's World* and Philip Pullman's *His Dark Materials* were ambitious projects that did not seem likely to have great commercial appeal. Yet both authors received the unqualified and enthusiastic support of their publishers. When asked, during lunch one day, by David Fickling what he would like to write, Pullman replied "*Paradise Lost* for teenagers in three volumes." Fickling's positive and "blatantly uncommercial response" committed Pullman to the project.[62] A publisher willing to take a risk on something apparently so "uncommercial" reminds us of Gaarder's publisher taking on *Sophie's World*. A retelling of *Paradise Lost* for children seemed as unlikely to become an international bestseller as "A Novel about the History of Philosophy." Gaarder was more surprised than anyone at the huge success of *Sophie's World*. The author had told his wife that he had to write the novel even though it would not be read by many people and they would not make any money on it. During a conversation on October 2, 2002, Gaarder told me that when his publisher agreed to publish it, he sent him a postcard to thank him for taking such an "uncommercial book." *Sophie's World* turned out to be the "most commercial" book ever published in Norway, constituting about twenty-five per cent of all book sales.

Some very interesting publishing is being done by small presses. The British small press scene is particularly vibrant and producing books of very high quality. PS Publishing, which was founded in Leeds in 1999 by Peter Crowther, specializes in novella-length fiction from the fantasy, science fiction, and horror genres. It quickly established itself as one of Britain's leading small presses, and has won the British Fantasy Award for Best Small Press almost every year since 2001. Another successful small press is Crowswing Books, which was originally founded by Sean Wright as an outlet for his own books, but now also publishes those by other authors. Wright's goal is to publish "quality limited edition fiction by quality writers" who can contribute "another imaginative and visionary dimension" to Crowswing.[63] The commercial success of Crowswing surprised many people in the publishing industry, as it was entirely the result of word-of-mouth sales. In the beginning, there was no advertising budget whatsoever. Wright works closely with independent booksellers and major chains, doing a lot of personal public relations work. A large amount of the business takes place through the Crowswing online bookshop. Many self-published books are first sold on the eBay auction site and by independent booksellers, before gradually finding their way into mainstream chains like Waterstone's and Amazon.

Self-publishing is a route taken by a number of crossover authors, as it has now become quite acceptable, even fashionable, to do so. G. P. Taylor, a vicar-turned-author, broke self-publishing ground in Britain when he brought out his debut novel *Shadowmancer* with his small press Mount Publishing in October 2002. Taylor opted to self-publish, at a cost of £3,500 (he sold his Harley-Davidson to finance it), when he was told that no publisher would be interested in a parable about Christianity and black magic set in the eighteenth century. The debut author managed to get the book available through all the major book wholesalers as well as the main book retailers. He also went to all the local book-shops and offered to do book signings, and convinced the local papers to write articles. Taylor's self-published novel was a huge word-of-mouth success. *Shadowmancer* was an unexpected runaway bestseller that took Britain by storm and turned the vicar into a very popular fantasy writer. A review in the *Times*, quoted on the Shadowmancer website, described the novel as "the biggest event in children's fiction since Harry Potter." It was referred to as the "Christian Harry Potter." G. P. Taylor was the first of the so-called New Independent Wave of British Children's Authors to be signed up to major publishing houses. Although it was highly unusual to be contracting for new titles a month before the release of the first novel, Faber & Faber offered him a £3.5 million publishing deal in the United Kingdom for *Shadowmancer* and a further six novels. Subsequently, the author received a $500,000 deal with G. P. Putnam's, a division of Penguin Group (USA), as well as a seven-figure film deal with Universal Pictures. *Shadowmancer* spent fifteen weeks at number one on the paperback bestseller list in Britain. Taylor's novel garnered impressive media coverage, both in Britain and in the United States. The media hype and pre-publication excitement in the United States was so great that G. P. Putnam's went back to print twice before the novel even went on sale. *Shadowmancer* became a *New York Times* number one bestseller and is translated into more than forty languages. Commenting on the amazing speed at which *Shadowmancer* sold in the first nine months or so after its launch (more than 2.6 million copies worldwide), Will Atkinson, head of international sales at Faber & Faber, stated that "could not have been possible if only children were buying."[64]

Sean Wright has been an extremely successful self-publisher. His first book, a limited edition of *Jesse Jameson and the Golden Glow* in May 2003, sold out before it hit the shelves. It was followed closely by the second book in the Alpha to Omega series, *Jesse Jameson and the Bogie Beast*, in October of that year. When *The Twisted Root of Jaarfindor*, his first "teenage-adult crossover book," was published in 2004, the leading British bookseller Waterstone's wanted to feature it in their Christmas promotion on a nationwide scale, so they reserved the entire first print run of three thousand copies, many of which were sold by word of mouth during the ten-week promotion. This was a remarkable achievement for a small press, which garnered national exposure shortly thereafter in the *Guardian* and the *Observer*. In the "New Wave of Children's Authors—One Year On," an article Wright posted on his Weblog on February 21, 2005, the author puts these sales figures in perspective by comparing them to Jonathan Stroud's highly promoted *Golem's Eye*, which sold only six hundred more copies in the same period. Wright's novel was later shortlisted for the British Fantasy Award in 2005. The author says that Foyles, the world's most famous bookshop, and Hatchards, London's oldest bookshop, have played a very important role in Crowswing's success by giving his books prime exposure. The hardback edition of 250 copies of *The Twisted Root of Jaarfindor* sold out at Hatchards, where Wright was a Hatchards Author of the Year in 2005, along with writers like Nina Bawden, Fredrick Forsyth, and John Grisham. Within twenty-four hours of announcing his debut adult novel *Jaarfindor Remade*, the full colour illustrated version, which had a print run of only fifty copies worldwide, sold out, five months before its release date of August 2006.

When a novel is self-published, it does not necessarily have to fit neatly into a generic or age category. Wright is an author of books for children, young adults, and adults. Much of his fiction is aimed at mid-teens and older. In an interview with Nick Gifford, posted on the Infinity Plus website, the author described *Wicked Or What?*, published in 2005, as his third "teenage-adult crossover sci-fi/fantasy book." There is a great deal of structural experimentation in Wright's books, which deal with difficult themes such as time, memory, mind games, mental illness, altered states of consciousness, paranoid delusions, or, as the author put it in his interview with Gifford, "a lot of mind-related issues that have become something of a taboo." They are not an easy read but the author does not intend them to be. Wright's fiction ignores the conventions of formulaic writing, borrowing from the genres of fantasy, science fiction, and horror. *The Twisted Root of Jaarfindor* is described as his first "teenage-adult sci fi/fantasy/horror novel." According to the author, *Wicked Or What?* is inspired by three legendary figures in fantasy, horror, and sci-fi fiction: Ray Bradbury, Mervyn Peake, and Philip K. Dick. The same blurring of these generic boundaries characterizes *New Wave of Speculative Fiction: The What If Factor*, a collection of short fiction by authors who write outside the formula. Edited by Wright and published by Crowswing in 2005, the volume was a small run paperback limited edition of only three hundred copies. Wright, who claims to have coined the phrase New Wave of British Children's Authors, is becoming somewhat of a legend in British literary circles. Other authors who are considered to be part of this new wave include Dominic Mieville, Charmian Hussey, and Gill Arbuthnott, who all self-published books between October 2002 (the release of *Shadowmancer*) and October 2003 (the release of the second *Jesse Jameson* novel), a period that Wright feels, according to the previously cited article on his Weblog, will come to be seen as a "Golden Age of Independent Book Publishing."

There has been a great deal of talk about the small press scene in Britain, but it is active in the United States as well. The debut novelist Michael Hoeye put all his own savings into self-publishing his first children's book, *Time Stops for No Mouse*. The writer's first proof edition of one thousand copies, issued in 1999, was followed by an edition under his own Terfle Books imprint in 2000. By 2001, the book had sold more than ten thousand copies. In a heated auction involving three other major publishers, Penguin Putnam won hardcover and paperback rights for *Time Stops for No Mouse* and two sequels, including the previously self-published *The Sands of Time* (2001), for a reported $1.8 million. Hoeye wrote *Time Stops for No Mouse* for his wife while she was away on a lengthy business trip, and the reader senses that it was written for the author's pleasure rather than with an eye to any particular readership. It became the first book in the Hermux Tantamoq Adventures, an action-adventure-mystery series about a rodent watchmaker-turned-sleuth. The chic, offbeat thriller, which is set in an urban world of talking rodents that is reminiscent of early twentieth-century New York, was followed by *The Sands of Time*, in which Hermux engages in an Indiana Jones-style adventure to a prehistoric kingdom of cats. Hoeye did not stop at the third novel, *No Time Like Show Time* (2004), but went on to publish *Time to Smell the Roses* in 2007. Published for a juvenile audience, the tales have a simple style, short chapters, fast-paced plots, and charmingly eccentric characters. The novels have been commended for not talking up or down to readers, which explains why they appeal equally to children and adults. The nostalgic atmosphere, sophisticated wit, and satiric social commentary give the books a layer to be savoured by older children and adult readers. The author estimates that half of his readers are adults. On the Penguin website, the wide-ranging age recommendations for various editions of Hoeye's novels include eight to twelve years, one to eighteen years, juvenile/adult, and adult.

The most successful self-published book to date in the United States is Christopher Paolini's *Eragon*, which was self-published several months before G. P. Taylor's *Shadowmancer*. In early 2002, *Eragon* was released by the family's publishing company, Paolini International. After months on the road promoting the book, Paolini sold the world rights for *Eragon* and two unwritten sequels to Knopf/Random House for a deal reportedly worth more than $500,000. The Knopf edition was released in August 2003 with a great deal of hype. By necessity, self-published authors are obliged to engage in extensive self-publication, but that is not to say that other authors do not get very involved in the promotion of their books. Many authors do regular public readings, school and library visits, and bookstore signings. They also participate in the rising number of literary conferences. In many of these contexts, adult and children's writers now appear together, which helps children's authors reach an adult audience.

Advances, Sales Figures, and Print Runs

Traditionally, advances for children's books have been quite low. Even *The Lord of the Rings*, which was not released for children, was published under a profit-sharing arrangement according to which Tolkien would not receive an advance or royalties until the books had broken even, after which he would take a large share of the profits. J. K. Rowling received a meagre £2,500 advance from Bloomsbury Children's Books for *Harry Potter and the Philosopher's Stone*. Her agent, Christopher Little, who spent approximately a year sending the manuscript to about a dozen larger publishers like Penguin and HarperCollins, had advised Rowling not to be too optimistic. After its acceptance by Bloomsbury, Barry Cunningham, her first editor, told her that she would never get rich writing children's books. The American rights to the still unknown first book were sold to Scholastic at the Bologna Book Fair in 1997 for a six-figure sum that was not disclosed until later. The $105,000 sum that Rowling received from Scholastic was quite high for a children's book at that time.

Rowling opened the door for large advances on children's books. Since Rowling's blockbuster hit, authors of children's titles with crossover potential are now getting the kinds of advances previously only given to bestselling adult authors like Danielle Steele or John Grisham. Five-, six-, even seven-figure deals are no longer uncommon. Amounts such as these are not recouped by selling only to the children's market. In the previous chapter, we saw that adult authors who take up writing for children may command the same big advances and film deals that they had in the adult fiction sphere, as in the case of P. B. Kerr. Others, like Paver, receive much larger advances for their children's books than they did for their adult novels. However, many authors obtaining these large advances have no track record at all, for example, Eoin Colfer, the Irish ex-teacher who wrote *Artemis Fowl*, or Zizou Corder, the mother-and-daughter team who wrote *Lionboy*. The publishing rights to the fantasy novel *The Dreamwalker's Child*, by Steve Voake, a West Country headmaster, were snapped up in 2003 after a furiously fought auction between four major publishers. For world rights to *Time Stops for No Mouse*, Michael Hoeye received "the record sum received for a children's book" from Penguin Putnam. The first ninety pages of *The Amulet of Samarkand* were the subject of a bidding war between four publishers, and the film rights were optioned by Miramax, resulting in a deal reportedly worth more than £2 million for the albeit established children's author Jonathan Stroud. Lian Hearn received "a substantial six-figure sum" (reportedly about £300,000) for *Across the Nightingale Floor* after a fierce bidding war that was eventually won by the combined financial clout of the adult and children's divisions of Macmillan. The movie deal from Universal was estimated at $3.6 million. Some publishers, including Rowling's British publisher Bloomsbury, have expressed the fear that the huge advances now demanded by authors and their agents will have a negative impact on future publishing programs, resulting in a decrease in the number of books published.

Many of the authors now being offered large advances are writing specifically for a young audience. After Rowling, the most successful children's author in Britain is Jacqueline Wilson, whose books will certainly never be read by adults. Yet she has sold over twenty million copies of her books in the United Kingdom alone, where she is the most borrowed author in libraries and had four of her titles in the top 100 most popular books in the BBC's Big Read poll. Other hugely popular children's books that command large advances include the American author Meg Cabot's *The Princess Diaries*, which imitates the adult chick lit genre, and the British author Georgia Byng's novels about Molly Moon, which were a highly publicized purchase by Macmillan.

No author in the near future, either for children or adults, is likely to receive the kind of profits that J. K. Rowling earns. She has become the first U.S.-dollar billionaire author in history. Early on, sales of the Potter books shattered all previous records in children's publishing and began toppling adult records. The fourth book in the Harry Potter series established a world record for the largest initial print run in the history of publishing (3.8 million in the United States alone). To put things in perspective, Scholastic's 650,000-copy print run of the previous Harry Potter novel had seemed wildly excessive. The average children's novel in the United States has a first printing of ten to fifteen thousand. *Harry Potter and the Goblet of Fire* became the fastest-selling book of all time. Even before it hit the bookshelves, Amazon.com had pre-sold eight times as many copies as its previous high, which was for John Grisham's *The Brethren*. On its release day, British bookshops and Internet sites sold almost as many hardback copies as the third book sold in its first full year of publication, far surpassing any previous records. In the United States, Scholastic also broke all publishing sales records, selling nearly three million copies in the first weekend. The subsequent books in the series continued to set new records. In the United States, the initial print run of *Harry Potter and the Order of the Phoenix* was close to seven million copies (it was raised to 8.5 million to satisfy demand), while those figures rose to just under eleven million for the sixth and twelve million for the seventh (the latter also proved to be insufficient and was increased to fourteen million). Within twenty-four hours of its release in Britain, *Harry Potter and the Half-Blood Prince* sold more than two million copies, while sales of *Harry Potter and the Deathly Hallows* during the same period were three million. In the United States, Scholastic moved more than eight million copies of the final novel on the first day, while Amazon.com had more than two million pre-orders. Worldwide sales of the series, as of September 2007, were in excess of 350 million copies.

Although the sales figures for the Harry Potter books tend to overshadow all others, many crossover books have reached mega-numbers in recent years. The one-million-copy first print run of Christopher Paolini's *Eldest* by Random House in 2005 is outstanding, even when compared with the fifth *Harry Potter* released the same year in a print run of seven million. In its first month of sales in Fall 2004, the eleventh volume of Lemony Snicket's A Series of Unfortunate Events, *The Grim Grotto* sold over one million copies in the United States alone. In keeping with the pessimistic publicity campaign, Snicket was purportedly "inconsolable" and "hiding in a corner." By May 2007, more than fifty-five million copies of A Series of Unfortunate Events had been sold around the world.

Although only a relatively small percentage of children's books win the coveted "crossover" handle, the potential of children's books in general has been dramatically altered. Thanks to the crossover phenomenon, publishing for children and young adults is the most exciting area of the global publishing industry. It is also, along with graphic novels, the fastest growing. For the first time in publishing history, children's titles are knocking adult titles from the top of bestseller lists and outselling authors like John Grisham. The top spots on Amazon.com's general bestseller list regularly include children's books. Although sales of children's books now exceed sales of adult fiction for many bookstores and online book retailers, not all of the news with regard to children's book sales has been good since the beginning of the Potter phenomenon. Along with the widespread euphoria, there has also been widespread concern that Harry Potter has not helped the children's market, but only the author and publisher of the Harry Potter books. Although more copies of *Harry Potter and the Goblet of Fire* were sold in a single year than any other book in the annals of publishing, it seems that overall numbers of children's books purchased actually declined by five million in Britain between 2000 and 2001. According to a report released in April 2002 by industry analysts Book Marketing Ltd. in Britain, sales of children's books had been virtually flat at about £425 million per year since the Potter phenomenon began. It seems that Rowling was collecting the cash that would normally have gone to other children's authors. A survey published by British children's authors in 2005 was titled "Not All of Us Are Rowling in It."[65] In addition, the huge sales of *Harry Potter* were due in large part to adults buying the books. In spite of some doom and gloom, particularly in the British market, sales of children's books worldwide seem to have skyrocketed and there has been an unprecedented boom in children's publishing, which shows no sign of slowing after the publication of the last *Harry Potter*.

The Marketing of Crossovers

Rowling's phenomenal success is often attributed to the aggressive marketing for which Bloomsbury is well known. Although this is only part of the answer, the Potter effect has had a monumental impact on the publishing and marketing of major children's titles. Contrary to adult books, few children's books, even by the most successful authors, had received more than very modest marketing prior to *Harry Potter*. Large-scale publicity campaigns, especially in non-book related outlets, were virtually unheard of. Traditionally, a novel published for children or young adults had a much longer sales and shelf life than an adult novel and cost less to produce, because it did not have to be supported by publicity and marketing. At the same time, children's and young adult books got less bookstore and review attention than adult books. Children's books required more time to establish themselves in the market. *Harry Potter* led the way for big, market-led blockbusters that do not fit the traditional sales pattern of children's books. The pressures that were once reserved only for the adult book market now exist in children's book publishing. Multi-book contracts that facilitate sustained marketing have become a very common strategy in children's publishing.

In a business that is now highly competitive, marketing strategies have become very sophisticated. There has been a huge increase in the amount of money being spent on the marketing of children's books, especially those with crossover potential. Children's publishers are now using the hard-sell techniques that were previously used only in the adult sector. The work of publicity departments has changed dramatically. Publicists now play such an important role that in-house teams of publicists are not sufficient and many publishers now also employ an extensive number of freelance publicists. Media-savvy marketing on the part of publishing houses builds buzz that translates into sales. This high-profile marketing has resulted in market-led literary successes. However, it has also led to concern about the ability of publishers to maintain the full range and quality of children's books in this climate. Almost every highly successful book in large markets is now the object of a strong, well-planned campaign. When the first book in Eoin Colfer's Artemis Fowl series was published in 2001, the major retailers were looking for another Harry Potter and worked closely with Puffin to heavily promote the book. For Lian Hearn's *Across the Nightingale Floor*, Pan Macmillan launched a massive marketing campaign in which the younger readers' and adult readers' markets were targeted separately. The publishing company reportedly spent about five million dollars on publicity for the novel. The mystery surrounding the identity of the real author, Gillian Rubenstein, added to the excitement surrounding its launch. The large publishers who can afford to market their authors strongly have a tremendous advantage. In 2004, Scholastic launched their worldwide marketing campaign of P. B. Kerr's trilogy The Children of the Lamp, which was backed by $250,000 in the United States and the United Kingdom. The same year, Scholastic supported Cornelia Funke's *Dragon Rider* with a $150,000 marketing campaign, including a national print and radio advertising campaign and a national publicity campaign. Such an extensive marketing campaign in the United States for a non-English-language children's novel was quite exceptional. Christopher Paolini's *Eldest* came out in 2005 backed by a $500,000 publicity campaign, the largest ad budget ever for Random House's children's division. Bloomsbury mounted a £1 million advertising campaign for *Harry Potter and the Half-Blood Prince*. One would think that a marketing campaign for the seventh and final *Harry Potter* was superfluous, but Scholastic supported its launch with a multi-million dollar campaign under the rather unexciting banner "There Will Soon Be 7." The final novel was released on the day of the tenth anniversary of the publication of the first book in the series. Even marketing campaigns for adult novels that cross over have become more extensive. Bloomsbury won two major British trade awards in 2005 for the huge marketing and publicity campaign that launched Susanna Clarke's *Jonathan Strange & Mr Norrell*.

The effectiveness of the Potter publicity machine has been extraordinary. Bloomsbury have played very cleverly to Rowling's youthful fans. On the publication day of *Harry Potter and the Prisoner of Azkaban*, sales were not allowed until 3:45 p.m., the implication being that children would be playing hooky if the book was available earlier. The strategy was so successful that when the book went on sale, bookstores all over Britain were packed with young readers still in their school uniforms, many of them reading on the floor, unable to wait until they got the book home. The launch of the fourth novel was marked by a four-day promotional trip around Britain in an antique steam train done up like the Hogwarts Express, but there have been no such tours or signings for subsequent books. Rowling has made it very clear she dislikes the circus that accompanies the launch of a new book. In contrast, Jonathan Stroud, who made a round-the-world publicity tour after he completed his Bartamaeus Trilogy, enjoys the promotional duties that seem to be such a chore to Rowling.

Publicists have come up with no end of gimmicks to promote promising crossover books. Kevin Crossley-Holland carries around a polished black pebble in a velvet bag, produced by Scholastic to mark the publication of *The Seeing Stone* in the United States in 2001.

A silence campaign was adopted for the fourth book in the Harry Potter series. This was not, however, a new marketing strategy. It had already been used in Australia in 1999 by Pan Macmillan when they published the final volume of John Marsden's Tomorrow series, *The Other Side of Dawn*. All details of the book, including the title, were kept secret until its release on October 1, 1999, while Australian teenagers everywhere waited with bated breath. In the case of *Harry Potter and the Goblet of Fire*, the effectiveness of this strategy was demonstrated on a global scale. No advance copies were sent out for review. For months, all that was known were two facts offered by the author: a character would die and Harry would start to show an interest in girls. The author also wrote a series of one-word clues on a postcard for a charity auction, where it raised £28,680. It was only a few weeks prior to the release of the book that the title and cover jacket were leaked. The silence campaign was continued for subsequent books in the series. The title of the seventh and final book, *Harry Potter and the Deathly Hallows*, was announced on December 21, 2006 via a special Christmas-themed hangman puzzle on Rowling's website, and confirmed shortly afterwards by the book's publishers.

The security surrounding the publication of the Harry Potter books has been unprecedented in publishing history. A high-level security operation was set up in Britain and the United States to guard the printing plants, storage warehouses, and the distribution to booksellers of *Harry Potter and the Goblet of Fire*. Anyone with access to advance copies had to sign confidentiality letters. The effort to keep the plot secret was the subject of injunctions and the embargo was strictly enforced. Despite these precautions, about twenty copies found their way onto Wal-Mart bookshelves in Virginia a week early, and one lucky fan found herself a media star. The huge security operation surrounding the publication of the fifth novel covered the globe and was said to be on a military scale suitable for the guarding of state secrets. Those involved were under gag orders to prevent leaks, and rumours were that only two people within the publishing house had read the novel. Rowling sued a U.S. newspaper for revealing plot details after a couple managed to buy a copy from a store in Brooklyn before its release date.

Every aspect of the sales and marketing of the Harry Potter books seemed to break new ground. In an unprecedented move, Chapters, who controls about fifty per cent of Canadian book sales, contracted with Canada Post for Saturday home delivery of ten thousand pre-ordered copies of *Harry Potter and the Goblet of Fire* on July 8, 2000. Ever since the fourth book was launched at midnight, bookstores opened for business at that hour on publication day to sell the subsequent books. Booksellers have also orchestrated increasingly elaborate theme parties. Launches are becoming ever more inventive, reminiscent of the sensational launching of designer clothes. Puffin had a top-secret Fowl Day in 2002 to launch Eoin Colfer's second title in the Artemis Fowl series. Many booksellers threw Harry Potter-style parties for the launch of Paolini's *Eldest* in 2005. When the fifth Harry Potter book was released, thirty lucky fans spent the night at Alnwick Castle (Northumberland), one of the on-screen Hogwarts, where they were given their own copies at midnight. For the same novel, the world's largest book launch was held at London's Royal Albert Hall in front of 4,000 fans. The sixth novel was launched in Edinburgh, where seventy fortunate children were invited to Edinburgh Castle —transformed into Hogwarts School of Witchcraft and Wizardry—to hear the author read the first chapter and to feast on Potter treats.

Harry Potter made the marketing of major child-to-adult crossover books a global affair. Bloomsbury called *Harry Potter and the Order of the Phoenix* "the world's most anticipated book." The fifth novel in the series was launched in 150 countries at one minute past midnight, British Summer Time on June 21, 2003, the shortest night of the year. Simultaneous worldwide publication is now a marketing strategy widely used in the children's book industry, especially for heavily marketed crossover blockbusters. In 2003, publishers in more than twenty countries simultaneously released their editions of Jonathan Stroud's *The Amulet of Samarkand* with a great deal of hype. According to Lynn Waggoner, director of sales and marketing for Disney Publishing, it was largely because of the simultaneous worldwide release that Hyperion did what is called in the industry a "laydown" or on-sale date for Stroud's novel.[66] Laydowns are a common practice with adult trade publishers, but that year, children's publishers also began widely adopting the formula. Other crossover novels with laydown dates in Fall 2003 included *Inkheart* by Cornelia Funke, *Loamhedge*— the sixteenth Redwall novel—by Brian Jacques, and *The Slippery Slope*—the tenth novel in A Series of Unfortunate Events—by Lemony Snicket. By focusing publicity and promotion, either nationally or internationally, on a specific date, publishers turn the release of a book into a major publishing event in the hope of creating an out-of-the-gate bestseller.

Publishers are now spending their marketing dollars in a very broad environment. Marketing campaigns routinely include, among others, retail merchandising kits, consumer and trade advertising, and extensive media and online promotions. A significant percentage of the marketing budget is devoted to promoting children's books to adults. Advertisements and other forms of publicity are designed to target primarily adult readers. The July 2000 issue of *Maclean's* that put Harry on the cover carried a Chapters.ca advertisement on the inside of the cover that was addressed directly to adults: "Just remember to give it back to your kids when you're done." Marketing Pullman's trilogy for adults in Britain was a challenge to the children's publisher Scholastic, but after the novel's success with adults in the United States, they nonetheless undertook to capture the attention of this new market. When *The Subtle Knife* came out, Scholastic bought a huge poster site in the Oxford railway station, as well as several poster sites in other railway stations throughout Britain, and the hardback was placed in railway bookshops, where they began to sell extremely well, much to the company's surprise. The promotion of books on public transportation became a common occurrence. The publication of the paperback edition of *Harry Potter and the Goblet of Fire* involved a poster campaign on London buses. HarperCollins ran a huge, unconventional marketing campaign for Lemony Snicket's A Series of Unfortunate Events, in which bad publicity was used to promote the books. Throughout the series, the author discouraged readers from reading his books ("Under no circumstances should anyone be reading these books for entertainment"), and was unconsolable when they did not heed his warnings. "Where is Lemony Snicket?" posters promoted the latest novel in the series. Interestingly, it seems that the first ever series of television advertisements for a children's book in Britain did not occur until 2001. It was not for *Harry Potter* or any other super crossover title, rather it was a Puffin ad for Roald Dahl.

In the past few years, the publishing industry has begun to move into online marketing, using new technology to promote their authors and books. Publishers have recognized the importance of interactive websites, Internet advertising, and online promotions. In 2005, HarperCollins used an innovative marketing campaign to promote the twelfth Snicket, *The Penultimate Pearl*, demonstrating the potential of online marketing strategies. About three months before the release of the book, an event website, TheNamelessNovel.com, was created that gave fans an opportunity to interact with the series. Daily trivia questions and games based on the previous eleven books provided clues that allowed the many fans who visited the site day after day to solve a puzzle revealing the title of the "nameless novel." Moving promotions online is a logical step since kids spend so much time on the Internet, points out Jim McKenzie, who was appointed director of online marketing for HarperCollins Children's Books in 2005. After the successful Snicket campaign, he admitted that HarperCollins hoped to stay on top of the trend.[67]

Harry Potter's U.S. publisher, Scholastic, is also moving a large amount of its print-advertising budget in order "to get directly to kids . . . through Internet advertising," says Suzanne Murphy, vice president, trade marketing. Murphy also states the obvious fact that is now being widely acknowledged by publishers: "They're definitely an online generation. In order to get kids to read our books, we need to be online too."[68] On Scholastic's website, kids can read bonus material, learn about authors in Q&As, and join groups like the booklovers club Flashlight Readers. But kids are not the only audience that publishers are trying to reach through online promotions. McKenzie admits that part of the marketing goal with HarperCollins's event website for *The Penultimate Pearl* was getting readers of all ages interested in Lemony Snicket. Seventy-eight percent of the visitors to the site were over the age of thirteen, although most were probably older teenagers rather than adults, says McKenzie.[69] A database of interested consumers can be obtained much more easily through website promotions than print advertising. Tens of thousands of fans signed up for the HarperCollins e-newsletter and author-tracker updates about Snicket during the 2005 promotion. Pop ups and banners have been used extensively to promote crossover books such as Cornelia Funke's *Inkspell* and Rowling's Harry Potter books. The new technologies are changing the way books are promoted and advertised, and crossover books have been particularly targeted in the early stages of this development.

Many critics feel that books are getting lost in the hype and the marketing machine. There is certainly an over-marketing of some titles. The successful crossover cannot be achieved through marketing alone. If the book does not have that special magic, no amount of marketing wizardry will turn it into a crossover hit. The author of the article "Once Upon a Time in the Marketing Department ..." warns: "Some of those books optimistically targeted at 'all age groups' may end up attracting none at all."[70] In this technological age, it is important not to underestimate the power of word of mouth, which now includes the virtual word of mouth of the online community. Word of mouth remains the most effective strategy for promoting a book. Although it is easy to forget at the end of the most heavily marketed blockbuster in history, kids were way ahead of the media coverage and the merchandising of the Harry Potter books. Marketing of the boy wizard did not really get underway until 1999. Philip Pullman's *His Dark Materials* was published without any hype whatsoever, yet gained an early, loyal following long before the publicity that came with winning the 2001 Whitbread Book of the Year. Likewise, Mark Haddon's *The Curious Incident of the Dog in the Night-Time* attracted the attention of the public thanks to word of mouth prior to winning the Whitbread or being longlisted for the Booker. At Christmas 2003 (the Whitbread was announced in January 2004), the adult version of Haddon's novel outsold such authors as John le Carré and Patricia Cornwell. Despite the huge advertising budget, the online community and word of mouth have been credited with much of the phenomenal success of Christopher Paolini's *Eragon*. Word of mouth is the main marketing strategy of small presses and authors who self-publish. G. P. Taylor's *Shadowmancer* also attests to its effectiveness. Another powerful influence, which combines word of mouth with the new media, are television talk shows like *The Oprah Winfrey Show* in the United States and *Richard & Judy* in Britain, both of which have their own book clubs. These leading talk show hosts now play a major role in bringing books to the attention of a wide, diverse audience, and crossover books figure prominently in their selections. Jennifer Donnelly was relatively unknown in Britain when she won the Carnegie Medal for *A Gathering Light*, but she gained enormous popularity when it was selected as one of the six novels on Richard and Judy's "Summer Read" in 2004. Although book industry insiders are sceptical about the credibility of recommendations by talk show hosts, they been extremely influential in increasing book sales. Malcolm Gladwell argues that this kind of "personalized recommendation" represents "the future of marketing, not its past," as readers feel the need for guidance in the age of infinite information.[71]

Booksellers and their Buyers

Booksellers play a very important role in the crossover phenomenon. Crossover books pose a dilemma for bookstores, who have to decide how to label these books. "Potential crossover books always face the problem that the two publishing industries run in separate but parallel universes," says Mark Haddon, who has had firsthand experience with both.[72] However, those worlds are now intersecting at certain points. If publishers refuse to categorize a crossover book, as they are doing with increasing frequency, booksellers still have to decide where to shelve the book, in the children's, young adult, or adult sections, or perhaps in more than one section. After the first novel in Pullman's trilogy started attracting an adult audience, some bookshops in Britain began putting it in adult fantasy as well as in children's fiction, which certainly extended the adult readership. Science fiction and fantasy authors such as Tolkien, Terry Pratchett, and Walter Moers have always been shelved in the adult section, but they are also read by children, so large bookshops have been putting them in the children's section as well.

Promoting a book in dual markets poses a number of problems. In 1997, the vice-president of merchandising at Barnes & Noble admitted that her stores were "not proactively selling kids' books to adults." Their message to publishers at the time was the following: "if you think you have a crossover book, you need to position it that way." When the sales representative would reply that it was listed in both catalogues, her response was that she needed to know where it should be in their particular stores.[73] If the book is published in two editions or listed in both the adult and children's catalogues, there is perhaps more pressure to double-shelve the book. However, double-shelving requires more space and larger quantities of the book, but industry insiders say that bookstores are now carrying less stock across the board. In 2004, Philippa Dickinson of Random House Children's Books maintained that "retailers don't like crossover novels very much . . . , because they can't be sure whether to put them in the adults' or children's section—and they don't often want to put them in both." The opposite view was expressed, one year earlier, by Suzy Jenvey, the editorial director of children's books at Faber & Faber. According to her, "retailers are happy for books to jump from one department to another," whereas ten years earlier, "that would never have happened."[74]

In fact, some booksellers were already looking for ways to promote crossover titles as early as 1997. That year, Hyperion had a concentrated promotion of children's books written by established adult novelists. A bookstore campaign, titled "Introduce your favorite writer to your favorite reader," included shelf talkers, table cards and bookmarks to place in the adult fiction section to encourage customers to browse in the children's section. It was Geist's hope that the promotion would encourage booksellers to shelve these books in both sections.[75] Some booksellers were already incorporating all types of children's books in adult displays, but they were certainly the exception. Stephanie Wolfe, children's buyer at University Bookstore in Seattle, who worked on the Children's Book Council's selection panel to create their annual catalogue of crossover titles in 1997, said that up until that time most of the cross-merchandising had been with picturebooks. It was the young adult category that was the most difficult for booksellers to help cross over in those years. When the Children's Book Council launched its "Not Just for Children Anymore!" catalogue, a selection of "110 Children's Books that Adults Will Enjoy and Buy for Themselves," at the Bookexpo America convention in 1997, it issued a challenge to booksellers to identify and merchandise crossover books. That challenge was taken up and the situation changed so dramatically in the following years that the Children's Book Council quit publishing the catalogue in 2002. Some online booksellers have introduced crossover categories. For example, BookBrowse.com has an "Adult-Teen Crossover" category that is described as "books that are targeted at adults but are likely to be of interest/ suitable for teens." A "Listmania!" list on Amazon.com is entitled "Fantasy Books for Adults in Denial." Libraries also now create lists of crossover titles, for example, Christchurch City Libraries' list of "Children's Books for Adults and Children" posted on their website.

Bookstores have been accustomed to strictly defined categories. However, crossover books do not fit neatly into age categories and often defy generic categories as well. When a book cannot be categorized in Germany, they say: "You can't put this book into a drawer." German booksellers want to do precisely that, according to Ralf Isau. In an e-mail message on May 22, 2007, the author told me his novels do not fit in a single "drawer" or under a specific label. In Germany, booksellers consider *The Neverending Story* to be a juvenile book and shelve it in the children's section, so they automatically consider all other novels set in the world of Phantásia, including Isau's, to be juvenile books. However, German bookstores have what is called the "allgemeine Reihe" (general line), in which you find fiction that is not limited by genres such as "fantasy," "science fiction," or "mystery," and that is mainly addressed to adult readers. "Many adults would never go to the juvenile literature section, but they rummage through the 'allgemeine Reihe,'" says Isau. That is not only the case in Germany, according to Melvin Burgess, who believes that "fantasy shelves are the only part of the bookshop which is browsed freely by kids, teenagers, adults."[76] However, in many countries, adults are now regularly visiting the children's sections of bookstores as well as libraries.

Just as books are crossing over from the children's to the adult sections of bookstores and vice versa, so, too, are readers. Prior to Rowling's Harry Potter books, the children's sections of bookshops and libraries were not frequented by teenagers, much less by adults. Many bookstores, including the Indigo chain in Canada, still display young adult fiction with baby literature, which discourages many teenage readers from visiting the section. Some bookstores have remedied this problem by creating two children's book sections. When employees at the two-level Winnipeg bookstore, McNally Robinson for Kids, found that high school readers were reluctant to visit the teen section (12–18) upstairs because it was in the kids' section, the store set up a new, "grittier" PG-15 section downstairs near the adult books. In addition to young adult books that deal with heavier topics, the section includes adult books, both those that are traditionally read by teenagers, such as *The Catcher in the Rye*, *Pride and Prejudice*, and more contemporary works like Kazuo Ishiguro's *Never Let Me Go* and Miriam Toews's *A Complicated Kindness*, the irreverent coming-of-age story of a wry sixteen-year-old who rebels against the conventions of a strict Mennonite community in rural Manitoba. Convinced that many young readers are daunted by adult literature sections, the owner of McNally Robinson for Kids claims it is "kind of a stepping stone."[77] On the Barnes & Noble website, there is a separate "teen bookstore." Like many bookstores, some libraries are now also refusing to clearly indicate which books are for children. At the municipal library of Leipzig in Germany, the young adult section is positioned well away from the children's section and it is not called a "youth section." It is simply an area where young adults can find what interests them: young adult novels, adult novels, detective fiction, science fiction and fantasy, horror (notably the highly popular Stephen King), as well as reference works, magazines, books about computers, CD-ROMs, and so forth. Many young adult authors are very conscious of the shelving dilemma faced by booksellers and libraries. As the content of young adult novels becomes more "adult," booksellers hesitate to put them in the children's section. Excellent examples are Melvin Burgess's gritty, controversial novels, such as *Junk*, about teenage heroin addiction, or *Doing It*, about teenage sexuality. Burgess himself admits: "Booksellers find it hard placing my books because they don't necessarily want the tits and arse next to the Three Little Pigs."[78]

In the years since the release of the fourth *Harry Potter* in 2000, booksellers have become increasingly used to the idea of books crossing from one section to another. The incentive was certainly there, as children's books with adult appeal have become very big business for book retailers. It is now quite common to find bestselling children's books prominently shelved next to adult books in bookstores. At the same time, adult novels are being displayed in the children's and young adult sections of many bookstores.

Many first editions of crossover novels have become much sought after collectibles that are commanding very high prices on the rare books market, much of which is conducted on eBay and other auction sites. Even mainstream bookstores have also gotten involved. The British bookseller Waterstone's has identified children's books as *the* hot collectible right now. However, the collectability of J. R. R. Tolkien's *The Hobbit*, mentioned earlier, indicates that this is not a new phenomenon. As a service to its customers, Waterstone's organizes signings of authors they think will be successful. Sean Wright was one of those authors. Waterstone's offered an exclusive limited first paperback edition of *The Twisted Root of Jaarfindor*. The fact that these first editions are signed by the author greatly increases their value, but the signed books are sold at the cover price rather than an inflated collector's price. "We're a book retailer, not a racketeer," said George Grey, manager of the children's department at Waterstone's in 2004.[79] At the other end of the spectrum, first editions of J. K. Rowling's *Harry Potter and the Philosopher's Stone*, which had a first edition print run of just five hundred, have sold for as much as $37,000. Even unread signed deluxe hardback first editions of *Harry Potter and the Goblet of Fire*, which was printed in the hundreds of thousands, have sold for $2,000.

Rowling is certainly not the only collectible crossover author. The July 2004 edition of the prestigious publication *Book and Magazine Collector* featured an article entitled "Rowling's Rivals: The New Collectables." The article is devoted to the "highly collectable novels" of the "new wave of children's authors," whose first editions are commanding high prices that are in an upward spiral. Their list of fifteen of the world's most collectible modern children's authors includes J. K. Rowling, Philip Pullman, Lemony Snicket, G. P. Taylor, Eoin Colfer, Charmian Hussey, Cornelia Funke, Dominic Mieville, Steve Augarde, Christopher Paolini, P. D. Moredun, Garth Nix, Gill Arbuthnot, Philip Reeve, and Sean Wright.[80] The fact that Charmian Hussey, Dominic Mieville, Gill Arbuthnot, and Sean Wright are included with authors like Rowling, Pullman, and Funke shows the power of self-publishing when it comes to collectible crossover titles. When G. P. Taylor self-published the first edition of *Shadowmancer*, he was obviously quite conscious from the outset of the value of a limited initial print run. Apparently he signed first editions and gave them to members of his congregation who were in financial difficulty, knowing that they would be able to sell them on eBay for a substantial amount (some copies later sold for over £1,000). When a hardcover first edition of the novel sold for $11,000 on eBay, Will Atkinson, head of international sales at Faber & Faber, pointed out that was "not the kind of spare change a kid would have."[81] In his interview with Nick Gifford on the Infinity Plus website, Sean Wright equates the sales of his books to collecting old and rare issues of the Marvel Comics, in other words, a nostalgia thing. Another collectible author is Michelle Paver. The cover price of her *Wolf Brother* is £8.99 but, with the author's signature and drawing of a wolf paw print, it sells on the Internet for about €1,000. It is obviously not children who are forking out these sums for collectible children's books. With more than a hint of irony, Jill Insley warns collectors of these children's/crossover books: "Once you have purchased your prize, do everything you can to keep the children away from it."[82]

Globalization of the Marketplace

Dan Hade, Jack Zipes, and a number of other critics have expressed their concern about the current children's publishing situation in the United States, where a handful of large companies now dominate the children's publishing industry. Even more disturbing is the way in which the huge companies of the English-speaking world in general dominate the global literary scene. This is best indicated by the universal phenomenon of the Harry Potter books, which have been published in more than two hundred countries. Would such a phenomenon have been possible if the books had not been produced in an English-speaking country? Some French critics feel that Rowling's series could never have originated in France, simply because they do not respect the norms and conventions of children's literature. It has even been suggested that without the introduction of the cultural phenomenon of Hallowe'en into France a few years earlier, the Harry Potter books would not have been nearly as popular there. In any case, their success has had a huge impact on French readers and French publishing in general, as they have had around the globe. Muriel Tiberghien, director of the journal *Livres, jeunes aujourd'hui*, attributes the "adultization" of literature to the English-speaking countries. Pointing out that the age category of "young adults" did not exist before the 1990s, she claims that the French discovered this literature principally in the United States.[83] The huge impact that she feels foreign literature, notably English-language literature, has had on French literature, is chiefly in the sphere of crossover fiction. Authors who initially wrote only for adults and cross over without understanding the "constraints" of children's literature, introduce a more emancipated style of writing. Although Tiberghien seems to view this particular influence of the English-language publishing world on foreign markets in a negative light, many others, like Michi Strausfeld, consider this "liberation" of literature to be a very positive development. Continental European publishers and critics, including Tiberghien herself, often cite Roald Dahl as being an author who has done a great deal to emancipate children's literature in countries like France and Spain.[84]

Critics such as Jack Zipes and Jean Perrot rightly point out that globalization has resulted in a certain homogenization of literature that facilitates the crossing of borders.[85] Literature has become more easily adaptable to all readers, languages, cultures, and, most notably, markets. The perceived erasure of cultural difference is alarming to many literary critics, who feel that national specificities are played down, if not absent altogether. There are obviously many exceptions to such generalizations. Even the Harry Potter books retain a strong British colouring that Rowling was unwilling to sacrifice in the cinematographic adaptation. Initially, Rowling refused all offers from film companies, finally agreeing to Warners because they promised to be faithful to the book. Apparently Stephen Spielberg was rejected because he had wanted to make the film more American, whereas Chris Columbus pledged to maintain the

Britishness of the novels. Although the books are based on universal archetypes, the British school system clearly structures life at the Hogwarts School of Witchcraft and Wizardry.

The English-language dominance of the global literary market is often seen as largely to blame for this trend toward literary homogenization. Many writers and publishers in less developed countries nonetheless feel that the success of Rowling's series has had a positive impact on the children's publishing industry in general. Dianne Hofmeyr believes that is the case in South Africa, but at the same time she laments the fact that bookstores there "still fill their shelves with so many imports."[86] In this era of globalization, when the publishing industry seems to be preoccupied with economics rather than literature, the director of Las Tres Edades is convinced that readers of all ages, children as well as adults, need a mental shift away from nationalistic feelings of self-sufficient superiority and toward an open receptiveness to other cultures. Many other critics have specifically accused the United States and Britain of this kind of cultural narrow-mindedness. Strausfeld begins by looking at the situation from the perspective of a country within the European community, but goes on to point out that over 3,000 million of the world's population are in India, China, and Latin America.[87] Yet scandalously few books from these countries get published abroad. Literature from the so-called developing countries rarely reaches American or British readers.

Paradoxically, globalization is only making this problem more acute. Many works that are bestsellers in their country of origin, and often in many other countries as well, have never been translated into English. Even works by major, award-winning authors all too often remain completely unknown in the English-speaking world. In contrast, the works of important American and British authors tend to be translated rapidly into most major European languages. A consideration of the global book market reveals a troubling discrepancy in the proportion of translations produced from one country to another. Whereas eighty per cent of the books published in Finland are translations, that figure drops to a mere three per cent in Great Britain and only one per cent in the United States.[88] In our so-called global age, publishers in English-speaking countries need to be convinced of the importance of publishing translations of foreign books, particularly crossover books that reach a wide audience. Rowling and Pullman are known the world over, but how many readers in the English-speaking world are familiar with even the names of Dominique Demers, Ljubko Deresh, Tormod Haugen, Wim Hofman, Bart Moeyaert, Haruki Murakami, Yury Olesha, or Andreas Steinhöfel. Yet, they are major crossover authors, whose novels are bestsellers not only in their own countries but often in many others as well. Even earlier books that have become modern classics and are regularly reissued in new editions in their country of origin have often had a dismal fate in Britain and North America. Although excellent translations of Tournier's *Friday and Robinson* and Michael Ende's *The Neverending Story* exist, the books have never been widely read in the English-speaking world. The latter is largely known to the North American public through the 1984 film version that deviates so drastically from the novel that the author himself initiated legal proceedings. Ende laments in particular the "Americanization" of his bestselling novel in the cinematographic adaptation. If foreign books do manage to get translated, often they do not stay in print for very long. One exception is Antoine de Saint-Exupéry's *The Little Prince*, but it is unique in that it was written and first published in the United States, and has enjoyed equal success in English and French. In France, the second bestselling children's book after *The Little Prince* is Tournier's *Friday and Robinson*, which has sold millions of copies there, but in the United States it wasn't even reprinted after a small initial print run. The crossover phenomenon has nonetheless helped to bring some foreign authors to the attention of the English-speaking world and even to put them on bestseller lists, one of the most notable examples being Cornelia Funke.

As director of Siruela's Las Tres Edades, Michi Strausfeld is dedicated to widening the horizons of Spanish readers of all ages by publishing crossover fiction from as many countries as possible. One can only hope that more publishers in other countries will adopt this laudable publishing policy, which demonstrates what true globalization should and could be. Perhaps the most we can hope for in the English-language market is that other publishers share the goal formulated by Gillie Russell, Fiction Publishing Director of HarperCollins Children's Books, that of "turning the culturally important into the commercially successful."[89]

Chapter Seven
Paratexts and Packaging

I don't think books have changed. Certainly the way we package books has changed beyond all recognition.

Marion Lloyd, ReadersVoice.com interview

Until recent years, adult and children's books had a very different look. In most cases, it was possible to immediately differentiate a book for children from a book for adults. Even young adult titles were generally quite recognizable by their appearance. Such distinctions are now largely a thing of the past. Marion Lloyd, who returned to Pan Macmillan to run their children's fiction list before becoming Associate Publisher at Pan, has been working in the publishing industry since the 1970s. In an interview posted on the ReadersVoice website in July 2005, Lloyd said that she does not think children's books have changed, but the way books are packaged "has changed beyond all recognition." To illustrate her point, she claimed not to have published a children's book with a picture of a child on it for years. "We're much more sophisticated in the way we package them. Our books look 'older' [i.e. like a book for adults] than they used to." Many children's and young adult books are now indistinguishable from adult books.

Crossover books are big business for publishers, as we saw in the previous chapter. How to package and position these books in the market is a vitally important question that has been occupying publishers for some time. Publishers have tried a variety of marketing strategies. In some cases, they have opted for a single edition that is sold into both adult and children's sections. With increasing frequency, they have done two separate editions of a book. In these cases, the editions have sometimes been simultaneous, but more often one edition follows the other, generally the adult edition after the children's edition. Often publishers hope that young adults will discover the novel in the adult section on their own, and that, likewise, adults will find the young adult novel in the children's section. One of the concerns of publishing a book in dual markets is expressed in the *Children's and Writers' Yearbook 2006*: "Publishers certainly don't want to cannibalise their own book sales."[1]

Crossover (Re)Packaging

In order to position a book as a crossover, publishers often specify somewhere in the paratext that it is meant for a diverse audience, often in conjunction with comparisons to previous crossover successes such as those of Rowling and Pullman. This is frequently done in the blurb on the cover or dustjacket. Such crossover recommendations have become increasingly common since the late 1990s. Often quotations from prestigious newspapers are used to attract adult readers to young adult novels. The cover of *Firesong*, the third volume in William Nicholson's trilogy, quotes an excerpt from the *Daily Telegraph*: "Nicholson's imaginative skill will delight readers across the ages."

Publishers have also become more wary of specifying a genre that implies a certain readership or indicating an age category on the cover or jacket. The Dutch author Edward van de Vendel tells how a seventeen-year-old student asked his teacher of Dutch language and literature if he could read the adolescent novel *De dagen van de bluegrassliefde* (The days of bluegrass love, 1999) for his literature class. In 2000, the novel received the Gouden Zoen (Golden kiss), a Dutch award given to the best novel for readers between the ages of twelve and fifteen. After skimming the book and reading the blurbs, the teacher refused because students were not allowed to read "youth novels" for class. The following day, the student returned to the teacher with Van de Vendel's *Gijsbrecht* (1998), a retelling of a famous old Dutch play, for which the author had won the same award the previous year. This time the student was given permission to read it because, writes Van de Vendel, "the publisher had been wise enough not to put the word 'youth novel' on the cover."[2]

Forewords, prefaces, introductions, afterwords, notes, and other forms of paratexts often suggest, or even explicitly mention, a certain readership. When Antonio Skármeta's adult text "Tema de clase" was published as the picturebook *The Composition* by the Venezuelan publisher Ediciones Ekaré, it underwent a number of paratextual changes. Most notably, a long explanatory note, entitled "Dictatorship," was included after the story to help young readers understand what it means to live under such a government. When Joy Kogawa rewrote her novel *Obasan* for children, *Naomi's Road* was preceded by a highly didactic prefatory letter, providing a historical context that would have been better left to the text. Retrospectively, Kogawa regrets having included the letter at the publisher's request. In keeping with the goals of the second version of Beatrice Culleton's *April Raintree*, a paratextual document was added in the form of an introduction. Likewise, many of the books published in Siruela's Las Tres Edades crossover series were later brought out in the Colección Escolar with pedagogical paratexts. The children's edition of J. M. G. Le Clézio's *Pawana* contains an afterword in which the author explains the genesis of the story and the intertextual relationship between his text and Melville's. When *Sirandanes*, a collection of traditional riddle-poems from Mauritius published for an adult audience by Le Clézio and his wife Jemia in 1990, was issued in a children's edition by Seghers Jeunesse in 2005, it included a new afterword by Danielle Henky. According to the publisher, the afterword was intended to make the riddles accessible to the largest possible number of readers. However, the new edition was entirely superfluous. In both editions, the riddles appear in Creole along with a French translation, and are followed by a short Creole lexicon. Le Clézio himself illustrated the book with very simplistic watercolours. It is quite probable that young readers appreciate the collection as much as, if not more than, adults, since riddles are an important part of children's culture.

In some cases, explanatory notes have even been added on the copyright page of picturebooks, even though that element of the paratext is least likely to catch the attention of a child reader. The copyright page of *Antipoden*, the picture-book by Ernst Jandl and Norman Junge, provides an explanation of the origin and meaning of the word *Antipoden*, but unless an adult co-reader informs children that it means "opposite feet," they will read the picturebook without the piece of information that the author, illustrator, or publisher felt was impor-tant enough to include on the copyright page. In a similar manner, the copyright page of *Einer, der nichts merkte* contains an explanation of the complicated planograph technique used by Käthi Bhend in the illustrations.

Explanatory notes are not only added when an adult text crosses over to a young audience, however. When "Amandine, or The Two Gardens" was published in the adult collection *The Fetishist*, Tournier included, in the form of a long note, an interview, entitled "Le sang des fillettes" (The blood of little girls), that had appeared in *Le Monde* when the children's edition was published the preceding year. The author seems to feel that, whereas children are able to understand the initiatory meaning of the tale instinctively, there is a need to point it out explicitly to adult readers. For the same reason, the subtitle "an initiatory tale" was added in the adult collection. In a reverse phenomenon, the genre "nouvelle" was indicated under the title *La famille Adam* when the story was published as a picturebook. It is paradoxical that the generic descriptor was added to the children's version when Tournier states insistently that the *nouvelle* is not a suitable genre for children. It was for that reason that the story was not included in the children's collection *Sept contes*. Perhaps the subtitle serves as a warning to adults who are thinking of buying the picturebook for children. In some cases, the same paratext appears for both audiences. The afterword that Tournier added to the picturebook *Angus*, drawing attention to Victor Hugo's hypotext, was retained, as a long note, when the tale was included in both his children's and adult collections.

Even a dedication can seem to imply a crossover readership for a book. In the picturebook *Einer, der nichts merkte*, only well-read adults will understand the meaning of Käthi Bhend's dedication, "For the cat," an allusion to Robert Walser's nomadic years in Bern. However, the illustrator extends the dedication in a manner that can be appreciated by children: throughout the illustrations, she adds a cat that is not present in the text. A classic example of a crossover dedication is Saint-Exupéry's double dedication of *The Little Prince*, "to Léon Werth" and "to Léon Werth when he was a little boy," clearly giving the book a dual address. Although the second dedication is supposedly a "correction" of the first, the author leaves both, as well as his apology to young readers for dedicating the book to a "grown-up," his reasons for doing so, and his explanation that "all grown-ups were once children," so that the dedication page reads like a transparent palimpsest.

Illustrations obviously play an essential role in determining a book's audience. In many countries, illustrated books, however lengthy and complex, often tend to be classified as children's books even though they may address a crossover audience. The scope of this study does not allow an extensive examination of this important aspect of the crossover phenomenon, which also includes the rapidly developing field of graphic novels. Crossover fiction, both classic and contemporary, includes a significant number of illustrated works. *Alice in Wonderland*, with its memorable illustrations by John Tenniel, is one of the most striking examples. Already it is difficult to imagine Michelle Paver's Chronicles of Ancient Darkness series without the realistic drawings by Geoff Taylor. Many crossover works have been illustrated by the authors themselves, including Kipling's *Just So Stories* and Tolkien's *The Hobbit*. Saint-Exupéry's luminous illustrations for *The Little Prince* are inseparable from the text of this unique book. His image of the much-loved little prince is a visual icon that is familiar the world over. More recently, Carmen Martín Gaite illustrated her novel *Caperucita en Manhattan*, and Philip Pullman did stamp-sized black-and-white art for a later edition of *His Dark Materials*.

In some cases, the presence of illustrations plays an important role in the novel's eventual readership. Wim Hofman illustrates his lengthy, poetic retelling of Snow White, *Zwart als inkt is het verhaal van Sneeuwwitje en de zeven dwergen* (Black as ink is the story of Snow White and the seven dwarfs), with over one hundred drawings in red and black ink. The Dutch author and illustrator subjects the well-known tale to intense psychological examination and explores the nightmare side of childhood experience. Taking the poisoned apple is a deliberate attempt at suicide, a theme that is suggested on the cover by the black lines through a child-like drawing of a girl. The awarding of two major children's book prizes (the Gouden Griffel or Golden Pencil and the prestigious Woutertje Pieterse Prize) to *Zwart als inkt* in 1998 sparked a great deal of discussion with regard to the target audience. In the Netherlands, where the cover bears the two prize stickers, *Zwart als inkt* is read mostly by children and women, according to the author, who insists that he does not write for a particular audience. The presentation of the German edition is almost identical with the exception of the absence of the children's prize stickers, but the author points out that it targets a dual audience of children and adults.[3]

Like Hofman, Clive Barker is an accomplished artist. He was also a bestselling adult author, film producer, and director, before he published *Abarat* in 2002. In the mid-1990s, he began working on the large, sumptuous paintings that would be included in his The Books of Abarat quartet. Over one hundred paintings made their way into the first book of the series. Originally, Barker began the work as a single volume based on the idea of a traditional medieval Book of Hours. It was a children's book that he hoped would reach "the adult audience." According to the author's website, it was to be "the literary equivalent of Fantasia,"one of his favourite movies. From the outset, his intention was to create a fantasy world that, like Narnia, Middle-earth, or Oz, would speak to readers of all ages. In his full-coloured illustrations, the artist presents a strange world of fantastical hybrid creatures that have been compared to those of Lewis Carroll and Dr. Seuss. The paintings generally appeal to all ages, but it is chiefly among the younger generation that he finds his cult following. In a review on the Trashotron website, Rick Kleffel suggests that "the illustrations lift the book a level beyond the usual illustrations in a children's book" and "serve to make the book a lot more appealing to anyone of any age." Some adults find the characters too grotesque even though the landscapes are quite beautiful. The stories in Barker's The Books of Abarat quartet actually grew out of the paintings that preceded them. This was also the case for Christine Nöstlinger's novel *Hugo, das Kind in den besten Jahren: Phantastischer Roman nach Bildern von Jörg Wollmann* (1983), which was inspired by the fantastic graphics of Jörg Wollmann.

Yann Martel would like to see a revival of the art of illustrating adult books. A competition to find an illustrator for *Life of Pi*, co-sponsored by Canongate and the *Times* newspaper of London, was launched in October 2005. Some felt it was a strategy to attract more publicity to the bestselling novel. Sixteen hundred artists from around the world entered the competition and a panel chose six finalists, from which the author selected the winner, the Croatian artist Tomislav Torjanac. Martel claims it is "adult art," despite the cute pictures of animals that would look right at home in a children's picturebook. One reviewer warns parents that in spite of its "child-friendly" look, the illustrated version of Martel's novel is not meant for children.[4] However, young adults were already reading the novel, so the illustrations can only make it more appealing for that audience.

Many adult texts are subsequently illustrated to facilitate the crossover to children. When the illustrations are an integral part of the original text, as in the case of Hofman and Barker, for example, it is not appropriate to consider them as paratextual elements. This becomes even more obvious with regard to picturebooks, in which the illustrations constitute a visual text that shares the narrative role with the verbal text. However, in the case of adult texts illustrated at a later date for children, the illustrations are a form of paratext. Michel Tournier's *Le miroir à deux faces* demonstrates quite well how the addition of illustrations can not only make an adult text accessible to children, but also retain the original adult audience. Alain Gauthier's sumptuous illustrations for *Le miroir à deux faces* are typical of the French artist's very distinctive style, which is characterized by ethereal figures in a dreamlike, surreal atmosphere. Tournier told me in a conversation on July 6, 1995, that he considers Gauthier's illustrations quite beautiful but much too "severe" and "melancholic," and not sufficiently "illustrative" to be suitable for young readers. On the other hand, the author believes that the illustrations Gauthier did for an earlier edition of *La Fugue du petit Poucet*, which is also included in the collection, are much more "accessible" to children, even though they are also in his distinctive surrealistic style. *Le miroir à deux faces* was published by Seuil Jeunesse, the children's division of Seuil, but the superb picturebook seems to appeal to adults more than children. Many contemporary picturebooks appeal to both children and adults, but that is the subject of another book in progress devoted to "Crossover Picturebooks."

The repackaging of books has often allowed them to find a new audience. Two years after the successful release of Carmen Martín Gaite's *Caperucita en Manhattan*, two stories that had appeared for children in the 1980s were published together, under the title *2 cuentos maravillosos* (2 wonder tales), in Las Tres Edades series, before also appearing in their paperback series for adults. Sometimes this formula entails the packaging together of two texts that were originally published for different readerships. The Norwegian author Ragnar Hovland offers an interesting example of this crossover packaging. His adult novel *Alltid fleire dagar* (Always another day), originally released for adults in 1979, was published in 1993 together with his young adult novel *Mercedes* in a single volume that was aimed at young adults. In the case of the Flemish author Henri Van Daele, the repackaging resulted in a crossover in the other direction. Almost all of Van Daele's works have been published by Lannoo as books for young readers, age twelve and up. In 1995, his autobiographical stories for young readers, along with a previously unpublished story about his adolescence, were collected in a single volume, entitled *Een tuin om in te spelen* (A garden to play in), to mark Van Daele's fiftieth birthday. The weighty volume of 1,283 pages was not published for young readers, but was described as *jeugdherinneringen* (memories of youth). His earlier writings for children and adolescents were thus widely read by an adult audience. In the Dutch journal *Literatuur zonder leeftijd* (Literature without age), Peter van den Hoven describes the book as "a wonderful present for the author, but also for all readers," both "young and old."[5] Van Daele has since published his first novel for adults, *Woestepet* (a nickname meaning Wildcap, 2002). In a similar manner, Robert Cormier's anthology *Eight Plus One*, published in 1980, introduced adults to short stories that had previously been published for young adults. Although these stories had initially appeared in a variety of magazines for adults, they had since been published elsewhere for young adults. The author prefaces each story in the collection with reflections on his writing that are of interest to both young readers and adults. The author's introductory note suggests that he had a crossover audience in mind. In 1991, the anthology was reissued in the young adult imprint Laurel-Leaf, but the publisher claims that the nine stories are "to be savored by readers of all ages." The collection received the World of Reading Readers' Choice Award, sponsored by Silver Burdett & Ginn, a particularly notable achievement because young readers voted for Cormier to receive the prize.

Although it is not an obvious case of crossover packaging, a trilogy by the Irish writer Edna O'Brien crossed over when it was reissued for a new generation. The first novel in the trilogy, *The Country Girls*, based on the author's own experiences about being educated in a convent, was an immediate success when it was first published in 1960. It was followed by two sequels: *The Lonely Girl* (1962; later published as *Girl with Green Eyes*) and *Girls in Their Married Bliss* (1964). Published for adults, the books were considered very provocative and the young Irish Catholic girls who read them at that time felt very daring indeed. Many of O'Brien's novels were banned in Ireland. In 1986, *The Country Girls Trilogy and Epilogue* was reissued in New York, by Farrar, Straus, in a single volume with a new epilogue. The trilogy is now seen more as young adult literature and it is read primarily by teenage girls. In Australia, Pan Macmillan began issuing John Marsden's young adult bestsellers of the Tomorrow series in an edition for adults. Bloomsbury adopted the opposite strategy, bringing out Susanna Clarke's 800-page adult novel, *Jonathan Strange & Mr Norrell*, in a box set of three volumes, perhaps in the hope of capturing more young adult readers.

The importance of the packaging of a book in determining its audience is perhaps best illustrated by the works of Dominique Demers. She was a highly successful children's author in Quebec before becoming a crossover author and eventually an author for adults as well. She has had the same novels on best-selling lists for both children and adults. Demers's popular Marie-Lune trilogy for adolescents tells the story of a fifteen-year-old girl's tempestuous passage to adulthood. The first novel in the trilogy, *Un hiver de tourmente* (A turbulent winter), was published in 1992 by La courte échelle, in their series Roman+. However, the two sequels, *Les grands sapins ne meurent pas* (The large firs do not die) and *Ils dansent dans la tempête* (They dance in the storm), were brought out, in 1993 and 1994 respectively, by the publisher Québec/Amérique. The move from La courte échelle, the leading children's publisher in Quebec, to Québec/Amérique, which, as was already mentioned, specializes in books for adults, played a crucial role in Demers's new status as a crossover author and later as an author for adults.

The Marie-Lune novels were hugely popular with young readers, as indicated by children's choice awards, such as the Communication-jeunesse Livre préféré des jeunes (Young people's favourite novel), which Demers won three years in a row, beginning in 1992–93, for each volume in the trilogy in turn. The crossover appeal of the series was clearly demonstrated by the "Coup de cœur" poll in 1997, when the first two volumes were chosen as the favourite novels not only in the category of adolescents aged thirteen to seventeen, but also for the age group eighteen to a hundred and eight. At the same time, the books in the trilogy garnered more traditional literary awards, including the 1993 Mr. Christie's Book Award for the first two novels, and the 1995 Prix Québec/Wallonie-Bruxelles for children's literature for the second novel. Although the books in the Titan series, in which the Marie-Lune trilogy appeared, are aimed primarily at adolescents, they often appeal to adults, according to Québec/Amérique's children's catalogue.

When Demers's publisher noticed that adults were reading the novels of the hugely popular trilogy "on the sly, without even the pretext of being a teacher, a bookseller, or a librarian," he decided to combine the three volumes into one, under a new title, and publish it for adults.[6] The Quebecois publisher brought out the single-volume adult edition of Demers's young adult trilogy in 1997, well before Rowling's *Harry Potter* spawned the trend of repackaging young adult fiction for adults. Although the text of the adult edition was identical, important changes were made to the paratext. A new title transformed the protagonist, Marie-Lune, into *Marie-Tempête*. A new foreword by Jacques Allard claims that the three young adult novels were really "a novel about adolescence in three parts," in other words, a "real" novel (9). The author's dedication "to all young people ..." was eliminated from the edition for adults.

According to Demers, the appearance of a young adult novel in a series for adults was a "first," at least in Quebec, where *Marie-Tempête* topped the adult bestseller list. Other sequences of juvenile novels have since been published in Quebec in a single volume for the adult market. In 1999, the publisher Michel Quintin put out two children's novels by Benjamin Simard—*Ben* (1997) and *Expédition Caribou* (1998)—in a single volume suitable for adults, entitled *Ben Caribou*. *Marie-Tempête* was a huge success in France, where readers did not realize that the novel was originally written for adolescents, a fact that greatly amuses the author. The popular trilogy was also adapted for television in Quebec. In spite of the success of the trilogy with adult readers, Demers realized, on publishing *Un hiver de tourmente* in 1992, that, in her case, writing for children and adolescents would never be "a springboard" toward writing for adults, but rather a "final goal." She is nonetheless convinced that the "ultimate test" of the quality of a manuscript is that of "a second target public." All the author's manuscripts are put to this test: she reads her "novels for adolescents to adults" and her "novels for adults to adolescents."[7] Thus Demers regularly practises what could be called "the crossover test."

Francesca Lia Block's Weetzie Bat books also offer an interesting case of crossover repackaging. The first book in the series was published for adults, but the collection of hip tales about growing up in Los Angeles was subsequently targeted at a young adult audience. However, they have also attracted a large adult audience, particularly from the trendy, under thirty-five crowd. In 1997, Joanna Cotler, publisher of Joanna Cotler Books at HarperCollins, told an interviewer that the crossover appeal of the Weetzie Bat books had been building for quite some time. Citing reviews in publications like New York's *The Village Voice*, she claimed that "Block always comes to mind in discussions about crossover books."[8] In order to capitalize on the adult appeal, HarperCollins reissued the Weetzie books with a more adult look in 1998. They were combined in a single paperback edition with a new title, *Dangerous Angels: The Weetzie Bat Books*, and a quote from *Spin* magazine calling it "a sensualist's paradise." It was also given a reading-group brochure like their adult books. HarperCollins included the book in both its adult and children's catalogues. The hip young trend-setting adults in their twenties and early thirties who are indulging their pop-culture tastes and embracing authors like Block do not demand the subdued, alternative jackets that many adult readers expect.

Simultaneous Publication for Two Audiences

Publishers do not always wait to see that a book is attracting another audience before publishing an edition for a second readership. Although the practice is much rarer, some books are published simultaneously for two audiences. In 1997, Québec/Amérique engaged in another editorial experiment, publishing Dominique Demers's novel *Maïna* simultaneously in an adult series and a juvenile series. This novel constituted another "first" in Quebec publishing history. In fact, it is difficult to find a comparable example in any country until several years later. In a letter written to me on July 13, 1999, Demers pointed to *Maïna* as a good example of the "blurred borders" between children's fiction and adult fiction. She had written the novel for adolescents approximately four-teen years and up, feeling that the project was a little too demanding for younger readers due to the prehistoric context and the anthropological information. *Maïna* is an adventure story about a pre-pubescent Native American who lives 3,500 years ago on Quebec's Côte-Nord. It falls into the genre of the prehistoric novel, whose prototype is *La guerre du feu* (*The Quest for Fire*), a novel published for adolescents in 1909, by the Belgian science fiction writer J. H. Rosny Sr. *Maïna* is also a coming-of-age story, in which the arrival of another tribe obliges the protagonist to confront intolerance and racism, but also the power and pain of love.

A few weeks after submitting the manuscript of *Maïna*, Demers received a phone call from her publisher to congratulate her on "finally having written an adult novel." When the author protested that *Maïna* was a young adult novel, he said that her young audience could read it in a series for adults. The success of the *Marie-Tempête* experiment led Demers to propose that the two volumes of *Maïna* be combined under a single title for adults, but that they also appear, as planned, in two volumes for adolescents. When her publisher asked why that was necessary, Demers replied that most adolescents—the audience for whom she had written the novel—would be discouraged by the thickness of the book if it was not published in two paperback volumes.[9] Many authors would agree with Demers, but the success of the later Harry Potter books proves otherwise.

Québec/Amérique accepted Demers's proposal with regard to *Maïna* and the novel also appeared for adolescents in the series Titan+, which is targeted at readers fourteen years and up (Titan without the plus sign is for twelve years and up). Curiously, the Québec/Amérique catalogue does not try to bill the books in this series for a crossover audience, as they did for the Titan series for younger readers, but rather for "young people of 14 years and up" who are "between adolescence and adulthood" (17). As with *Marie-Tempête*, not a single comma was changed and only paratextual differences distinguish the two editions. The author completely rewrote the foreword for the adult edition, eliminating, for example, the phrase dedicating the work "to all young people who like reading" (11). *Maïna* was equally well received by adult and adolescent audiences.

Demers does not believe, however, that *Maïna*'s success with both audiences means that literature for adolescents is merely a question of format and number of pages. In spite of the novel's success with adults (it spent weeks at the top of the bestseller list), Demers still insists that *Maïna* is really a young adult novel. It involves a runaway, a quest for identity, a coming of age, an initiation to sexuality, and the first serious questions concerning spirituality. The author feels that it has all the qualities of a novel for adolescents and is firmly rooted in their fantasies, dreams, fears, and secret desires. The enthusiastic reaction of young readers certainly confirms the author's view. The two volumes of the edition for adolescents were chosen as the favourite book of young readers in 1997, winning the Livre préféré des jeunes, Communication-Jeunesse 1997. At the same time, like many novels for adolescents, *Maïna* was also able "to cross the border of age groups to reach adults."[10]

Publishers eager to take advantage of the current boom in juvenile fiction are pushing the limits and releasing juvenile titles written with older audiences in mind. Whereas Demers maintained that *Maïna* had been written for young adults, Mark Haddon insists that in writing *The Curious Incident of the Dog in the Night-Time* his intention was to write a novel for adults, in the hope of getting out of the "ghetto" of children's literature. Unlike Pullman, who fights to pull children's literature out of the "ghetto," Haddon sought to escape into literary fiction for adults. Prior to *The Curious Incident of the Dog in the Night-Time*, Haddon was a successful children's author, with seventeen books to his name. The novel's runaway success so completely overshadowed his earlier works that the bestselling author was frequently referred to as a "first-time author."[11] In an exclusive author interview on Powell's website, Haddon admitted to Dave Weich that he was both surprised and disappointed when his agent suggested that, since the novel had a teenage protagonist, they try it "with both adult and children's publishers." After the success of his novel, Haddon talked about his "coming out as a writer," as if his entry into the world of adult fiction marked his coming of age as an author. Making the crossover from being a children's author to an adult author was, in his words, "like going across Death Valley in a Bacofoil suit." During this discouraging period, Haddon wrote five unpublished and, according to him, unpublishable novels, and also changed agents. While he was writing children's books, he suffered from "a frustrated literary ambition," which he describes in the following terms: "I felt for years that I had my little cold face pressed to the windowpane of the House of Literature and they were all in there: Julian ... Martin .... And then it was as if someone opened the door and I sort of tumbled down the hallway and ended up in the Jacuzzi."[12] Haddon nonetheless seemed determined to write an adult novel that could not be marketed to young readers. Perhaps this is because his bestseller has been described as a children's book "which doubled as his first adult novel."[13] After *The Curious Incident of the Dog in the Night-Time*, Haddon began writing an adult novel, with the working title "Blood and Scissors," that he claimed had "no crossover appeal whatsoever," even though the novel about a man suffering a nervous breakdown would have the same mix of darkness and humour. In 2006, the novel was published for adults under the title *A Spot of Bother*. When asked if he didn't run the risk of losing his younger readers, Haddon replied: "Younger readers do become the older readers quite soon."[14]

Although Haddon saw *The Curious Incident of the Dog in the Night-Time* more as an adult book, his publishers sensed the novel's commercial potential with two entirely different audiences and marketed it as both a literary novel and a young adult novel. When so much was made of its crossover appeal, the author dismissed this as being "nothing more than a marketing and media construct."[15] Haddon's novel was hailed as being unique in publishing. It may have been, as one critic claimed, "the first book to have been published simultaneously in two imprints—one for children and one for adults," but it was not, as Amanda Craig and others suggested, the first novel "published simultaneously as both adult and children's fiction."[16] Such claims fail to take into account what was happening beyond the English-language market. It may have been the first instance in Britain, but, as Demers's *Maïna* attests, the phenomenon had already occurred elsewhere. Two publishers at Random House did parallel editions of Haddon's novel: Jonathan Cape for the adult market and David Fickling Books for the teenage market. Its dual publication made it a true "crossover book" in the eyes of British reviewers. In the United States, however, only an adult edition was released to target the literary market, where it was received with wide acclaim. Likewise, the novel was published in Australia only in an adult edition.

In 2003, *The Curious Incident of the Dog in the Night-Time* was called "the big crossover hit book of the year," a book whose "genuine cross-over success echoes the *Harry Potter* phenomenon."[17] It garnered a wide adult audience in Britain when it not only won the fiction section of the Whitbread prize as an adult novel and then won the overall Whitbread prize, but was also longlisted for the Man Booker prize. John Carey, the Booker chairman, lamented that his fellow judges failed to put it on the shortlist. After taking the United Kingdom by storm, Haddon's novel became an unexpected international bestseller. It has sold in excess of twelve million copies worldwide, and has been published in more than forty countries. Haddon's novel met with rave reviews from all quarters and won prizes in both children's and adult spheres. At the British Book Awards in 2003, he took both the Children's Book of the Year and the Literary Fiction Award. By 2005, it was being called a "crossover classic" by an Indian journalist.[18]

In spite of the inevitable comparisons with *Harry Potter*, Haddon's book is very different. Some readers have found the unusual coming-of-age story reminiscent of *To Kill a Mockingbird* or *The Catcher in the Rye*, a book that influenced Haddon, but it remains highly original. Firmly anchored in realism, the awkwardly titled novel is narrated by a fifteen-year-old boy with Asperger's syndrome, a form of autism. The novel appeals to a very diverse audience, including readers of crime, young adult fiction, and literary fiction. The author believes that the widespread interest in his book is largely due to the fact that readers have to fill in the book's many gaps. The highly unusual narrator, who does not understand metaphor and never explains, invites each reader to interpret the story in his or her own way. Because Haddon adopts the very simple sentence structure in which Christopher attempts to communicate, the story is accessible to young readers. The mathematics that are woven throughout the narrative explain part of the novel's appeal. Middle-aged male readers, in particular, would write to Haddon pointing out logical errors, and the author admits that a couple of the "more glaring mathematical errors" were corrected.[19]

Scott MacDonald, staff writer for publishing trade magazine *Quill & Quire*, says publishers are averse to releasing a title for two audiences simultaneously. He explains: "It might sound like a great opportunity to sell it both ways, but instead, [publishers] worry that it will fall through the cracks. They worry that if they market it both ways, neither one will work and the book will just disappear."[20] Although this is a legitimate concern, a number of publishers have taken the risk and been rewarded by having the same book on bestselling lists for both children and adults.

Judging a Book by its Cover

The idea of publishing a book with different covers for two separate markets was not born with *Harry Potter*. After observing strong sales to young adult readers of Sandra Cisneros's *The House on Mango Street* and David Guterson's *Snow Falling on Cedars*, which were both marketed as adult books, Carl Lennertz, director of marketing of the Knopf Group, contacted booksellers asking for suggestions about hardcover young adult novels that Vintage could pick up in paperback primarily for adults. Although it was still in the "preliminary stages," in 1997, Lennertz was recommending "'the radical notion' of publishing two editions of the same book: one for the young adult market and one for adults. Each would have a different cover and price points."[21]

Bloomsbury did not delay in responding to adults' enthusiasm for *Harry Potter and the Philosopher's Stone*, publishing an edition of the novel packaged to appeal specifically to adult readers. The only differences between the adult and children's editions, with the exception of the price (adults were expected to pay more), are of a paratextual nature. As is often the case, the adult version has a more sober cover design so that adults feel comfortable reading it in public. A Swedish colleague who ordered three books from Amazon in Great Britain was surprised to receive the first volume in the edition for adults, with its sober, black and silver cover, and the two others in the brightly coloured children's editions. The mention of the Nestlé Smarties Book Prize, which was proudly displayed on the children's edition, was eliminated from the adult edition to avoid association with a prize reserved for children's fiction, and replaced by an excerpt from the *Times*. In France, the Harry Potter books were published by Gallimard's children's department in their paperback series Folio Junior, but they also appeared in a larger format that they marketed "for adults."[22] From the fourth volume onward, the books were given a more sophisticated look that was appropriate for adults as well as children. In Germany, the books were also released in two editions with different covers.

The publisher's choice of jacket design can play a crucial role in determining whether a book reaches a crossover audience. The dust jacket of Philip Pullman's *Northern Lights* offers an excellent example. The beautiful cover illustration that Eric Rohmann did for the U.S. edition has been used successfully in many other countries because it works well as a crossover cover. In the United States, the adult paperback was nonetheless given a different cover, which is far less attractive but decidedly more subtle. In an e-mail message on May 7, 2000, Pullman told me he had just returned from a signing of the first two volumes of the trilogy at a science fiction festival in St. Malo, where he had discovered that his French audience was composed of both adults and children, even though the books were published by Gallimard Jeunesse. Impressed by the French publication, the author once again pointed to the Rohmann jackets that create books "an adult need not be embarrassed to be seen with." In Germany, the trilogy was first published in hardcover by the children's publisher Carlsen. The paperback was brought out a year or so later by Heyne, one of Germany's largest paperback publishing houses, which does not publish children's books. In another e-mail message on May 22, 2007, Pullman said he did not know if the German publisher was deliberately attempting to attract adult readers, but he thought the first book looked "pretty grown-up in its German livery." This is confirmed by the fact that Heyne adopted the cover illustrations of Carlsen's first editions and still continues to use them, although Carlsen's recent editions have new cover illustrations. In contrast, the Hungarian jacket, which depicts a child of six in a pink woolly cardigan with a tear rolling down her cheek, is a "grotesquely inappropriate" choice, according to the author, who stated in an e-mail message on May 5, 2000, that it makes an adult audience "impossible." In 1998, Pullman had expressed the view that ideally there would be two different covers for the same book to appeal to the two markets. In Britain, Scholastic eventually gave *His Dark Materials* a new look for adults, repackaging the original children's covers in new adult-oriented jackets so that adults need not suffer the "indignity" of being seen reading a children's book in public. When an attractive boxed set with great paintings on the covers was in the works, the author said he hoped it would look "quite unlike a children's book" and be "the sort of thing adults are not embarrassed to be seen reading."[23]

In the wake of Pottermania, many children's books have been repackaged for an adult market. In light of the huge success of G. P. Taylor's *Shadowmancer*, Faber & Faber launched an edition for adults in February 2004. The style of the cover is not strikingly different from the young adult edition, issued the previous year, but it announces the novel as "the number one bestseller," without indicating on which particular list. HarperCollins brought out Garth Nix's The Abhorsen Trilogy in two editions in the United States, a young adult edition and an adult edition, in their Eos imprint, that had more subdued, symbolic covers. The two German editions of Isabel Allende's *City of the Beasts* were issued with different covers. The more subtle cover of the adult edition emphasizes the well-known author's name, which appears in very large, red letters on a white background, accompanied only with a small image of a jaguar in the lower right-hand corner. The children's cover, on the other hand, is more colourful, with the partial heads of a jaguar and an eagle in the foreground and the mysterious city in the background, while the author's name is quite inconspicuous. In 2006, Orion began issuing Kevin Crossley-Holland's Arthur trilogy for adults in their Phoenix imprint, again with more sober, adult-looking covers. The cover of *The Seeing Stone*, for example, bears only a simple coat of arms.

Publishers in other countries also began this repackaging strategy in the late 1990s. In 1999, Querido published Bart Moeyaert's *It's Love We Don't Understand* as a young adult novel in paperback, but with a cover they thought would attract an adult audience. After seven reprintings as such, the highly successful novel was reissued on their adult list in 2006 as a hardback with a different, but similar cover. Moeyaert's first collection of poems, *Verzamel de liefde* (the title is a word play: Gather the love/Gathered love), followed a similar path. It was first published on their children's list in softcover in 2003, but, after five reprintings, was reissued in a hardback edition, with a new cover, on the adult list. Moeyaert is not the only Querido author to have the same titles on both the children's and adult lists. Anne Provoost's *In the Shadow of the Ark* is now in its third printing in the softcover young adult edition, but, in 2007, it was also published on the adult list in a new hardback edition, with a completely different cover. The same thing happened in the United States, where it was initially published by Scholastic's Arthur A. Levine imprint.

The award-winning novel *Die Mitte der Welt* (*The Center of the World*), by the German children's author Andreas Steinhöfel, was published in 1998 by Carlsen Verlag, a publisher specializing in children's books. Although it is recommended on their website for readers fourteen years of age and up, Antje Richers of Carlsen told me in an e-mail message on March 31, 2006, that it was never accorded an age category and was seen as an "All-age-Titel." It was the first Carlsen book to be viewed as "a 'fiction and poetry book' AND a children's book by the book industry." Although there had been earlier examples, *Die Mitte der Welt* was the first novel to be highly successful in reaching a crossover audience, she stated in another e-mail message on April 3, 2006. The very lengthy novel (464 pages) is narrated in the first person by seventeen-year-old Phil, who is struggling with his homosexuality and his dysfunctional family in a conservative community. Hailed as a sophisticated literary novel, it has had great acclaim nationally and internationally from both critics and readers. In 1999, it won the prestigious Buxtehuder Bulle award for best young adult novel in Germany and was shortlisted for the Deutscher Jugendliteraturpreis.

Some reviewers have suggested that Steinhöfel's lengthy novel, which deals with passion, sex, and intimacy in very lyrical prose, is only for sophisticated readers. Two years after its release for young adults, *The Center of the World* appeared as a paperback for a general audience with Fischer Verlag. Unlike many other such repackaging endeavours, it was reissued with the same cover illustration, but with the genre "Roman" (novel) clearly indicated in large letters following the title. In German bookshops, Steinhöfel's novel is found in both the children's and adult sections. The English edition, which did not appear until 2005, was published only for a young adult audience. In 2007, it was reissued in the Laurel-Leaf imprint, which, according to the Random House website, is committed to "providing teens with quality literature in an accessible, mass-market format." Some online bookselling sites nonetheless market it for young people and adults. *Die Mitte der Welt* was reportedly being adapted as a feature film by the director Vanessa Jopp, who, on reading the book, knew that she wanted to see this "intense family story" on the screen. The film is expected to be "an adult *Forget America*," "a more mature film" than her first feature film, because *The Center of the World* is "more of a family drama à la John Irving than a coming-of-age tale."[24] In 2001, Steinhöfel published *Defender: Geschichten aus der Mitte der Welt* (Defender: Stories from the centre of the world, 2001), a follow-up that takes the form of a collection of short stories in which characters from the novel reappear. Although *Defender* is also read by young people and adults, it has been less successful than the novel with both audiences.

Another author in the German-language area who was the object of a similar crossover repackaging is the acclaimed Austrian author Renate Welsh. In 2002, she published the novel *Dieda oder Das fremde Kind* (That girl, or the strange child). It was published as a young adult novel in Austria, where it won the 2003 Österreichischen Kinder- und Jugendbuchpreis (Austrian child and youth book prize). In Germany, the novel was initially released for young adults by Oetinger, but three years later it was brought out by another publisher as an adult novel. Although the cover of the adult edition was different, like the children's edition it depicted the young protagonist (it seems that in Europe children can still be depicted on the cover of both children's and adult novels). *Dieda* is a stark and moving autobiographical novel about a seven-year-old girl who lives with the family of her stepmother in a village in Austria at the end of World War II. She blames herself for her real mother's death from a brain tumour and she feels entirely unwelcome in her new home, where she responds only to "that girl." Welsh often addresses the plight of girls and women in a patriarchal Austrian society. Although it was more officially recognized as a crossover work, *Dieda* is not Welsh's only novel that falls into that category. During a conversation on April 13, 2007, the author admitted to me that her earlier novel *Johanna* (1979), which won the Deutscher Jugendliteraturpreis and became a classic, is not really for children, but it has never been published in an edition for adults.

In 2007, the Danish author Sanne Munk Jensen published the provocatively titled novel *En dag skinner solen også på en hunds røv* (One day the sun will also shine on a dog's arse), in which the story of a young woman's difficult life is gradually pieced together through a week's diary entries. The novel was initially released and marketed for young adults by Gyldendal, but it was reviewed with a crossover audience in mind. In a review in the Danish newspaper *Weekendavisen*, quoted on the publisher's website, Damian Arguimbau writes that it is one-third young adult book, one-third adult novel, and one-third generational novel. Later the novel was reprinted in Gyldendal's dual audience Pocket series, alongside authors such as Philip Roth and Karen Blixen. The cover illustrations reflect the different target groups, as the young adult edition has a manga-style cover designed to appeal to teenagers, whereas the paperback has a more sophisticated, double image of a young woman's face and a quotation from a review that appeared in Denmark's oldest newspaper. However, the quotation from the review, "Per-fucking-fekt" (Per-fucking-fect), a combination of "perfect" and "fucking," appears in a speech bubble and it is actually a quote from the novel itself.

The tweaking of the cover imagery does not work only in one direction. In some cases, the cover is changed to attract an audience of young readers. Haddon's *The Curious Incident* got separate covers for the two audiences in Britain, where the cover for young adults is brighter and mentions the *Guardian* Children's Fiction Prize, while the cover of the adult edition quotes the *Independent*. In conceiving a new packaging for Lori Lansens's *The Girls*, Marion Garner, publisher of Vintage Canada, says that consideration was given "to the YA appeal" so that it could be pitched to that market as well.[25] This is reflected in the changes to the cover. On the original Knopf hardcover, the title was placed in a very wide orange band, with only small images of the eyes of young girls peaking out above the band on the top edge and mouths showing below the bottom edge. The Vintage paperback, on the other hand, has a large silhouette of a female that wraps around the spine. It also bears an enthusiastic endorsement by Isabel Allende, who is familiar to young readers as well as adults.

It is important to note, however, that publishers do not always feel the need to change the cover when a book is released for another audience. When the English translation of Rafik Schami's *Damascus Nights* was published for adults, Farrar, Straus & Giroux retained the cover illustration of the original German children's edition, a brightly coloured picture of Damascus roof tops by the innovative Swiss illustrator Étienne Delessert. Some critics have suggested retrospectively that publishers need not have bothered issuing young adult books with two covers, particularly in the case of the Harry Potter books. As the book review editor for the *Independent* of London, Boyd Tonkin, put it: "Such was Harry's heft that the smart executive lost in a gaudy-jacketed children's edition became as common a sight on commuter trains as brollies and brief-cases."[26] However, attitudes can vary greatly from one market to another. Although British adults may be willing to be seen reading children's books in public, that is not necessarily the case in all countries. In Germany, it was not until the sixth *Harry Potter* that the children's and the adult editions appeared simultaneously (in October 2005), with very different covers. There was suddenly a perceived need to provide adults with their own edition right from the outset.

Separate adult covers were a particularly welcome addition in the Asia Pacific market. After noticing that adults in Asia were willing to pay more for the illustrated cover of Meg Cabot's *The Princess Diaries* than the pink one featuring a tiara, Maeyee Lee, Asia Pacific marketing director of Simon & Schuster, asked them why and was told: "We don't want to feel embarrassed reading books with kiddy covers on the subway home." When Lee asked her bosses why they could not do "an adult cover for [their] crossovers too," it was decided they would do so. The covers of Simon & Schuster's popular Samurai Girl series, which featured bright "kiddy photographs," were changed to more subtle illustrations in cool hues. Sales worldwide doubled almost immediately. According to Lee, this proves that "people do judge a book by its cover." Adult demand for Simon & Schuster's Mates, Dates series, with titles such as *Designer Divas*, was so high that Lee had to put them on their adult order form as well. In March 2004, they had printed more than one million copies of Mates, Dates, all of which sold out worldwide.[27] Adults were able to save face behind their new adult covers.

Publishers who cannot afford two editions can rebrand a title simply by adding it to their adult catalogue in the case of a children's book or their children's catalogue in the case of an adult book. Like many publishers in smaller markets, most Canadian publishers cannot afford the luxury of recasting their covers for a second audience. When McClelland & Stewart discovered that the novel *Midnight at the Dragon Café*, published in 2004 by Toronto writer Judy Fong Bates, appealed to young adult readers, it was added to the company's children's imprint, Tundra Books. For Christmas 2005, McClelland & Stewart's director of publicity and marketing, Bruce Walsh, gave Canadian Kristen den Hartog's third adult novel *Origin of Haloes* to his two nieces, aged fifteen and seventeen, who loved it. He says the themes—falling in love with a teacher and getting pregnant—appeal to a young audience. The result was that *Origins of Haloes* was also added to Tundra's children's catalogue. Walsh claims that it is up to the individual to decide whether he or she is "a reader of young adult fiction or . . . a young reader of adult fiction."[28] However, when the publisher includes a title in both their adult and children's catalogues, thus pitching it to both audiences, they are not leaving the decision to the reader.

The strategy of giving adults their own edition of a children's book if it is found to appeal to them does not help publishers pitch a new book into the market. That is why some publishers started putting a book into both their adult and children's catalogues from the outset. *The Moth Diaries*, published in 2002 by the American critic Rachel Klein, was picked up in Britain by Faber & Faber, whose editorial director of children's books, Suzy Jenvey, says publishers buy a book because they are "passionate about it." Later, they are obliged "to define its market" and "to categorise it." Faber & Faber deliberately did not do that with Klein's book, which appeared in 2004 in both their general catalogue and their children's catalogue.[29] Apparently the other two bidders for the rights to Klein's book were adult publishers. Some reviewers feel that the neo-gothic psychological chiller set in a girls' boarding school is targeted at 15- to 25-year-olds, an age category that does not officially exist in publishing terms. Many believed that Klein's audience would be mostly young female readers. The appeal to an older audience and the publisher's decision to put it in their adult catalogue can be explained in part by the fact that, although much of the book consists of the obsessive diary entries of a sixteen-year-old during her junior year at an exclusive girls' boarding school in the late 1960s, these are framed by the observations of the same woman many years later.

One of the first books ever to be marketed simultaneously to adults and children was Lian Hearn's *Across the Nightingale Floor*, the first novel in the Tales of the Otori trilogy, which was published in 2002. The novel was sent to Pan Macmillan by the author's agent "as a teenage book, a book for young adults," but they sensed that it was "one of those rare books that absolutely has an audience which is as wide as it can possibly be, from . . . 12 year olds right through to the adult market." They snapped up the U.K. rights to the novel in a fierce bidding war, with the intention of featuring it as the lead hardcover title on both its adult and children's lists in Fall 2002. In her July 2005 interview on the Readers Voice website, Marion Lloyd claims that Pan Macmillan "pioneered" the "trend of the crossover book" in the marketing of Hearn's novel. It was the first book published simultaneously across Pan's adult and children's lists, but, according to Lloyd, this had never been done previously. Pan Macmillan's very focused marketing strategy to reach both audiences would be adopted subsequently by other publishers.

Some publishers avoid categorizing any of their books. Although it is a children's books imprint, David Fickling Books is one such publisher. Linda Newbery's *Set in Stone*, a book with two alternating narrators in their twenties, was published on David Fickling's list, but the author said she "certainly wouldn't describe it as a children's book." In an interview posted on the WordMavericks website, she explains: "Fortunately, David doesn't make such distinctions. To him, a book is a book, and doesn't have to be 'aimed' at anyone in particular." In recent years, books intended primarily for children are often not classified clearly as children's books. Many publishers no longer include any indications regarding age category in their books.

The similar packaging of books for adults and young readers maintains the ambiguity and facilitates the back and forth between audiences, allowing publishers to capture a crossover audience without the cost of two editions. Although some countries still publish children's books with very unsophisticated covers (Pullman's example of the Hungarian cover of *Northern Lights* is a case in point), it is now standard practice to give a much more adult look to the covers of young adult and even children's fiction. They no longer follow the traditional aesthetic that made a children's book immediately recognizable. The traditional illustrated book jackets are being replaced by glossy covers that often feature computer generated graphics and/or photographs. Children's novels are now commonly issued in subdued jackets, which are often symbolic in nature. The covers of Anthony Horowitz's series about the teenage spy Alex Rider have very simple images, such as a lightning bolt, a gunsight, a scorpion, and a stylized angel. The cover of Louis Sachar's *Holes* depicts the protagonist, but the caricatural profile of the head at the bottom of the page is cropped off, leaving only a red cap worn backwards, an ear, and a disturbing eye that stares fixedly at the reader. The cover of the Bloomsbury edition was even more adult, depicting a large green lizard against the red desert and the blue sky. The jackets of children's books have become much more sophisticated and can now proudly take their place in the adult section if they should happen to find their way there by accident or design. The intent is not only to convince adults that this is literature for all ages, but also to allow adults to unashamedly have them on their bookshelves or read them in public. Commenting on today's covers in the WordMavericks interview, Linda Newbery states: "Covers are so sophisticated now, too, that adults will pick up books from teenage or 'young adult' lists without realising there's any distinction—and maybe there shouldn't be one." The trend is a global one. The covers of the young adult novel *The Song of an Innocent Bystander*, published by Ian Bone in 2000, are very different in Australia, Britain, and the United States, but they are all quite adult looking.

Publishers are particularly concerned that covers not be too young or too gendered. When the third volume of Kate Constable's Chanters of Tremaris trilogy was released in 2005, the covers were redesigned in Australia because it was felt that the original covers were "too young." While the author believes that is true, she admits that she loved the distinctive drawings and gorgeous colours of the original covers. In fact, she told me, in an e-mail message on April 27, 2006, that she had a dispute with the publishers over the redesign because she felt that something more akin to the American covers would have greater appeal. In the United States, the jackets have a portrait of the young heroine on the cover and are less apt to catch an adult's eye in the bookshop. She feels that the muted Australian jackets, which emphasize the dreamy settings of the novels and look very adult, are "a bit bland and sterile, though very tasteful." This is true of many of today's covers, designed to avoid shocking an adult audience. In an attempt to appease Constable, who wanted more of a human element in the picture, they finally put a shadowy girl's face on the cover of the first book. The Australian publisher was very wary of making the covers too "girly" and scaring off any potential male readers. As in Bone's case, the covers are very different in each territory, but they are not uniformly pitched at a crossover market. The current Australian covers of the Chanters of Tremaris books are slanted toward a more sophisticated audience, the American covers are aimed squarely at young teenage girls (and are very successful), and the Danish covers are more childish and almost manga in style.

In recent years, many older books have been reissued with covers that appeal to a crossover audience. A striking example is *The Lord of the Rings*, which now features covers with shots from the Peter Jackson films. The packaging and repackaging of crossover fiction has become a very important aspect of the crossover phenomenon.

Epilogue
Causes and Consequences of the Current Crossover Craze

What we're seeing is books dropping into a popular cultural mainstream way of life in the way they haven't done before.

Suzy Jenvey, qtd. in Jasper Rees, "We're All Reading Children's Books"

Some sceptics still wonder if the crossover bubble will burst and if the whole crossover trend is not just a fad that will disappear as quickly as it came now that the last Harry Potter book has been published, or at least once the last movie has been released. In a 2002 article in *Publishers Weekly*, Julia Eccleshare formulated the question that many in the literary world were asking in the early years of Pottermania and that a large number still continue to ask: "Does the newly invented 'crossover market' really exist?"[1] Others question whether such runaway successes will endure and be read by future generations. As we have seen in this study, crossover fiction does not consist merely of a few exceptional children's fantasy titles that have enchanted today's adults. Rather, it is an extensive body of diverse, cross-generational literature, with a very long history, that is finally being recognized as a flourishing and significant genre by writers, readers, publishers, and critics around the world.

The crossover craze that took the world by storm in the late 1990s, as Potter-mania set in, has very quickly become almost the literary norm. It no longer seems appropriate to speak of "crossover fever," although Julia Eccleshare still refers to the phenomenon in those terms in 2005.[2] The Potter phenomenon has heralded a new age in the publishing industry. The full impact of the Rowling revolution was not immediately evident, but has only revealed itself with time. In the early stages, publishers and writers attempted to come up with copycat titles in the hope of imitating the runaway bestseller. The media speculated on the "next J. K. Rowling," suggesting as contenders for the title Lemony Snicket, Eoin Colfer, Jonathan Stroud, Christopher Paolini, and Michelle Paver, among others. Earlier books, notably *The Lord of the Rings*, were repackaged to appeal to the Potter generation. Since the success of the first *Harry Potter*, there has been a steady stream of exciting, groundbreaking events in the publishing industry. Rowling's books broke all previous publishing records. Her reading from the fourth novel to an audience of over 20,000 at the SkyDome stadium in Toronto as part of the Harbourfront Centre's International Festival of Authors in 2000 earned an entry in the Guinness Book of Records for the world's largest ever author reading. Despite Harry Potter's domination of the crossover scene and despite the accompanying commercial hype that tended to completely overshadow any literary considerations, a more subtle, profound, and lasting transformation has nonetheless been taking place in the world of crossover books. Now that the series is completed, the Potter phenomenon will gradually fade, but Rowling's super crossover has left a lasting mark on the publishing industry as well as on literature and culture in general.

The literary landscape has changed dramatically in recent years. Up until recently, children's literature received very little in the way of exposure, hype, and marketing. The huge success of a few super crossover books raised the profile of children's literature and gave it an entirely new status. Children's publishing has had new life injected into it, as the commercial potential of the children's market has been recognized by writers and publishers alike. As Anne Fine puts it, "what had been a quiet backwater [prior to the Harry Potter craze] was suddenly mainstream."[3] Writing for children is certainly no longer what many previously saw as a marginalized ghetto. In fact, many feel that the status of children's literature is finally being elevated to that of adult fiction. Children's literature and children's authors had long been ignored by mainstream literary reviewers, but they are now gaining respect in the literary establishment and enjoying a much higher profile in the media. Children's books are contenders for prestigious mainstream literary awards. The sphere of juvenile fiction is now attracting new talent who, a decade earlier, might not have considered writing for children. The new status of children's literature and the general phenomenon of crossover literature is one of the most striking and significant cultural markers of our times. A mere decade ago, few would have foreseen this children's literature boom. In the mid-1990s, no one would have predicted that the highest profile figure in children's culture would be a literary character or that one of the most famous people on the globe would be a children's author.

Children's literature is not only receiving new recognition, it is being enthusiastically embraced by adult readers, adult writers, literary critics, publishers, and the media. Children's fiction is seen to make a valuable contribution to the general literary scene, into which it is infusing new energy. The impact of the crossover phenomenon on the field of children's literature in general is immeasurable. At the same time, it is widely acknowledged that this is a very exciting period for the publishing industry in general, for the most part due to crossover books. This is expressed by Suzy Jenvey, editorial director of children's books at Faber & Faber, in the remark that serves as an epigraph to this epilogue: "What we're seeing is books dropping into a popular cultural mainstream way of life in the way they haven't done before."[4] Crossover fiction continues to break new ground in the literary and publishing worlds. It is transforming literary systems, canons, awards, bestseller lists, concepts of readership, the status of authors, the publishing industry, and bookselling practices.

Children's books had to change in order to survive in a world of multimedia, where so many other forms of entertainment vie for the attention of young and old alike. A few years ago, many critics, convinced that children's literature was in its last throws, were predicting the decline of the children's book industry. In our technological civilization, we are immersed in easily acquired entertainment and culture has largely become a global commodity. At a 1997 Modern Language Association forum I organized on "The State of Children's Books in this Millennium and the Next," in which authors, illustrators, publishers, curators, and scholars from numerous countries participated, crossover literature seemed to emerge as a survival technique for the book in the face of the threatening forces of the visual media in this global economic and technological age. The Canadian author Tim Wynne-Jones expressed his belief that story would survive the perilous threat that seemed to be looming toward the end of the millennium.[5] Less than three years later, Wynne-Jones, along with Kenneth Oppel, would provide the "opening act" before Rowling read from the fastest-selling story of all time at the world's largest ever author reading. There no longer seemed to be any doubt about the survival of story and the book. In a talk delivered in 2002, Jostein Gaarder also reflected on the fate of "story" when "literature—and the book—come up against competition from new media like television, video, computers, the internet, etc." Although he believes that we do not yet really understand the impact that information technology will have on our lives and our civilization in general, his view nonetheless echoed that of Wynne-Jones: "The only thing of which I am certain is that the story will survive."[6] Harry Potter turned millions of children hooked on video games and television into avid readers. The crossover phenomenon has firmly established that books and literature will continue to occupy an important place in the cultural panoply of the digital age.

Many hypotheses have been put forward to try to explain the current crossover trend, particularly the wide appeal of children's books to adult readers. However, it is probably a combination of many different factors. The author Linda Newbery offers a quintessentially simple explanation for the phenomenon in an interview posted on the Wordmavericks website: "Mainly I think it's because adults are realizing what a lot of good fiction is published on lists for children and young people! I expect this has been going on for a long time with those in the know, like librarians, but at last publishers and bookshops are realising, and capitalising on it." Many people tend to point immediately to the financial factors that Newbery makes secondary to literary merit. There is no doubt that authors and publishers have finally wakened up to the commercial potential of having their books bought by much larger numbers of readers from a wider range of ages. Children's books are being deliberately pitched to adult readers. Publishers and booksellers are making it much easier for adults to buy children's books. Young adult and children's books are displayed in adult sections of bookstores and the sophisticated covers often make it impossible to distinguish them from adult books. The more cynical see the crossover trend only as a commercial and marketing phenomenon. There have been a multitude of articles in the press with titles such as "Harry Potter and the Art of Making Money," in which Philip Hensher expresses a view shared by many people: "The whole J. K. Rowling thing long ago passed out of the realm of literature into accountancy."[7] Scholars, too, often see *Harry Potter* and the other super crossovers essentially as a marketing and mass media phenomenon. However, these books are, as Philip Nel rightly points out with regard to *Harry Potter* in particular, "both a marketing phenomenon and a literary phenomenon."[8] Unfortunately, it is often very difficult to separate the two, and the former often obscures the latter. Harry Potter may be more familiar to marketing students than literary students in universities, where the boy wizard constitutes a common case study in marketing classes.

The crossover tag is considered by some to be simply a means of validating a children's book and increasing its perceived literary value. However, crossover books existed long before the tag was invented and the market recognized. Those who suggest that adults are reading crossovers merely to see what all the hype is about ignore the fact that it was adults reading children's books that created the hype in the first place. Some cynics have suggested that adult readers of crossovers are Rowling wannabes checking out the successful formula, although this could not possibly explain the huge numbers of adults reaching for children's books. Adult readers of children's fiction have been referred to as "tourists" in the world of kid lit, but, in fact, they seem to have become permanent residents.

Harry Potter ushered in what has been declared by many critics to be a new golden age for children's literature. A 2001 article in the *Guardian* described it in the following terms: "This is at best a bronze age for literary fiction, with the behemoths of yesteryear (Rushdie, Amis, Barnes) stuck in repetitive middle age. It is, however, turning into rather a golden age for children's fiction."[9] Critics often speak of the golden age of British children's fiction in the latter half of the nineteenth century, an age that produced great children's/crossover classics such as *Alice in Wonderland* and *Peter Pan*. In 2003, S. F. Said linked the current golden age, not only to the golden age introduced about a century earlier by Rudyard Kipling, but also to the "golden age" of the 1960s, which featured authors like Ursula Le Guin, Alan Garner, and Susan Cooper. In Said's mind, the common denominator is myth.[10] Michel Tournier also believes that the "mythic dimension" makes writing accessible to readers of all ages because of its multilayered nature that appeals, on one level to a child, and on another to a metaphysician.[11] Myth provides the ultimate vehicle for authors who wish to address a cross-generational audience. Said rightly attributes the vast mass appeal of "the great crossovers—literary or cinematic" to the fact that they "take their mythic dimension very seriously" and not to the fact that they were "engineered to make the maximum possible amount of money."[12] Despite the hype and commercialization, the new golden age of children's literature is producing crossovers that take their mythic dimension very seriously indeed. One has only to think of Philip Pullman's *His Dark Materials* or Lian Hearn's Tales of the Otori. Crossovers offer archetypes that speak to the subconscious in ways that adult fiction often does not. With the development of children's literature, myths, legends, and fairy tales were largely excised from the adult canon and relegated to the children's library. Adults are now reclaiming their right to these so-called children's stories.

There are still those who refuse to recognize crossover fiction as "serious literature." In a review of *I'm Not Scared*, the British writer George Walden speaks disparagingly of "those who sell us film-books and kidult writing as serious literature."[13] This is quite ironic because Niccolò Ammaniti's novel was published as a highly acclaimed adult novel in Italy. Popular crossover books are often seen merely as "escapist pap" and the adults who read them are accused of seeking nothing but escapism between their covers. The escapist label is most often attached to hugely popular fantasy novels in the vein of *Harry Potter*. Some commentators think that this trend is a direct result of a hectic lifestyle that encourages adults to turn to lighter reading. Maeyee Lee, Asia Pacific marketing director of Simon & Schuster, sees this happening in the Asian market. According to her, surveys have shown that "adults are using crossovers to destress quickly in bite-sized moments snatched from frenetic schedules."[14] However, the adoption of such literature by adults is often viewed in a more negative light, as a sign of their unwillingness to accept responsibility or their uncertainty about the future. A number of more cynical critics point to "the infantilisation of adult culture," or the intellectual degradation or dumbing down of culture in general. In an article entitled "Dumbing Down American Readers," the American critic Harold Bloom, author of *The Western Canon*, claims that the Harry Potter books, like Stephen King's novels, are a sign of the dumbing down of American literature, culture, and society.[15] The success of Rowling's books is, according to Anthony Holden, additional proof that the British are "increasingly dragged down to the lowest common denominator by the purveyors of all forms of mindless mass entertainment."[16] Describing the phenomenon in terms of "children's culture hijacked by the childish," a journalist in the *Times* wrote that Rowling's true readership was being shoved aside by adults "who presumably never got over being too dumb for Tolkien."[17] Likewise, in an article entitled "Harry Potter and the Childish Adult," the novelist A. S. Byatt scathingly attacked the childish and uncultured adult readers of *Harry Potter*, who "don't have the skills to tell ersatz magic from the real thing."[18]

Today's society is seen by many to be full of immature, infantilized adults who, they believe, are driving the crossover trend. A number of terms, generally portmanteau words, have been coined to refer to these "children who won't grow up," including kidults, adultescents, middlescents, and middle youths.[19] While the rise in child-to-adult crossovers is due in part to a market of trend-setting adults in the under thirty-five age group who are indulging their pop-culture tastes, adults of all ages are reading children's books. A number of British authors who write solely for adults have expressed consternation, even anger, at all the adults reading *Harry Potter*. It is perhaps as much sour grapes as highbrow snobbery that has led novelists like A. S. Byatt, Philip Hensher, and others to ridicule and patronizingly lecture "adult Potterers." In the British newspaper the *Independent*, Howard Jacobson described his irresistible urge to knock copies of *Harry Potter* out of the hands of adult readers.[20] Jonathan Myerson devoted a lengthy article to "the sad grown-ups" who are reading children's books. He pronounces the adult crossover "pathetic" and says that if he had his way, all books would carry "a heavy-print literacy warning: 'This Is A Children's Book, Designed For Under Elevens. It May Seriously Damage Your Credibility.'" This author seriously damages his own credibility by so completely misunderstanding the crossover phenomenon and underestimating both children's literature and child readers. In his view, children's books have absolutely nothing to offer adult readers, who, he adamantly claims, do not share the interests and problems of children. He virtually denies the possibility of such a thing as crossover fiction: "This is why different books are written for these two tribes; there is barely any genuine or useful crossover between the agendas." He even goes so far as to suggest that the worst adult book—"the flimsiest of science fiction or the nastiest of horror stories"—is better for an adult reader than the best children's book, because "at least they are constructed from the building bricks of adult experience." He chides the children's author who would be foolish enough to believe that a child reader would "understand, let alone enjoy," complex plotting. "You're supposed to grow out of children's books," Myerson condescendingly informs adult readers, advising them to choose fiction written specifically for their "adult age group." In the early days of the adult crossover, adults at least realized it was "shaming to read a kids' book," but in 2003, he writes, "we have the appalling spectacle of city brokers and merchant bankers block-booking seats in cinemas for their staff outings."[21] Philip Pullman took issue with Myerson's scathing article in a film made exclusively for the 2001 Whitbread Book Awards.

A very different perspective on adults reading children's books in public is presented by Pef in *La grande aventure du livre* (The great adventure of the book), which the popular children's author (he also writes for adults) was commissioned to write in 1984 for a campaign on the book and young people organized by the French Ministry of Youth and Sports. In a passage devoted to reading on the metro, a national pastime in France, the child narrator claims that "we children" never read in the metro because people watching provides such a fantastic spectacle (9). He describes the scene created by a woman laughing hysterically as she reads a small book and Pef's humorous drawing shows curious onlookers crowded around her attempting to see what she is reading with such enjoyment. The reaction of the adults, who find it strange that the woman should be reading a picturebook, is contrasted with that of the young narrator, who is quite proud because "it was a children's book that was going very well with a grown-up" (10). In 1984, an adult reading a children's book might have been an unusual sight on the French metro, but since *Harry Potter*, it has become a common occurrence there, as in so many other countries. Adults no longer even bother to try to hide the cover from fellow passengers, as the stigma attached to adults reading children's books has disappeared. Only those who have not read children's books in a very long time could believe that their appeal with adults is a sign of dumbing down. Works such as Pullman's *His Dark Materials* have stemmed many such claims. Writers, publishers, and critics now widely agree that some of the very best fiction is being written and published for young readers. Suzy Jenvey claims that this trend is not "infantilisation," but rather a "change in popular culture."[22] The crossover phenomenon actually began much earlier with television shows, films, and video games. It simply took longer to move into the literary arena, where it has nonetheless had a much higher profile. Although crossover films were drawing huge audiences of children, teenagers, and adults well before Potter-mania did the same for crossover books, the subject has not yet attracted the attention of scholars in the field of film studies.

Many critics feel that it is out of nostalgia that adults turn to children's books, which evoke their own childhood. Often contemporary children's books contain themes that are reminiscent of their favourite childhood books. Some scholars attribute this widespread nostalgia in society to globalization. In an essay entitled "Global and Local Cultures," Mike Featherstone identifies the first such period of nostalgia as 1880–1920, which roughly coincides with the first golden age of children's literature. According to him, "a second phase of nostalgia can be related to the late twentieth-century phase of globalization which has taken place since the 1960s and is associated by many commentators with postmodernism." For the latter, this nostalgia in contemporary society reflects the postmodern loss of reference points, a loss that can lead people to develop "art forms to recreate some golden age." Although Featherstone does not discuss literature, his description of "postmodern spaces" is somewhat reminiscent of certain crossovers: "They encourage the adult to be childlike again, and allow the child to play with simulated ranges of adult experiences."[23] The British psychotherapist Adam Phillips, who is hugely respected by literary London, believes that "many adults are drawn to children's fiction because they feel robbed of that idyllic childhood, and long to return to a state of innocence and omnipotence."[24] In her 1984 study *The Case of Peter Pan, or The Impossibility of Children's Fiction*, Jacqueline Rose argued that children's books are not really for children, but are written by nostalgic adults. Similarly, the current crossover trend is attributed by some to a kind of Peter Pan syndrome. Boyd Tonkin asks if "this vogue for 'crossover' fiction [is] the sign of a culture full of jaded Peter Pans, eager to blot out the heartache of post-adolescent life in an orgy of infantile regression?" He is convinced, however, that this is not at all the case: "Rather, it's a matter of adult readers (and adult authors) recovering within themselves the special intensity, and the special focus, of the pre-adolescent vision. The aim is not to resurrect a vanished 'innocence,' but to enrich a fragmented present with a shared past. Every reader in the world, after all, either has been—or remains—a child, with access at some level to the child's capacity for rapture, terror, boredom and excitement. This is, perhaps, the only sort of universality that literature can claim."[25] Tonkin rightly emphasizes the "shared past" that links children, teenagers, and adults in the generation-spanning stories of crossover fiction.

Adults are not seeking a return to a state of innocence through children's books. Often it is far from an idyllic childhood that is being represented in crossover novels, as those by authors such as Robert Cormier, Tormod Haugen, Bart Moeyaert, and Anne Provoost attest. On the contrary, many are very painful coming-of-age stories. The adolescent coming of age and attempting to understand the bewildering adult world is a common theme in literature. These books attract adult readers as well as young readers because they focus on the transformation of children into adults. They are stories about lifechange and transformation that are equally relevant for adolescents, middle-aged adults, or seniors. More so than in previous decades, perhaps, today's society acknowledges and accepts that metamorphosis and maturation are not exclusively limited to adolescents.

While some critics see the "infantilization" of adults as the major cause of the crossover phenomenon, others point to the "adultization" of today's children and young adults. A number of new terms, such as "tweenager," "tween," and "tweenie," have been coined to refer to children who are seen to be growing up too quickly. The crossover trend is often attributed to the fact that children's fiction in general is becoming more "adult," as children and adolescents become increasingly sophisticated. Over the past decade or so, a number of critics have described the "adultization" of children's literature in Denmark, France, and other Western countries.[26] Until the late 1990s, critics tended to stress the distinctiveness of children's literature. In his 1992 study *The Pleasures of Children's Literature*, Perry Nodelman wrote: "While the book concentrates on the ways in which children's literature is distinct from other kinds, it does so in the belief that the differences are less significant than the similarities, that the pleasures of children's literature are essentially the pleasures of all literature."[27] Today many authors and scholars insist rather that children's literature is *not* distinct from other genres. Why should only children's literature follow determined rules? It is first and foremost literature, and it should have the same artistic freedom as other literature. Contemporary children's authors often avoid the conventions and codes that have traditionally governed the genre of children's literature, thus forging new paths for crossover literature. In countries that do not have a long tradition of children's literature or where it is still in its early stages, the lack of models gives writers a freedom that is not experienced by Western writers. That is the case in South Africa, according to Dianne Hofmeyr, who claims that the books of South African writers have "a raw energy that is not found in other children's books."[28] This may explain why books like her *Boikie, You Better Believe It* and K. Sello Duiker's *Thirteen Cents* are so easily adopted by both children and adults.

It has often been said that J. K. Rowling broke all the rules for a conventional children's book, particularly with regard to the length and the darkness of the subject matter. Even the first Harry Potter novel was rejected by numerous publishers chiefly because they felt it was too long, at about 90,000 words. As the series progressed, Rowling wrote ever longer books that challenged the bias about children's ability to read lengthy novels. Her fourth instalment was called the longest children's book in existence. At 255,000 words, *Harry Potter and the Goblet of Fire* was almost as long as the first three novels combined. At least one bookseller urged Raincoast, Rowling's Canadian publisher, to divide the 636-page book in two. The Harry Potter books demonstrated unequivocally that children could easily and eagerly devour 700-page novels and still demand more. However, they only confirmed what many children's writers had been saying for years about children's desire and need to be challenged. Prior to Rowling, other authors had convincingly made the case with lengthy and far more complex novels, including Michael Ende's *The Neverending Story* (428 pages) and Jostein Gaarder's *Sophie's World* (508 pages). Although the Harry Potter books made the point on a much more global scale, the rules for conventional children's books, which Rowling was seen to have transgressed, had actually all been broken in much earlier works. Since the overwhelming success of her books, however, page counts of children's books have grown exponentially in most Western markets.

While adult fiction has remained very compartmentalized (literary fiction, romance, mystery, science fiction, and so forth), children's literature has been pushing at the boundaries for many years. Crossover works often challenge borderlines of all sorts, crossing traditional generic boundaries as well as conventional age boundaries. In 1995, Ursula Le Guin observed that "the genres are all merging."[29] This hybridization of traditional genres is characteristic of much contemporary crossover fiction. Jostein Gaarder's *Sophie's World*, published in 1991, blends mystery with fantasy. Tormod Haugen's 1989 novel *Skriket fra jungelen* (The cry from the jungle), which is subtitled "A film novel," borrows heavily from cinematographic techniques, while blending fantasy, realism, thriller, and science fiction. Philip Pullman's treatment of moral issues in *His Dark Materials* elevates his work above such clear-cut generic categories as "fantasy." Unusual generic blends are being pushed into the mainstream by the crossover phenomenon. Stephenie Meyer's debut novel, *Twilight* (2005), offered a new twist on the horror genre, and the vampire novel in particular. Meyer's story about a young girl whose new boyfriend turns out to be a vampire transcends the boundaries of the horror genre, blending terror and suspense with romance and a certain eroticism. With its realistic framework, the Twilight series appeals to readers, both young adults and adults, who are not usually vampire story fans, or even readers of the fantasy or horror genres. Another interesting innovation is the scholarly apparatus that some authors use to great effect in their fiction for both children and adults. Jonathan Stroud's Bartamaeus Trilogy and Susanna Clarke's *Jonathan Strange & Mr Norrell* both contain lengthy footnotes that appeal especially, but not exclusively, to an older audience.

Children's authors whose works cross over to adults often use complex narrative techniques, such as genre blending, metafiction, and polyfocalization, with more audacity than their counterparts writing exclusively for adults. The innovative experimentation in children's and young adult fiction—strongly influenced by the new technologies—was demonstrated by Eliza Dresang in her 1999 study *Radical Change: Books for Youth in a Digital Age*. Many critics have pointed to the influence of postmodernism on children's books, not only in the West, but also in Russia, Japan, and many other countries. Since young readers often understand the ludic dimension of postmodernism better than adults and are more adept with interactive texts, the literary playing field has been levelled. Characters in today's children's fiction are not good and bad or black and white, but complex and ambiguous, as Pullman's trilogy clearly illustrates. Authors do not hesitate to introduce a large number of secondary characters and young readers may be more capable than adults of keeping them all straight in their minds. The clearly delineated plots of conventional children's literature have been replaced by complex plots with multiple, interwoven story lines. The complicated plot in Pullman's *His Dark Materials* became increasingly so with each novel, and Rowling also allowed her plot to become more complex as the Harry Potter series progressed. The extensive child-to-adult crossover that has attracted so much attention in recent years is largely due to the fact that today's children's and young adult books are complex and multilayered texts that invite readings on various levels. Mike Bryan, senior vice-president of sales at Penguin International, rightly points out that crossovers take a great deal of craftsmanship and skill because they have to be written "on many levels."[30] Diverse readers have different responses to these texts, but these are not necessarily the result of age, but rather of individual sensibilities (imaginative, intellectual, and emotion capacities; sense of humour; and so forth). Children, teenagers, and adults read crossover texts from their different perspectives and they may get very different things from them, but they all take equal pleasure from the reading experience.

When the success of the Harry Potter books focused unprecedented attention on the field of children's books, many adults were surprised to find them much darker and more disturbing than they had imagined. Today's children's authors do not hesitate to present a more pessimistic view of the world. In writing *The Curious Incident of the Dog in the Night-Time*, Mark Haddon claims that he wanted to get rid of the "little invisible ring of safety" that characterizes children's fiction and to say to the reader "This is the real world, bad things might happen."[31] The attitude of many contemporary authors is in stark contrast to that expressed by Isaac Bashevis Singer in 1977: "I try to give a happy ending to a story for a child because I know how sensitive a child is. If you tell a child that a murderer or a thief was never punished or never caught, the child feels that there is no justice in the world altogether."[32] Even in the 1970s, not all children's authors shared Singer's opinion. According to Richard Adams, "one must at all costs tell the truth to children, not so much about mere physical pain and fear, but about the really unanswerable things—what Thomas Hardy called 'the essential grimness of the human situation.'"[33] Robert Cormier's first young adult novel was rejected by numerous publishers for its pessimistic ending, and his subsequent works consistently described the dark underside of adolescence. Since the outset of his career, Tormod Haugen has never hesitated to use discomforting themes because he wants to depict life as it really is, rather than the way adults want children to believe it is. Daniel Handler defines dark literature as books containing "a heightened level of chaos." He feels that critics object to the highly chaotic world that he created in A Series of Unfortunate Events, in which the innocent, young Baudelaire orphans unjustly undergo an inordinate amount of sorrow, despair, pain, and suffering, far exceeding that of any Dickens orphan. In his view, however, "most children's books aren't nearly dark enough, given the randomness and chaos of the real world." Many writers echo Handler's view that it is essential to give children the truth, even when it is dark and painful. Often they seek to portray not only the darkness in the world, but also the darkness within. Francesca Lia Block believes "in the importance of expressing and acknowledging the darkness inside us, and that includes the darkness in young people."[34]

Not all crossover writers are of this opinion, however. Some claim that children should feel safe and not be confronted with all the world's evils until a later age. Michael Hoeye, the author of the Hermux Tantamoq Adventures, was quoted decrying the availability of "ultradark" entertainment for children in USA Today.[35] Even those in favour of representing the darker side of life feel that it is necessary to include an element of hope. Katherine Paterson states categorically: "I cannot, will not, withhold from my young readers the harsh realities of human hunger and suffering and loss, but neither will I neglect to plant that stubborn seed of hope." Likewise, Ursula Le Guin says: "there's a certain type of hopelessness that I just can't dump on kids. On grown-ups sometimes."[36] Mike Cadden argues convincingly that ethical considerations and what he calls "the continuum of hope" determine genre and audience for Le Guin.[37] In their comparison of young adult and adult novels about adolescence, Helma van Lierop-Debrauwer and Neel Bastiaansen-Harks found that the main difference was the presence of hope and a more optimistic worldview in most young adult novels, although there were a few exceptions.[38] Many authors of children's literature and crossover fiction feel a strong sense of authorial responsibility toward their readers.

The darkness in children's literature is not as new as many people seem to think. Bestselling, even canonical, children's books over the years have frequently featured death and violence. The fairy tales of Perrault, the Brothers Grimm, and Andersen are full of cruelty, violence, and death. The same can be said of *Alice in Wonderland* and *Peter Pan*. One critic calls Peter Pan "a borderline psychopath, prone to creepy . . . pronouncements, such as 'I forget them after I kill them' or 'Death will be an awfully big adventure.'"[39] Death pervades the beloved children's book *Charlotte's Web*. It is often the dark children's literature that most marks both child and adult readers. Beverly Horowitz, vice-president and publisher of Knopf Delacorte Dell Young Readers Group (a division of Random House Children's Books), feels the broader issue is the way we now define the readership of these books: "Perhaps the truth is not that children's books are darker than they used to be, but that younger kids are now reading dark books." Horowitz has worked with Robert Cormier and Philip Pullman, and she has noticed "a trend of younger readers tackling books that were not intended for their age group." She rightly stresses the fact that children of the same age are not necessarily ready for the same reading material.[40] Some reviewers have cautioned parents about letting nervous children read Neil Gaiman's *Coraline*, but children themselves love the book. The author justifies the frightening subject by pointing to the Brothers Grimm: "There's nothing in *Coraline* that is as scary or as awful or as nightmarish as what you'll find in 'Hansel and Gretel.'" Furthermore, he feels that "kids are much better than adults at censoring themselves and even protecting themselves from harmful stuff."[41] Today, many children have been somewhat desensitized to violence by the other media—television, films, video games, the Web—with which books must now compete. A novel has the advantage, however, of allowing time for a more profound consideration of these troubling issues. Many people would argue that today's darker children's fiction merely reflects the darker world in which children now live.

The themes dealt with in today's children's fiction are very wide-ranging and often quite contentious. Freeing themselves from the rigid moral codes and taboos that had long governed children's literature, many authors no longer offer the standard fare of children's books, but explore more "adult" themes. "A Children's Writer with Adult Topics" is the title of an article devoted to Philip Pullman, but it applies equally well to many contemporary children's authors.[42] Among the wide range of controversial topics now dealt with in children's books are sexuality, pregnancy, incest, sexual abuse, suicide, cruelty, murder, terrorism, racism, genocide, war, disease, and death. This emancipation happened more quickly in some countries than in others, most notably in the Nordic countries. For more than twenty years, the Swedish author Peter Pohl has consistently presented difficult themes such as violence, death, and loneliness, in books that rarely have a happy ending. Tormod Haugen's acclaimed novel about suicide, *Vinterstedet*, was published in Norway in 1984.

Young adult fiction in particular is more explicit in its subject matter than in the past. Dianne Hofmeyr's young adult novel *Blue Train to the Moon* (1993) deals with the subject of being in love and H.I.V. positive, while Michelle Paver does not hesitate to offer realistic descriptions of the plague in the Chronicles of Ancient Darkness. Hofmeyr's *Boikie You Better Believe It* (1994) and Meg Rosen's bestseller *How I Live Now* (2004), which was heralded by some as the best crossover novel since Mark Haddon's *The Curious Incident of the Dog in the Night-Time*, are both stories about terrorism. Robert Cormier's *Tunes for Bears to Dance to* (1992) and Markus Zusak's *The Book Thief* (2005) deal with the horrors of the Holocaust. Julia Alvarez describes her children's novel *Before We Were Free* (2002) as *The Diary of Anne Frank* for the Latin American crowd. The idea for her novel about twelve-year-old Anita's life in the Dominican Republic during the repressive regime of El Jefe, Rafael Trujillo, came to Alvarez after examining a list of books about the Holocaust for young readers and wondering why such literature was absent in her culture. Although she initially questioned the appropriateness of writing about the torture of people in the Dominican underground for a young audience, Alvarez eventually decided that since it was part of life, it should be written down.[43] The British author Janni Howker uses the ancient sign of a spiral on a menhir as an analogy of both writing and reading, as writer and reader alike must engage in the exploration of "the dark corridor of the mind." According to Bart Moeyaert, many adults object to novels of this kind: "You can't give children a dark corridor with no bright end in sight." The fear is that young people will "commit suicide or lose their way." Suggesting that two parallel lines might best represent the books for young people that adults would sanction, the author points out that young people do not want boring books any more than adults do.[44] The serious, often profound, subjects of books by authors like Moeyaert resonate with adults as well as young people.

A number of authors who crosswrite children and adults have claimed that the basic, perhaps only, difference between their adult and children's fiction is that the latter contains no sex. The American author Robert Heinlein once said his juvenile science fiction was so good because he wrote the best possible novel for adults he could and then left out the sex.[45] More recently, P. B. Kerr made a similar claim, posted on the Scholastic website, with regard to his first children's novel, *The Akhenaten Adventure*. While it is true that children's authors cannot rely on sex to keep a reader's attention, it is no longer necessarily left out in contemporary children's and young adult fiction. In fact, sexuality, and even eroticism, was introduced into fiction for young readers in the 1970s and 1980s. We have already seen the erotic suggestiveness of Michel Tournier's picturebook *Pierrot*, published in 1979. Nor was sexuality completely absent from much earlier children's literature. For example, in the novel *Peter and Wendy*, J. M. Barrie refers to fairies staggering through the forest "on their way home from an orgy."[46] However, the subject has been treated in an increasingly explicit manner since the 1970s. Adult mediators frequently question the appropriateness of such material for young readers. Judy Blume's young adult fiction has long been banned by school boards due to its frank treatment of sexuality. When I commented on the fact that some libraries catalogue the second volume of the Sally Lockhart series—published in 1987—in adult fiction, while the other volumes are catalogued as young adult fiction, Pullman told me in an e-mail message on November 5, 2005: "it's probably to do with sex—it usually is." It is in *The Shadow in the North* that the unwed protagonist becomes pregnant.

Lian Hearne's Tales of the Otori series deals not only with sexuality, but with rape, violence, homosexuality, sadism, and torture, and these themes give the novel its adult feel. It has been suggested that Hearn's books break with the children's literature model, in that they include violence and sexuality, but they are by no means the first to do so. Cormier has fought many censorship battles because his novels contain both, but the author insists that nothing in his novels is "gratuitous or titillating for the sake of titillating." Even in *Tenderness*, which concerns "a sexually precocious girl and a serial killer with a predisposition for necrophilia," he claims to have relied for the most part on "suggestion."[47] In her series, Hearn strove consciously for "that matter-of-fact acceptance of sexuality," in order to reflect faithfully a period in Japanese culture when it was quite common for young men to frequent brothels and engage in casual sexual relationships with other men.[48] She deals with this adult material in a restrained manner, without developing it unnecessarily. In *The Amber Spyglass*, sexual desire between Will and Lyra is described with exquisite subtleness by Pullman, who feels child readers can handle the ambiguity. Although such scenes are now much more common in children's and young adult fiction, they still provoke controversy. Certain adult readers criticized a rather explicit sex scene in Linda Newbery's 2002 novel *The Shell House*, but, in the Wordmavericks interview, the author defends its presence, saying that "if you're going to include sex in a teenage novel, you shouldn't 'cop out' by being coy about it." Believing the scene to be "entirely appropriate," the author is convinced that readers who have actually read that far into the book will not be shocked by the episode. Like many authors, she objects to such scenes being taken out of context by angry parents assuming the role of censors rather than readers. Children's books are coming under much closer scrutiny by adults as a result of the unprecedented attention focused on them by the crossover phenomenon.

The broadening horizons of children's literature have blurred the distinction between children's fiction and adult fiction, and facilitated the crossover in both directions. In the 1980s, Tournier complained bitterly that he was unable to reach his "major public, which is young people, in foreign countries," particularly the United States, because publishers of children's books around the world insist on complete "conformity." The French author claimed that the children's book trade "operates by laws that absolutely ban all genuine literary creativity."[49] In the 1970s and early 1980s, Tournier may have had good reason to complain about the great divide that separated the avant-garde world of adult books from the more conservative world of children's books, characterized by its strict, well-defined guidelines. Today, there are very few, if any, taboo subjects in literature published for young readers, and this fact makes it easier for adult fiction to cross over to children. In a sense, this is a return to the situation that existed prior to the creation of a separate literature for children. Maurice Sendak reminds us that the tales collected by the Grimm Brothers appeal to all ages because they are "about the pure essence of life—incest, murder, insane mothers, love, sex."[50]

The key to the current crossover phenomenon seems to lie largely in the art of storytelling. The success of crossover titles is attributed over and over to the power of the story. Like so many crossover novels, *Across the Nightingale Floor* is, as the dustjacket claims, "a work of transcendent storytelling with an appeal that crosses genres, genders, and generations." The need for story is timeless and the crossover phenomenon is proving that it is also "ageless." Adults, as well as children, need stories. Francis Spufford, the author of the 2002 best-selling memoir *The Child that Books Built*, claims that narrative thinking is as hardwired in humans as language acquisition. As one commentator put it, "We are story-telling, story-listening apes."[51] Many critics argue that the writers and publishers of so-called literary fiction have long neglected the story. Spufford, who reread all his childhood favourites while writing the book, believes that children's books fill a need for compelling stories currently missing in adult fiction. He blames modernism for promoting experimentation at the expense of a good narrative. "What's happening now is a return to the story in its strongest sense, to the primal excitement of wanting to know what happens next."[52] In the twentieth century, storytelling was not a high priority in literary fiction. This barely tolerant attitude toward story is expressed in E. M. Forster's famous "Yes—oh dear, yes—the novel tells a story."[53] In the 1950s, Alain Robbe-Grillet declared character and plot to be dead in the novel, but, fortunately, they never died in children's literature. When Pullman won the Carnegie Medal for *Northern Lights* in 1996, he attacked Britain's adult novelists in his acceptance speech (posted on the Random House website), claiming that many had lost the art of telling a good story and were actually embarrassed by stories. "Only in children's literature is the story taken seriously," he asserted. Children's authors continue to satisfy their readers' yearning for a good story because "in a book for children you can't put the plot on hold while you cut artistic capers for the amusement of your sophisticated readers." Adult writers wanting to deal directly in stories were forced to move into genre fiction, such as crime or science fiction, "where no one expects literary craftsmanship."

Commenting, in 2003, on the increasingly "abstruse and remote" nature of literary fiction, the children's author S. F. Said wrote: "As modernism moved into postmodernism, high literature became so bogged down in theory that it became dull at best, meaningless at worst." This is contrasted with children's literature of the same period, which offered "vivid, bold storytelling of a profundity and scope that dwarfed any Booker Prize winner's."[54] More than a decade earlier, one Booker Prize winner eloquently expressed his discontent with what was happening in contemporary fiction. In *Haroun and the Sea of Stories*, Salman Rushdie objects to the way in which many writers, even children's authors, are polluting the Sea of Stories: "Certain popular romances have become just long lists of shopping expeditions. Children's stories also." (83). *Haroun and the Sea of Stories* is a defence of the art of the storyteller, which appeals widely to all ages. Rushdie is an exception to the general rule expressed in 1999 by Philip Pullman: "There are very few writers of what one might call the literary Booker Prize short-list novel who are good at stories and who think stories are important."[55] The question that "baffles" Jonathan Myerson, that is, why do avid adult readers "sandwich" children's books between "McEwan and Balzac, Roth and Dickens," is answered by the author himself when he proudly holds up his own "difficult, unreadable . . . novels."[56] Many readers and authors have expressed their frustration with a great deal of adult literary fiction and its self-conscious "literariness," which can make very dull reading. There is now a widespread rejection of reflexive literary novels by authors such as Milan Kundera. Critics, writers, and readers alike have strongly stated their disappointment with hyped literary novels like Margaret Atwood's *The Blind Assassin*, the Booker Prize winner in 2000. It was the very next year that *The Amber Spyglass* became the first children's book to be longlisted for the Booker Prize. This nomination led one journalist to write in the *Guardian*: "Segregation of genres may remain valid commercially and as a filter for parents. In judging the best writing, it is now redundant."[57] Although Pullman's novel did not receive the Booker, it did win the Whitbread Book of the Year Award, becoming the first children's book winner since the award's inception to claim the overall prize. With children's books now being nominated for some of the world's most prestigious literary prizes, perhaps even the world of high literature has finally acknowledged that adults, as well as children, appreciate a good story. The divide between award-winning literary fiction and popular crossover fiction has narrowed in recent years to the point where some works now manage to successfully bridge the two worlds.

Adults are rediscovering the pleasure of a good story in children's books, where it remains as important as ever. "More and more adults are realising that some children's writers are maybe providing something that adult authors aren't," writes David Almond, who identifies that "something" as "the power of narrative." As he puts it, "a discipline comes with making sure the page keeps turning." Julia Alvarez agrees that the secret of writing for children is "getting to the bones of the story, the bones of what keeps a person turning the page."[58] Crossover authors all point to story as the source of the widespread appeal with readers of all ages. Jonathan Stroud distinguishes adult fiction from children's fiction on the basis of story: "A lot of adult fiction hasn't got such a strong narrative drive. A successful book for children must have a strong narrative." Children's authors realize that they have a demanding, discerning audience.

"The kid is not going to be impressed by trendy, pretentious, hifalutin stuff which some adults will be enraptured by," affirms Stroud.[59]

As early as the 1970s, critics were already pointing out the restraints put on adult writers and the freedom offered by children's literature. In 1976, Miles McDowell wrote: "It has been argued, indeed, that present day 'adult' writers are peculiarly restricted to themes of personal relationships, or to man in society, and that to be free to write of adventure, of fantasy, of initiation and personal growth, to write of a period other than our own, to explore some of the great archetypal experiences such as the quest or the great dichotomous morality patterns, a writer must turn to children's fiction, or to the adult 'pulp' market."[60] This situation was not confined to the English-speaking world; critics elsewhere were making similar observations. In *La infancia recuperada* (*Childhood Regained: The Art of the Storyteller*), also published in 1976, the Spanish philosopher and writer Fernando Savater contrasts the cynical or disenchanted manipulator of sophisticated literary forms with the true storyteller, who knows that "storytelling is incurably ingenuous . . . [with an] ingenuousness [that] is fundamentally etymological: it comes from that Latin *ingenuus* whose etymological meaning is 'noble, generous' and, specifically, 'freeborn,' as stories are freely born and freely transmitted in the noble and generous task of storytelling."[61] Stories transcend any kind of boundaries, including those of age. As we have seen, many authors claim they do not write for an age, they write for the story. Crossover writers invite intergenerational readers into their fictions, readers who are defined not so much by their age, or even by common experience and knowledge, but rather by "a capacity to enjoy stories as places where the adult and child can happily cohabit."[62] Their fiction offers challenging and engaging stories for young and old alike.

At the other end of the spectrum from literary fiction, and equally unsatisfying for many readers, are popular blockbuster adult novels that offer nothing but story. The best fiction, whether it is adult, young adult, or children's, feeds our desire for a satisfying narrative while at the same time offering deeper psychological and philosophical reflections. Although Mike Bryan of Penguin International believes that the most successful crossovers offer "corking good escapist fun," he insists that they also contain "serious messages about values."[63] Crossover authors agree that writing for children allows them to take on the essential issues that are important to them. Whereas Myerson states categorically that a children's novel cannot provide "truths about human life" or "psychological understanding," many crossover writers believe that they are, in fact, the only books that can.[64] Pullman explains why he writes for children: "Children's books still deal with the huge themes which have always been part of literature—love, loyalty, the place of religion and science in life, what it really means to be human. Contemporary adult fiction is too small and too sterile for what I'm trying to do."[65] Admitting that he would be "a little embarrassed to write a grown-up book that dealt directly with alternative moral universes," William Nicholson states: "Issues of God and heaven, life and death, are central to our lives but [as adults] we're shy of talking about them. When you write for children, though, you can go roaring into these incredibly important stories."[66] Adults want to be able to deal with these subjects as well, and crossover books like those of Nicholson, Pullman, and Almond allow them to do so.

Crossover authors have been asking young readers to reflect on challenging philosophical questions for generations, in works that have become classic favourites with all ages, *Alice in Wonderland*, *Watership Down*, *The Mouse and His Child*, and *Le Petit Prince*, to name only a few. In his book *Secret Gardens: A Study of the Golden Age of Children's Literature* (1985), Humphrey Carpenter attributes the golden age of children's fiction after 1860 in large part to the *Zeitgeist* or spirit of the time, characterized by a search for something to fill the void left by a loss of religious faith.[67] Some commentators have suggested that the current golden age is the result of a similar phenomenon. Many contemporary crossover books have a spiritual dimension and deal with challenging metaphysical and existential issues, notable examples being the works of Jostein Gaarder and Philip Pullman. Critics often tend to attribute the adult appeal of these books to the weighty philosophical content. However, readers of all ages struggle with metaphysical concerns and ask the big questions about where we come from and where we go. Maija-Liisa Harju rightly argues that such topics should not be seen as being out of reach for children, because "grappling with existential questions is a challenge humans of all ages must face throughout their life-stages."[68] William Nicholson believes that fantasy literature is filling a spiritual need in adult readers, but he acknowledges that it also appeals to children: "There is a type of psycho-spiritual adventure story that appeals very strongly to quite a wide age group—10–30." A bookseller once told the author of The Wind on Fire trilogy that he could sell his books equally well "in the Mind Body Spirit section."[69] David Almond has been attributed with creating a genre all of his own, a unique blend of spirituality and gritty, urban realism sometimes referred to as mystical realism, which has great appeal for adults as well as young readers. The search for meaning has no age limit.

Crossover fiction acknowledges that different generations share experiences, knowledge, desires, and concerns. Rachel Falconer points out that critics like Jacqueline Rose fail to take into consideration "the continuum between children's and adults' experience."[70] In her 1986 essay, Rebecca West states that Luigi Malerba's fiction allows us to fix our attention on "the metaphorical slash that both separates and joins the terms *adults/children*."[71] While differences are acknowledged in crossover literature, they are considered insignificant in comparison to the similarities. There is a move away from the polarization of children and adults toward a recognition of the continuity that connects readers of all ages. There is not a schismatic divide between child and adult readers, but rather "a continuum of understanding," wrote Carole Scott in her 1999 essay in *Transcending Boundaries*.[72] Maija-Liisa Harju uses the term "the crossover continuum" to refer to the philosophical space created by crossover fiction, a space in which readers of all ages can meet to share their common experience.[73] In resisting the traditional boundaries created between child and adult literatures, crossover fiction offers a shared reading experience for all ages. This shared enthusiasm for story and reading obviously has very positive social and cultural effects. Many children's authors have lamented the great divide between the worlds of adults and children. Bart Moeyaert often evokes "the irreconcilability of his own childlike empire and the adult universe." Jostein Gaarder feels that in many societies, perhaps particularly in some Western countries, there has been an alarming end to "shared experience *across the generation gap.*" In his view, children, parents, and grandparents tend to live increasingly in their own worlds.[74] Crossover literature brings the generations together, providing common points of reference. This sharing of culture by readers of all ages promotes cross-generational exchange and understanding.

Crossover books offer good stories written in a style that ranges from acceptably grown-up to highly sophisticated. The prose is often skilfully crafted, detailed, and full of evocative imagery. Reviewers feel that some children's books have been so slanted to an adult audience that they require adult competencies, and make intellectual and emotional demands thought to be inappropriate for children. Most children's authors disagree. Encouraging writers, in the 1990s, to "forget about target groups" and give young readers "a good story," the Danish author Kim Fupz Aakeson stated: "It's all right to provoke children with something they don't understand or get a bit wrong. Neither does it matter if a children's book contains something that is perhaps only for the adult reader."[75] While Bart Moeyaert was still a very young writer experimenting with narrative content and structures in Belgium in the early 1980s, he consciously chose what the critic Annemie Leysen terms "adult writing for children and youth." Through his skilful use of language and imagery, "a simple story turns into . . . a genuine literary work of art." Even his books for young children are written with the same artistic rigour as his young adult/crossover titles. Books by authors like Moeyaert may sometimes be less accessible for young readers, but they "tap uncharted depths in children."[76] It is commonly acknowledged that Moeyaert inspired many authors in the Dutch-speaking countries to create a more "literary" writing for children. Well before the current crossover phenomenon changed the status of children's literature, his innovation and persistent crusade greatly contributed to the increased stature not only of Flemish children's literature, but of Flemish literature in general. Both national and international critics and reviewers who previously considered children's literature to be a minor literary genre began showing enthusiastic interest thanks to crossover authors such as Bart Moeyaert and Anne Provoost in Belgium, Tormod Haugen and Jostein Gaarder in Norway, Wim Hofman in the Netherlands, and Dominique Demers in Quebec.

Even when crossover authors use a prose that is relatively simple from a syntactical and lexical point of view, the text is often quite challenging on a conceptual level. The most successful crossover authors refuse to make everything accessible on the surface of the story. This is well illustrated by Garth Nix's

"Iceberg" theory of fantasy, according to which the story is merely the visible tip of the iceberg and the reader should sense the remaining ninety per cent below the surface. In Nix's opinion, too many fantasy writers fall into the trap of over explaining, losing "the mythic, the sense of mystery."[77] Thought-provoking crossover novels raise many questions that remain unanswered. Most crossover texts contain thought-provoking concepts that engage the reader—adult or child—on an intellectual as well as an emotional level. They are stimulating and enlightening for, and accessible to, both adult and young readers.

While young readers do not have to understand everything in a text (adult readers may not either), many critics feel that today's young readers generally have more literary competence than their predecessors. Children of the twenty-first century are savvy consumers exposed to the same cultural and marketing influences as adults. Many contemporary children's authors talk about the difficulty of writing for today's highly critical and demanding kids, who do not like being patronized. "Write down to them and you risk alienating the audience," insists Richard Peck, winner of the 2001 Newbery Medal.[78] Convinced that preeen readers are the most difficult audience of all, Carl Hiaasen asked for an escape clause in his two-book contract with Knopf so he could bail if *Hoot* was a failure. Many writers over the years have refused to make concessions to the child reader, feeling that they could and should be reading up. Challenging texts can be very empowering, even magical for children. In a series of "seven small stories" or anecdotes, Bart Moeyaert reflects on the accessibility of literary texts to young readers. In "The French Chekhov," the author demonstrates that "difficult or literary language does not exclude a reader by definition," by describing his own experience at a French production of *The Seagull* in Brussels. Although "the language of the bird" took him by surprise and he did not understand half of the performance, the evening turned out to be an extraordinary feast for mind, heart, and senses. For Moeyaert, accessibility is not a question of age, but of attitude. In an anecdote entitled "The Happy Girl," the author describes his encounter with a ten-year-old girl who told him how much she liked one of his more difficult novels. To his horror, Moeyaert found himself making the same assumptions as so many other adults and "parroting" their oft repeated statement: "This book is inaccessible for ten-year-olds." In his view, the repetition of such ideas gives them credence and validity, so that eventually they become true.[79]

The crossover phenomenon raises a very basic, yet essential, question: Is there a correct age to read a book? The same phenomenon answers the question: Absolutely not. Why should age be a prerequisite of reading? Readers cannot be lumped into rigidly defined age categories. Why should children be told that a book is out of their reach? While one ten-year-old child may read *The Lord of the Rings* with pleasure and understanding, the next ten-year-old may barely be able to read. Young readers do not feel the need to know if a book is "for children"; they simply read what interests and appeals to them, and reject what does not. Adults, on the other hand, have traditionally felt more uncomfortable with books that were not clearly "for adults." Why should adults feel embarrassed to read *Winnie-the-Pooh* in middle age? No one tells us that Goethe's *Werther* or James Joyce's *A Portrait of the Artist as a Young Man* should be read by adults in their formative years or that Thomas Mann's *Der Tod in Venedig* or Marcel Proust's *A la recherche du temps perdu* should be read by seniors.

Crossover books transcend the conventionally recognized barriers within the fiction market. They demonstrate the narrative form's remarkable ability to reach across ages, defying our classifications of writer, reader, and text. There is a very long tradition of adults and children claiming the same stories as their own. "Young people have always read books that were aimed at adults and vice versa," stated Mark Haddon, whose novel *The Curious Incident of the Dog in the Night-Time* was marketed simultaneously for both audiences.[80] Contemporary literature is now shifting away from age as a defining category. In this technological age, both print and electronic media have broken from traditional age boundaries. Writers and publishers are refusing to make distinctions between children's fiction and adult fiction, between child readers and adult readers, just as television producers, filmmakers, and game designers are creating entertainment for all ages. In today's culture, there is a tendency to no longer see certain material as appropriate or inappropriate for specific age categories, but rather to acknowledge the multiple audiences of different ages who can appreciate the same work. Children, teenagers, and adults become part of a community where age doesn't matter. From books and films, to television shows and video games, the same works are proving to be equally appealing to and meaningful for children, teenagers, and adults.

Notes

Introduction

1. "2001: A Year in Books," *Guardian Unlimited*, 2001, http://books.guardian. co.uk/quiz/questions/0,5957,623142,00.html (accessed June 30, 2007).
2. S. F. Said, "The Godfather of Harry Potter," *Daily Telegraph*, December 8, 2002.
3. Judith Rosen, "Breaking the Age Barrier," *Publishers Weekly*, September 8, 1997, 28.
4. *The Letters of John Gay*, ed. C. F. Burgess (Oxford: Oxford University Press, 1966), 60.
5. Selma Lanes, *The Art of Maurice Sendak* (New York: Harry N. Adams, 1980), 206.
6. Declan Kiberd, "Literature, Childhood and Ireland" (paper presented at the Congress of the International Research Society of Children's Literature, Dublin, Ireland, August 13–17, 2005). This quotation did not find its way into the published paper.
7. Zohar Shavit, *Poetics of Children's Literature* (Athens, GA: University of Georgia Press, 1987), 71.
8. Bettina Kümmerling-Meibauer, "Crosswriting as a Criterion for Canonicity: The Case of Erich Kästner," in *Transcending Boundaries: Writing for a Dual Audience of Children and Adults*, ed. Sandra L. Beckett (New York: Garland, 1999), 25, n. 11.
9. The first time a foreign title is mentioned, an English translation will follow in parentheses. If an English translation exists, the English title will be given in italics for a book and in roman type with quotation marks for texts published in journals or elsewhere; otherwise, the translation of the title is mine and will appear in roman type only. All translations in this book are mine unless otherwise indicated.
10. Qtd. in Jacques Demougin, ed., *Dictionnaire de la littérature française et francophone*, vol. 1.1 (Paris: Larousse, 1987), 100.
11. Gabriel d'Aubarède, "Écrire pour les enfants," *Les Nouvelles Littéraires*, March 22, 1956, 4.

12. See U. C. Knoepflmacher, "The Balancing of Child and Adult: An Approach to Victorian Fantasies for Children," *Nineteenth-Century Fiction* 37, no. 4 (March 1983): 497–530.

13. Michel Tournier, "Michel Tournier: comment écrire pour les enfants," *Le Monde*, December 24, 1979, 19.

14. Stuart Hannabuss, "Books Adopted by Children," in *International Companion Encyclopedia of Children's Literature*, ed. Peter Hunt (London: Routledge, 1996), 424.

15. Jostein Gaarder, "Books for a World without Readers?" (paper presented at the International Board on Books for Young People (IBBY) Congress, Basel, Switzerland, September 29–October 2, 2002).

16. S. F. Said, "The Grown-up World of Kidult Books," *Daily Telegraph*, January 11, 2003.

17. Philip Ardagh, "Wrap It Up," *Guardian*, December 20, 2003.

18. Dante, "Reading into Crossover Trends," the *Straits Times*, March 8, 2004, http://www.hisdarkmaterials.org/article411.html (accessed April 2, 2006).

19. See, for example, Helma van Lierop-Debrauwer and Neel Bastiaansen-Harks, *Over grenzen: De adolescentenroman in het literatuuronderwijs* (Delft: Eburon, 2005), 19. In light of its current literary and cultural importance, crossover fiction has received surprisingly little scholarly attention. This can be explained in part by the fact that the majority of critics and scholars work within either the adult or children's literature spheres, and their research does not "cross over." *Over grenzen* (across borders) is one of the few studies that crosses over, comparing books that are traditionally separated by the boundaries between adult and juvenile fiction. Much of the existing critical literature is devoted to authors who address children and adults in separate works rather than to crossover texts.

20. Kate Kellaway, "The Race for Both Older and Younger Readers in One Book," *Observer*, April 11, 2004.

21. Debbie Taylor, "The Potter Effect," *Mslexia* 14 (Summer/Autumn 2002).

22. Henry Steele Commager, "When Majors Wrote for Minors," *The Saturday Review*, May 10, 1952, 10.

23. Malerba's children's and adult fiction often contain the same themes, concepts, and humour. Not only do adults read his children's books, but some of his works for adults—the story collections *La scoperta dell'alfabeto* (The discovery of the alphabet, 1963) and *Dopo il pescecane* (After the shark, 1979), and the novel *Il Pataffio* (Hodge-Podge, 1978)—are read by young readers. See Rebecca West, "Come One, Come All: Luigi Malerba's Diffuse Fictions," *The Lion and the Unicorn* 10 (1986): 95–107.

24. Mike Cadden defines the "crossover writer" as "the writer who writes for both children and adults," but the term is used in this study only to refer to authors who reach both audiences with the same works. See Cadden,

"Speaking to Both Children and Genre: Le Guin's Ethics of Audience," *The Lion and the Unicorn* 24, no. 1 (January 2000): 132.

25. Ana Maria Machado, "Words to Bridge Gaps: Children's Books as a Bridge between Adults and Children" (paper delivered at the International Board on Books for Young People (IBBY) Congress, Basel, Switzerland, September 29– October 2, 2002).

26. Rosen, "Breaking the Age Barrier," 28.

27. Kellaway, "The Race for Both Older and Younger Readers in One Book."

28. E-mails from Antje Richers, March 31, 2006 and April 3, 2006.

29. Eva Glistrup, "Children's Literature in Denmark: Trends and Currents in the 1990s" (paper presented at the 63rd International Federation of Library Associations and Institutions Annual Conference, August 31–September 5, 1997), http:// www.ifla.org/IV/ifla63/63glie.htm (accessed September 8, 2005).

30. Boyd Tonkin, "Once Upon a Time in the Marketing Department ... ," *Independent* (London), November 8, 2002.

31. See the section on "Shifting Boundaries Between Children's and Adult Literature," in *Reflections of Change: Children's Literature Since 1945*, ed. Sandra L. Beckett (Westport: Greenwood, 1997), 33–54.

32. See Maria Nikolajeva, "Exit Children's Literature," *The Lion and the Unicorn* 22, no. 2 (1998): 221–36. She writes: "we must acknowledge that, sooner or later, children's literature will be integrated into the mainstream and disappear" (p. 233).

33. C. S. Lewis, "On Three Ways of Writing for Children," in *Only Connect: Reading on Children's Literature*, ed. Sheila Egoff, G. T. Stubbs, and L. F. Ashley (Toronto: Oxford University Press, 1969), 210.

34. Michel Tournier, "Écrire pour les enfants," in *Pierrot ou les secrets de la nuit*, Enfantimages (Paris: Gallimard, 1979); "Writing for Children is No Child's Play," *UNESCO Courier* 6 (June 1982): 34.

35. Shavit, *Poetics of Children's Literature*, 37; Dagmar Grenz, "E. T. A. Hoffmann as an Author for Children and Adults or the Child and the Adult as Readers of Children's Literature," *Phaedrus* 13 (1988): 94.

36. Katharine Jones, "Getting Rid of Children's Literature," *The Lion and the Unicorn* 30, no. 3 (September 2006): 305.

37. Emer O'Sullivan, "The Fate of the Dual Addressee in the Translation of Children's Literature," *New Comparison* 16 (Autumn 1993): 119.

38. Kiberd, "Literature, Childhood and Ireland," in *Expectations and Experiences: Children, Childhood and Children's Literature*, ed. Clare Bradford and Valerie Coghlan (Litchfield: Pied Piper Press, 2007), 24.

39. West, "Come One, Come All: Luigi Malerba's Diffuse Fictions," 95–97.

40. Salman Rushdie, "*The Wizard of Oz*," Film Classics (London: British Film Institute, 1992): 18.

41. Dominique Demers, "Enfant lecteur, adolescent lecteur, adulte lecteur: frontières mouvantes, exigences mythiques et désirs bien réels," in

Littérature de jeunesse et Fin de siècle, ed. Glen Campbell and Eileen Lohka (Winnipeg: Presses Universitaires de Saint-Boniface, 2007), 27.

42. Andre Mayer, "Sharing the Love: How Publishers are Re-branding Adult Fiction for Younger Readers," CBC, March 14, 2006, http://www.cbc.ca/arts/books/youngadultfiction.html (accessed December 6, 2006).

43. See Shavit, *Poetics of Children's Literature*, 33–59.

44. Aubarède, "Écrire pour les enfants," 1.

45. Michel Tournier, "Les enfants dans la bibliothèque," interview with Jean-François Josselin, *Le Nouvel Observateur*, December 6, 1971, 56; Michel Tournier, "Michel Tournier face aux lycéens," *Le Magazine Littéraire* 226 (January 1986): 21.

46. See Édith Madore, "Les 'écrivains' et les 'auteurs jeunesse,'" *Tangence* 67 (Autumn 2001): 23–33. The author borrows the title of her paper from Denis Côté.

47. Aidan Chambers, "Ways of Telling," in *Booktalk: Occasional Writing on Literature and Children* (London: The Bodley Head, 1985), 92–115.

48. Dominique Noguez, *Le grantécrivain et autres textes* (Paris: Gallimard, 2000), 9, 13.

49. Grenz, "E. T. A. Hoffmann as an Author for Children and Adults or the Child and the Adult as Readers of Children's Literature," 96, n. 34.

50. Peter Hunt, "Roald Dahl (1916–1990)," in *Children's Literature* (Malden: Blackwell Publishing, 2001), 56.

51. Suzi Feay, "The Tale of Genji for the Potter Generation," *Independent on Sunday*, November 28, 2004. There are, of course, other reasons for adopting a pen name when writing for children. In the case of the French author Pierre Ferrier, the short pen name Pef, which he uses to sign his popular children's books, was probably chosen merely to amuse his young audience and to lessen the distance between author and reader.

52. Vanessa E. Jones, "Young-Adult Books Are No Longer Child's Play for Bestselling Authors," *Boston Globe*, September 19, 2002, D1; her italics.

53. Ibid.

54. See Rachel Falconer, "Crossover Literature," in *International Companion Encyclopedia of Children's Literature*, ed. Peter Hunt, 2nd ed., 2 vols. (London: Routledge, 2004), 556–75; Sandra L. Beckett, "Crossover Books," in *The Oxford Encyclopedia of Children's Literature*, ed. Jack Zipes, 4 vols. (New York: Oxford University Press, 2006), 1: 369–70.

55. Nicholas Clee, "Can the Magic Last Forever?" *Independent* (London), September 15, 2004.

1. Adult-to-Child Crossover Fiction

1. See, for example, Jan Susina, "Editor's Note: Kiddie Lit(e): The Dumbing Down of Children's Literature," *The Lion and the Unicorn* 17, no. 1 (June 1993): v–ix.

2. Kiberd, "Literature, Childhood and Ireland," 17.
3. Jochen Weber, "Pasando les límites: All-Age-Books, Crossover-Literature y otras tendencias actuales de la literatura para jóvenes lectores" (paper presented at the 1er Congreso Nacional de Lectura y Escritura: Escuela y Literatura Infantil, Durango, Mexico, May 16–18, 2004).
4. SFFWorld, "Interview with Anne McCaffrey," May 8, 2000, SFFWorld, http://www.sffworld.com/interview/49p0.html (accessed July 6, 2007).
5. David Gemmell, "No Shades of Grey," *Guardian*, May 10, 2003.
6. Ibid.
7. Luc Reid, "Susanna Clarke's *Jonathan Strange & Mr Norrell*: Magic Chuses to Reemerge in Regency England," Strange Horizons, September 27, 2004, http://www.strangehorizons.com/reviews/2004/09/susanna_clarkes.shtml (accessed March 16, 2007).
8. John Hodgman, "Susanna Clarke's Magic Book," *New York Times*, August 1, 2004.
9. Ibid.
10. Karen Robinson, "Dark Art of Writing Books that Win Minds," *Sunday Times*, January 27, 2002.
11. Ralf Isau, e-mail message to author, May 22, 2007.
12. Kate Kellaway, "Autistic Differences," *Observer*, April 27, 2003.
13. Sandra L. Beckett, *De grands romanciers écrivent pour les enfants* (Montréal: PUM, 1997), 290, 298.
14. Leslie Wilson, e-mail message to author, April 12, 2006.
15. Mayer, "Sharing the Love: How Publishers are Re-branding Adult Fiction for Younger Readers."
16. Ibid.
17. Haruki Murakami, "A Conversation with Haruki Murakami, Author of *Sputnik Sweetheart*," Random House, http://www.randomhouse.com/catalog/display.pperl?isbn=9780375726057&view=auqa (accessed November 11, 2007).
18. Michel Tournier, "Quand Michel Tournier récrit ses livres pour les enfants," *Le Monde*, December 24, 1971, 7.
19. Tournier, "Writing for Children is No Child's Play," 34.
20. Marianne Payot, "L'Entretien: Michel Tournier," *Lire* (October 1996): 34. After the publication of *Le miroir des idées* (The mirror of ideas) in 1994, Tournier told me, during a conversation in July of that year, that he had failed because the philosophical essay was inaccessible to readers of less than sixteen years of age.
21. Deborah Ross, "Soap and the Serious Writer," *Independent* (London), February 4, 2002.
22. Beckett, *De grands romanciers écrivent pour les enfants*, 267.
23. Ibid., 293, 299.
24. Jérôme Garcin, "Interview avec Michel Tournier," *L'Événement du Jeudi*, January 9–15, 1986.

25. Riana Scheepers, e-mail to author, June 24, 2007.
26. Annari van der Merwe, "K. Sello kuiker: 13 April 1974–19 January 2005," LitNet: In Memorium, January 20, 2005, http://www.oulitnet.co.za/inmemoriam/duiker_dies.asp (accessed May 9, 2007).
27. Rosemary Stone, "Editorial," *Books for Keeps*, no. 135 (July 2002): 3.
28. Frank McConnell, "Sandman," *Commonweal*, October 20, 1995.
29. Liam McDougall, "*Life of Pi* Hits One Million Sales as Spielberg Eyes Movie Chance," *Sunday Herald*, August 10, 2003.
30. Margaret Atwood, "A Tasty Slice of Pi and Ships," *Sunday Times*, May 5, 2002.
31. David Robinson, "Publisher Keeps His Faith in Scotland," *Scotsman*, September 16, 2003.
32. James Poniewozik, "A Nursery Rhyme of Vengeance," *Time*, October 25, 2002; Gail Caldwell, review of *The Little Friend*, by Donna Tartt, *Boston Globe*, October 27, 2002.
33. Mayer, "Sharing the Love: How Publishers are Re-branding Adult Fiction for Younger Readers."
34. Ibid.
35. Samivel, "*L'Âne Culotte* et l'univers onirique d'Henri Bosco," *Les Cahiers de l'Amitié Henri Bosco* 11 (April–October 1976): 77.
36. An examination of the manuscript in 1997 revealed that it contains three versions of the foreword, including a good, typed copy, suggesting that it was the publisher rather than the author who decided to omit it, feeling no doubt that a text addressed specifically to adults had no place in a book that was part of a children's series.
37. Henri Bosco, "Les enfants m'ont dicté les livres que j'ai écrits pour eux," *Les Nouvelles Littéraires* 1631 (December 4, 1958): 4.
38. Likewise, in *The Boy and the River*, the reception of Grandpa Savinien's simple tale by the villagers of all ages—from the village elders to the youngest child—can be seen as a *mise en abyme* of the reception of the frame story, destined to delight both children and adults.
39. Henri Bosco, *Diaire*, October 1955 and 1958. A letter Bosco wrote in 1963 mentions the cycle that goes from *L'Âne Culotte* to *Bargabot*, and a footnote in the French edition of *The Boy and the River* refers readers who want to get to know Hyacinthe better to *L'Âne Culotte*, suggesting that the latter initiates the cycle. English-speaking children, however, will have no knowledge of the earlier novel, as the footnote was omitted from the translation, undoubtedly because *L'Âne Culotte* has never appeared in English.
40. Henri Bosco, "Henri Bosco voyageur. Le séjour en Grèce (juin–juillet 1963)" [Lettres à Henri Ehret], ed. Claude Girault, *Cahiers Henri Bosco* 21 (1981): 26, note 2.
41. Kümmerling-Meibauer, "Crosswriting as a Criterion for Canonicity: The Case of Erich Kästner," 17. See entire article on pp. 13–30.
42. See Bettina Kümmerling-Meibauer, "Annäherungen von Jugend- und

Erwachsenenliteratur: Die schwedische Jugendliteratur des 80er und frühen 90er Jahre," *Der Deutschunterricht* 46 (1996): 68–81.

43. Laurent Chabin, "La littérature jeunesse: littérature ou sous-littérature," in *Littérature de jeunesse et Fin de siècle*, ed. Campbell and Lohka, 41.

44. Weber, "Pasando les límites: All-Age-Books, Crossover-Literature y otras tendencias actuales de la literatura para jóvenes lectores."

45. Beckett, *De grands romanciers écrivent pour les enfants*, 281. "Barberousse" also appeared, in a slightly different form, in the *La Nouvelle Revue Française* in 1984.

46. It originally appeared in *Nash sovremennik* as *Vniz po techeniiu* (Downstream) in 1972, but was republished later that same year in a slightly revised form with its new title and an added subtitle, *Ocherk odnoi poezdki* (The sketch of a journey). This edition included *Den' gi dlia Marii* (Money for Maria) and *Poslednii srok* (The final hours).

47. *Histoire du livre de jeunesse d'hier à aujourd'hui, en France et dans le monde* (Paris: Gallimard Jeunesse, 1993), 70.

48. Demougin, ed., *Dictionnaire de la littérature française et francophone*, vol. 1, 100.

49. Georges Lemoine, letter to author, January 21, 2003. Tournier has also said that love stories do not interest children (Tournier, unpublished interview with author, July 6, 1995).

50. J. M. G. Le Clézio, letter to Georges Lemoine, January 22, 1990; Georges Lemoine, e-mail message to author, November 3, 2007.

51. Mello is convinced that if an adult does not like a story, a child probably will not like it either (Roger Mello, e-mail message to author, September 26, 2003).

52. Monika Osberghaus, "Vor kurzer oder langer Zeit lebte einer, der nichts merkte: Käthi Bhends Robert-Walser-Bilderbuch," *Frankfurter Allgemeine Zeitung*, January 17, 2004, 36.

53. Jochen Weber, e-mail message to author, January 22, 2007.

54. Michel Tournier, "Le sang des fillettes," *Le Monde*, December 9, 1977, 31.

55. Serge Koster, *Michel Tournier* (Paris: Henri Veyrier, 1986), 158.

56. Michel Tournier, interview with author, July 1995.

57. Antonio Skármeta, "Cuando la ficción nace del infierno," *Imaginaria* 101, April 30, 2003.

58. Beckett, *De grands romanciers écrivent pour les enfants*, 284.

59. *Guardian Unlimited* Books, "The Greatest Gifts," *Guardian Unlimited*, December 2006, http://books.guardian.co.uk/booksoftheyear2004/page/0,,1363149,00.html (accessed April 25, 2007).

60. See Grisel Pires dos Barros, "El cuento de Navidad de Auggie Wren," *Imaginaria* 144, December 22, 2004.

61. Lise Kildegaard, "'Three Square Stories' by Louis Jensen," *Translation* 2 (Fall 2007): 71–79.

62. Monica C. Madsen, "'At sætte livets forunderlighed på ord,' interview med forfatter Louis Jensen," *Læsningens magi: Om børn, bøger og læselyst*, vol. 1 (Copenhagen: Biblioteksstyrelsen, 2003), 7, reprinted as "'The Wondrous Beauty of Life,' interview with author Louis Jensen," trans. Vibeke Cranfield, *Scandinavian Public Library Quarterly* 37, no. 1 (2004): 17; Glistrup, "Children's Literature in Denmark: Trends and Currents in the 1990s."

63. Tournier, "Michel Tournier face aux lycéens," 21.

64. Sandra L. Beckett, "Entretien avec Michel Tournier," *Dalhousie French Studies* 35 (Summer 1996): 71.

65. Alexander Sager, "And the Winner Is ... ," SignandSight.com, September 28, 2005, http://www.signandsight.com/features/290.html (accessed June 13, 2007).

66. "Ted Hughes's Crow," *The Listener*, July 30, 1970.

2. Rewriting for Another Audience

1. Marguerite Yourcenar, *Œuvres romanesques*, Bibliothèque de la Pléiade (Paris: Gallimard, 1990), 1219.

2. Tournier, "Les Enfants dans la bibliothèque," 57.

3. Gérard Genette, *Palimpsests: Literature in the Second Degree* (Lincoln: The University of Nebraska Press, 1997), 374.

4. Anna Forné, *La piratería textual: Un estudio hipertextual de "Son vacas, somos puercos" y "El médico de los piratas" de Carmen Boullosa* (Lund: Romanska Institutionen, 2001).

5. Diane Lafrance, "Cécile Gagnon et la réécriture pour jeunes: Du *Chemin Kénogami* à *C'est ici, mon pays*," "L'écrivain/e pour la jeunesse et ses publics" (paper presented at the Congrès de l'ACFAS, Université de Montréal, May 15–19, 2000).

6. Kathleen Donohue, "'Free-falling' and 'Serendipity': An Interview with Joy Kogawa," *Canadian Children's Literature/Littérature canadienne pour la jeunesse* 84 (1996): 41.

7. Ibid., 41, 42.

8. Meg Harper, "Using It or Losing It ... Exploring Your Creativity," *Scattered Authors' Society Newsletter*, April 2006.

9. Beckett, *De grands romanciers écrivent pour les enfants*, 284.

10. Shavit, *Poetics of Children's Literature*, 44. Shavit offers a much more detailed comparison of the two versions in her study (see pp. 43–59).

11. Ibid., 45.

12. Tournier, "Writing for Children is No Child's Play," 33. For a more detailed study of this novel, see Sandra L. Beckett, "Michel Tournier Retells the Robinson Crusoe Myth: *Friday and Robinson: Life on Speranza Island*," in *Beyond Babar: The European Tradition in Children's Literature*, ed. Sandra L. Beckett and Maria Nikolajeva (Lanham: Scarecrow, 2006), 157–89.

13. Beckett, *De grands romanciers écrivent pour les enfants*, 277–78.
14. Ibid., 265–66.
15. Tournier, "Quand Michel Tournier écrit ses livres pour les enfants."
16. Garcin, "Interview avec Michel Tournier."
17. Genette, *Palimpsests*, 374. For a more detailed analysis of Genette's interpretation of *Friday*, see Sandra L. Beckett, "From the Art of Rewriting to the Art of Crosswriting Child and Adult: The Secret of Michel Tournier's Dual Readership," in *Voices from Far Away: Current Trends in International Children's Literature Research* 24, ed. Maria Nikolajeva (Stockholm: Centrum för barnkulturforskning, 1995), 15.
18. Payot, "L'Entretien: Michel Tournier," 33–34.
19. *Histoire du livre de jeunesse d'hier à aujourd'hui, en France et dans le monde*, 88.
20. See Michel Tournier, "Écrire pour les enfants," interview with Jean-Marie Magnan, *La Quinzaine Littéraire*, December 16–31, 1971, 13; Tournier, "Les enfants dans la bibliothèque," 57.
21. Genette, *Palimpsests*, 424.
22. Tournier, "Les enfants dans la bibliothèque," 57.
23. Michel Tournier, "Discussion" during "Table ronde sur la littérature pour enfants," in *Images et signes de Michel Tournier*, ed. Arlette Bouloumié and Maurice de Gandillac (Paris: Gallimard, 1991), 308.
24. Michel Tournier, *The Wind Spirit: An Autobiography*, trans. Arthur Goldhammer (Boston: Beacon Press, 1988), 183.
25. Ibid., 156–57, Tournier's italics.
26. Beckett, *De grands romanciers écrivent pour les enfants*, 285–86.
27. Tournier, "Writing for Children is No Child's Play," 34.
28. Gilles Lapouge, "Michel Tournier s'explique," *Lire* 64 (December 1980): 45.
29. Michael Worton, "Michel Tournier and the Masterful Art of Rewriting," *PN Review* 11, no. 3 (1984): 25.
30. Tournier, "Michel Tournier face aux lycéens," 21.
31. Beckett, "Entretien avec Michel Tournier," 67; Michel Tournier, unpublished interview with author, July 6, 1995.

3. Child-to-Adult Crossover Fiction

1. Mayer, "Sharing the Love: How Publishers are Re-branding Adult Fiction for Younger Readers."
2. Demers, "Enfant lecteur, adolescent lecteur, adulte lecteur: frontières mouvantes, exigences mythiques et désirs bien réels," 300.
3. See Jasper Rees, "We're All Reading Children's Books," *Daily Telegraph*, November 17, 2003.
4. The situation in children's literature, where literary children's books win major awards and are accepted by the literary establishment while

popular children's books are not seen as literature, reflects that of adult literature. Authors like Stephen King and Jeffrey Archer will never win the Booker.

5. Shavit, *The Poetics of Children's Literature*, 37, 179.

6. Hans-Heino Ewers, "The Adult as Co-Reader and Reader of Children's Literature" (paper presented at the 8th IRSCL Congress, Cologne, Germany, September 28–October 2, 1987), published under the title "Das doppelsinnige Kinderbuch: Erwachsene als Leser and Mitleser von Kinderliteratur," *Fundevogel* 41–42 (1987): 8–12.

7. C. S. Lewis, *Of Other Worlds: Essays and Stories*, ed. Walter Hooper (London: Geoffrey Bles, 1966), 15.

8. W. H. Auden, "Today's 'Wonder-World' Needs Alice," *The New York Times Magazine*, July 1, 1962, 137.

9. Bosco, "Les enfants m'ont dicté les livres que j'ai écrit pour eux." Bosco, *Diaire*, between July and October 1957. Bosco's journal, manuscripts, and other writings are kept at the Fonds de documentation Henri Bosco at the Université de Nice.

10. See Maria Nikolajeva, *Children's Literature Comes of Age: Toward a New Aesthetic* (New York: Garland, 1996).

11. Tournier, "Les enfants dans la bibliothèque," 56.

12. Ana Maria Machado, "Words to Bridge Gaps: Children's Books as a Bridge between Adults and Children" (paper presented at the IBBY Congress, Basel, Switzerland, September 29–October 3, 2002).

13. Jostein Gaarder, "Books for a World without Readers?"

14. Dalya Alberge, "Children's Tale Works Magic on Whitbread," *The Times*, January 23, 2002.

15. Jürgen Martini discusses this in the context of Nigerian children's literature, explaining that the writer sees himself or herself as a teacher of both adults and children. See Martini, "The Novelist as a Teacher: Children's Books by Well-Known Nigerian Authors" (paper presented at the 8th IRSCL Congress, Cologne, Germany, September 28–October 2, 1987).

16. Theodor Brüggemann and Otto Brunken, eds., *Handbuch zur Kinder- und Jugendliteratur: Vom Beginn des Buchdrucks bis 1570* (Stuttgart: Metzler, 1987), 3.

17. Grenz, "E. T. A. Hoffmann as an Author for Children and Adults or the Child and the Adult as Readers of Children's Literature," 93.

18. O'Sullivan, "The Fate of the Dual Addressee in the Translation of Children's Literature," 118.

19. E. T. A. Hoffmann, "Nußknacker und Mausekönig," in *Kinder-Märchen* by C. W. Contessa, Friedrich Baron de la Motte Fouqué and E. T. A. Hoffmann, ed. Hans-Heino Ewers (Stuttgart: Reclam, 1987), 294.

20. See Grenz, "E. T. A. Hoffmann as an Author for Children and Adults or the Child and the Adult as Readers of Children's Literature," 91–96.

21. Hans-Heino Ewers, "Epilogue," in *Kinder-Märchen*, 327–50.

22. Robert Louis Stevenson, "The Art of Writing," in *Essays on the Art of Writing* (London: Chatto & Windus, 1905), 23.

23. David Daiche, *Robert Louis Stevenson and His World* (London: Thames and Hudson, 1973), 56.

24. Patrick Scott and Roger Mortimer, with assistance from Bruce Bowlin, "Robert Louis Stevenson, 1850–1894" (exhibition, Thomas Cooper Library, University of South California, Summer 1994–Spring 1995), University of South Carolina, http://www.sc.edu/library/spcoll/britlit/rls/rls3.html (accessed June 21, 2007).

25. Aubarède, "Écrire pour les enfants," 4; qtd. in Demougin, ed., *Dictionnaire de la littérature française et francophone*, 100.

26. Maija-Liisa Harju, "Tove Jansson and the Crossover Continuum" (Ph.D. course paper, McGill University, 2007).

27. W. Glynn Jones, *Tove Jansson* (Boston: Twayne Publishers, 1984), 3; Harju, "Tove Jansson and the Crossover Continuum."

28. Harju, "Tove Jansson and the Crossover Continuum."

29. Christine Wilkie-Stibbs, "Russell Hoban," in *The Oxford Encyclopedia of Children's Literature*, ed. Zipes, vol. 2, 298.

30. Eva-Maria Metcalf, "Concepts of Childhood in Peter Handke's *Kindergeschichte* and Christine Nöstlinger's *Hugo, das Kind in den besten Jahren*," in *Wandlungen des Literaturbegriffs in den Deutschsprachigen Ländern seit 1945*, ed. Gerhard P. Knapp and Gerd Labroisse (Amsterdam: Rodopi, 1988), 291, 298.

31. Serge Koster, *Michel Tournier* (Paris: Henri Veyrier, 1986), 150; Mary Blume, "A Laughing Provocateur Is Launched in Britain," *International Herald Tribune*, December 30, 1983, 7.

32. Tournier, "Michel Tournier: comment écrire pour les enfants," 19; Tournier, "Writing for Children is No Child's Play," 34.

33. Ray J. Parrott Jr., "Aesopian Language," in *Modern Encyclopedia of Russian and Soviet Literature*, vol. 1 (Gulf Breeze, FL: Academic International Press, 1977), 39. See Larissa Tumanov, "Writing for a Dual Audience in the Former Soviet Union: The Aesopian Children's Literature of Kornei Chukovskii, Mikhail Zoshchenko, and Daniil Kharms," in *Transcending Boundaries: Writing for a Dual Audience of Children and Adults*, ed. Beckett, 129–48.

34. Tumanov, "Writing for a Dual Audience in the Former Soviet Union," 129–30.

35. Lev Loseff, *On the Beneficence of Censorship: Aesopian Language in Modern Russian Literature* (Munich: Otto Sagner, 1984), 86.

36. Felicity Ann O'Dell, *Socialisation Through Children's Literature: The Soviet Example* (Cambridge: Cambridge University Press, 1978), 57.

37. Tumanov, "Writing for a Dual Audience in the Former Soviet Union," 136–37.

38. Rebecca Domar, "The Tragedy of a Soviet Satirist: The Case of Zoshchenko," in *Through the Glass of Soviet Literature*, ed. Ernest Simmons (New York: Columbia University Press, 1953), 205.

39. See Arkady Belinkov, "The Soviet Intelligentsia and the Socialist Revolution: On Yury Olesha's *Envy*," *The Russian Review* 30, no. 4 (October 1971), 356–68.

40. See Lilia Ratcheva-Stratieva, "Earth Hanging in Infinity: Janusz Korczak's *King Matt the First*," in *Beyond Babar: The European Tradition in Children's Literature*, ed. Beckett and Nikolajeva, 1–20.

41. James Fenton, "Keeping Up with Salman Rushdie," *New York Review of Books* 38, no. 6 (March 28, 1991): 31.

42. Jean-Pierre Durix, "The Gardener of Stories: Salman Rushdie's *Haroun and the Sea of Stories*," in *Reading Rushdie: Perspectives on the Fiction of Salman Rushdie*, ed. M. D. Fletcher (Amsterdam: Rodopi, 1994), 343.

43. Catherine Cundy, *Salman Rushdie* (Manchester: Manchester University Press, 1996), 88.

44. Rushdie, "*The Wizard of Oz*," 18.

45. Thomas Swann, *A. A. Milne* (Boston: Twayne, 1971), 66.

46. Frederick C. Crews, *The Pooh Perplex: A Freshman Casebook. In Which It Is Discovered that the True Meaning of the Pooh Stories Is Not as Simple as Is Usually Believed, But for Proper Elucidation Requires the Combined Efforts of Several Academicians of Varying Critical Persuasions* (New York: E. P. Dutton, 1963), ix.

47. Ann Thwaite, *A. A. Milne: His Life* (London: Faber & Faber, 1991), 318.

48. O'Sullivan, "The Fate of the Dual Addressee in the Translation of Children's Literature," 112.

49. Ibid., 113, 119. O'Sullivan points out that Rowohlt had already introduced Pooh into German adult discourse with his column "Pooh's Corner" in the weekly newspaper *Die Zeit*, in which he adopts the naive perspective of a bear to comment on political, cultural, and social matters (113).

50. The survey of "All-Time Bestselling Children's Books," edited by Diane Roback and Jason Britton and compiled by Debbie Hochman, appeared in *Publishers Weekly* on December 17, 2001. The lists are based on sales figures from national sales in the United States from the original date of publication through the end of 2000.

51. Andrew O'Hehir, "The Book of the Century," part 1, Salon.com, June 4, 2001, http://archive.salon.com/books/feature/2001/06/04/tolkien/ (accessed March 24, 2007).

52. Krysia Diver, "A Lord for Germany," *Sydney Morning Herald*, October 5, 2004.

53. Philip Toynbee, "Dissension among the Judges," *Observer*, August 6, 1961. The quotation from the *Sunday Times* is quoted on the Barnes and Noble website.

54. Qtd. in S. F. Said, "The Godfather of Harry Potter"; Vernon Harwood,

"Interview: Richard Adams," part 1, BBC Radio Berkshire, http://www.bbc.co.uk/berkshire/content/articles/2007/03/16/richard_adams_interview_feature.shtml (accessed May 11, 2007).

55. S. F. Said, "The Godfather of Harry Potter."

56. See Ulli Pfau, *Phantásien in Halle 4/5: Michael Endes 'Unendliche Geschichte' und ihre Verfilmung* (Munich: Deutscher Taschenbuch Verlag, 1984), 92.

57. Dieter Petzold, "A Neverending Success Story? Michael Ende's Return Trip to Fantasia," in *Beyond Babar: The European Tradition in Children's Literature*, ed. Beckett and Nikolajeva, 234.

58. Qtd. in Irene Garland, "Jostein Gaarder," in *Britannica Book of the Year*, 1995, Encyclopedia Britannica Online, http://britannica.com/eb/article-9115358/Gaarder-Jostein (accessed May 11, 2007).

59. Roger-Pol Droit, "La philosophie comme jeu d'enfant," *Le Monde*, February 24, 1995; review of *Sophie's World*, by Jostein Gaarder, *The Washington Post Book World*, cited in the blurb of the U.S. paperback edition of *Sophie's World*.

60. Review of *Sophie's World*, by Jostein Gaarder, *Daily Telegraph*, qtd. in the blurb of the English paperback edition of *Through a Glass, Darkly*.

61. Gaarder, "Books for a World without Readers?"

62. Susan Salter Reynolds, review of *The Solitaire Mystery*, by Jostein Gaarder, *Los Angeles Times*, July 21, 1996.

63. David Templeton, "Dark Days: Ghouls and Goblins, Mayhem and Murder—It's Just Kids' Stuff," *North Bay Bohemian*, March 14–20, 2002.

64. Tara Pepper, "Not Just for Children," *Newsweek International*, February 2, 2006.

65. Bel Mooney, "Writing through Ages," *Times*, August 28, 2002.

66. See, for example, Taylor, "The Potter Effect."

67. Julia Eccleshare, *A Guide to the Harry Potter Novels* (London: Continuum, 2002), 106.

68. Jumana Farouky, "J. K. Rowling," *Time* (Europe) 168, no. 21 (November 13, 2006).

69. Jane Nissen, *The Bookseller*, March 2000.

70. Qtd. in Wendy Parsons and Catriona Nicholson, "Talking to Philip Pullman: An Interview," *The Lion and the Unicorn* 23, no. 1 (1999): 123.

71. Amanda Craig, *Window into Souls*, by Philip Pullman, *New Statesman*, September 26, 1997, 66.

72. S. F. Said, "The Grown-up World of Kidult Books."

73. See John Ezard, "Harry Potter Toppled in Sales Charts," *Guardian*, June 2, 2003.

74. Nicolette Jones, "Twice the Appeal," *The Children's Bookseller*, September 10, 1999: 22.

75. David Lister, "Pullman Wins Whitbread for Children's Fantasy," *Independent* (London), January 23, 2002.

76. Helena de Bertodano, "I Am of the Devil's Party," *Sunday Telegraph*, January 27, 2002; James Naughtie, "*Northern Lights*," Radio 4's Book Club, May 7, 2000.

77. Parsons and Nicholson, "Talking to Philip Pullman," 122.

78. Claudia FitzHerbert, "This Author Is Original and Also Dangerous," *Daily Telegraph*, January 23, 2002.

79. For example, Bel Mooney claims "all the 'crossover' titles involve magical quests" ("Writing through Ages").

80. Jonathan Hunt, "Redefining the Young Adult Novel," *The Horn Book Magazine* 83, vol. 2 (March–April 2007): 141–47.

81. Lierop-Debrauwer and Bastiaansen-Harks, *Over grenze: De adolescenten-roman in het literatuuronderwijs*.

82. "1990 Hans Christian Andersen Awards," *Bookbird* 3 (1990): 3.

83. Tor Fretheim, "Merkel, Donna og retten til å bli hørt og sett," *Bokspeilet* 2 (1986): 4.

84. Anne Born, "Tormod Haugen, *Vinterstedet*—The Winter Place: Synopsis" (unpublished review written at the request of Gyldendal, 1984).

85. See, for example, Angela Carew, "Anne Provoost: *In the Shadow of the Ark*," *Kirkus Reviews* (July 2004).

86. Ilene Cooper, "Find More Like This: *In the Shadow of the Ark*," *Booklist* 100, nos. 19–20 (June 1–15, 2004): 1721.

87. NSW Ministry for the Arts, "2005 NSW Premier's Literary Awards," http://www.arts.nsw.gov.au/awards/LiteraryAwards/2005%20awards/2005 shortlist.htm (accessed June 15, 2007).

88. Elaine Williams, "Home-grown Heartaches," *The Times Educational Supplement*, November 21, 2003.

89. Sam Birch, "Set in Success," February 27, 2007, http://vision.york.ac.uk/index.php?option=com_content&task=view&id=148 (accessed March 12, 2007).

90. Adèle Geras, "Hotel du lac," review of *A Gathering Light*, by Jennifer Donnelly, *Guardian*, June 7, 2003.

91. Karen Magnuson Beil, "Interview with Jennifer Donnelly," *The Children's Literature Connection*, http://www.childrensliteratureconnection.org/resources-info.asp?ID=7 (accessed March 15, 2007).

92. Madelyn Travis, "Foundlings on Stage," Booktrust, http://www.book trusted.co.uk/articles/documents.php4?articleid=40 (accessed June 15, 2007).

93. Julia Eccleshare, "Inside the Outsider," *Guardian*, May 17, 2003.

94. Joanna Briscoe, "So What's the Real Story?" *Independent* (London), May 15, 2003.

95. Sean Merrigan, "Interview with Clare Sambrook: Author of *Hide & Seek*," Edit Red, http://www.editred.com/Uploads/st_37256_Interview_with_Clare_Samb (accessed May 9, 2007).

96. Bruce Fulton, "Kori: *The Beacon Anthology of Korean American Fiction*," *Pacific Affairs* 75, no. 4 (Winter 2002/2003): 660–61.

97. See Richard Flynn, "'Affirmative Acts': Language, Childhood, and Power in June Jordan's Cross-Writing," *Children's Literature* 30 (2002): 159–85.

4. All Ages Fantasy

1. John Gardner, "Interview: Discworld Author Terry Pratchett," *New Zealand Herald*, October 26, 2002.
2. Nicholas Clee, "Can the Magic Last Forever?" *Independent* (London) September 15, 2004.
3. Rees, "We're All Reading Children's Books."
4. Farah Mendlesohn, *Diana Wynne Jones: Children's Literature and the Fantastic Tradition* (New York: Routledge, 2005), xiii.
5. Ursula K. Le Guin, "Dreams Must Explain Themselves," in *The Language of the Night: Essays on Fantasy and Science Fiction*, ed. Susan Wood (New York: G. P. Putnam's Sons, 1979), 55. Mike Cadden claims that Le Guin reserves the genre of fantasy for children and that "there are few outright fantasies for adults," whereas there are "no real science fiction tales for children" among her texts ("Speaking to Both Children and Genre: Le Guin's Ethics of Audience," 134). However, he admits that she may allow "her age-based genres to blur" in her young adult fiction (136).
6. Gardner, "Interview: Discworld Author Terry Pratchett."
7. Raymond H. Thompson, "Interview with Alan Garner," 1989, in "Taliesin's Successors: Interviews with Authors of Modern Arthurian Literature," The Camelot Project, http://www.lib.rochester.edu/camelot /intrvws/garner.htm (accessed October 11, 2007).
8. Todd Gilchrist, "Howl's Moving Castle," IGN Entertainment, June 9, 2005, http://movies.ign.com/articles/624/624042p1.html (accessed June 26, 2007).
9. The Long Patrol Club, "An Interview with Stuart Moore," http://www. longpatrolclub.com/interviews/stuartmoore.html (accessed November 18, 2007).
10. Maria Nikolajeva, "Children's, Adult, Human … ?" in *Transcending Boundaries: Writing for a Dual Audience of Children and Adults*, ed. Beckett, 65.
11. Amanda Craig, "Window into Souls," *New Statesman*, September 26, 1997, 66; William Waldegrave, Review of *The Subtle Knife* by Philip Pullman, *The Week*, September 1997.
12. Parsons and Nicholson, "Talking to Philip Pullman," 131.
13. Michelle Pauli, "A Kind of Magic," *Guardian*, October 7, 2005.
14. Ibid.
15. Claire Armitstead, "Arthur Reborn," *Guardian*, September 29, 2001.
16. Michael Kipen, "Chabon's Fantasy League: Baseball Saves the Day in an Adventure for Kids and Adults," *San Francisco Chronicle*, September 15, 2002.

17. Suzi Feay, "The Tale of Genji for the Potter Generation," *Independent on Sunday*, November 28, 2004.
18. Sandra Comino, "Entrevista con Liliana Bodoc," *Imaginaria*, July 7, 2004.
19. Samit Basu, "On Flights of Fantasy," *Telegraph* (Calcutta), August 6, 2005.
20. Karen McVeigh and Lesley Walker, "Pratchett Casts a Bitter Spell on Rivals," *Scotsman*, July 13, 2002.
21. Terry Pratchett, comment posted September 27, 1993, Alt.Fan.Pratchett, http://groups.google.com/group/alt.fan.pratchett/msg/3b119fcb1984cb53 (accessed May 18, 2007).
22. Jane Langton, Review of *Handles*, by Jan Mark, *The New York Times*, July 28, 1985.
23. Jan Mark, "Jan Mark," *Books for Keeps* 25 (March 1984): 12–13; "Jan Mark," Biography, http://biography.jrank.org/pages/1875/Mark-Jan-1943.html (accessed August 17, 2007).
24. Damian Kelleher, "Caught in the Crossover," *The Times Educational Supplement*, October 11, 2002.
25. Jack Zipes, *Sticks and Stones: The Troublesome Success of Children's Literature from Slovenly Peter to Harry Potter* (New York: Routledge, 2001), 177.
26. See Maria Nikolajeva, *From Mythic to Linear: Time in Children's Literature* (Lanham: Scarecrow, 2000), 231.
27. Julia Eccleshare considers this evolution up to book four in *A Guide to the Harry Potter Novels* (pp. 18–31).
28. Parsons and Nicholson, "Talking to Philip Pullman," 124–26.
29. Kaja Perina, "Lemony Snicket: Reversal of Fortune," *Psychology Today* 37, no. 6 (November–December 2004): 104.
30. Sandy Auden, "Get 'Em Reading Fantasy at an Early Age: New Teen Fiction Hits the Shelves," The Alien Online, September 14, 2002, http://www.thealienonline.net/ao_060.asp?baa=1&tid=1&scid=6&iid=997 (accessed April 9, 2006).

5. Authors Crossing Over

1. Rees, "We're All Reading Children's Books."
2. John Ezard, "Fully Booked," *Guardian*, January 24, 2002.
3. Jones, "Young-Adult Books Are No Longer Child's Play for Bestselling Authors."
4. "Lemony Snicket's The Grim Grotto Surpasses 1.1 Million Copies Sold," *PR Newswire*, October 21, 2004.
5. David Abrams, "The Mask Behind the Man," *January Magazine*, June 2002, http://januarymagazine.com/kidsbooks/lemony2002.html (accessed April 9, 2006).
6. Jones, "Young-Adult Books Are No Longer Child's Play for Bestselling Authors," D1.

7. Kipen, "Chabon's Fantasy League: Baseball Saves the Day in an Adventure for Kids and Adults."

8. Tonkin, "Once Upon a Time in the Marketing Department ..."

9. Petro Matskevych and Kseniya Sladkevych, "The All-European Tendency: Yesterday's Teenagers Become 'Adult' Authors" (paper presented at the International Symposium "Visualizing the Child in Children's Fiction," Lviv, Ukraine, April 12, 2007).

10. See Juliet McMaster, "'Adults' Literature,' by Children," *The Lion and the Unicorn* 25, no. 2 (April 2001): 277–99.

11. Ibid. The spelling "Freindship" is retained in the title of most editions.

12. Ibid., 285.

13. Bart Moeyaert, "A Talk with TBB (Internet), United States," in IBBY Belgium Flemish Section nomination dossier for the Hans Christian Andersen Award 2002.

14. Malcolm Knox, "Writers Coming of Age," *Sydney Morning Herald*, May 10, 2003.

15. Rees, "We're All Reading Children's Books."

16. See blurb of *Ich habe einfach Glück*.

17. Matskevych and Sladkevych, "The All-European Tendency: Yesterday's Teenagers Become 'Adult' Authors."

6. Publishers and the Marketplace

1. Kelleher, "Caught in the Crossover."

2. Taylor, "The Potter Effect."

3. Clee, "Can the Magic Last Forever?"

4. Said, "The Grown-up World of Kidult Books."

5. Tonkin, "Once Upon a Time in the Marketing Department..."

6. Julia Donaldson, *Children's Writers' and Artists' Yearbook 2006* (London: A&C Black, 2006), 107.

7. Pepper, "Not Just for Children."

8. Julia Eccleshare, "Crossing Over," *Literature Matters*, June 2005, http://www.britishcouncil.org/arts-literature-matters-3-eccleshare.htm (accessed April 2, 2006).

9. Clee, "Can the Magic Last Forever?"

10. Dante, "Reading into Crossover Trends."

11. Mayer, "Sharing the Love: How Publishers are Re-branding Adult Fiction for Younger Readers."

12. John Rowe Townsend, *A Sense of Story: Essays on Contemporary Writers for Children* (Philadelphia: J. B. Lippincott, 1971), 10.

13. Garan Holcombe, "Mark Haddon," 2004, British Council, http://www.contemporarywriters.com/authors/?p=auth3E38026813f8c194E5NnW1CF3087 (accessed March 31, 2006). By extension, this logic would mean that any novel written by an adult was necessarily for adults and that only

teenagers and children could write young adult and children's novels respectively.

14. Demers, "Enfant lecteur, adolescent lecteur, adulte lecteur: frontières mouvantes, exigences mythiques et désirs bien réels," 17.
15. Harry Kullman, "Att skriva för bra," *Skolbiblioteket* 6 (1964): 208.
16. Jones, "Young-Adult Books Are No Longer Child's Play for Bestselling Authors," D1.
17. Michael Rosen, "Home and Away—Writing and Performing Poetry for Children," paper presented at the Congress of the International Research Society of Children's Literature, Dublin, Ireland, August 13–17 (2005).
18. Fretheim, "Merkel, Donna og retten til å bli hørt og sett."
19. Born, "Tormod Haugen, *Vinterstedet*—The Winter Place: Synopsis."
20. "Bibliothèque blanche," *Bulletin de la NRF* 75 (November 1953): 16; Jacques Lemarchand, "Livres pour enfants," *Bulletin de la NRF* 144 (December 1950): 13b–14a.
21. Lemarchand, "Livres pour enfants," 13b–14a.
22. Ibid., 14a; italics are mine.
23. "La Bibliothèque blanche," *Bulletin de la NRF* [1966?]; italics are mine.
24. Josselin, "Les enfants dans la bibliothèque," 56.
25. *Histoire du livre de jeunesse d'hier à aujourd'hui, en France et dans le monde,* 69.
26. Beckett, "Entretien avec Michel Tournier," 68.
27. For a more detailed look at Calvino as a crosswriter, see Alida Poeti, "Crossing Borders: Calvino in the Footprints of Collodi," in *Transcending Boundaries: Writing for a Dual Audience of Children and Adults,* ed. Beckett, 201–13.
28. Le Guin, "Dreams Must Explain Themselves," 45.
29. Jones, "Young-Adult Books Are No Longer Child's Play for Bestselling Authors," D1.
30. Ibid.
31. Demers, "Enfant lecteur, adolescent lecteur, adult lecteur: frontières mouvantes, exigences mythiques et désirs bien réels," 21, 25. Demers explains her talent as a storyteller by the fact that she learned the craft by reading thousands of children's books.
32. See O'Sullivan, "The Fate of the Dual Addressee in the Translation of Children's Literature," 109–19.
33. Rosen, "Breaking the Age Barrier," 29–30.
34. Lapouge, "Michel Tournier s'explique," 45; Tournier, "Writing for Children is No Child's Play," 33.
35. Beckett, *De grands romanciers écrivent pour les enfants,* 265.
36. Guitta Pessis Pasternak, "Tournier le sensuel," *Le Monde,* August 13, 1984.
37. Joseph H. McMahon, "Michel Tournier's Texts for Children," *Children's Literature* 13 (1985): 168.

38. Demers, "Enfant lecteur, adolescent lecteur, adulte lecteur: frontières mouvantes, exigences mythiques et désirs bien réels," 30–31.

39. Antonio Ventura, "Michi Strausfeld: Entrevista a Michi Strausfeld, directora de la colección 'Las Tres Edades' de Siruela," *Babar*, May 1, 2005, http://revistababar.com/web/index.php?option=com_content&task=view&id=229&Itemid=51 (accessed March 28, 2007).

40. Ibid.

41. Michi Strausfeld, "Las Tres Edades: de ocho a ochenta y ocho años," *CLIJ* 50 (May 1993): 44–45.

42. Ibid. A detailed analysis of this novel can be found in Sandra L. Beckett, *Recycling Red Riding Hood* (New York: Routledge, 2002), 308–31.

43. Carmen Martín Gaite, "Entrevista: Carmen Martín Gaite," *CLIJ* 26 (March 1991): 7.

44. [*Caperucita en Manhattan*], *Peonza* 40 (May 1997).

45. Alberto García-Teresa, "José Maria Merino," May 30, 2002, http://www.bibliopolis.org/articulo/merino.htm (accessed May 25, 2007). A shortened version of the interview was published in *2001* (September–October 2002).

46. Ventura, "Michi Strausfeld: Entrevista a Michi Strausfeld, directora de la colección 'Las Tres Edades' de Siruela."

47. Danielle Thaler, "Littérature de jeunesse: un concept problématique," *Canadian Children's Literature/Littérature canadienne pour la jeunesse* 83 (Autumn 1986): 28.

48. Taylor, "The Potter Effect."

49. See Zipes, *Sticks and Stones*, 51–54.

50. Andrew Blake, *The Irresistible Rise of Harry Potter* (London: Verso, 2002), 88.

51. Dan Hade, "Stories as Commodities" (paper presented at the international conference "Perspectives contemporaines du roman pour la jeunesse," Institut International Charles Perrault, Eaubonne, France, December 1–2, 2000). Published in French as "Des histoires qui sont aussi des marchandises," in *Perspectives contemporaines du roman pour la jeunesse*, ed. Virginie Douglas (Paris: L'Harmattan, 2003), 46.

52. Elizabeth Mehren, "Reading by 9: Toy Tie-ins Rate an 'A' with Children's Book Publishers," *Los Angeles Times*, December 23, 1998, A1.

53. Briscoe, "So What's the Real Story?"

54. Hade mentioned this in his paper, "Stories as Commodities," but it did not find its way into his essay in the proceedings of the conference.

55. Robert McCrum, "Not for Children," *Observer*, October 22, 2000.

56. Tomas Kellner, "Harry Potter and the Vanishing Brand Magic," *Forbes Magazine*, July 14, 2005.

57. "Dianne Hofmeyr," Children's Literature Research Unit, University of South Africa, http://www.childlit.org.za/boikie.html (accessed March 25, 2006).

58. Parmy Olson, "Bloomsbury Ready to Close the Book on Harry Potter?" *Forbes Magazine*, April 3, 2007.
59. Liam McDougall, "*Life of Pi* Hits One Million Sales as Spielberg Eyes Movie Chance," *Sunday Herald*, August 10, 2003.
60. Hade, "Des histoires qui sont aussi des marchandises," 55.
61. Taylor, "The Potter Effect."
62. Parsons and Nicholson, "Talking to Philip Pullman," 124–26.
63. Nick Gifford, "An Interview with Sean Wright," Infinity Plus, http://www.infinityplus.co.uk/nonfiction/intsw.htm (accessed April 3, 2006).
64. Dante, "Reading into Crossover Trends."
65. See John Ezard, "Harry Potter and the Stony Broke Authors," *Guardian*, July 14, 2005.
66. Shannon Maughan, "The Lowdown on Laydowns: Publishers Embrace One-Day Laydown Dates for Big Books This Season," *Publishers Weekly*, September 1, 2003.
67. Kimberly Maul, "Snicket Buzz About Newly Named Novel Was Fostered Online, Offering a Sign of What's to Come," *Book Standard*, October 18, 2005.
68. Ibid.
69. Ibid.
70. Tonkin, "Once Upon a Time in the Marketing Department …"
71. Malcolm Gladwell, "The Science of the Sleeper," *The New Yorker*, October 4, 1999.
72. Rees, "We're All Reading Children's Books."
73. Rosen, "Breaking the Age Barrier," 28–31.
74. Clee, "Can the Magic Last Forever?"; Rees, "We're All Reading Children's Books."
75. See Rosen, "Breaking the Age Barrier," 29.
76. Rees, "We're All Reading Children's Books."
77. Mayer, "Sharing the Love: How Publishers are Re-branding Adult Fiction for Younger Readers."
78. Rees, "We're All Reading Children's Books."
79. Jill Insley, "Once Upon a Time This Book Was Born," *Observer*, December 5, 2004.
80. Stuart Webb, "Rowling's Rivals: The New Collectables," *Book and Magazine Collector* 244, July 2004.
81. Dante, "Reading Into Crossover Trends."
82. Insley, "Once Upon a Time This Book Was Born."
83. Muriel Tiberghien, "Table Ronde" (round table presented at the international conference on "Perspectives contemporaines du roman pour la jeunesse," Institut International Charles Perrault, Eaubonne, France, December 1–2, 2000).
84. Ibid.
85. See Zipes, *Sticks and Stones*; Jean Perrot, *Mondialisation et littérature de jeunesse* (Paris: de la Librairie, 2008).

86. "Dianne Hofmeyr," Children's Literature Research Unit, University of South Africa.
87. Ventura, "Michi Strausfeld."
88. Emer O'Sullivan, "Internationalism, the Universal Child and the World of Children's Literature," in *International Companion Encyclopedia of Children's Literature*, ed. Hunt, 2nd ed., vol. 1, 22.
89. Julia Eccleshare, "A Golden Time for Children's Books," *Publishers Weekly*, February 18, 2002.

7. Paratexts and Packaging

1. Donaldson, *Children's Writers' and Artists' Yearbook 2006*, 107.
2. Helma van Lierop-Debrauwer, "Terra Incognita? Adolescent Fiction in the Higher Classes in Secondary Education" (paper presented at the 8th Biennial Conference of the International Society for the Empirical Study of Literature (IGEL), Pécs, Hungary, August 21–24, 2002).
3. Conversation with Wim Hofman, April 5, 2000; e-mail message from Wim Hofman, October 11, 2000.
4. Paul Gessell, "Adult Art Fills Illustrated Edition of Yann Martel's *Life of Pi* Novel," *Vancouver Sun*, November 17, 2007.
5. Peter van den Hoven, "Een Vlaamse reus: Over de levensverhalen van Henri van Daele," *Literatuur zonder leeftijd* 39 (1996): 356.
6. Demers, "Enfant lecteur, adolescent lecteur, adulte lecteur: frontières mouvantes, exigences mythiques et désirs bien réels," 28.
7. Ibid.
8. Rosen, "Breaking the Age Barrier," 29.
9. Demers, "Enfant lecteur, adolescent lecteur, adulte lecteur: frontières mouvantes, exigences mythiques et désirs bien réels," 29–30.
10. Ibid.
11. See Dante, "Reading into Crossover Trends."
12. Amanda Craig, "Mark Haddon," *Sunday Times*, February 2004; Kate Kellaway, "Autistic Differences," *Observer*, April 27, 2003.
13. John Ezard, "Favouite Haddon wins Whitbread," *Guardian*, February 28, 2004.
14. Rees, "We're All Reading Children's Books."
15. Holcombe, "Mark Haddon."
16. Ibid; Craig, "Mark Haddon."
17. Mike Shuttleworth, "A Curious Bestseller," *The Age*, February 14, 2004, http://www.theage.com.au.articles/2004/02/11/1076388428007.html (accessed March 29, 2006).
18. Basu, "On Flights of Fantasy."
19. Shuttleworth, "A Curious Bestseller."
20. Mayer, "Sharing the Love: How Publishers are Re-branding Adult Fiction for Younger Readers."

21. Rosen, "Breaking the Age Barrier," 29.
22. Dominique Caron, "La magie de J. K. Rowling," *Le libraire* 1, no. 6 (April 2000): 41.
23. Parsons and Nicholson, "Talking to Philip Pullman," 125–26.
24. "*Die Mitte der Welt*," Film-Archive, http://www.german-cinema.de/archive /filmi_view.php?film_id=1243 (accessed March 25, 2006).
25. Mayer, "Sharing the Love: How Publishers are Re-branding Adult Fiction for Younger Readers."
26. Tonkin, "Once Upon a Time in the Marketing Department …"
27. Dante, "Reading into Crossover Trends."
28. Mayer, "Sharing the Love: How Publishers are Re-branding Adult Fiction for Younger Readers."
29. Rees, "We're All Reading Children's Books."

Epilogue: Causes and Consequences of the Current Crossover Craze

1. Julia Eccleshare, "A Golden Time for Children's Books," *Publishers Weekly*, February 18, 2002.
2. Eccleshare, "Crossing Over."
3. Anne Fine, "The Big Picture," British Council Arts, www.britishcouncil. org/arts-literature-matters-3-fine.htm (accessed April 25, 2006).
4. Rees, "We're All Reading Children's Books."
5. Tim Wynne-Jones, "The Survival of the Book," *Signal 87* (September 1998): 160–66.
6. Gaarder, "Books for a World without Readers?"
7. Philip Hensher, "Harry Potter and the Art of Making Money," *Independent* (London), June 19, 2003.
8. Philip Nel, "Is There a Text in This Advertising Campaign? Literature, Marketing, and Harry Potter," *The Lion and the Unicorn* 29, no. 2 (2005): 236.
9. "Literary Expansion: Children's Books Break through the Barrier," *Guardian*, August 18, 2001.
10. Said, "The Grown-up World of Kidult Books."
11. Tournier, *The Wind Spirit*, 156–57.
12. Said, "The Grown-up World of Kidult Books."
13. George Walden, "A Child's View, Again," *Daily Telegraph*, January 26, 2003.
14. Dante, "Reading into Crossover Trends."
15. Harold Bloom, "Dumbing Down American Readers," *Boston Globe*, September 24, 2003. See also his article "Can 35 Million Book Buyers Be Wrong? Yes," *The Wall Street Journal*, July 11, 2000, A26.
16. Anthony Holden, "Why Harry Potter Doesn't Cast a Spell over Me," *Observer*, June 25, 2000.

17. Barbara Ellen, "Access Small Areas," *Times*, November 15, 2001.
18. A. S. Byatt, "Harry Potter and the Childish Adult," *New York Times*, July 7, 2003.
19. See Frank Furedi, "The Children Who Won't Grow Up," *Spiked*, July 29, 2003.
20. Howard Jacobson, "Adults Should Not Toady to the Taste of Tots," *Independent* (London), July 5, 2003.
21. Jonathan Myerson, "Harry Potter and the Sad Grown-ups," *Independent* (London), November 14, 2001.
22. Rees, "We're All Reading Children's Books."
23. Mike Featherstone, "Global and Local Cultures," in *Mapping the Futures: Local Cultures, Global Change*, ed. Jon Bird, Barry Curtis, Tim Putnam, George Robertson, and Lisa Tickner (London: Routledge, 1993), 177, 180.
24. Pepper, "Not Just for Children."
25. Tonkin, "Once Upon a Time in the Marketing Department . . ."
26. See Eva Glistrup, "Children's Literature in Denmark: Trends and Currents in the 1990s"; Muriel Tiberghien, "Table Ronde."
27. Perry Nodelman, *The Pleasures of Children's Literature* (New York and London: Longman, 1992), 11. See also Myles McDowell, "Fiction for Children and Adults: Some Essential Differences," *Children's Literature in Education* 4, no. 1 (March 1973): 50–63.
28. "Dianne Hofmeyr," Children's Literature Research Unit, University of South Africa.
29. William Walsh, "I Am a Woman Writer; I Am a Western Writer: An Interview with Ursula Le Guin," *The Kenyon Review* 17, nos. 3–4 (1995): 198.
30. Dante, "Reading into Crossover Trends."
31. Craig, "Mark Haddon."
32. Isaac Bashevis Singer, "Isaac Bashevis Singer on Writing for Children," *Children's Literature* 6 (1977): 12–13.
33. Richard Adams, "Some Ingredients of *Watership Down*," in *The Thorny Paradise: Writers on Writing for Children*, ed. Edward Blishen (Harmondsworth: Kestrel Books, 1975), 165.
34. Templeton, "Dark Days: Ghouls and Goblins, Mayhem and Murder —It's Just Kids' Stuff."
35. Jones, "Young-Adult Books Are No Longer Child's Play for Bestselling Authors," D1.
36. Katherine Paterson, *Gates of Excellence: On Reading and Writing Books for Children* (New York: Elsevier/Nelson Books, 1981), 38; Larry McCaffery and Sinda Gregory, "An Interview with Ursula Le Guin," *Missouri Review* 7 (1984): 82.
37. See Mike Cadden, *Ursula K. Le Guin Beyond Genre: Fiction for Children and Adults* (New York: Routledge, 2005): 135–46. This chapter is a revision of

his article "Speaking to Both Children and Genre: Le Guin's Ethics of Audience."

38. See Van Lierop-Debrauwer and Bastiaansen-Harks, *Over grenzen: De adolescentenroman in het literatuuronderwijs.*

39. Templeton, "Dark Days: Ghouls and Goblins, Mayhem and Murder—It's Just Kids' Stuff."

40. Ibid.

41. Jones, "Young-Adult Books Are No Longer Child's Play for Bestselling Authors," D1

42. Thomas Penny, "A Children's Writer with Adult Topics," *Telegraph,* February 23, 2001.

43. Jones, "Young-Adult Books Are No Longer Child's Play for Bestselling Authors," D1.

44. Bart Moeyaert, "Seven Small Stories," paper presented at the Seminar "Coming Home in Children's Literature," Roehampton Institute, London, May 12–13, 2000.

45. Sue Bursztynski, "Return to Tremaris," review of *The Waterless Sea,* by Kate Constable. *January Magazine,* August 2003, http://januarymagazine. com/SFF/waterlesssea.html (accessed April 20, 2007).

46. J. M. Barrie, *Peter Pan in Kensington Gardens / Peter and Wendy* (Oxford: Oxford University Press, 1999), 132.

47. Mitzi Myers, "'No Safe Place to Run To': An Interview with Robert Cormier," *The Lion and the Unicorn* 24, no. 3 (2000): 450.

48. Feay, "The Tale of Genji for the Potter Generation."

49. Susan Petit, "An Interview with Michel Tournier: 'I Write Because I Have Something to Say,'" in *Michel Tournier's Metaphysical Fictions* (Amsterdam/Philadelphia: John Benjamins Publishing Co., 1991), 178–79; Tournier, "Writing for Children is No Child's Play," 33.

50. Lanes, *The Art of Maurice Sendak,* 206.

51. Taylor, "The Potter Effect."

52. Ibid.

53. E. M. Forster, *Aspects of the Novel* (New York: Harcourt, Brace, 1956), 26.

54. S. F. Said, "The Grown-up World of Kidult Books."

55. Parsons and Nicholson, "Talking to Philip Pullman," 122.

56. Myerson, "Harry Potter and the Sad Grown-ups."

57. "Literary Expansion: Children's Books Break through the Barrier."

58. Rees, "We're All Reading Children's Books"; Jones, "Young-Adult Books Are No Longer Child's Play for Bestselling Authors," D1.

59. Rees, "We're All Reading Children's Books."

60. Myles McDowell, "Fiction for Children and Adults: Some Essential Differences," *Children's Literature in Education* 4, no. 1 (March 1973): 53.

61. Fernando Savater, *Childhood Regained: The Art of the Storyteller.* Trans.

Frances M. López-Morillas (New York: Columbia University Press, 1982), 7.

62. West, "Come One, Come All: Luigi Malerba's Diffuse Fictions," 103.

63. Dante, "Reading into Crossover Trends."

64. Myerson, "Harry Potter and the Sad Grown-ups."

65. Julia Eccleshare, "Northern Lights and Christmas Miracles," *Books for Keeps* 100 (September 1996): 15.

66. Pepper, "Not Just for Children."

67. Humphrey Carpenter, *Secret Gardens: A Study of the Golden Age of Children's Literature* (Boston: Houghton Mifflin, 1985), 13.

68. Harju, "Tove Jansson and the Crossover Continuum."

69. Rees, "We're All Reading Children's Books."

70. Falconer, "Crossover Literature," 572.

71. West, "Come One, Come All: Luigi Malerba's Diffuse Fictions," 102; her italics.

72. Carole Scott, "Dual Audience in Picturebooks," in *Transcending Boundaries: Writing for a Dual Audience of Children and Adults*, ed. Beckett, 102.

73. Harju, "Tove Jansson and the Crossover Continuum."

74. Annemie Leysen, "About Flemish and Dutch Literature," in *A Companion to Dutch and Flemish Letters*, translated from the Dutch by David Colmer and Paul Vincent (N.p.: Stichting Frankfurter Buchmesse, 1997), 46; Gaarder, "Books for a World without Readers?"; his italics.

75. Glistrup, "Children's Literature in Denmark: Trends and Currents in the 1990s."

76. Leysen, "About Flemish and Dutch Literature."

77. Garth Nix, "Garth Nix: Digging into Fantasy," *Locus, the Magazine of the Science Fiction & Fantasy Field*, January 2003, 76–78.

78. Jones, "Young-Adult Books Are No Longer Child's Play for Bestselling Authors," D1.

79. Bart Moeyaert, "Seven Small Stories."

80. Holcombe, "Mark Haddon."

Bibliography

Primary Sources

Adams, Douglas. *The Hitch-Hiker's Guide to the Galaxy.* London: Pan, 1979.

Adams, Richard. *Watership Down: A Novel.* London: Rex Collings, 1972.

———. *Tales from Watership Down.* London: Hutchinson, 1996.

Akunin, Boris [Grigory Shalvovich Chkhartishvili]. *Azazel.* Moscow: Zakharov, 1998. Translated by Andrew Bromfield under the title *The Winter Queen* (New York: Random House, 2003).

Alain-Fournier [Henri Alban-Fournier]. *Le Grand Meaulnes.* Paris: Émile-Paul frères, 1913.

Alcott, Louisa May. *Little Women.* Boston: Roberts Bros., 1868.

Allende, Isabel. *La Cuidad de las Bestias.* Barcelona: Montena, 2002. Translated by Margaret Sayers Peden under the title *City of the Beasts* (New York: HarperCollins, 2002).

———. *El Reino del Dragón de Oro.* Barcelona: Plaza & Janés, 2003. Translated by Margaret Sayers Peden under the title *Kingdom of the Golden Dragon* (New York: HarperCollins, 2004).

———. *El Bosque de los Pigmeos.* Barcelona: Montena, 2004. Translated by Margaret Sayers Peden under the title *Forest of the Pygmies* (New York: HarperCollins, 2005).

Almond, David. *Skellig.* London: Hodder Children's Books, 1998.

———. *Heaven Eyes.* London: Hodder Children's Books, 2000.

———. *The Fire-Eaters.* London: Hodder Children's Books, 2003.

Alvarez, Julia. *Before We Were Free.* New York: Knopf Books for Young Readers, 2002.

Alye parusa. Dir. Aleksandr Ptushko. Soviet Union: Ministerstvo Kinematografii, 1961.

Ambjørnsen, Ingvar. *Hvite niggere.* Oslo: Cappelen, 1986.

Ammaniti, Niccolò. *Io non ho paura.* Torino: Einaudi, 2001. Translated by Jonathan Hunt under the title *I'm Not Scared* (Edinburgh: Canongate, 2003).

Anderson, M. T. *The Astonishing Life of Octavian Nothing, Traitor to the Nation.* Cambridge, MA: Candlewick Press, 2006.

Arkady, Gaydar. *Golubaya chashka.* Moscow: Detizdat, 1936. Translated under the title *The Blue Cup* (Moscow: Moscow Raduga Publishers, 1988).

———. *Timur ego komanda.* Moscow and Leningrad: Detzidat, 1941. Published in English as *Timur and His Squad* (Moscow: Novosti Press Agency Publishing House, 1988).

Around the World in Eighty Days. Dir. Frank Coraci. Perf. Jackie Chan. Burbank, California: Buena Vista Pictures, 2004.

Ashford, Daisy. *The Young Visiters.* Preface by J. M. Barrie. London: Chatto & Windus, 1919.

Astaf'ev, Viktor. *Poslednii poklon.* Perm: Knizhnoe izdatelstvo, 1968.

———. *Babushkin prazdnik.* Moscow: Sovetskaia Rossia, 1983.

Atwood, Margaret. *The Blind Assassin.* Toronto: McClelland & Stewart, 2000.

Auster, Paul. *El cuento de Navidad de Auggie Wren.* Illus. Isol. Buenos Aires: Sudamericana, 2003. Published in English as *Auggie Wren's Christmas Story.* New York: Henry Holt, 2004.

Aymé, Marcel. *Le puits aux images.* Paris: Gallimard, 1932.

———. *Les contes du chat perché.* Paris: Gallimard, 1939.

———. *Le passe-muraille.* Paris: Gallimard, 1943.

———. *Derniers contes du chat perché.* Illus. Lesley Queneau. Paris: Gallimard, 1958.

———. *Les bottes de sept lieues et autres nouvelles.* Paris: Gallimard, 1988.

Barker, Clive. *Abarat.* New York: Joanna Cotler Books/HarperCollins, 2002.

——. *Abarat: Days of Magic, Nights of War.* New York: Joanna Cotler Books/HarperCollins, 2004.

Barrie, J. M. *Peter Pan in Kensington Gardens / Peter and Wendy.* Oxford: Oxford University Press, 1999.

Bates, Judy Fong. *Midnight at the Dragon Café.* Toronto: McClelland & Stewart, 2004.

Baum, L. Frank. *The Wonderful Wizard of Oz.* Illus. W. W. Denslow. Chicago and New York: G. M. Hill Co., 1900.

Beake, Lesley. *A Cageful of Butterflies.* Cape Town, SA: Maskew Miller Logman, 1989.

——. *Song of Be.* Cape Town: Maskew Miller Logman, 1991.

Beckman, Gunnel. *Medan katten var borta.* Stockholm: Bonniers, 1960.

Bertagna, Julie. *Exodus.* London: Young Picador, 2002.

——. *Zenith.* London: Young Picador, 2007.

Bichsel, Peter. *Kindergeschichten.* Neuwied: Luchterhand, 1969.

——. *Ein Tisch ist ein Tisch.* Illus. Angela von Roehl. Frankfurt am Main: Suhrkamp, 1995.

Bjugn, Sissel and Fam Ekman. *Jente i bitar.* Oslo: Det Norske Samlaget, 1992.

Block, Francesca Lia. *Weetzie Bat.* New York: Harper & Row, 1989.

——. *Dangerous Angels: The Weetzie Bat Books.* New York: HarperCollins, 1998.

Bodoc, Liliana. *Los días del venado.* Buenos Aires: Grupo Editorial Norma, 2000.

——. *Los días de la sombra.* Buenos Aires: Grupo Editorial Norma, 2002.

——. *Los días del fuego.* Buenos Aires: Grupo Editorial Norma, 2004.

Bone, Ian. *The Song of an Innocent Bystander.* Camberwell, Vic. and London: Penguin, 2000.

Bosco, Henri. *L'Âne Culotte.* Paris: Gallimard, 1937.

——. *L'Âne Culotte.* Paris: Club des Jeunes Amis du Livre, 1956.

——. *Hyacinthe.* Paris: Gallimard, 1940.

——. *Le Mas Théotime.* Paris: Gallimard, 1945. Translated by Mervyn Savill under the title *The Farm Theotime* (London: Francis Aldor, 1946).

——. *L'enfant et la rivière.* Illus. E. Jalbert-Edon. Algiers and Paris: Charlot, 1945. Translated by Gerard Hopkins under the title *The Boy and the River* (New York: Pantheon Books, 1956).

——. *Le Jardin d'Hyacinthe.* Paris: Gallimard, 1945.

——. *La clef des champs.* Illus. Jacques Houplain. Algiers: Éditions de l'Empire, 1956.

——. *Le renard dans l'île.* Paris: Gallimard, 1956. Translated by Gerard Hopkins under the title *The Fox in the Island* (London: Oxford University Press, 1958).

——. *Bargabot* [followed by] *Pascalet.* Paris: Gallimard, 1958.

——. *Barboche.* 1957. London: Oxford University Press, 1959.

——. *Mon compagnon de songes.* Paris: Gallimard, 1967.

——. *Tante Martine.* Paris: Gallimard, 1972.

Boullosa, Carmen. *Son vacas, somos puercos.* Mexico: Era, 1991. Translated by Leland H. Chambers under the title *They're Cows, We're Pigs* (New York: Grove Press, 1997).

——. *El médico de los piratas: bucaneros y filibusteros en el Caribe.* Madrid: Siruela, 1992.

Brasme, Anne-Sophie. *Respire.* Paris: Fayard, 2001. Translated by Rory Mulholland under the title *Breathe* (London: Weidenfeld & Nicolson, 2003).

Brooks, Kevin. *Martyn Pig.* Frome: Chicken House, 2002.

——. *Lucas.* Frome: Chicken House, 2003.

——. *Kissing the Rain.* Frome: Chicken House, 2004.

——. *Candy.* Frome: Chicken House, 2005.

Brouillet, Chrystine. *Le collectionneur.* 16/96. Montréal: La courte échelle, 1995.

——. *C'est pour mieux t'aimer, mon enfant.* 16/96. Montréal: La courte échelle, 1996.

——. *Les fiancées de l'enfer.* 16/96. Montréal: La courte échelle, 1999.

——. *Soins intensifs.* 16/96. Montréal: La courte échelle, 2000.

Brown, Dan. *Angels & Demons.* New York: Pocket Books, 2000.

——. *The Da Vinci Code.* New York: Doubleday, 2003.

Burchill, Julie. *Sugar Rush.* London: Young Picador, 2004.

Byng, Georgia. *Molly Moon's Incredible Book of Hypnotism.* London: Macmillan Children's, 2002.

Calvino, Italo. *Il barone rampante.* Turin: Terza, 1957. Translated by Archibald Colquhoun under the title *The Baron in the Trees* (New York: Random House, 1959).

——. *Marcovaldo ovvero le stagioni in città.* Illus. Sergio Tofano. Turin: Einaudi, 1963.

Card, Orson Scott. *Ender's Shadow.* New York: Tom Doherty Associates Book, 1999.

Carroll, Lewis. *Alice's Adventures in Wonderland.* Illus. John Tenniel. London: Macmillan, 1865.

Chabon, Michael. *Summerland.* New York: Miramax Books/Hyperion Books for Children, 2002.

Chambers, Aidan. *Breaktime.* London: Bodley Head, 1978.

——. *Postcards from No Man's Land.* London: Bodley Head, 1999.

——. *This Is All: The Pillow Book of Cordelia Kenn.* London: Bodley Head, 2005.

Charlotte's Web. Dir. Gary Winick. Los Angeles: Paramount Pictures, 2006.

Chevalier, Tracy. *The Girl with a Pearl Earring.* New York: Dutton, 1999.

Christensen, Lars Saabye. *Beatles.* Oslo: Cappelen, 1984.

Chukovsky, Kornei. *Skazki.* Moscow: Detskaia Literatura, 1993.

Cisneros, Sandra. *The House on Mango Street.* Houston: Arte Publico Press, 1983.

Clarke, Susanna. *Jonathan Strange & Mr Norrell.* Illus. Portia Rosenberg. London: Bloomsbury, 2004.

——. *The Ladies of Grace Adieu.* London: Bloomsbury, 2006.

Colfer, Eoin. *Artemis Fowl.* London: Viking, 2001.

——. *Artemis Fowl: The Arctic Incident.* London: Puffin, 2002.

——. *Artemis Fowl: The Eternity Code.* London: Puffin, 2003.

——. *The Supernaturalist.* New York: Miramax Books/Hyperion Books for Children, 2004.

——. *The Artemis Fowl Files.* London: Puffin, 2004.

——. *Artemis Fowl: The Opal Deception.* London: Puffin, 2005.

——. *Artemis Fowl and the Lost Colony.* London: Puffin, 2006.

——. *Artemis Fowl: The Graphic Novel.* Adapted by Eoin Colfer and Andrew Donkin. Illus. Giovanni Rigano. New York: Hyperion, 2007.

Constable, Kate. *The Singer of All Songs.* Crows Nest, N. S. W.: Allen & Unwin, 2002.

——. *The Waterless Sea.* Crows Nest, N. S. W.: Allen & Unwin, 2004.

——. *The Tenth Power.* Crows Nest, N. S. W.: Allen & Unwin, 2005.

Cooper, Susan. *Over Sea, Under Stone.* London: Jonathan Cape, 1965.

——. *The Dark is Rising.* New York: Atheneum, 1973.

——. *Greenwitch.* New York: Atheneum, 1974.

——. *The Grey King.* New York: Atheneum, 1975.

——. *Silver on the Tree.* New York: Atheneum, 1977.

Corder, Zizou [Louisa Young and Isabel Adomakoh Young]. *Lionboy.* London and New York: Puffin, 2003.

——. *Lionboy: The Chase.* London and New York: Puffin, 2004.

——. *Lionboy: The Truth.* New York: Dial Books, 2005.

Cormier, Robert. *Now and at the Hour.* New York: Coward-McCann, 1960.

——. *The Chocolate War.* New York: Pantheon, 1974.

——. *I Am the Cheese.* New York: Knopf, 1977.

——. *After the First Death.* New York: Pantheon, 1979.

——. *Eight Plus One.* New York: Pantheon Books, 1980.

——. *Beyond the Chocolate War.* New York: Knopf, 1985.

——. *Tunes for Bears to Dance to.* New York: Delacorte, 1992.

——. *Tenderness.* New York: Delacorte Press, 1997.

Côté, Denis. *Les parallèles célestes.* Montréal: Québec/Amérique, 1983.

Crazy. Dir. Hans-Christian Schmid. Munich: Claussen & Wöbke Filmproduktion GmbH, 2000.

Crossley-Holland, Kevin. *The Seeing Stone.* London: Orion, 2000.

——. *At the Crossing-Places.* London: Orion, 2001.

——. *King of the Middle March.* London: Orion, 2003.

——. *Gatty's Tale.* London: Orion, 2006.

Culleton, Beatrice. *In Search of April Raintree.* Winnipeg: Pemmican, 1983.

——. *April Raintree.* Winnipeg: Pemmican, 1984.

Dahl, Roald. *Kiss Kiss.* New York: Alfred A. Knopf, 1960.

——. *Danny the Champion of the World.* Illus. Jill Bennett. New York: Alfred A. Knopf, 1975.

Demers, Dominique. *Un hiver de tourmente.* Montréal: La courte échelle, 1992.

——. *Les grands sapins ne meurent pas.* Montréal: Québec/Amérique Jeunesse, 1993.

——. *Ils dansent dans la tempête.* Montréal: Québec/Amérique Jeunesse, 1994.

——. *Maïna.* Montréal: Québec/Amérique, 1997.

——. *Maïna. Tome 1: L'appel des loups.* Montréal: Québec/Amérique Jeunesse, 1997.

——. *Maïna. Tome 2: Au pays de Natak.* Montréal: Québec/Amérique Jeunesse, 1997.

——. *Marie-Tempête.* Montréal: Québec/Amérique, 1997.

——. *Le Pari.* Montréal: Québec/Amérique, 1999.

——. *Là où la mer commence.* Paris: Robert Laffont, 2001.

Den Hartog, Kristen. *Origin of Haloes.* Toronto: McClelland & Stewart, 2005.

Deresh, Ljubko. *Культ* (Cult). Lviv: Calvaria, 2002.

——. *Поклоніння ящірці* (Worshipping the lizard). Lviv: Calvaria, 2004.

Diamant, Anita. *The Red Tent.* New York: A Wyatt Book for St. Martin's Press, 1997.

Dickinson, Peter. *Suth's Story.* New York: Grosset & Dunlap, 1998.

——. *Noli's Story*. New York: Grosset & Dunlap, 1998.
——. *Po's Story*. New York: Grosset & Dunlap, 1998.
——. *The Kin*. Illus. Ian Andrew. London: Macmillan Children's Books, 1998.
——. *Mana's Story*. New York: Grosset & Dunlap, 1999.
——. *The Kin*. Illus. Ian Andrew. New York: G. P. Putnam's Sons, 2003.
Dines, Carol. *The Queen's Soprano*. Orlando: Harcourt, 2006.
Donnelly, Jennifer. *The Tea Rose*. New York: Thomas Dunne, 2002.
——. *A Northern Light*. San Diego: Harcourt, 2003. Published in the United Kingdom as *A Gathering Light*. London: Bloomsbury, 2003.
——. *The Winter Rose*. New York: Hyperion, 2007.
Dros, Imme. *Ongelukkig verliefd*. Amsterdam: Querido, 1995.
Duiker, K[abelo] Sello. *Thirteen Cents*. Cape Town: David Philips, 2000.
——. *The Quiet Violence of Dreams*. Cape Town: Kwela, 2001.
——. *The Hidden Star*. Cape Town: Umuzi, 2005.
Edelfeldt, Inger. *Brev till nattens drottning*. Stockholm: AWE/Geber, 1985.
Eliot, T. S. *Old Possum's Book of Practical Cats*. London: Faber & Faber, 1939.
——. *Old Possum's Book of Practical Cats*. Illus. Edward Gorey. London: Faber & Faber, 1982.
Ende, Michael. *Die unendliche Geschichte*. Illus. Roswitha Quadflieg. Stuttgart: Thienemann, 1979. Translated by Ralph Manheim under the title *The Neverending Story* (London: Allen Lane, 1983).
Engdahl, Sylvia. *This Star Shall Abide*. Illus. Richard Cuffari. New York: Atheneum, 1972.
——. *Beyond the Tomorrow Mountains*. Illus. Richard Cuffari. New York: Atheneum, 1973.
——. *The Doors of the Universe*. New York: Atheneum, 1981.
——. *Children of the Star*. Stone Mountain, GA: Meisha Merlin Publishing, 2000.
Eragon. Dir. Stefen Fangmeier. Los Angeles: Fox 2000 Pictures, 2006.
Falling. Dir. Hans Herbots. Antwerp: Acasa Esana, 2001.
Fenkl, Heinz Insu and Walter K. Lew, eds. *The Beacon Anthology of Korean American Fiction*. Boston: Beacon Press, 2001.
Funke, Cornelia. *Drachenreiter*. Illus. by the author. Hamburg: Dressler, 1997. Translated by Anthea Bell under the title *Dragon Rider* (Frome: Chicken House, 2004).
——. *Herr der Diebe*. Illus. by the author. Hamburg: Dressler, 2000. Translated by Oliver Latsch under the title *The Thief Lord* (Frome: Chicken House, 2002).
——. *Tintenherz*. Illus. by the author. Hamburg: Dressler, 2003. Translated by Anthea Bell under the title *Inkheart* (Frome: Chicken House, 2003).
——. *Tintenblut*. Illus. by the author. Hamburg: Dressler, 2005. Translated by Anthea Bell under the title *Inkspell* (Frome: Chicken House; New York: Scholastic, 2005).
——. *Tintentod*. Illus. by the author. Hamburg: Dressler, 2007.
Gaarder, Jostein. *Kabalmysteriet*. Illus. Hilde Kramer. Oslo: Aschehoug, 1990. Translated by Sarah Jane Hall under the title *The Solitaire Mystery* (New York: Farrar, Straus, and Giroux, 1996).
——. *Sophies verden*. Oslo: Aschehoug, 1991. Translated by Paulette Møller under the title *Sophie's World* (New York: Farrar, Straus, and Giroux, 1994).
——. *Julemysteriet*. Oslo: Aschehoug, 1992. Translated by Elizabeth Rokkan under the title *The Christmas Mystery* (New York: Farrar, Straus, and Giroux, 1998).
——. *I et speil, i en gåte*. Oslo: Aschehoug, 1993. Translated by Elizabeth Rokkan under the title *Through a Glass, Darkly* (London: Dolphin, 1996).
——. *Hallo, er det noen der?* Oslo: Aschehoug, 1996. Translated by James Anderson under the title *Hello, Is Anybody There?* (New York: Farrar, Straus, and Giroux, 1998).
——. *Vita Brevis: Floria Aemilias brev til Aurel Augustin*. Oslo: Aschehoug, 1996. Translated by Anne Born under the title *That Same Flower: Floria Aemilia's Letter to Saint Augustine* (New York: Farrar, Straus, and Giroux, 1998).
——. *Maya*. Oslo: Aschehoug, 1999. Translated by James Anderson under the title *Maya* (London: Phoenix, 2000).
——. *Sirkusdirektørends datter*. Oslo: Aschehoug, 2001. Translated by James Anderson under the title *The Ringmaster's Daughter* (London: Weidenfeld & Nicolson, 2002).
——. *Appelsinpiken*. Oslo: Aschehoug, 2003. Translated by James Anderson under the title *The Orange Girl* (London: Weidenfeld & Nicolson, 2004).
Gagnon, Cécile. *Le chemin Kénogami*. Montréal: Québec/Amérique, 1994.
——. *C'est ici, mon pays*. Castor Poche. Paris: Flammarion, 1999.
——. *Un arbre devant ma porte*. Montréal: Québec/Amérique, 1999.
Gaiman, Neil. *Neverwhere*. London: BBC, 1996.
——. *Stardust*. Illus. Charles Vess. London: Titan, 1998.

———. *Coraline*. Illus. Dave McKean. London: Bloomsbury, 2002.

———. *Anansi Boys*. London: Review, 2005.

Gándara, Alejandro. *El final del cielo*. Illus. Ops. Madrid: Siruela, 1990.

Garner, Alan. *Red Shift*. London: Collins, 1973.

Gavin, Jamila. *Coram Boy*. London: Mammoth, 2000.

———. *The Blood Stone*. London: Egmont, 2003.

Gaydar, Arkady. *Golubaya chashka*, Moscow: Detizdat, 1936. Translated by Musia Renbourn under the title *The Drummer Boy, and Two Other Stories* (London: Hutchinson's Books for Young People, 1947).

———. *Timur i ego komanda*. Moscow and Leningrad: Detzidat, 1941. Translated under the title *Timur and His Squad* (Moscow: Foreign Languages Pub. House, 1948).

Gemmell, David. *Legend*. London: Century Hutchinson, 1984.

———. *Hero in Shadows*. London: Corgi, 2000.

Geras, Adèle. *Troy*. London: Scholastic, 2000.

———. *Ithaka*. Oxford: David Fickling Books, 2005.

Gestel, Peter van. *Nachtogen*. Baarn: De Fontein, 1996.

Giono, Jean. "Le petit garçon qui avait envie d'espace." *Les jolis contes N.P.C.K.* Vol. 6. Vevey, Switzerland: Société des produits Nestlé S.A., 1949.

———. *L'homme qui plantait des arbres*. Illus. Willi Glasauer. Paris: Gallimard, 1983.

———. *L'homme qui plantait des arbres*. Illus. Frédérick Back. Montréal: Les Entreprises Radio Canada; Paris: Gallimard; Saint-Laurent: Lacombe, 1989.

———. *The Man Who Planted Trees*. Illus. Michael McCurdy. White River Junction, VT: Chelsea Green Publishing, 1985.

Goethe, Johann Wolfgang von. *Die Leiden des jungen Werthers*. Leipzig: in der Weygandschen Buchhandlung, 1774.

———. *Das Hexen-Einmal-Eins*. Illus. Wolf Erlbruch. Munich: Carl Hanser, 1998.

Grahame, Kenneth. *The Wind in the Willows*. New York: Scribner's Sons, 1908.

Grin, Alexander. *Alye parusa*. Moscow and Petrograd: L. D. Frenkel, 1923. Translated by Thomas P. Whitney under the title *Scarlet Sails*. Illus. Esta Nesbitt (New York: Scribner, 1967).

Guerrero, Pablo. *Mi laberinto*. Illus. Emilio Urberuaga. Madrid: Kókinos, 2003.

Guimarães Rosa, João. "Fita verde no cabelo." In *Ave, palavra*. Rio de Janeiro: José Olympio, 1970.

———. *Fita verde no cabelo: nova velha estória*. Illus. Roger Mello. Rio de Janeiro: Nova Fronteira, 1992.

Haddon, Mark. *The Sea of Tranquility*. Illus. Christian Birmingham. London: HarperCollins Children's Books, 1996.

———. *The Curious Incident of the Dog in the Night-Time*. London: Jonathan Cape, 2003.

———. *The Curious Incident of the Dog in the Night-Time*. London: David Fickling Books, 2003.

———. *The Talking Horse and the Sad Girl and the Village Under the Sea*. London: Picador, 2005.

———. *A Spot of Bother*. London: Jonathan Cape, 2006.

Haptie, Charlotte. *Otto and the Flying Twins*. London: Hodder Children's Books, 2002.

Hartnett, Sonya. *Wilful Blue*. Ringwood, Vic.: Viking, 1994.

———. *Thursday's Child*. Ringwood, Vic.: Penguin, 2000.

———. *Of a Boy*. Camberwell, Vic.: Viking, 2002.

———. *Surrender*. Camberwell, Vic.: Penguin Group Australia, 2005.

Hartog, Kristen den. *Origin of Haloes*. Toronto: McClelland & Stewart, 2005.

Haugen, Tormod. *Nattfuglene*. Oslo: Gyldendal, 1975. Translated by Sheila La Farge under the title *The Night Birds* (New York: Delacorte, 1982).

———. *Zeppelin*. Oslo: Gyldendal, 1976. Translated by David R. Jacobs under the title *Zeppelin* (London: Turton & Chambers, 1991). Published in the United States as *Keeping Secrets* (New York: HarperCollins, 1994).

———. *Vinterstedet*. Oslo: Gyldendal, 1984.

———. *Romanen om Merkel Hanssen og Donna Winter og den store flukten*. Oslo: Gyldendal, 1986.

———. *Skriket fra jungelen*. Oslo: Gyldendal, 1989.

———. *Tsarens juveler*. Oslo: Gyldendal, 1992.

———. *Georg og Gloria (og Edvard)*. Oslo: Gyldendal, 1996.

———. *I lyset fra fullmånen*. Oslo: Gyldendal, 2001.

Hauru no ugoku shiro. Dir. Hayao Miyazaki. Tokyo: Studio Ghibli, 2004. Released in English as *Howl's Moving Castle*. Co-director Rick Dempsey. Emeryville, Calif.: Pix (English dubbing), 2005.

Hearn, Lian [Gillian Rubenstein]. *Across the Nightingale Floor*. Sydney: Hodder, 2002.

———. *Grass for His Pillow*. Sydney: Hodder Headline, 2003.

——. *Brilliance of the Moon.* Sydney: Hodder Headline, 2004.
——. *The Harsh Cry of the Heron.* Sydney: Hachette Australia, 2006.
——. *Heaven's Net is Wide.* Sydney: Hachette Australia, 2007.
Hennig von Lange, Alexa. *Relax.* Hamburg: Rogner und Bernard bei Zweitausendeins, 1997.
——. *Ich bin's.* Hamburg: Rogner und Bernard bei Zweitausendeins, 2000.
——. *Ich habe einfach Glück.* Hamburg: Rogner & Bernard bei Zweitausendeins, 2001.
——. *Woher ich komme.* Berlin: Rowohlt, 2003.
——. *Erste Liebe.* Berlin: Rowohlt, 2004.
——. *Warum so traurig?* Berlin: Rowohlt, 2005.
Herr der Diebe. Dir. Richard Claus. Burbank, Calif: Warner Brothers, 2006.
Hesselholdt, Christina. *Køkkenet gravkammeret & landskabet.* Copenhagen: Rosinante, 1991.
Hiaasen, Carl. *Hoot.* New York: Knopf, 2002.
——. *Flush.* New York: Knopf, 2005.
His Dark Materials: The Golden Compass. Dir. Chris Weitz. New York: New Line Cinema, 2007. Aka
    His Dark Materials: Northern Lights (UK).
Hoban, Russell. *The Mouse and His Child.* Illus. Lillian Hoban. New York: Harper & Row, 1967.
Høeg, Peter. *Frøken Smillas fornemmelse for sne.* Copenhagen: Rosinante, 1992. Translated by Tiina
    Nunnally under the title *Smilla's Sense of Snow* (New York: Farrar, Straus, and Giroux, 1993).
Hoeye, Michael. *Time Stops for No Mouse: A Hermux Tantamoq Adventure.* Portland, OR: Terfle
    Books, 2000.
——. *The Sands of Time: A Hermux Tantamoq Adventure.* Portland, OR: Terfle Books, 2001.
——. *No Time Like Show Time: A Hermux Tantamoq Adventure.* New York: G. P. Putnam's, 2004.
——. *Time to Smell the Roses: A Hermux Tantamoq Adventure.* New York: G. P. Putnam's, 2007.
Hoffman, Mary. *City of Masks.* London: Bloomsbury, 2002.
——. *City of Stars.* London: Bloomsbury, 2003.
——. *City of Flowers.* London: Bloomsbury, 2005.
Hoffmann, E. T. A. *Nutcracker.* Illus. Maurice Sendak. Trans. Ralph Manheim. New York: Crown,
    1984.
——. "Nußknacker und Mausekönig." In *Kinder-Märchen* by C. W. Contessa, Friedrich Baron de
    la Motte Fouqué and E. T. A. Hoffmann. Ed. Hans-Heino Ewers. Stuttgart: Reclam, 1987.
    66–144.
Hofman, Wim. *Zwart als inkt is het verhaal van Sneeuwwitje en de zeven dwergen.* Amsterdam:
    Antwerp: Querido, 1998.
Hofmeyr, Dianne. *Blue Train to the Moon.* Cape Town: Maskew Miller Longman, 1993.
——. *Boikie You Better Believe It.* Cape Town: Tafelberg, 1994.
——. *The Waterbearer.* Cape Town: Tafelberg, 2001.
——. *Fish Notes and Star Songs.* London: Simon & Schuster, 2005.
Hoot. Dir. Wil Shriner. New York: New Line and Walden, 2006.
Hopkins, Cathy. *Designer Divas.* London: Simon & Schuster, 2003.
Hovland, Ragnar. *Alltid fleire dagar.* Oslo: Det Norske Samlaget, 1979.
——. *Alltid fleire dagar og Mercedes.* Oslo: Det Norske Samlaget,1993.
Hughes, Ted. *Crow: From the Life and Songs of the Crow.* London: Faber, 1970.
Io non ho paura. Dir. Gabriele Salavtores. Milan and Rome: Colorado Film Production, 2003.
Irving, John. *A Widow for One Year.* Media, PA: Unicycle Press, 1998.
——. *Ein Geräusch, wie wenn einer versucht, kein Geräusch zu machen.* Illus. Tatjana Hauptmann.
    Zürich: Diogenes, 2003. Translated under the title *A Sound Like Someone Trying Not to Make a
    Sound* (New York: Doubleday Books for Young Readers, 2004).
Isau, Ralf. *Di Träume des Jonathan Jabbok.* Stuttgart: Thienemann, 1995.
——. *Das Museum der gestohlenen Erinnerungen.* Stuttgart: Thienemann, 1997.
——. *Der Kreis der Dämmerung. Teil I.* Stuttgart: Thienemann, 1999.
——. *Der Kreis der Dämmerung. Teil II.* Stuttgart: Thienemann, 2000.
——. *Der Kreis der Dämmerung. Teil III.* Stuttgart: Thienemann, 2001
——. *Der Kreis der Dämmerung. Teil IV.* Stuttgart: Thienemann, 2001.
——. *Pala und die seltsame Verflüchtigung der Worte.* Stuttgart: Thienemann, 2002.
——. *Der silberne Sinn.* Bergisch Gladbach: Ehrenwirth, 2003.
——. *Die geheime Bibliothek des Thaddäus Tillmann Trutz.* Munich: Droemer Knaur, 2003.
Ishiguro, Kazuo. *Never Let Me Go.* London: Faber, 2005.
Jacques, Brian. *Redwall.* Illus. Gary Chalk. London: Hutchinson Children's, 1986.
——. *Loamhedge.* New York: Philomel, 2003.
——. *Redwall: The Graphic Novel.* Adapted by Stuart Moore. Illus. Bret Blevins. Philomel, 2007.
Jandl, Ernst. *Fünfter sein.* Illus. Norman Junge. Weinheim and Basel: Beltz & Gelberg, 1997.

Translated under the title *Next Please*. London: Hutchinson Children's Books, 2001.
——. *Antipoden*. Illus. Norman Junge. Weinheim and Basel: Beltz & Gelberg, 1999.
——. *Ottos Mops*. Illus. Norman Junge. Weinheim and Basel: Beltz & Gelberg, 2001.
Jansson, Tove. *Trollvinter*. 1957. Translated by Thomas Warburton under the title *Moominland Midwinter* (London: Ernest Benn, 1958).
——. *Pappan och havet*, 1965. Translated by Kingsley Hart under the title *Moominpappa at Sea* (London: Ernest Benn, 1966).
——. *Sent i November*, 1970. Translated by Kingsley Hart under the title *Moominvalley in November* (London: Ernest Benn, 1971).
——. *Sommerboken*. Stockholm: Albert Bonniers; Helsingfors: Schildt, 1972. Translated by Thomas Teal under the title *The Summer Book* (London: Hutchinson, 1975).
Jensen, Louis. *Hundrede historier*. Copenhagen: Gyldendal, 1992.
——. *Hundrede nye historier*. Copenhagen: Gyldendal, 1995.
——. *Nøgen*. Copenhagen: Gyldendal, 1995.
——. *Den kløvede mand*. Copenhagen: Gyldendal, 1999.
——. *Hundrede splinternye historier*. Copenhagen: Gyldendal, 2000.
——. *Hundrede firkantede historier*. Copenhagen: Gyldendal, 2002.
——. *Hundrede meget firkantede historier*. Copenhagen: Gyldendal, 2005.
——. *Hundrede helt & aldeles firkantede historier*. Illus. Lillian Brøgger. Copenhagen: Gyldendal, 2007.
Jensen, Sanne Munk. *En dag skinner solen også på en hunds røv*. Copenhagen: Gyldendal, 2007.
Jones, Diana Wynne. *Charmed Life*. London and Basingstoke: Macmillan, 1977.
——. *The Chronicles of Chrestomanci*. New York: HarperCollins, 2001.
——. *Conrad's Fate*. London: HarperCollins, 2005.
——. *The Pinhoe Egg*. New York: Greenwillow Books, 2006.
Jordan, June. *Who Look at Me*. Illustrated with 27 paintings. New York: Cromwell, 1969.
Juul, Pia. *Lidt ligesom mig*. Copenhagen: Dansklærerforeningens Forlag, 2004.
Käpt'n Blaubär–Der Film. Dir. Hayo Freitag. Berlin: Senator Films, 1999.
Kästner, Erich. *Emil und die Detektive*. Illus. Walter Trier. Berlin-Gruenewald: Williams & Co., 1929. Translated by May Massee under the title *Emil and the Detectives* (Garden City, NY: Doubleday, Doran & Co., 1930).
——. *Fabian: Die Geschichte eines Moralisten*. Stuttgart and Berlin: Deutsche Verl. Anst., 1931. Translated by Cyrus Brooks under the title *Fabian: The Story of a Moralist* (London: Jonathan Cape, 1932).
——. *Die Konferenz der Tiere*. Nach einer Idee von Jella Lepman. Illus. Walter Trier. Zurich: Europa Verlag, 1949. Based on an idea by Jella Lepman. New York: David McKay, 1949. Translated by Zita de Schauensee under the title *The Animals' Conference*.
Kemmler, Melanie. *Der hölzerne Mann*. Berlin: Aufbau-Verlag, 2003.
Kerner, Charlotte. *Blueprint: Blaupause*. Weinheim: Beltz & Gelberg, 1999. Translated by Elizabeth D. Crawford under the title *Blueprint* (Minneapolis: Lerner Publications Company, 2000).
Kerr, P. B. *The Akhenaten Adventure*. London: Scholastic, 2004.
——. *The Blue Djinn of Babylon*. London: Scholastic, 2005.
——. *The Cobra King of Kathmandu*. London: Scholastic, 2006.
——. *The Day of the Djinn Warriors*. London: Scholastic, 2007.
Keulen, Mensje van. *De rode strik*. Amsterdam: Atlas, 1994.
Kharms, Daniil [Daniil Iuvachiov]. *Letiat po Nebu Shariki*. Ed. A. A. Aleksandrov and N. M. Kavin. Krasnoiarsk: Krasnoiarskoe Knizhnoe Izdatel'stvo, 1990.
Kim, Helen. *The Long Season of Rain*. New York: Henry Holt, 1996.
Kingsley, Charles. *The Water-Babies: A Fairy Tale for a Land-Baby*. Illus. J. Noel Paton. London and Cambridge: Macmillan & Co., 1863.
Kita, Morio [Sokichi Saito]. *Dokutoru Manbo kokaiki*. Tokyo: Chuo Koronsha, 1960. Translated by Ralph F. McCarthy under the title *Doctor Manbo at Sea* (Tokyo: Kodansha International, 1987).
——. *Yoru to kiri no sumi de*. Tokyo: Shinchosha, 1960.
——. *Funanori Kupukupu no boken*. Tokyo: Shueisha, 1962. Translated by Ralph F. McCarthy under the title *The Adventures of Kupukupu the Sailor*. Illus. Miyuki Kiyomura (Tokyo: Kodansha International, 1985).
Klein, Rachel. *The Moth Diaries*. Washington, D. C.: Counterpoint, 2002.
Kogawa, Joy. *Obasan*. Toronto: Lester & Orpen Dennys, 1981.
——. *Naomi's Road*. Illus. Matt Gould. Toronto: Oxford University Press, 1986.
——. *Naomi no michi*. Trans. Asami Michiko. Tokyo: Shogakukan, 1988.
——. *Itsuka*. Toronto: Viking, 1992.

Die Konferenz der Tiere. Dir. Curt Linda. Munich, Linda Film, 1969.

Korczak, Janusz [Henryk Goldszmit]. *Król Maciuś Pierwszy* (1923). Warsaw: Nasza Księgarnia, 1955. Adapted by Edith and Sidney Sulkin under the title *Matthew, the Young King* (New York: Roy Publishers, 1945). Also available in a translation by Richard Lourie under the title *King Matt the First* (New York: Farrar, Straus, and Giroux, 1986).

———. *Król Maciuś na wyspie bezludnej* (1923). Warsaw: Nasza Księgarnia, 1957.

———. *Kiedy znów będęmaly.* Warsaw: Nasza Księgarnia, 1961. Translated by E. P. Kulaviec under the title *When I Am Little Again* (Lanham: University Press, 1992).

Kullman, Harry. *Natthämtaren.* Stockholm: Rabén & Sjögren, 1962.

Kuroyanagi, Tetsuko. *Madogiwa no Totto-chan.* Tokyo: Kodansha, 1981. Translated by Dorothy Britton under the title *Totto-chan: The Little Girl at the Window* (Tokyo: Kodansha International, 1982).

Lansens, Lori. *The Girls.* Toronto: Alfred A. Knopf, 2005.

Lebert, Benjamin. *Crazy.* Cologne: Kiepenheuer und Witsch, 1999. Translated by Carol Brown Janeway under the title *Crazy* (New York: Knopf, 2000).

———. *Der Vogel ist ein Rabe.* Cologne: Kiepenheuer und Witsch, 2003. Translated by Peter Constantine under the title *The Bird Is a Raven* (New York: Knopf, 2005).

Le Clézio, J. M. G. *Le Procès-verbal.* Paris: Gallimard, 1963.

———. *Mondo et autres histoires.* Paris: Gallimard, 1978.

———. *L'Inconnu sur la terre.* Paris, Gallimard, 1978.

———. *Désert.* Paris: Gallimard, 1980.

———. *Lullaby.* Folio Junior. Paris: Gallimard, 1980.

———. *La ronde et autres faits divers.* Paris: Gallimard, 1982.

———. *Balaabilou.* Paris: Gallimard, 1985.

———. *Celui qui n'avait jamais vu la mer.* Folio Junior. Paris: Gallimard, 1988.

———. *La grande vie* [followed by] *Peuple du ciel.* Folio Junior. Paris: Gallimard, 1990.

———. *Sirandanes.* Paris: Seghers, 1990.

———. *Sirandanes.* Paris: Seghers Jeunesse, 2005.

———. *Villa Aurore* [followed by] *Orlamonde.* Folio Junior. Paris: Gallimard, 1990.

———. *Voyage au pays des arbres.* Folio Cadet Rouge. Paris: Gallimard, 1990.

———. *Peuple du ciel.* Paris: Gallimard, 1991.

———. *Pawana.* Paris: Gallimard, 1992.

———. *Pawana.* Illus. Georges Lemoine. Lecture Junior. Paris: Gallimard, 1995.

Lee, Harper. *To Kill a Mockingbird.* Philadelphia: Lippincott, 1960.

Lee, Tanith. *Red as Blood, or Tales from the Sisters Grimmer.* New York: DAW Books, 1983.

Le Guin, Ursula K. *A Wizard of Earthsea.* Illus. Ruth Robbins. Berkeley, CA: Parnassus Press, 1968.

Lewis, C. S. *The Lion, the Witch and the Wardrobe: A Story for Children.* Illus. Pauline Baynes. London: Geoffrey Bles, 1950.

Lieshout, Ted van. *Gebr.* Amsterdam: Van Goor, 1996. Translated by Lance Salway under the title *Brothers* (London: Collins Flamingo, 2001).

London, Jack. *The Call of the Wild.* New York and London: The Macmillan Company, 1903.

———. *The Sea-Wolf.* New York and London: The Macmillan Company, 1904.

———. *White Fang.* New York and London: The Macmillan Company, 1905.

The Lord of the Rings: The Fellowship of the Ring. Dir. Peter Jackson. New York: New Line Cinema, 2001.

The Lord of the Rings: The Two Towers. Dir. Peter Jackson. New York: New Line Cinema, 2002.

The Lord of the Rings: The Return of the King. Dir. New York: New Line Cinema, 2003.

Malerba, Luigi. *La scoperta dell'alfabeto.* Milan: Bompiani, 1963.

———. *Il pataffio.* Milan: Bompiani, 1978.

———. *Dopo il pescecane.* Milan: Bompiani, 1979.

Mankell, Henning. *Hunden som sprang mot en stjärna.* Stockholm: Rabén & Sjögren, 1990.

Marie-Tempête. Dir. Denis Malleval. Paris: Escazal Films, 2000.

Mark, Jan. *The Ennead.* Harmondsworth: Kestrel Books, 1978.

———. *Divide and Rule.* Harmondsworth: Kestrel Books, 1979.

———. *Aquarius.* Harmondsworth: Kestrel Books, 1982.

———. *The Eclipse of the Century.* London: Scholastic, 1999.

———. *Useful Idiots.* Oxford: David Fickling, 2004.

———. *Riding Tycho.* London: Macmillan, 2005.

Marsden, John. *Tomorrow, When the War Began.* Chippendale, N. S. W.: Pan Macmillan, 1993.

———. *The Dead of the Night.* Chippendale, N. S. W.: Pan Macmillan, 1994.

———. *The Third Day, the Frost.* Sydney: Pan Macmillan, 1995.

———. *Darkness, Be My Friend.* Sydney: Pan Macmillan, 1996.
———. *Burning for Revenge.* Sydney: Pan Macmillan, 1997.
———. *The Night Is for Hunting.* Sydney: Pan Macmillan, 1998.
———. *The Other Side of Dawn.* Sydney: Pan Macmillan, 1999.
———. *While I Live.* Sydney: Pan Macmillan, 2003.
———. *Incurable.* Sydney: Pan Macmillan, 2005.
———. *Circle of Flight.* Sydney: Pan Macmillan, 2006.
Martel, Yann. *Life of Pi.* Toronto: Knopf Canada, 2001.
Martín Gaite, Carmen. *El cuarto de atrás.* Barcelona: Destino, 1978.
———. *Cuentos completos.* Madrid: Alianza, 1978.
———. *El castillo de las tres murallas.* Illus. Juan Carlos Eguillor. Barcelona: Lumen, 1981.
———. *El pastel del diablo.* Illus. Nuria Salvatella. Barcelona: Lumen, 1985.
———. *Caperucita en Manhattan.* Madrid: Siruela, 1990.
———. *2 cuentos maravillosos.* Madrid: Siruela, 1992.
Martinez, Victor. *Parrot in the Oven, mi vida.* New York: HarperCollins, 1996.
McCaffrey, Anne. *Dragonflight.* New York: Ballantine Books, 1968.
———. and Todd McCaffrey. *Dragon's Kin.* New York: Del Rey/Ballantine Books, 2003.
Meck, Anoeschka von. *Vaselinetjie.* Cape Town: Tafelberg, 2004.
Melissa P. Dir. Luca Guadagnino. Rome: Bess Movie, 2005.
Merino, José María. *Novela de Andrés Choz.* Madrid: Editorial Magisterio Español, 1976.
———. *El oro de los sueños: Crónica de las aventuras verdaderas de Miguel Villacé Yolotl.* Madrid: Alfaguara, 1986.
———. *La tierra del tiempo perdido: Crónica de las aventuras verdaderas de Miguel Villacé Yolotl.* Madrid: Alfaguara, 1987.
———. *Las lágrimas del sol: Crónica de las aventuras verdaderas de Miguel Villacé Yolotl.* Madrid: Alfaguara, 1989.
———. *Las crónicas mestizas.* Madrid: Alfaguara, 1992.
———. *Los trenes del verano.* Las Tres Edades. Madrid: Siruela, 1992.
Mésseder, João Pedro. *Palavra que voa.* Illus. Gémeo Luís [Luís Mendonça]. Lisbon: Caminho, 2005.
Meyer, Stephenie. *Twilight.* New York: Little, Brown and Company, 2005.
Middelhauve, Gertraud. *Dichter erzählen Kindern.* Cologne: Middelhauve, 1966.
———. *Dichter Europas erzählen Kindern.* Cologne: Middelhauve, 1972.
Mikhalkov, Sergey. *Dyadya Stepa.* Moscow: Detizdat, 1936. Translated by Eugene Felgenhauer under the title *Uncle Steeple and Other Poems.* Illus. F. Lemkul (Moscow: Progress Publishers, 1974).
Millán, José Antonio. *Base y el generador misterioso (una aventura digital).* Illus. Arnal Ballester. Las Tres Edades. Madrid: Siruela, 2002.
Millás, Juan José. *Papel mojado.* Illus. Mario Lacoma. Madrid: E. G. Anaya, 1983.
Milne, A. A. *Winnie-the-Pooh.* Illus. Ernest H. Shepard. London: Methuen, 1926.
———. *The House at Pooh Corner.* Illus. Ernest H. Shepard. London: Methuen, 1928.
"Die Mitte der Welt." Film-Archive, http://www.german-cinema.de/archive/filmi_view.php?film_id=1243 (accessed March 25, 2006).
Miyazawa, Kenji. *Chūmon no Ōi Ryōriten.* Tokyo: Kogensha/Sharyo-Shuppan-bu, 1924.
———. "Ginga tetsudo no yoru." In *Miyazawa Kenji zenshū dai san kan.* Vol. 3. Tokyo: Bunpodo, 1934.
———. *Wildcat and the Acorns and Other Stories.* Trans. John Bester. Tokyo: Kodansha International, 1985.
———. *Night Train and Other Stories.* Trans. John Bester. Illus. Makoto Obo. Tokyo: Kodansha International, 1987.
———. *The Night Hawk Star.* Adapted by Helen Smith. Illus. Junko Marimoto. Sydney: Random House, 1991.
Moers, Walter. *Die 13½ Leben des Käptn Blaubär: die halben Lebenserinnerungen eines Seebären; unter Benutzung des "Lexikons der erklärungsbedürftigen Wunder, Daseinsformen und Phänomene Zamoniens und Umgebung" von Abdul Nachtigaller.* Frankfurt am Main: Eichborn, 1999. Translated by John Brownjohn under the title *The 13½ Lives of Captain Bluebear: Being the Demibiography of a Seagoing Bear, with Numerous Illustrations and Excerpts from the "Encyclopedia of the Marvels, Life Forms and Other Phenomena of Zamonia and its Environs" by Professor Abdullah Nightingale* (London: Secker & Warburg, 1999).
———. *Wilde Reise durch die Nacht.* Frankfurt am Main: Eichborn, 2001. Translated by John Brownjohn under the title *A Wild Ride through the Night* (London: Secker & Warburg, 2003).
———. *Die Stadt der Träumenden Bücher: Ein Roman aus Zamonien von Hildegunst von Mythenmetz.*

Munich: Piper Verlag, 2004. Translated by John Brownjohn under the title *The City of Dreaming Books* (London: Harvill Secker, 2006).

Moeyaert, Bart. *Duet met valse noten.* Averbode/Apeldoorn: Altiora, 1983.

——. *Suzanne Dantine.* Averbode/Apeldoorn: Altiora, 1989. Revised edition under the title *Wespennest.* Amsterdam: Querido, 1997. Translated by David Colmer under the title *Hornet's Nest* (Asheville, N. C.: Front Street, 2000).

——. *Kus me.* Averbode/Apeldoorn: Altiora, 1991.

——. *Blote handen.* Illus. Peter van Poppel. Amsterdam: Querido, 1995. Translated by David Colmer under the title *Bare Hands* (Asheville, N. C.: Front Street, 1998).

——. *Het is de liefde die we niet begrijpen.* Cover Gerd Dooreman & Andy Huysmans. Amsterdam/Antwerp: Querido, 1999. Translated by Wanda Boeke under the title *It's Love We Don't Understand* (Asheville, N. C.: Front Street, 2001).

——. *Broere: de oudste, de stilste, de echste, de verste, de liefste, de snelste en ik.* Illus. Gerda Dendooven. With CD recording of the theatre production of the same name. Amsterdam: Querido, 2000. Translated by Wanda Boeke under the title *Brothers: the oldest, the quietest, the realest, the farthest, the nicest, the fastest, and I* (Asheville, N. C.: Front Street, 2005).

Montero, Rosa. *El nido de los sueños.* Illus Alfonso Ruano Martín. Las Tres Edades. Madrid: Siruela, 1991.

Morgan, Sally. *My Place.* Fremantle, W. A.: Fremantle Arts Centre Press, 1987.

——. *Wanamurraganya: The Story of Jack McPhee.* Fremantle, W. A.: Fremantle Arts Centre Press, 1989.

——. *Sally's Story.* Ed. Barbara Ker Wilson. Fremantle, W. A.: Fremantle Arts Centre Press, 1990

——. *Arthur Corunna's Story.* Ed. Barbara Ker Wilson. Fremantle, W. A.: Fremantle Arts Centre Press, 1990.

——. *Mother and Daughter: The Story of Daisy and Gladys Corunna.* Ed. Barbara Ker Wilson. Fremantle, W. A. : Fremantle Arts Centre Press, 1990.

Morgenstern, Christian. *Galgenlieder.* Monaco: Bruno Cossirer, 1905. Translated by Max Knight under the title *Christian Morgenstern's Galgenlieder: A Selection* (Berkeley and Los Angeles: University of California Press, 1963).

——. *Das große Lalulā.* Illus. Norman Junge. Berlin: Aufbau-Verlag, 2004.

Mori, Kyoko. *Shizuko's Daughter.* New York: Henry Holt, 1993.

——. *One Bird.* New York: Henry Holt, 1995.

Morpurgo, Michael. *Kensuke's Kingdom.* Illus. Michael Foreman. London: Heinemann Young Books, 1999.

——. *Private Peaceful.* London: Collins, 2003.

Müller, John, ed. *De perfecte puber.* Alphen aan den Rijn: Magazijn de Bijenkorf, 1991.

Murakami, Haruki. *Hitsuji o meguru bōken.* Tokyo: Kodansha, 1982. Translated by Alfred Birnbaum under the title *A Wild Sheep Chase* (Tokyo and New York: Kodansha International, 1989).

——. *Noruwei no mori.* Tokyo: Kodansha, 1987. Translated by Alfred Birnbaum under the title *Norwegian Wood* (Tokyo: Kodansha, 1989). Later edition translated by Jay Rubin (London: Harvill, 2000).

——. *Andāguraundo.* Tokyo: Kodansha, 1997–98. Translated by Alfred Birnbaum and Philip Gabriel under the title *Underground* (London: Harvill, 2002).

——. *Kami no kodomo-tachi wa mina odoru.* Tokyo: Shinchosha, 2000. Translated by Jay Rubin under the title *After the Quake* (New York: Vintage International, 2000).

Newbery, Linda. *The Shell House.* Oxford: David Fickling, 2002.

——. *Sisterland.* Oxford: David Fickling, 2003.

——. *Set in Stone.* Oxford: David Fickling, 2006.

Nicholson, William. *The Wind Singer.* London: Egmont, 2000.

——. *Slaves of the Mastery.* London: Egmont, 2001.

——. *Firesong.* London: Egmont, 2002.

Nix, Garth. *Sabriel.* Sydney: HarperCollins, 1995.

——. *Lirael: Daughter of the Clayr.* Crows Nest, N. S. W.: Allen & Unwin, 2001.

——. *Abhorsen.* Crows Nest, N. S. W.: Allen & Unwin, 2003.

——. *Mister Monday.* Crows Nest, N. S. W.: Allen & Unwin, 2003.

——. *Grim Tuesday.* Crows Nest, N. S. W.: Allen & Unwin, 2004.

——. *Drowned Wednesday.* Crows Nest, N. S. W.: Allen & Unwin, 2005.

——. *Across the Wall: Stories of the Old Kingdom and Beyond.* Crows Nest, N. S. W.: Allen & Unwin, 2005.

——. *Sir Thursday.* Crows Nest, N. S. W.: Allen & Unwin, 2006.

——. *Lady Friday.* Crows Nest, N. S. W.: Allen & Unwin, 2007.

Nöstlinger, Christine. *Konrad oder Das Kind aus der Konservenbüchse.* Illus. Frantz Wittkamp. Hamburg: Oetinger, 1975. Translated by Anthea Bell under the title *Conrad: The Factory-Made Boy* (London: Andersen Press, 1976).

——. *Andreas oder Die unteren sieben Achtel des Eisberges: Familienroman aus der Wiederaufbauzeit.* Weinheim: Beltz & Gelberg, 1978.

——. *Hugo, das Kind in den besten Jahren: Phantastischer Roman nach Bildern von Jörg Wollmann.* Weinheim: Beltz & Gelberg, 1983.

——. *Gretchen Sackmeier.* Würzburg: Arena, 1999.

Nye, Naomi Shihab. *The Space between Our Footsteps: Poems and Paintings from the Middle East.* New York: Simon & Schuster Books for Young Readers, 1998.

O'Brien, Edna. *The Country Girls.* London: Hutchinson, 1960.

——. *The Lonely Girl.* London: Jonathan Cape, 1962. Published as *Girl with Green Eyes.* London: Penguin, 1964.

——. *Girls in Their Married Bliss.* London: Jonathan Cape, 1964.

——. *The Country Girls Trilogy and Epilogue.* New York: Farrar, Straus, and Giroux, 1986.

Olesha, Yury Karlovich. *Tri tolstyaka.* Illus. Mikhail Dobuzhinsky. Moscow and Leningrad: Zemlya i fabrica, 1928. Translated by Aimée Anderson under the title *Complete Short Stories and Three Fat Men* (Anne Arbor, Mich.: Ardis, 1979).

——. *Zavist.* Moscow and Leningrad: Zemlya i fabrica, 1928. Translated by P. Ross under the title *Envy* (London: Westhouse, 1947).

Oppel, Kenneth. *Colin's Fantastic Video Adventure.* Illus. Tony Blundell. Harmondsworth, Middlesex: Penguin, 1985.

——. *Silverwing.* New York: Simon & Schuster Books for Young Readers, 1997.

——. *Sunwing.* New York: Simon & Schuster Books for Young Readers, 2000.

——. *Firewing.* New York: Simon & Schuster Books for Young Readers, 2003.

——. *Airborn.* Toronto: HarperCollins, 2004.

——. *Skybreaker.* Toronto: HarperCollins, 2005.

——. *Darkwing.* Toronto: HarperCollins, 2007.

O'Shea, Pat. *The Hounds of Morrigan.* London: Oxford University Press, 1985.

Panarello, Melissa. *Cien colpi di spazzola prima di andare a dormire.* Rome: Fazi, 2003. Translated by Lawrence Venuti under the title *100 Strokes of the Brush Before Bed* (New York: Black Cat, 2004).

Paolini, Christopher. *Eragon.* New York: Alfred A. Knopf, 2002. Originally published: Paolini International, LLC, 2002.

——. *Eldest.* New York: Knopf, 2005.

Paver, Michelle. *Wolf Brother.* Illus. Geoff Taylor. London: Orion Children's, 2004.

——. *Spirit Walker.* Illus. Geoff Taylor. London: Orion Children's, 2005.

——. *Soul Eater.* Illus. Geoff Taylor. London: Orion Children's, 2006.

——. *Outcast.* Illus. Geoff Taylor. London: Orion Children's, 2007.

Paz, Octavio. *My Life with the Wave.* Trans. and adapted for children by Catherine Cowan. Illus. Mark Buehner (New York: Lothrop, 1997).

Peake, Mervyn. *Titus Groan.* London: Eyre & Spottiswoode, 1946.

——. *Gormenghast.* London: Eyre & Spottiswoode, 1950.

——. *Titus Alone.* London: Eyre & Spottiswoode, 1959.

Pef [Pierre Ferrier]. *La grande aventure du livre.* Paris: Gallimard, 1984.

Pierce, Tamora. *Alanna: The First Adventure.* New York: Atheneum, 1983.

——. *Lioness Rampant.* New York: Atheneum, 1988.

Pierre, D. B. C. *Vernon God Little.* London: Faber & Faber, 2003.

Plante, Raymond. *Projections privées.* 16/96. Montréal: La courte échelle, 1997.

——. *La nomade.* 16/96. Montréal: La courte échelle, 1999.

——. *Novembre, la nuit.* 16/96. Montréal: La courte échelle, 2000.

——. *Baisers voyous.* 16/96. Montréal: La courte échelle, 2001.

Pohl, Peter. *Regnbågen har bara åtta färger.* Stokholm: AWE: Geber, 1986.

——. *Janne, min vän.* Stockholm: AWG, 1985. Translated by Laurie Thompson under the title *Johnny My Friend* (Woodchester Stroud: Turton & Chambers, 1991).

——. *Vi kallar honom Anna.* Stockholm: AWE: Geber, 1987.

——. *Medan regnbågen bleknar.* Stockholm: Alfabeta, 1989.

——. *De stora penslarnas lek.* Stockholm: Alfabeta, 1989.

——. *Vilja växa.* Stockholm: Alfabeta, 1994.

——. *Klara papper är ett måste.* Stockholm: Rabén Prisma, 1998.

Pratchett, Terry. *The Colour of Magic.* Gerrards Cross: Smythe, 1983.

——. *The Amazing Maurice and His Educated Rodents*. London: Doubleday, 2001.

——. *The Wee Free Men*. London: Doubleday, 2003.

Pressler, Mirjam. *Novemberkatzen*. Weinheim: Beltz & Gelberg, 1982.

——. *Wenn das Glück kommt, muß man ihm einen Stuhl hinstellen*. Weinheim: Beltz & Gelberg, 1994. Translated by Elizabeth D. Crawford under the title *Halinka* (New York: Henry Holt, 1998).

——. *Shylocks Tochter: Venedig im Jahre 1568*. Frankfurt am Main: Alibaba, 1999. Translated by Brian Murdock under the title *Shylock's Daughter* (New York: Phyllis Fogelman Books, 2001).

——. *Malka Mai*. Weinheim: Beltz & Gelberg, 2001. Translated by Brian Murdock under the title *Malka* (London: Picador, 2002).

Prévert, Jacques. *Contes pour enfants pas sages*. Paris: Le Pré aux Clercs, 1947.

——. *La pêche à la baleine*. Illus. Henri Galeron. Paris: Gallimard, 1979.

——. *Page d'écriture*. Illus. Jacqueline Duhême. Paris: Gallimard, 1980.

——. *En sortant de l'école*. Illus. Jacquline Duhême. Paris: Gallimard, 1981.

——. *Le gardien du phare aime trop les oiseaux*. Illus. Jacqueline Duhême. Paris: Gallimard, 1984.

——. *L'opéra de la lune*. Illus. Jacqueline Duhême. Paris: Gallimard, 1986.

——. *Chanson des escargots qui vont à l'enterrement*. Illus. Jacqueline Duhême. Paris: Gallimard, 1988.

——. *Le cancre*. Illus. Jacqueline Duhême. Paris: Gallimard, 1989.

——. *Chanson pour les enfants l'hiver*. Illus. Jacqueline Duhême. Paris: Gallimard, 1992.

——. *Au hasard des oiseaux et d'autres poèmes*. Illus. Jacqueline Duhême. Paris: Gallimard, 1994.

——. *Étranges étrangers et autres poèmes*. Illus. Jacqueline Duhême. Paris: Gallimard, 2000.

——. *Le chat et l'oiseau*. Illus. Jacqueline Duhême. Paris: Gallimard, 2000.

Provoost, Anne. *Vallen*. Antwerp: Houtekiet, 1994. Translated by John Nieuwenhuizen under the title *Falling* (St. Leonards, N. S. W.: Allen & Unwin, 1997).

——. *De Arkvaarders*. Amsterdam: Querido. 2001. Translated by John Nieuwenhuizen under the title *In the Shadow of the Ark* (New York: Arthur A. Levine, 2004).

Prue, Sally. *Cold Tom*. Oxford: Oxford University Press, 2001.

Pullman, Philip. *The Ruby in the Smoke*. Oxford: Oxford University Press, 1985.

——. *The Shadow in the North*. Oxford: Oxford University Press, 1987.

——. *The Tiger in the Well*. London: Viking, 1991.

——. *The Tin Princess*. London: Penguin, 1994.

——. *Northern Lights*. London: Scholastic, 1995.

——. *Clockwork, or All Wound Up*. Illus. Peter Bailey. London: Doubleday, 1996.

——. *The Subtle Knife*. London: Scholastic, 1997.

——. *The Amber Spyglass*. London: Scholastic, 2000.

——. *Lyra's Oxford*. Oxford: David Fickling, 2003.

——. *His Dark Materials Omnibus*. New York: Knopf Books for Young Readers, 2007.

Quintana, Anton [Anton Adolf Kuyten]. *De bavianenkoning*. Amsterdam: Van Goor Jeudgboeken, 1982. Translated by John Nieuwenhuizen under the title *The Baboon King* (St. Leonards, N.S.W.: Allen & Unwin, 1998).

Rasputin, Valentin. *Vniz i vverkh po techeniiu*. Moscow: Sovetskaia Rossiia, 1972.

——. *Na reke Angare*. Illus. P. Bagina. Moscow: Malysh, 1980. Translated by Valentina G. Brougher and Helen C. Poot under the title "Downstream," in *Contemporary Russian Prose*. Ed. Carl and Ellendea Proffer (Ann Arbor: Ardis, 1982). 379–430.

Rees, Celia. *Witch Child*. London: Bloomsbury, 2000.

——. *Sorceress*. London: Bloomsbury, 2002.

Richler, Mordecai. *The Apprenticeship of Duddy Kravitz*. London and Amsterdam: Andre Deutsch, 1959.

Richter, Jutta. *Die Katze oder Wie ich die Ewigkeit verloren habe*. Munich: Hanser, 2006.

Rosen, Meg. *How I Live Now*. New York: Wendy Lamb Books, 2004.

Rosen, Michael. *Mind Your Own Business*. Illus. Quentin Blake. New York: S. G. Phillips, 1974.

——. *The Hypnotiser*. Illus. Andrew Tiffen. London: Deutsch, 1988.

Rosny, J. H. Sr. *La guerre du feu*. Paris: Je Sais Tout, 1909. Translated by Harold Talbott under the title *The Quest for Fire* (New York: Pantheon Books, 1967).

Rossetti, Ana. *Una mano de santos*. Las Tres Edades. Madrid: Siruela, 1997.

Rowling, J(oanne). K. *Harry Potter and the Philosopher's Stone*. London: Bloomsbury, 1997.

——. *Harry Potter and the Chamber of Secrets*. London: Bloomsbury, 1998.

——. *Harry Potter and the Prisoner of Azkaban*. London: Bloomsbury, 1999.

——. *Harry Potter and the Goblet of Fire*. London: Bloomsbury, 2000.

——. *Fantastic Beasts and Where to Find Them* by Newt Scamander. Foreword by Albus

Dumbledore. London: Bloomsbury and Obscurus Books, 2001.

——. *Quidditch through the Ages* by Kennilworthy Whisp. London: Bloomsbury and Whizz Hard Books, 2001.

——. *Harry Potter and the Order of the Phoenix.* London: Bloomsbury, 2003.

——. *Harry Potter and the Half-Blood Prince.* London: Bloomsbury, 2005.

——. *Harry Potter and the Deathly Hallows.* London: Bloomsbury, 2007.

Rushdie, Salman. *Haroun and the Sea of Stories.* London: Granta Books, 1990.

Sachar, Louis. *Holes.* New York: Farrar, Straus, and Giroux, 1998.

Saint-Exupéry, Antoine de. *Le Petit Prince.* New York: Reynal & Hitchcock, 1943. Translated by Katherine Woods under the title *The Little Prince* (New York: Reynal & Hitchcock, 1943).

Sambrook, Clare. *Hide & Seek.* Edinburgh: Canongate, 2005.

Schami, Rafik [Suheil Fadél]. *Erzähler der Nacht.* Weinheim: Beltz & Gelberg, 1989. Translated by Philip Böhm under the title *Damascus Nights* (New York: Farrar, Straus, and Giroux, 1993).

Scheepers, Riana. *Dulle Griet.* Cape Town: Tafelberg, 1991.

——. *Die heidendogters jubel.* Cape Town: Tafelberg, 1995.

——. *Blinde Sambok.* Cape Town: Tafelberg, 2001.

——. *Die avonture van wilde Willemientjie.* Cape Town: Tafelberg, 2006.

Schnurre, Wolfdietrich. "Die Prinzessin." In *Das Los unserer Stadt.* Olten: Walter, 1959. 73.

——. *Die Prinzessin kommt um vier.* Illus. Rotraut Susanne Berner. Berlin: Aufbau-Verlag, 2000.

The Seeker: The Dark is Rising. Dir. David L. Cunningham. Universal City, CA: Marc Platt Productions, 2007.

Simard, Benjamin. *Ben.* Waterloo, Québec: Michel Quintin, 1997.

——. *Expédition Caribou.* Waterloo, Québec: Michel Quintin, 1998.

——. *Ben Caribou.* Waterloo, Québec: Michel Quintin, 1999.

Singer, Nicky. *Feather Boy.* New York: Delacorte, 2001.

——. *Doll.* London: Collins Flamingo, 2003.

——. *The Innocent's Story.* Oxford: Oxford University Press, 2005.

Skármeta, Antonio. *La composición.* Illus. Alfonso Ruano. Caracas: Ed. Ekaré, 2000. Published in English as *The Composition* (Toronto: Groundwood, 2000).

Smoke. Dir. Wayne Wang. New York: Miramax, 1995.

Snicket, Lemony [Daniel Handler]. *The Bad Beginning.* New York: HarperCollins, 1999.

——. *Lemony Snicket: The Unauthorized Autobiography.* New York: HarperCollins, 2002.

——. *The Slippery Slope.* New York: HarperCollins, 2003.

——. *A Series of Unfortunate Events: The Blank Book.* Illus. Brett Helquist. New York: HarperCollins, 2004.

——. *The Grim Grotto.* New York: HarperCollins, 2004.

——. *A Series of Unfortunate Events: The Pessimistic Posters.* New York: HarperKids Entertainment, 2004.

——. *The Penultimate Pearl.* New York: HarperCollins, 2005.

——. *A Series of Unfortunate Events: The Beatrice Letters.* Illus. Brett Helquist. New York: HarperCollins, 2006.

——. *A Series of Unfortunate Events: The Notorious Notations.* Illus. Brett Helquist. New York: HarperCollins, 2006.

——. *A Series of Unfortunate Events: The Puzzling Puzzles.* New York: HarperCollins, 2006.

——. *13 Shocking Secrets You'll Wish You Never Knew About Lemony Snicket.* New York: HarperCollins, 2006.

——. *The End.* Illus. Brett Helquist. New York: HarperCollins, 2006.

——. *Horseradish: Bitter Truths You Can't Avoid.* Ed. Susan Rich. New York: HarperCollins, 2007.

Spencer-Smith, T. *The Man Who Snarled at Flowers: A Fantasy for Children.* Cape Town: Tafelberg, 1991.

Stanišić, Saša. *Wie der Soldat das Grammofon repariert.* Munich: Luchterhand Literaturverlag, 2006.

Star Wars. Dir. George Lucas. 20th Century Fox, 1977.

Steinhöfel, Andreas. *Die Mitte der Welt.* Hamburg: Carlsen, 1998. Translated by Alisa Jaffa under the title *The Center of the World* (New York: Delacorte Books for Young Readers, 2005).

——. *Defender: Geschichten aus der Mitte der Welt.* Hamburg: Carlsen, 2001.

Stevenson, Robert Louis. *Treasure Island.* London: Cassell & Co., 1883.

——. *A Child's Garden of Verses.* London: Longmans & Co., 1885.

——. *The Strange Case of Dr. Jekyll and Mr. Hyde.* London: Longmans, Green, and Co., 1886.

Stone, David Lee. *The Ratastrophe Catastrophe.* London: Hodder, 2003.

——. *The Coldstone Conflict.* London: Hodder, 2007.

——. [under the pen name David Grimstone]. *Davey Swag.* London: Hodder, 2008.

Streatfeild, Noel. *The Whicharts*. London: W. Heinemann, 1931.

——. *Ballet Shoes: A Children's Novel of the Theatre*. London: J. M. Dent & Sons, 1936.

Stroud, Jonathan. *The Amulet of Samarkand*. London: Doubleday, 2003.

——. *The Golem's Eye*. London: Doubleday, 2004.

——. *Ptolemy's Gate*. London: Doubleday, 2005.

Stuart Little. Dir. Robert Minkoff. Los Angeles: Burbank, Calif.: Columbia Pictures, 1999.

The Sword in the Stone. Dir. Wolfgang Reitherman. Walt Disney, 1963.

Tartt, Donna. *The Secret History*. New York: Knopf, 1992.

——. *The Little Friend*. New York: Knopf, 2002.

Taylor, G. P. *Shadowmancer*. London: Faber & Faber, 2003. Originally published: Cloughton: Mount, 2002.

——. *Wormwood*. London: Faber & Faber, 2004.

——. *Tersias*. London: Faber & Faber, 2005.

——. *The Curse of Salamander Street*. London: Faber & Faber, 2006.

——. and Dan Boultwood. *The Tizzle Sisters & Erik*. Illus. Cliff Wright. Herts: Markosia Enterprises, 2006.

Thompson, Colin. *Future Eden: A Brief History of Next Time*. London: Simon & Schuster, 1999.

——. *Laughing for Beginners*. Sydney: Sceptre, 2002.

——. *Space: The Final Effrontery*. South Melbourne: Lothian Books, 2005.

Toews, Miriam. *A Complicated Kindness*. Toronto: Alfred A. Knopf Canada, 2004.

Tolkien, J. R. R. *The Hobbit*. London: G. Allen & Unwin, 1937.

——. *The Fellowship of the Ring*. London: George Allen & Unwin, 1954.

——. *The Two Towers*. London: George Allen & Unwin, 1954.

——. *The Return of the King*. London: George Allen & Unwin, 1955.

Tony Takitani. Dir. Jun Ichikawa. Prod. Motoki Ishida. Tokyo, Wilco Co. Ltd., 2004.

Tournier, Michel. *Vendredi ou les limbes du Pacifique*. Paris: Gallimard, 1967. Translated by Norman Denny under the title *Friday, or The Other Island* (London: Collins, 1969). Published in the United States as *Friday* (Garden City, NY: Doubleday, 1969).

——. *Le Roi des Aulnes*. Paris: Gallimard, 1970. Translated by Barbara Bray under the title *The Erl-King* (London: Collins, 1972). Published in the United States as *The Ogre* (New York: Doubleday, 1972).

——. *Friday and Robinson: Life on Speranza Island*. New York: Alfred A. Knopf, 1972.

——. *Vendredi ou La Vie sauvage*. Paris: Gallimard, 1977. Translated by Ralph Manheim under the title *Friday and Robinson: Life on Speranza Island* (New York: Knopf, 1972).

——. *Amandine ou les deux jardins*. Illus. Joëlle Boucher. Paris: Éditions G.P., 1977.

——. *Le Vent Paraclet*. Paris: Gallimard, 1977. Translated by Arthur Goldhammer under the title *The Wind Spirit: An Autobiography* (Boston: Beacon Press, 1988).

——. *Le Coq de bruyère*. Paris: Gallimard, 1978. Translated by Barbara Wright under the title *The Fetishist* (New York: Doubleday, 1984).

——. *La Fugue du petit Poucet*. Paris: Éditions G.P., 1979.

——. *Gaspard, Melchior et Balthazar*. Paris: Gallimard, 1980. Translated by Ralph Manheim under the title *The Four Wise Men* (New York: Doubleday, 1982).

——. *Barbedor*. Enfantimages. Paris: Gallimard, 1980.

——. *Que ma joie demeure*. Illus. Jean Claverie. Enfantimages. Paris: Gallimard, 1982.

——. *Gilles et Jeanne*. Paris: Gallimard, 1983.

——. *Les Rois mages*. Folio Junior. Paris: Gallimard, 1983.

——. *Sept contes*. Folio Junior. Paris: Gallimard, 1984.

——. "Pierrot, or The Secrets of the Night." Translated by Margaret Higonnet. *Children's Literature* 13 (1985): 169–72.

——. *La goutte d'or*. Paris: Gallimard, 1986. Translated by Barbara Wright under the title *The Golden Droplet* (New York: Doubleday, 1987).

——. *Angus*. Illus. Pierre Joubert. Sens: Signe de Piste Éditions, 1988.

——. *Le médianoche amoureux*. Paris: Gallimard, 1989. Translated by Barbara Wright under the title *The Midnight Love Feast*. (London: Collins, 1991).

——. *Les contes du médianoche*. Folio Junior. Paris: Gallimard, 1989.

——. *La couleuvrine*. Lecture Junior. Paris: Gallimard, 1994.

——. *Le miroir à deux faces*. Paris: Seuil Jeunesse, 1994.

——. *Eléazar ou la source et le buisson*. Paris: Gallimard, 1996. Translated by Jonathan F. Krell under the title *Eleazar, Exodus to the West* (Lincoln, NE: University of Nebraska Press, 2002).

——. *Barberousse* [followed by] *La Reine blonde*. Folio Cadet. Paris: Gallimard, 2003.

Townsend, Sue. *The Secret Diary of Adrian Mole, Aged 13¾*. London: Methuen, 1982.

——. *The Growing Pains of Adrian Mole*. London: Methuen, 1984.

Troyat, Henri. "L'âme de Mélitone." Illus. Adrienne Ségur. In *Contes des pays de neige*. Paris: Flammarion, 1955.

Twain, Mark [Samuel Langhorne Clemens]. *The Adventures of Tom Sawyer*. Hartford, CT: American Publishing Co., 1876.

——. *Huckleberry Finn*. New York: Charles L. Webster, 1885.

——. *Tom Sawyer, Detective*. New York: Harper & Brothers, 1896.

Vallen. Dir. Hans Herbots. Antwerp: Acasa Esana Pictures, 2001.

Van Daele, Henri. *Een tuin om in te spelen*. Tielt: Lannoo, 1995.

——. *Woestepet*. Tielt: Lannoo, 2002.

Van de Vendel, Edward. *Gijsbrecht: naar Vondels Gysbreght van Aemstel*. Illus. Hanneke van der Hoeven. Amsterdam: Querido, 1998.

——. *De dagen van de bluegrassliefde*. Amsterdam: Querido, 1999.

Van der Vyver, Marita. *Griet skryf 'n sprokie*. Cape Town: Tafelberg, 1992. Translated by Catherine Knox under the title *Entertaining Angels* (London: Joseph, 1994).

——. *Dinge van 'n Kind*. Cape Town: Tafelberg, 1994. Translated by Madeleine Biljon under the title *Childish Things* (New York: Dutton, 1996).

Vegter, Anne. *Verse Bekken! Of Hoe Heel Kort zich in een kip vergiste, uit het wc-raam hing, het op een sluipen zette an andere avonturen van de rat*. Illus. Geerten ten Bosch. Amsterdam: Querido, 1990.

Verne, Jules. *Cinq semaines en ballon*. Paris: Pierre-Jules Hetzel, 1863.

——. *Voyage au centre de la terre*. Paris: Pierre-Jules Hetzel, 1864.

——. *De la terre à la lune*. Paris: Pierre-Jules Hetzel, 1865.

——. *Vingt mille lieues sous les mers*. Illus. Alphonse de Neuville. Paris: Pierre-Jules Hetzel, 1869–70.

——. *Le tour du monde en quatre-vingts jours*. Illus. Alphonse de Neuville and Léon Benett. Paris: Pierre-Jules Hetzel, 1873.

Walser, Robert. *Der Spaziergang*. Frauenfeld: Huber, 1917. Translated by Christopher Middleton and others under the title *The Walk* (London and New York: Serpent's Tail, 1992).

——. *Einer, der nichts merkte*. Illus. Käthi Bhend. Zurich: Atlantis, 2003.

——. Welsh, Renate. *Johanna*. Vienna: Jugend & Folk, 1979.

——. *Dieda oder Das fremde Kind*. Innsbruck and Vienna: Obelisk, 2002.

Welty, Eudora. *The Robber Bridegroom*. Garden City, NY: Doubleday, 1942.

White, E. B. (Elwyn Brooks). *Stuart Little*. Illus. Garth Williams. New York: Harper, 1945.

——. *Charlotte's Web*. Illus. Garth Williams. New York: Harper, 1952.

White, T. H. *The Sword in the Stone*. London: Collins, 1938.

——. *The Witch in the Wood*. New York: G. P. Putnam's Sons, 1939.

——. *The Ill-Made Knight*. New York: G. P. Putnam's Sons, 1940.

——. *The Once and Future King*. London: Collins, 1958.

——. *The Book of Merlyn*. Prologue by Sylvia Townsend Warner. Illus. Trevor Stubley. Austin and London: University of Texas Press, 1977.

Wilson, Leslie. *Last Train from Kummersdorf*. London: Faber & Faber, 2004.

Wright, Sean. *Jesse Jameson and the Golden Glow*. King's Lynn: Crowswing, 2003.

——. *Jesse Jameson and the Bogie Beast*. King's Lynn: Crowswing Books, 2003.

——. *The Twisted Root of Jaarfindor*. King's Lynn: Crowswing, 2004.

——. *Dark Tales of Time and Space*. King's Lynn: Crowswing, 2005.

——. *Wicked Or What?* King's Lynn: Crowswing, 2005.

——. *Jaarfindor Remade*. King's Lynn: Crowswing, 2006.

——. *Love Under Jaarfindor Spires*. King's Lynn: Crowswing, 2006.

——, ed. *New Wave of Speculative Fiction: The What If Factor*. [Norfolk]: Crowswing, 2005.

Yourcenar, Marguerite. *Nouvelles orientales*. Paris: Gallimard, 1938. Translated by Alberto Manguel, in collaboration with the author, under the title *Oriental Tales* (New York: Farrar, Straus, and Giroux, 1985).

——. *Comment Wang-Fô fut sauvé*. Illus. Georges Lemoine. Enfantimages. Paris: Gallimard, 1979.

——. *Comme l'eau qui coule*. Paris: Gallimard, 1982.

——. *Notre Dame-des-Hirondelles*. Illus. Georges Lemoine. Enfantimages. Paris: Gallimard, 1982.

——. *Œuvres romanesques*. Bibliothèque de la Pléiade. Paris: Gallimard, 1990.

——. *Une belle matinée*. Illus. Georges Lemoine. Folio junior. Paris: Gallimard, 2003.

Zoshchenko, Mikhail. *Twelve Stories*. Selected and annotated by Lesli LaRocco and Slava Paperno. Columbus, OH: Slavica, 1989.

Zusak, Markus. *The Book Thief*. Sydney: Picador, 2005.

Secondary Sources

Abrams, David. "The Mask Behind the Man." *January Magazine*, June 2002, http://january magazine.com/kidsbooks/lemony2002.html (accessed April 9, 2006).

Adams, Richard. "Some Ingredients of *Watership Down*." In *The Thorny Paradise: Writers on Writing for Children*. Ed. Edward Blishen. Harmondsworth: Kestrel Books, 1975. 163–73.

Alberge, Dalya. "Children's Tale Works Magic on Whitbread." *Times*, January 23, 2002.

Allsobrook, Marian. "Writers for Adults, Writers for Children." In *International Companion Encyclopedia of Children's Literature*. Ed. Peter Hunt. 2nd ed. Vol. 1. London: Routledge, 2004. 576–86.

Almansi, Guido. "Malherba and the Art of Storytelling." *Quaderni d'italianistica* 1 (1980): 157–70.

Anatol, Giselle Liza, ed. *Reading Harry Potter: Critical Essays*. Westport, CT: Praeger, 2003.

Apseloff, Marilyn. *They Wrote for Children Too: An Annotated Bibliography of Children's Literature by Famous Writers for Adults*. New York: Greenwood, 1989.

Ardagh, Philip. "Wrap It Up." *Guardian*, December 20, 2003.

Armitstead, Claire. "Arthur Reborn." *Guardian*, September 29, 2001.

Atwood, Margaret. "A Tasty Slice of Pi and Ships." *Sunday Times*, May 5, 2002.

Aubarède, Gabriel d'. "Écrire pour les enfants." *Les Nouvelles Littéraires*, March 22, 1956, 1, 4.

Auden, Sandy. "Get 'Em Reading Fantasy at an Early Age: New Teen Fiction Hits the Shelves." The Alien Online, September 14, 2002, http://www.thealienonline.net/ao_060.asp?baa=1&tid=1&scid=6&iid=997 (accessed April 9, 2006).

Auden, W. H. "Today's 'Wonder-World' Needs Alice." *The New York Times Magazine*, July 1, 1962, 137.

Barnes, Clive. "Is *Across the Nightingale Floor* a Crossover Title?" *Books for Keeps* 137 (November 2002): 4.

Barros, Grisel Pires dos. "El cuento de Navidad de Auggie Wren." *Imaginaria* 144, December 22, 2004.

Basu, Samit. "On Flights of Fantasy." *Telegraph* (Calcutta), August 6, 2005.

Beckett, Sandra L. "From the Art of Rewriting to the Art of Crosswriting Child and Adult: The Secret of Michel Tournier's Dual Readership." In *Voices from Far Away: Current Trends in International Children's Literature Research* 24. Ed. Maria Nikolajeva. Stockholm: Centrum för barnkulturforskning, 1995. 9–34.

——. "Entretien avec Michel Tournier." *Dalhousie French Studies* 35 (Summer 1996): 66–78.

——. "The Meeting of Two Worlds: Michel Tournier's *Friday and Robinson: Life on Speranza Island*." In *Other Worlds, Other Livres: Children's Literature Experiences*. Vol 2. Ed. Myrna Machet, Sandra Olën, and Thomas van der Walt. Pretoria: Unisa Press, 1996. 110–27.

——. "Crosswriting Child and Adult: Henri Bosco's *L'enfant et la rivière*." *Children's Literature Association Quarterly* 21, vol. 4 (Winter 1996–97): 189–98.

——. "Adresato dvejinimas dabartineje prancuzi literaturoje" (Contemporary French children's books). *Rubinaitis* (Vilnius) 2, no. 7 (1997): 13–18.

——. "Amandine Through the Looking Glass: Michel Tournier's 'Initiatory Tale' for Children." *Bookbird* 35, no. 2 (Summer 1997): 12–15.

——. *De grands romanciers écrivent pour les enfants*. Montréal: Les Presses de l'Université de Montréal; Grenoble: Editions littéraires et linguistiques de l'Université de Grenoble, 1997.

——. "La réécriture pour enfants de *Comment Wang-Fô fut sauvé*. Lectures transversales de Marguerite Yourcenar*. Ed. Rémy Poignault and Blanca Arancibia. Tours: Société Internationale d'Etudes Yourcenariennes, 1997. 173–85.

——. "Crossing the Borders: The 'Children's Books' of Michel Tournier and Jean-Marie Gustave Le Clézio." *The Lion and the Unicorn* 22, no. 1 (January 1998): 44–69.

——. "Crosswriting Child and Adult in France: Children's Fiction for Adults? Adult Fiction for Children? Fiction for All Ages?" In *Transcending Boundaries: Writing for a Dual Audience of Children and Adults*. Ed. Sandra L. Beckett. New York: Garland, 1999. 31–61.

——. "Livres pour tous: le flou des frontières entre fiction pour enfants et fiction pour adultes." *Tangence* 67 (Autumn 2001): 9–22.

——. *Recycling Red Riding Hood*. New York: Routledge, 2002. 308–31.

——. "Artists' Books for a Cross-Audience." In *Studies in Children's Literature 1500–2000*. Ed. Celia Keenan and Mary Shine Thompson. Dublin: Four Courts Press, 2004. 162–69.

——. "Crossover Books." In *The Oxford Encyclopedia of Children's Literature*. Ed. Jack Zipes. Vol. 1. New York: Oxford University Press, 2006. 369–70.

——. "Michel Tournier Retells the Robinson Crusoe Myth: *Friday and Robinson: Life on Speranza*

Island." In *Beyond Babar: The European Tradition in Children's Literature.* Ed. Sandra Beckett and Maria Nikolajeva. Lanham: Scarecrow, 2006. 157–89.

——, ed. *Reflections of Change: Children's Literature Since 1945.* Westport, CT: Greenwood, 1997.

——, ed. *Transcending Boundaries: Writing for a Dual Audience of Children and Adults.* New York: Garland, 1999.

——. and Maria Nikolajeva, eds. *Beyond Babar: The European Tradition in Children's Literature.* Lanham, Scarecrow, 2006.

Beil, Karen Magnuson. "Interview with Jennifer Donnelly." *The Children's Literature Connection,* http://www.childrensliteratureconnection.org/resources-info.asp?ID=7 (accessed March 15, 2007).

Belinkov, Arkady. "The Soviet Intelligentsia and the Socialist Revolution: On Yury Olesha's *Envy.*" *The Russian Review* 30, no. 4 (October 1971): 356–68.

Bertodano, Helena de. "I Am of the Devil's Party." *Sunday Telegraph,* January 27, 2002.

"Bibliothèque Blanche." *Bulletin de la NRF* 75 (November 1953): 16.

"La Bibliothèque Blanche." *Bulletin de la NRF* [1966?].

Birch, Sam. "Set in Success." February 27, 2007, http://vision.york.ac.uk/index.php?option=com_content&task=view&id=148 (accessed March 12, 2007).

Blake, Andrew. *The Irresistible Rise of Harry Potter.* London: Verso, 2002.

Bloom, Harold. *The Western Canon: The Books and School of the Ages.* New York: Harcourt Brace, 1994.

——. "Can 35 Million Book Buyers Be Wrong? Yes." *Wall Street Journal,* July 11, 2000, A26.

——. "Dumbing Down American Readers." *Boston Globe,* September 24, 2003.

Blume, Mary. "A Laughing Provocateur Is Launched in Britain." *International Herald Tribune,* December 30, 1983, 7.

Blume, Svenja. *Texte ohne Grenzen für Lesern jeden Alters: Zur Neustrukturierung des Jugendliteraturbegriffs in der literarischen Postmoderne.* Freiburg: Rombach, 2005.

Born, Anne. "Tormod Haugen, *Vinterstedet*—The Winter Place: Synopsis." 1984. Unpublished review written at the request of Gyldendal.

Bosco, Henri. "Les enfants m'ont dicté les livres que j'ai écrit pour eux." *Les Nouvelles Littéraires* 1631, December 4, 1958, 4.

——. "Henri Bosco voyageur. Le séjour en Grèce (juin–juillet 1963)" [Lettres à Henri Ehret], ed. Claude Girault, *Cahiers Henri Bosco* 21 (1981): 26, note 2.

Bradford, Clare and Valerie Coghlan, eds. *Expectations and Experiences: Children, Childhood and Children's Literature.* Litchfield: Pied Piper Press, 2007.

Briscoe, Joanna. "So What's the Real Story?" *Independent* (London), May 15, 2003.

Brüggemann, Theodor and Otto Brunken, eds. *Handbuch zur Kinder- und Jugendliteratur: Vom Beginn des Buchdrucks bis 1570.* Stuttgart: Metzler, 1987.

Bursztynski, Sue. "Return to Tremaris." Review of *The Waterless Sea,* by Kate Constable. *January Magazine,* August 2003, http://januarymagazine.com/SFF/waterlesssea.html (accessed April 20, 2007).

Byatt, A. S. "Harry Potter and the Childish Adult." *New York Times,* July 7, 2003.

Cadden, Mike. "Speaking to Both Children and Genre: Le Guin's Ethics of Audience." *The Lion and the Unicorn* 24, no. 1 (January 2000): 128–42.

——. *Ursula K. Le Guin Beyond Genre: Fiction for Children and Adults.* New York: Routledge, 2005.

Caldwell, Gail. Review of *The Little Friend,* by Donna Tartt. *Boston Globe,* October 27, 2002.

Campbell, Glen and Eileen Lohka, eds. with the collaboration of Sandra L. Beckett, Claude Romney, and Danielle Thaler. *Littérature de jeunesse et Fin de siècle.* Winnipeg: Presses Universitaires de Saint-Boniface, 2007.

Carew, Angela. "Anne Provoost: *In the Shadow of the Ark.*" *Kirkus Reviews,* July 2004.

Caron, Dominique. "La magie de J. K. Rowling." *Le libraire* 1, no. 6 (April 2000): 4.

Carpenter, Humphrey. *Secret Gardens: A Study of the Golden Age of Children's Literature.* Boston: Houghton Mifflin, 1985.

Carranza, Marcela. "Colección Clásicos Ilustrados." *Imaginaria* 186, August 2, 2006.

Carter, James, ed. *Talking Books: Children's Authors Talk about the Craft, Creativity and Process of Writing.* London: Routledge, 1999.

Chabin, Laurent. "La littérature jeunesse: littérature ou sous-littérature." In *Littérature de jeunesse et Fin de siècle.* Ed. Glen Campbell and Eileen Lohka with the collaboration of Sandra L. Beckett, Claude Romney, and Danielle Thaler. Winnipeg: Presses Universitaires de Saint-Boniface, 2007. 37–54.

Chambers, Aidan. "Ways of Telling." In *Booktalk: Occasional Writing on Literature and Children.* London: The Bodley Head, 1985. 92–115.

Cleaver, Pamela. "For Children or Adults?" *Books and Bookmen* (May 1975): 20–25.

Clee, Nicholas. "Can the Magic Last Forever?" *Independent* (London), September 15, 2004.

Comino, Sandra. "Entrevista con Liliana Bodoc." *Imaginaria*, July 7, 2004.

Commager, Henry Steele. "When Majors Wrote for Minors." *The Saturday Review*, May 10, 1952, 10–11, 44–46.

Cooper, Ilene. "Find More Like This: *In the Shadow of the Ark.*" *Booklist* 100, nos. 19–20 (June 1–15, 2004): 1721.

Copeland, Marion. "Crossover Animal Fantasy Series: Crossing Cultural and Species as Well as Age Boundaries." *Society and Animals* 11, no. 3 (November 2003): 287–98.

Craig, Amanda. "Window into Souls." *New Statesman*, September 26, 1997, 66.

———. "Mark Haddon." *Sunday Times*, February 2004.

Crews, Frederick C. *The Pooh Perplex: A Freshman Casebook. In Which It Is Discovered that the True Meaning of the Pooh Stories Is Not as Simple as Is Usually Believed, But for Proper Elucidation Requires the Combined Efforts of Several Academicians of Varying Critical Persuasions.* New York: E. P. Dutton, 1963.

———. *Postmodern Pooh.* New York: North Point Press, 2001.

Cummins, June. "Read Between the Lines for a Lesson in Consumer Coercion." *The Times Higher Education Supplement*, December 21, 2001, 20.

Cundy, Catherine. *Salman Rushdie.* Manchester: Manchester University Press, 1996.

Cunningham, Hugh. *Children and Childhood in Western Society Since 1500.* London and New York: Longman, 1995.

Daiche, David. *Robert Louis Stevenson and His World.* London: Thames and Hudson, 1973.

Dante. "Reading into Crossover Trends." *Straits Times*, March 8, 2004.

Demers, Dominique. "Enfant lecteur, adolescent lecteur, adulte lecteur: frontières mouvantes, exigences mythiques et désirs bien réels." In *Littérature de jeunesse et Fin de siècle.* Ed. Glen Campbell and Eileen Lohka with the collaboration of Sandra L. Beckett, Claude Romney, and Danielle Thaler. Winnipeg: Presses Universitaires de Saint-Boniface, 2007. 11–35.

Demougin, Jacques, ed. *Dictionnaire de la littérature française et francophone.* Vol. 1. Paris: Larousse, 1987.

"Dianne Hofmeyr." Children's Literature Research Unit, University of South Africa, http://childlit.org.za/boikie.html (accessed March 25, 2006).

Diver, Krysia. "A Lord for Germany." *Sydney Morning Herald*, October 5, 2004.

Dodds, Georges T. "The Tomorrow Series." SF Site, http://www.sfsite.com/02b/tom51.htm, 1998 (accessed May 19, 2007).

Domar, Rebecca. "The Tragedy of a Soviet Satirist: The Case of Zoshchenko." In *Through the Glass of Soviet Literature.* Ed. Ernest Simmons. New York: Columbia University Press, 1953. 201–43.

Donaldson, Julia. *Children's Writers' and Artists' Yearbook 2006.* London: A&C Black, 2006.

Doniger, Wendy. "Can You Spot the Source?" *London Review of Books*, February 17, 2000, 26–27.

Donohue, Kathleen. "'Free-falling' and 'Serendipity': An Interview with Joy Kogawa." *Canadian Children's Literature/Littérature canadienne pour la jeunesse* 84 (1996): 34–46.

Dresang, Eliza T. *Radical Change: Books for Youth in a Digital Age.* New York: The H.W. Wilson Company, 1999.

Droit, Roger-Pol. "La philosophie comme jeu d'enfant." *Le Monde*, February 24, 1995.

Dugast-Portes, Francine. "J-M. G. Le Clézio et la littérature de jeunesse." In *Culture, texte et jeune lecteur.* Ed. Jean Perrot. Nancy: Presses Universitaires de Nancy, 1993. 143–60.

Durix, Jean-Pierre. "The Gardener of Stories: Salman Rushdie's *Haroun and the Sea of Stories.*" In *Reading Rushdie: Perspectives on the Fiction of Salman Rushdie.* Ed. D. M. Fletcher. Amsterdam: Rodopi, 1994. 343–51.

Dusinberre, Juliet. *Alice to the Lighthouse: Children's Books and Radical Experiments in Art.* Basingstoke: Macmillan, 1999.

Eagleton, Terry. "Awakening from Modernity." *The Times Literary Supplement*, February 20, 1987.

Eccleshare, Julia. "Northern Lights and Christmas Miracles." *Books for Keeps* 100 (September 1996): 15.

———. "A Golden Time for Children's Books." *Publishers Weekly*, February 18, 2002.

———. *A Guide to the Harry Potter Novels.* London: Continuum, 2002.

———. "Inside the Outsider." *Guardian*, May 17, 2003.

———. "Crossing Over." *Literature Matters*, June 2005, http://www.britishcouncil.org/arts-literature-matters-3-eccleshare.htm (accessed April 2, 2006).

Eco, Umberto. *Opera aperta*. Milan: V. Bompiani, 1962. Translated by Anna Cancogni under the title *The Open Work* (Cambridge, MA: Harvard University Press, 1989).

Ellen, Barbara. "Access Small Areas." *Times*, November 15, 2001.

Ewers, Hans-Heino. "Epilogue." In C. W. Contessa, Friedrich Baron de la Motte Fouqué, and E. T. A. Hoffmann. *Kinder-Märchen*. Ed. Hans-Heino Ewers. Stuttgart: Reclam, 1987. 327–50.

———. "The Adult as Co-Reader and Reader of Children's Literature." Paper presented at the 8th IRSCL Congress, Cologne, Germany, September 28–October 2, 1987. Published under the title "Das doppelsinnige Kinderbuch: Erwachsene als Leser and Mitleser von Kinderliteratur." *Fundevogel* 41–42 (1987): 8–12.

———. "Grenzverwischungen und Grenzüberschreitungen: die Kinder- und Jugendliteratur auf dem Weg zu einer neuen Identität." *JuLit / Arbeitskreis für Jugendlierautur* 23, no. 3 (1997): 82–84.

———, ed. *Kinderliteratur und Moderne: ästhetische Herausforderungen für die Kinderliteratur im 20. Jahrhundert*. Weinheim and Munich: Juventa, 1990.

Ezard, John. "Fully Booked." *Guardian*, January 24, 2002.

———. "Harry Potter Toppled in Sales Charts." *Guardian*, June 2, 2003.

———. "Favourite Haddon wins Whitbread." *Guardian*, February 28, 2004.

———. "Harry Potter and the Stony Broke Authors." *Guardian*, July 14, 2005.

Falconer, Rachel. "Crossover Literature." In *International Companion Encyclopedia of Children's Literature*. Ed. Peter Hunt. 2nd ed. Volume I. London: Routledge, 2004. 556–75.

Farouky, Jumana. "J. K. Rowling." *Time* (Europe) 168, no. 21 (November 13, 2006).

Featherstone, Mike. "Global and Local Cultures." In *Mapping the Futures: Local Cultures, Global Change*. Ed. Jon Bird, Barry Curtis, Tim Putnam, George Robertson, and Lisa Tickner. London: Routledge, 1993. 169–87.

Feay, Suzi. "The Tale of Genji for the Potter Generation." *Independent on Sunday*, November 28, 2004.

Fenton, James. "Keeping Up with Salman Rushdie." *New York Review of Books* 38, no. 6 (March 28, 1991).

Fine, Anne. "The Big Picture." British Council Arts, http://www.britishcouncil.org/arts-literature-matters-3-fine.htm (accessed April 25, 2006).

Fitzgerald, Carol. "Garth Nix: Interview." KidsReads.com, April 14, 2004, http://www.kidsreads.com/authors/au-nix-garth.asp (accessed August 18, 2007).

FitzHerbert, Claudia. "This Author Is Original and Also Dangerous." *Daily Telegraph*, January 23, 2002.

Flynn, Richard. "'Affirmative Acts': Language, Childhood, and Power in June Jordan's Cross-Writing." *Children's Literature* 30 (2002): 159–85.

Forné, Anna. *La piratería textual: Un estudio hipertextual de "Son vacas, somos puercos" y "El médico de los piratas" de Carmen Boullosa*. Lund: Romanska Institutionen, 2001.

Forster, E. M. (Edward Morgan). *Aspects of the Novel*. New York: Harcourt, Brace, 1956.

France, Louise. "The Great Unknown." *Observer*, April 15, 2007.

Fretheim, Tor. "Merkel, Donna og retten til å bli hørt og sett." *Bokspeilet* 2 (1986): 4.

Fuchs, Sabine. "About a Factory-Made Boy: Christine Nöstlinger's Story about Conrad." In *Beyond Babar: The European Tradition in Children's Literature*. Ed. Sandra L. Beckett and Maria Nikolajeva. Lanham: Scarecrow, 2006. 191–207.

Fulton, Bruce. "Kori: *The Beacon Anthology of Korean American Fiction*." *Pacific Affairs* 75, no. 4 (Winter 2002/2003): 660–61.

Furedi, Frank. "The Children Who Won't Grow Up." *Spiked*, July 29, 2003.

Gaarder, Jostein. "Books for a World without Readers?" Paper presented at the International Board on Books for Young People (IBBY) Congress, Basel, Switerland, September 29–October 2, 2002.

Galef, David. "Crossing Over: Authors Who Write Both Children's and Adults' Fiction." *Children's Literature Association Quarterly* 20, no. 1 (1995): 29–35.

García-Teresa, Alberto. "José Maria Merino." May 30, 2002, http://www.bibliopolis.org/articulo/merino.htm (accessed May 25, 2007). A shortened version of the interview was published in *2001* (September–October 2002).

Garcin, Jérôme. "Interview avec Michel Tournier." *L'Événement du jeudi*, January 9–15, 1986.

Gardner, John. "Interview: Discworld Author Terry Pratchett." *New Zealand Herald*, October 26, 2002.

Garland, Irene. "Jostein Gaarder." In *Britannica Book of the Year*, 1995, Encyclopedia Britannica Online. http://britannica.com/eb/article-9115358/Gaarder-Jostein (accessed May 11, 2007).

Gay, John. *The Letters of John Gay*. Ed. C. F. Burgess. Oxford: Oxford University Press, 1966.

Gemmell, David. "No Shades of Grey." *Guardian*, May 10, 2003.

Genette, Gérard. *Palimpsests: Literature in the Second Degree.* Translated by Channa Newman and Claude Doubinsky. Lincoln: The University of Nebraska Press, 1997.

Géras, Adèle. "Hotel du lac." Review of *A Gathering Light* by Jennifer Donnelly, *Guardian,* June 7, 2003.

Gessell, Paul. "Adult Art Fills Illustrated Edition of Yann Martel's *Life of Pi* Novel." *Vancouver Sun,* November 17, 2007.

Gifford, Nick. "An Interview with Sean Wright." Infinity Plus, http://www.infinityplus.co.uk/nonfiction/intsw.htm (accessed April 3, 2006).

Gilchrist, Todd. "Howl's Moving Castle." IGN Entertainment, June 9, 2005, http://movies.ign.com/articles/624/624042p1.html (accessed June 26, 2007).

Gladwell, Malcolm. "The Science of the Sleeper." *The New Yorker,* October 4, 1999.

Glistrup, Eva. "Children's Literature in Denmark: Trends and Currents in the 1990s." Paper presented at the 63rd International Federation of Library Associations and Institutions Annual Conference, August 31–September 5, 1997.

Gray, Paul. "Wild About Harry." *Time* 154, no. 12, September 20, 1999, 46–52.

Grenby, Matthew Orville. "Adults Only? Children and Children's Books in British Circulating Libraries, 1748–1848." *Book History* 5 (2002): 19–38.

Grenz, Dagmar. "E. T. A. Hoffmann as an Author for Children and Adults or the Child and the Adult as Readers of Children's Literature." *Phaedrus* 13 (1988): 91–96.

——, ed. *Kinderliteratur – Literatur auch für Erwachsene?: Zum Verhältnis von Kinderliteratur und Erwachsenenliteratur.* Munich: Fink, 1990.

Gupta, Suman. *Re-Reading Harry Potter.* New York: Palgrave Macmillan, 2003.

Hade, Dan. "Des histoires qui sont aussi des marchandises." In *Perspectives contemporaines du roman pour la jeunesse.* Ed. Virginie Douglas. Paris: L'Harmattan, 2003. 37–56.

Hannabuss, Stuart. "Books Adopted by Children." In *International Companion Encyclopedia of Children's Literature.* Ed. Peter Hunt. London: Routledge, 1996. 422–32.

Harju, Maija-Liisa. "Tove Jansson and the Crossover Continuum." Ph.D. course paper, McGill University, 2007.

Harper, Meg. "Using It or Losing It … Exploring Your Creativity." *Scattered Authors' Society Newsletter,* April 2006.

Harwood, Vernon. "Interview: Richard Adams." Part 1. BBC Radio Berkshire. http://www.bbc.co.uk/berkshire/content/articles/2007/03/16/richard_adams_interview_feature.shtml (accessed May 11, 2007).

Heilman, Elizabeth E., ed. *Harry Potter's World: Multidisciplinary Critical Perspectives.* New York: RoutledgeFalmer, 2003.

Hensher, Philip. "Harry Potter and the Art of Making Money." *Independent,* June 19, 2003.

——. "A Crowd-Pleaser but No Classic." *Spectator,* July 12, 2003.

Histoire du livre de jeunesse d'hier à aujourd'hui, en France et dans le monde. Paris: Gallimard Jeunesse, 1993.

Hodgman, John. "Susanna Clarke's Magic Book." *New York Times,* August 1, 2004.

Holcombe, Garan. "Mark Haddon." British Council. 2004, http://www.contemporarywriters.com/authors/?p=auth3E38026813f8c194E5NnW1CF3087 (accessed March 31, 2006).

Holden, Anthony. "Why Harry Potter Doesn't Cast a Spell over Me." *Observer,* June 25, 2000.

Hoven, Peter van den. *Grensverkeer.* La Haye: NBLC, 1994.

——. "Een Vlaamse reus: Over de levensverhalen van Henri van Daele." *Literatuur zonder leeftijd* 39 (1996): 335–56.

Hunt, Jonathan. "Redefining the Young Adult Novel." *The Horn Book Magazine* 83, vol. 2 (March–April 2007): 141–47.

Hunt, Peter. *Children's Literature.* Malden, MA: Blackwell Publishing, 2001.

Hunt, Peter and Millicent Lenz. *Alternative Worlds in Fantasy Fiction.* London: Continuum, 2001.

Insley, Jill. "Once Upon a Time This Book Was Born." *Observer,* December 5, 2004.

Jacobson, Howard. "Adults Should Not Toady to the Taste of Tots." *Independent* (London), July 5, 2003.

"Jan Mark." Biography. http://biography.jrank.org/pages/1875/Mark-Jan-1943.html (accessed August 17, 2007).

Johnson, Rachel. "Read me a Dirty Story, Mummy." *Spectator,* July 24, 2004.

Johnson, Sarah. "The Outsider." Review of *Cold Tom,* by Sally Prue, *Times,* December 1–7, 2001.

Jones, Katharine. "Getting Rid of Children's Literature." *The Lion and the Unicorn* 30, no. 3 (September 2006): 287–315.

Jones, Louisa. "Children's Stories for Adults: Problems in Modern Poetic Fiction." *Proceedings: Pacific Northwest Conference on Foreign Languages.* Twenty-First Annual Meeting, April 3–4, 1970. Ed. Ralph W. Baldner. Vol XXI. Victoria: University of Victoria, 1970. 16–23.

Jones, Nicolette. "Twice the Appeal." *The Children's Bookseller,* September 10, 1999, 22.

Jones, Vanessa E. "Young-Adult Books Are No Longer Child's Play for Bestselling Authors." *Boston Globe,* September 19, 2002, D1.

Jones, W. Glynn. *Tove Jansson.* Boston: Twayne Publishers, 1984.

Kellaway, Kate. "Autistic Differences." *Observer,* April 27, 2003.

——. "The Race for Both Older and Younger Readers in One Book." *Observer,* April 11, 2004.

Kelleher, Damian. "Caught in the Crossover." *The Times Educational Supplement,* October 11, 2002.

Kellner, Tomas. "Harry Potter and the Vanishing Brand Magic." *Forbes Magazine,* July 14, 2005.

Kiberd, Declan. "Literature, Childhood and Ireland." In *Expectations and Experiences: Children, Childhood and Children's Literature.* Ed. Clare Bradford and Valerie Coghlan. Litchfield: Pied Piper Press & IRSCL, 2007. 13–26.

Kildegaard, Lise. "'Three Square Stories' by Louis Jensen." *Translation* 2 (Fall 2007) 71–79.

Kipen, Michael. "Chabon's Fantasy League: Baseball Saves the Day in an Adventure for Kids and Adults." *San Francisco Chronicle,* September 15, 2002.

Knoepflmacher, U. C. "The Balancing of Child and Adult: An Approach to Victorian Fantasies for Children." *Nineteenth-Century Fiction* 37, no. 4 (March 1983): 497–530.

Knoepflmacher, U. C. and Mitzi Myers, eds. "'Cross-Writing' and the Reconceptualizing of Children's Literary Studies." *Children's Literature* 25 (1997): vii–xvii.

Knox, Malcolm. "Writers Coming of Age." *Sydney Morning Herald,* May 10, 2003.

Koster, Serge. *Michel Tournier.* Paris: Henri Veyrier, 1986.

Kullman, Harry. "Att skriva för bra." *Skolbiblioteket* 6 (1964): 208–09.

Kümmerling-Meibauer, Bettina. "Annäherungen von Jugend- und Erwachsenenliteratur: Die schwedische Jugendliteratur des 80er und frühen 90er Jahre." *Der Deutschunterricht* 46 (1996): 68–81.

——. "The Status of Sequels in Children's Literature: *The Long Secret* and *The Chocolate War.*" In *Reflections of Change: Children's Literature Since 1945.* Ed. Sandra L. Beckett. Westport, Conn: Greenwood Press, 1997. 65–73.

——. *Klassiker der Kinder- und jugendliteratur. Ein internationales Lexikon.* 2 vols. Stuttgart, J. B. Metzler, 1999.

——. "Crosswriting as a Criterion for Canonicity: The Case of Erich Kästner." In *Transcending Boundaries: Writing for a Dual Audience of Children and Adults.* Ed. Sandra L. Beckett. New York: Garland, 1999. 13–30.

——. *Kinderliteratur, Kanonbildung und literarische Wertung.* Stuttgart: J. B. Metzler, 2003.

Lafrance, Diane. "Cécile Gagnon et la réecriture pour jeunes: Du *Chemin Kénogami* à *C'est ici, mon pays,*" "L'écrivain/e pour la jeunesse et ses publics." Paper presented at the Congrès de l'ACFAS, Université de Montréal, May 15–19, 2000.

Lanes, Selma. *The Art of Maurice Sendak.* New York: Harry N. Adams, 1980.

Langton, Jane. "Jane Langton's Latest Book for Young People is *The Fragile Flag.*" *The New York Times,* July 28, 1985.

——. Review of *Handles,* by Jan Mark, *New York Times,* July 28, 1985.

Lapouge, Gilles. "Michel Tournier s'explique." *Lire* 64 (December 1980): 28–46.

Larsen, Steffen. "Author Spotlight: Louis Jensen." *Bookbird* 37, no. 4 (1999): 53–56.

Lebedeva, Angela. "Sergey Mikhalkov: Our Living Classic." *Bookbird* 41, no. 3 (July 2003): 57–58.

Le Guin, Ursula K. "Dreams Must Explain Themselves." In *The Language of the Night: Essays on Fantasy and Science Fiction.* Ed. Susan Wood. New York: G. P. Putnam's Sons, 1979. 47–56.

Lemarchand, Jacques. "Livres pour enfants." *Bulletin de la NRF* 144 (December 1950): 13b–14a.

"Lemony Snicket's The Grim Grotto Surpasses 1.1 Million Copies Sold." *PR Newswire,* October 21, 2004.

Levitas, Ruth. "The Future of Thinking about the Future." In *Mapping the Futures: Local Cultures, Global Change.* Ed. Jon Bird, Barry Curtis, Tim Putnam, George Robertson, and Lisa Tickner. London: Routledge, 1993. 257–66.

Lewis, C. S. "On Stories." In *Of Other Worlds: Essays and Stories.* Ed. Walter Hooper. London: Geoffrey Bles, 1966. 3–200.

——. "On Three Ways of Writing for Children." In *Only Connect: Readings on Children's Literature.* Ed. Sheila Egoff, G. T. Stubbs, and L. F. Ashley. Toronto: Oxford University Press, 1969. 207–20.

Leysen, Annemie. "About Flemish and Dutch Literature." In *A Companion to Dutch and Flemish Letters.* Translated from the Dutch by David Colmer and Paul Vincent. N.p.: Stichting Frankfurter Buchmesse, 1997. 37–47.

Lierop-Debrauwer, Helma van. "Terra Incognita? Adolescent Fiction in the Higher Classes in Secondary Education." Paper presented at the 8th Biennial Conference of the International Society for the Empirical Study of Literature (IGEL), Pécs, Hungary, August 21–24, 2002.

———. and Neel Bastiaansen-Harks. *Over grenzen: De adolescentenroman in het literatuuronderwijs.* Delft: Eburon, 2005.

Lister, David. "Pullman Wins Whitbread for Children's Fantasy." *Independent* (London), January 23, 2002.

"Literary Expansion: Children's Books Break through the Barrier." *Guardian*, August 18, 2001.

The Long Patrol Club. "An Interview with Stuart Moore." http://www.longpatrolclub.com/interviews/stuartmoore.html (accessed November 18, 2007).

Loseff, Lev. *On the Beneficence of Censorship: Aesopian Language in Modern Russian Literature.* Munich: Otto Sagner, 1984.

Lurie, Alison. *Don't Tell the Grownups: Subversive Children's Literature.* Boston: Little, Brown, 1990.

Machado, Ana Maria. "Words to Bridge Gaps: Children's Books as a Bridge between Adults and Children." Paper presented at the International Board on Books for Young People (IBBY) Congress, Basel, Switzerland, September 29–October 2, 2002.

Mackay, Brad. "Hey Kids! No Comics! How the Comic Book Almost Disappeared." *CBC Arts Online*, February 3, 2005.

Madore, Édith. "Les 'écrivains' et les 'auteurs jeunesse.'" *Tangence* 67 (Autumn 2001): 23–33.

Madsen, Monica C. "'At sætte livets forunderlighed på ord.' Interview med forfatter Louis Jensen." *Læsningens magi: Om børn, bøger og læselyst.* Vol. 1. Copenhagen: Biblioteksstyrelsen, 2003. 7–9. Reprinted as "'The Wondrous Beauty of Life.' Interview with author Louis Jensen." Trans. Vibeke Cranfield. *Scandinavian Public Library Quarterly* 37, no. 1 (2004): 17–19.

Mark, Jan. "Jan Mark." *Books for Keeps* 25 (March 1984): 12–13.

———. "Jan Mark," Biography, http://biography.jrank.org/pages/1875/Mark-Jan-1943.html (accessed August 17, 2007).

Martín Gaite, Carmen. "Entrevista: Carmen Martín Gaite." *CLIJ* 26 (March 1991): 7–12.

Martini, Jürgen. "The Novelist as a Teacher: Children's Books by Well-Known Nigerian Authors." Paper presented at the 8th IRSCL Congress, Cologne, Germany, September 28–October 2, 1987.

Matskevych, Petro, and Kseniya Sladkevych, "The All-European Tendency: Yesterday's Teenagers Become 'Adult' Authors." Paper presented at International Symposium "Visualizing the Child in Children's Fiction," Lviv, Ukraine, April 12, 2007.

Maughan, Shannon. "The Lowdown on Laydowns: Publishers Embrace One-Day Laydown Dates for Big Books This Season." *Publishers Weekly*, September 1, 2003.

Maul, Kimberly. "Snicket Buzz About Newly Named Novel Was Fostered Online, Offering a Sign of What's to Come." *Book Standard*, October 18, 2005.

Mauri, Paolo. *Malerba.* Florence: La Nuova Italia, 1977.

Mayer, Andre. "Sharing the Love: How Publishers are Re-branding Adult Fiction for Younger Readers." CBC, March 14, 2006, http://www.cbc.ca/arts/books/youngadultfiction.html (accessed December 6, 2006).

McCaffery, Larry and Sinda Gregory. "An Interview with Ursula Le Guin." *Missouri Review* 7 (1984): 82.

McConnell, Frank. "Sandman." *Commonweal*, October 20, 1995.

McCrum, Robert. "Not for Children." *Observer*, October 22, 2000.

———. "Daemon Geezer." *Guardian*, February 20, 2002.

McDougall, Liam. "*Life of Pi* Hits One Million Sales as Spielberg Eyes Movie Chance." *The Sunday Herald*, August 10, 2003.

McDowell, Myles. "Fiction for Children and Adults: Some Essential Differences." *Children's Literature in Education* 4, no. 1 (March 1973): 50–63.

McMahon, Joseph H. "Michel Tournier's Texts for Children." *Children's Literature* 13 (1985): 154–68.

McMaster, Juliet. "'Adults' Literature,' by Children." *The Lion and the Unicorn* 25, no. 2 (April 2001): 277–99.

McVeigh, Karen and Lesley Walker. "Pratchett Casts a Bitter Spell on Rivals." *Scotsman*, July 13, 2002.

Mehren, Elizabeth. "Reading by 9: Toy Tie-ins Rate an 'A' with Children's Book Publishers." *Los Angeles Times*, December 23, 1998, A1.

Mendlesohn, Farah. *Diana Wynne Jones: Children's Literature and the Fantastic Tradition.* New York: Routledge, 2005.

Merrigan, Sean. "Interview with Clare Sambrook: Author of *Hide & Seek.*" Edit Red, http://www.editred.com/Uploads/st_37256_Interview_with_Clare_Samb (accessed May 9, 2007).

Merwe, Annari van der. "K. Sello Duiker: 13 April 1974–19 January 2005." LitNet: In Memorium, January 20, 2005. http://www.oulitnet.co.za/inmemoriam/duiker_dies.asp (accessed May 9, 2007).

Metcalf, Eva-Maria. "Concepts of Childhood in Peter Handke's *Kindergeschichte* and Christine Nöstlinger's *Hugo, das Kind in den besten Jahren.*" In *Wandlungen des Literaturbegriffs in den Deutschsprachigen Ländern seit 1945.* Ed. Gerhard P. Knapp and Gerd Labroisse. Amsterdam: Rodopi, 1988. 281–302.

Moeyaert, Bart. "Seven Small Stories." Paper presented at the seminar "Coming Home in Children's Literature," Roehampton Institute London, May 12–13, 1000.

———. "A Talk with TBB (Internet), United States." In IBBY Belgium Flemish Section nomination dossier for the Hans Christian Andersen Award 2002.

Mooney, Bel. "Writing through Ages." *Times*, August 28, 2002.

Moss, Stephen. "Let's Forget about 'Children's Writing.'" *Guardian*, January 23, 2002.

Murakami, Haruki. "A Conversation with Haruki Murakami, Author of *Sputnik Sweetheart.*" Random House. http://www.randomhouse.com/catalog/display.pperl?isbn=9780375726057& view=auqa (accessed November 11, 2007).

Myers, Mitzi. "'No Safe Place to Run To': An Interview with Robert Cormier." *The Lion and the Unicorn* 24, no. 3 (2000): 445–64.

Myerson, Jonathan. "Harry Potter and the Sad Grown-ups." *Independent* (London), November 14, 2001.

Naughtie, James. "*Northern Lights.*" Radio 4's Book Club, May 7, 2000.

Nel, Philip. *J. K. Rowling's Harry Potter Novels: A Reader's Guide.* New York and London: Continuum, 2001.

———. "Is There a Text in This Advertising Campaign? Literature, Marketing, and Harry Potter." *The Lion and the Unicorn* 29, no. 2 (2005): 236–67.

Nikolajeva, Maria. *Children's Literature Comes of Age: Toward a New Aesthetic.* New York: Garland, 1996.

———. "Exit Children's Literature." *The Lion and the Unicorn* 22, no. 2 (1998): 221–36.

———. "Children's, Adult, Human … ?" In *Transcending Boundaries: Writing for a Dual Audience of Children and Adults.* Ed. Sandra L. Beckett. New York: Garland, 1999. 63–80.

———. *From Mythic to Linear: Time in Children's Literature.* Lanham: Scarecrow, 2000.

"1990 Hans Christian Andersen Awards." *Bookbird* 3 (1990): 3.

Nissen, Jane. *The Bookseller*, March 2000.

Nix, Garth. "Garth Nix: Digging into Fantasy." *Locus, the Magazine of the Science Fiction & Fantasy Field*, January 2003. 76–78.

Nodelman, Perry. *The Pleasures of Children's Literature.* New York and London: Longman, 1992.

Noguez, Dominique. *Le grantécrivain et autres textes.* Paris: Gallimard, 2000.

Nöstlinger, Christine. "Die Richtung der Hoffnung." *Fundevogel* 9–10 (January 1985): 12.

NSW Ministry for the Arts. "2005 NSW Premier's Literary Awards." http://www.arts.nsw.gov.au/ awards/LiteraryAwards/2005%20awards/2005shortlist.htm (accessed June 15, 2007).

O'Dell, Felicity Ann. *Socialisation Through Children's Literature: The Soviet Example.* Cambridge: Cambridge University Press, 1978.

O'Hehir, Andrew. "The Book of the Century." Part 1. Salon.com, June 4, 2001, http://archive. salon.com/books/feature/2001/06/04/tolkien/ (accessed March 24, 2007).

Olson, Parmy. "Bloomsbury Ready to Close the Book on Harry Potter?" *Forbes Magazine*, April 3, 2007.

Osberghaus, Monika. "Vor kurzer oder langer Zeit lebte einer, der nichts merkte: Käthi Bhends Robert-Walser-Bilderbuch." *Frankfurter Allgemeine Zeitung*, January 17, 2004, 36.

O'Sullivan, Emer. "The Fate of the Dual Addressee in the Translation of Children's Literature." *New Comparison* 16 (Autumn 1993): 109–19.

———. "Internationalism, the Universal Child and the World of Children's Literature." In *International Companion Encyclopedia of Children's Literature.* Ed. Peter Hunt. 2nd ed. Volume I. London: Routledge, 2004. 13–15.

———. *Kinderliterarische Komparatistik.* Heidelberg: Winter, 2000. Translated by Anthea Bell under the title *Comparative Children's Literature* (New York: Routledge, 2005).

Parrott Jr., Ray J. "Aesopian Language." In *Modern Encyclopedia of Russian and Soviet Literature.* Vol. 1. Gulf Breeze, FA: Academic International Press, 1977. 39–45.

Parsons, Wendy and Catriona Nicholson. "Talking to Philip Pullman: An Interview." *The Lion and the Unicorn* 23, no. 1 (1999): 116–34.

Pasternak, Guitta Pessis. "Tournier le sensuel." *Le Monde*, August 13, 1984.

Paterson, Katherine. *Gates of Excellence: On Reading and Writing Books for Children.* New York: Elsevier/Nelson Books, 1981.

Pauli, Michelle. "A Kind of Magic." *Guardian,* October 7, 2005.

Payot, Marianne. "L'Entretien: Michel Tournier." *Lire* (October 1996): 32–40.

Penny, Thomas. "A Children's Writer with Adult Topics." *Telegraph,* February 23, 2001.

Pepper, Tara. "Not Just for Children." *Newsweek International,* February 2, 2006.

Perina, Kaja. "Lemony Snicket: Reversal of Fortune." *Psychology Today* 37, no. 6 (November–December 2004): 104.

Perrot, Jean. *Jeux et enjeux du livre d'enfance et de jeunesse.* Paris: Cercle de la Librairie, 1999.

——. *Mondialisation et littérature de jeunesse.* Paris: Cercle de la Librairie, 2008.

Petit, Susan. "An Interview with Michel Tournier: 'I Write Because I Have Something to Say.'" In *Michel Tournier's Metaphysical Fictions.* Amsterdam/Philadelphia: John Benjamins Publishing Co., 1991. 173–93.

Petzold, Dieter. "A Neverending Success Story? Michael Ende's Return Trip to Fantasia." In *Beyond Babar: The European Tradition in Children's Literature.* Ed. Sandra L. Beckett and Maria Nikolajeva. Lanham: Scarecrow, 2006. 209–40.

Pfau, Ulli. *Phantásien in Halle 4/5: Michael Endes 'Unendliche Geschichte' und ihre Verfilmung.* Munich: Deutscher Taschenbuch Verlag, 1984.

Poeti, Alida. "Crossing Borders: Calvino in the Footprints of Collodi." In *Transcending Boundaries: Writing for a Dual Audience of Children and Adults.* Ed. Sandra L. Beckett. New York: Garland, 1999. 201–13.

Poniewozik, James. "A Nursery Rhyme of Vengeance." *Time,* October 25, 2002.

Postman, Neil. *The Disappearance of Childhood.* New York: Delacorte, 1982.

Ratcheva-Stratieva, Lilia. "Earth Hanging in Infinity: Janusz Korczak's *King Matt the First.*" In *Beyond Babar: The European Tradition in Children's Literature.* Ed. Sandra L. Beckett and Maria Nikolajeva. Lanham: Scarecrow, 2006. 1–20.

Rees, Jasper. "We're All Reading Children's Books." *Daily Telegraph,* November 17, 2003.

Reid, Luc. "Susanna Clarke's *Jonathan Strange & Mr Norrell*: Magic Chuses to Reemerge in Regency England." *Strange Horizons,* September 27, 2004, http://www.strangehorizons.com/reviews/2004/09/susanna_clarkes.shtml (accessed March 16, 2007).

Reynolds, Kimberley, ed. *Modern Children's Literature: An Introduction.* Basingstoke: Palgrave, 2005.

Reynolds, Susan Salter. Review of *The Solitaire Mystery,* by Jostein Gaarder, *Los Angeles Times,* July 21, 1996.

Roback, Dianne and Jason Britton, eds. Compiled by Debbie Hochman. "All-Time Bestselling Children's Books." *Publishers Weekly,* December 17, 2001.

Robinson, David. "Publisher Keeps His Faith in Scotland." *Scotsman,* September 16, 2003.

Robinson, Karen. "Dark Art of Writing Books that Win Minds." *Sunday Times,* January 27, 2002.

Rose, Jacqueline. *The Case of Peter Pan, or The Impossibility of Children's Fiction.* London: Macmillan, 1984.

Rosen, Judith. "Breaking the Age Barrier." *Publishers Weekly,* September 8, 1997, 28–31.

——. "Growing Up." *Publishers Weekly,* February 21, 2005.

Rosen, Michael. "Home and Away—Writing and Performing Poetry for Children." Paper presented at the Congress of the International Research Society of Children's Literature, Dublin, Ireland, August 13–17, 2005.

Ross, Deborah. "Soap and the Serious Writer." *Independent* (London), February 4, 2002.

Rushdie, Salman. "Keeping up with Salman Rushdie." Interview with James Fenton. *New York Review of Books* 38, no. 6, March 28, 1991, 24–32.

——. "The Wizard of Oz." Film Classics. London: British Film Institute, 1992.

Sager, Alexander. "And the Winner Is … " SignandSight.com, September 28, 2005, http://www.signandsight.com/features/290.html (accessed June 13, 2007).

SFFWorld. "Interview with Anne McCaffrey," May 8, 2000. SFFWorld. http://www.sffworld.com/interview/49p0.html (accessed July 6, 2007).

Said, S. F. "The Godfather of Harry Potter." *Daily Telegraph,* December 8, 2002.

——. "The Grown-up World of Kidult Books." *Daily Telegraph,* January 11, 2003.

Samivel [Paul Gayet-Tancrède]. "*L'Âne Culotte* et l'univers onirique d'Henri Bosco." *Les Cahiers de l'Amitié Henri Bosco* 11 (April–October 1976): 76–80.

Savater, Fernando. *La infancia recuperada.* Madrid: Taurus, 1976. Translated by Frances M. López-Morillas under the title *Childhood Regained: The Art of the Storyteller* (New York: Columbia University Press, 1982).

Scott, Carole. "Dual Audience in Picturebooks." In *Transcending Boundaries: Writing for a Dual Audience of Children and Adults*. Ed. Sandra L. Beckett. New York: Garland, 1999.

Scott, Patrick and Roger Mortimer, with assistance from Bruce Bowlin. "Robert Louis Stevenson, 1850–1894." Exhibition, Thomas Cooper Library, University of South California, Summer 1994–Spring 1995. University of South Carolina, http://www.sc.edu/library/spcoll/britlit/rls/rls3.html (accessed June 21, 2007).

Shavit, Zohar. *The Poetics of Children's Literature*. Athens, GA: University of Georgia Press, 1987.

Sherman, Beatrice. "A Prince of Lonely Space." *New York Times*, April 11, 1943.

Shuttleworth, Mike. "A Curious Bestseller." *The Age*, February 14, 2004. http://www.theage.com.au.articles/2004/02/11/1076388428007.html (accessed March 29, 2006).

Singer, Isaac Bashevis. "Isaac Bashevis Singer on Writing for Children." *Children's Literature* 6 (1977): 9–16.

Skardhamar, Anne-Kari. "Angel, Star, Butterfly and Mirror: Philosophy for Children in *Through a Glass, Darkly*." *Bookbird* 2 (2006): 30–36.

Skármeta, Antonio. "Cuando la ficción nace del infierno." *Imaginaria* 101 (April 30, 2003).

Smadja, Isabelle and Pierre Bruno, eds. *Harry Potter: ange ou démon?* Paris: Presses Universitaires de France, 2007.

Spufford, Francis. *The Child that Books Built*. London: Faber & Faber, 2002.

Stevenson, Robert Louis. "The Art of Writing." In *Essays on the Art of Writing*. London: Chatto & Windus, 1905.

Stone, Rosemary. "Editorial." *Books for Keeps* 135 (July 2002): 3.

Strausfeld, Michi. "Las Tres Edades: de ocho a ochenta y ocho años." *CLIJ* 50 (May 1993): 44–45.

Summerskill, Ben. "Playtime as Kidults Grow Up at Last." *Observer*, July 23, 2000.

Susina, Jan. "Editors Note: Kiddie Lit(e): The Dumbing Down of Children's Literature." *The Lion and the Unicorn* 17, no. 1 (June 1993): v–ix.

Swann, Thomas. *A. A. Milne*. Boston: Twayne, 1971.

Swart, Genevieve. "Enigma Unmasks with Her Final Saga." *Sydney Morning Herald*, October 30, 2006.

Taylor, Charles. "This Sorcery Isn't Just for Kids." *Salon Magazine*, February 20, 2002.

Taylor, Debbie. "The Potter Effect." *Mslexia* 14 (Summer/Autumn 2002).

"Ted Hughes's Crow." *The Listener*, July 30, 1970.

Templeton, David. "Dark Days: Ghouls and Golbins, Mayhem and Murder—It's Just Kids' Stuff." *North Bay Bohemian*, March 14–20, 2002.

Thaler, Danielle. "Littérature de jeunesse: un concept problématique." *Canadian Children's Literature/Littérature canadienne pour la jeunesse* 83 (Autumn 1986): 26–38.

Thompson, Raymond H. "Interview with Alan Garner," 1989. In "Taliesin's Successors: Interviews with Authors of Modern Arthurian Literature." The Camelot Project. http://www.lib.rochester.edu/camelot/intrvws/garner.htm (accessed October 11, 2007).

Thwaite, Ann. *A. A. Milne: His Life*. London: Faber & Faber, 1991.

Tiberghien, Muriel. "Table Ronde." Round table presented at the international conference on "Perspectives contemporaines du roman pour la jeunesse," Institut International Charles Perrault, Eaubonne, France, December 1–2, 2000.

Tonkin, Boyd. "Once Upon a Time in the Marketing Department … " *Independent* (London), November 8, 2002.

Tournier, Michel. "Les enfants dans la bibliothèque." Interview with Jean-François Josselin. *Le Nouvel Observateur*, December 6, 1971, 56–57.

———. "Écrire pour les enfants." Interview with Jean-Marie Magnan. *La Quinzaine Littéraire*, December 16–31, 1971, 11–13.

———. "Quand Michel Tournier récrit ses livres pour les enfants." *Le Monde*, December 24, 1971, 7.

———. "Le sang des fillettes." *Le Monde*, December 9, 1977, 31.

———. "Écrire pour les enfants." In *Pierrot ou les secrets de la nuit*. Enfantimages. Paris: Gallimard, 1979.

———. "Michel Tournier: comment écrire pour les enfants." *Le Monde*, December 24, 1979, 19.

———. "Michel Tournier: avant tout, plaire aux enfants." In *Barbedor*. Enfantimages. Paris: Gallimard, 1980.

———. "Writing for Children is No Child's Play." *UNESCO Courier* 6, June 1982, 33–34.

———. "Michel Tournier face aux lycéens." *Le Magazine Littéraire* 226, January 1986, 20–25.

———. *The Wind Spirit: An Autobiography*. Translated by Arthur Goldhammer. Boston: Beacon Press, 1988.

———. "Discussion" during "Table ronde sur la littérature pour enfants." In *Images et signes de Michel*

Tournier. Ed. Arlette Bouloumié and Maurice de Gandillac. Paris: Gallimard, 1991. 303–09; 316–21.

Townsend, John Rowe. *A Sense of Story: Essays on Contemporary Writers for Children.* Philadelphia: J. B. Lippincott, 1971, 10.

Toynbee, Philip. "Dissension among the Judges." *Observer,* August 6, 1961.

Travis, Madelyn. "Foundlings on Stage." Booktrust, http://www.booktrusted.co.uk/articles/documents.php4?articleid=40 (accessed June 15, 2007).

Tucker, Nicholas. "The Rise and Rise of Harry Potter." *Children's Literature in Education* 30, no. 4 (December 1999): 221–34.

——. *Darkness Visible: Inside the World of Philip Pullman.* Cambridge: Wizard Books, 2003.

Tumanov, Larissa Klein. "Between Literary Systems: Authors of Literature for Adults Write for Children". Ph.D., University of Alberta, 1999.

——. "Writing for a Dual Audience in the Former Soviet Union: The Aesopian Children's Literature of Kornei Chukovskii, Mikhail Zoshchenko, and Daniil Kharms." In *Transcending Boundaries: Writing for a Dual Audience of Children and Adults.* Ed. Sandra L. Beckett. New York: Garland, 1999. 129–48.

"2001: A Year in Books." Guardian Unlimited, 2001. http://books.guardian.co.uk/quiz/questions/0,5957,623142,00.html (accessed June 30, 2007).

Ventura, Antonio. "Michi Strausfeld: Entrevista a Michi Strausfeld, directora de la colección 'Las Tres Edades' de Siruela." *Babar,* May 1, 2005, http://revistababar.com/web/index.php?option=com_content&task=view&id=229&Itemid=51 (accessed March 28, 2007).

Waldegrave, William. Review of *The Subtle Knife,* by Philip Pullman. *The Week,* September 1997.

Walden, George. "A Child's View, Again." *Daily Telegraph,* January 26, 2003.

Wall, Barbara. *The Narrator's Voice: The Dilemma of Children's Fiction.* New York: St. Martin's Press, 1991.

Walsh, William. "I Am a Woman Writer; I Am a Western Writer: An Interview with Ursula Le Guin." *The Kenyon Review* 17, nos. 3–4 (1995): 192–205.

Webb, Stuart. "Rowling's Rivals: The New Collectables." *Book and Magazine Collector* 244, July 2004.

Weber, Jochen. "Pasando les límites: All-Age-Books, Crossover-Literature y otras tendencias actuales de la literatura para jóvenes lectores." Paper presented at the 1er Congreso Nacional de Lectura y Escritura: Escuela y Literatura Infantil, Durango, Mexico, May 16–18, 2004.

West, Rebecca. "Come One, Come All: Luigi Malerba's Diffuse Fictions." *The Lion and the Unicorn* 10 (1986): 95–107.

Whited, Lana A., ed. *The Ivory Tower and Harry Potter: Perspectives on a Literary Phenomenon.* Columbia: University of Missouri Press, 2002.

Wilkie-Stibbs, Christine. "Russell Hoban." In *The Oxford Encyclopedia of Children's Literature.* Ed. Jack Zipes. Vol. 2. New York: Oxford University Press, 2006. 298.

Williams, Elaine. "Home-grown Heartaches." *The Times Educational Supplement,* November 21, 2003.

Worton, Michael. "Michel Tournier and the Masterful Art of Rewriting." *PN Review* 11, no. 3 (1984): 24–25.

"Writers of Adult Literature Who Also Write for Children." Special issue of *The Lion and the Unicorn* 2, no. 1 (1978).

Wynne-Jones, Tim. "The Survival of the Book." *Signal* 87 (September 1998): 160–66.

——. "Tigers and Poodles and Birds, Oh My!" *The Horn Book Magazine* 80, no. 3 (May–June 2004): 265–75.

Zipes, Jack. *Sticks and Stones: The Troublesome Success of Children's Literature from Slovenly Peter to Harry Potter.* New York: Routledge, 2001.

Index